CACREP Standards	Sangganjanavanich, Introduction to Professional Counseling	Watson, Counseling Assessment and Evaluation	Conyne, Group Work Leadership	Parsons, Becoming a Skilled Counselor	Parsons, Counseling Theory	Wong, Counseling Individuals Through the Life Span	Duan, Becoming a Multiculturally Competent Counselor	Wright, Research Methods for Counseling	Tang, Career Development and Counseling	Scott, Counselor as Consultant	Zhang, Field Experience	Sheperis, Ethical Decision Making
1. Professional Orientation and Ethical Practice	1a 1b 1d 1e 1f 1g 1h 1i 1j	1j	1b 1j	1b 1d 1e 1j	1j	1j	1j	1j	1b 1j	1b 1j	1b 1c 1d 1e 1f 1g 1h 1i 1j	1b 1d 1e 1f 1g 1h 1i 1j
2. Social and Cultural Diversity	2c 2f 2g	2g	2d 2e 2g	2b 2c 2g	2c 2e 2g	2a 2b 2c 2d 2e 2g	2c 2e 2f 2g	2g	2g	2d 2g	2d	2d 2f
3. Human Growth and Development			3f		3b	3a 3b 3c 3d 3e 3f 3g	3d 3e		3c			
4. Career Development		4f							4a 4b 4c 4d 4e 4f 4g	4c	4b 4c 4e 4g	
5. Helping Relationships	5a 5b 5c 5f 5g 5h		5b 5c 5d 5e	5a 5b 5c 5d	5b 5c 5d 5e 5g	5b	5b 5e		5b 5c	5b 5c 5f 5g 5h	5c 5d 5e 5f 5g	5d 5e
6. Group Work			6a 6b 6c 6d 6e								6d 6e	6a 6b 6c 6d 6e
7. Assessment		7a 7b 7c 7d 7e 7f 7g	7b	7b		7f		7c 7d 7e			7g	
8. Research and Program Evaluation								8a 8b 8c 8d 8e			8d 8e 8f	8e

Counseling and Professional Identity

Series Editors: Richard D. Parsons, PhD, and Naijian Zhang, PhD

Becoming a Skilled Counselor—Richard D. Parsons and Naijian Zhang

Research Methods for Counseling: An Introduction—Robert J. Wright

Group Work Leadership: An Introduction for Helpers—Robert K. Conyne

Introduction to Professional Counseling—Varunee Faii Sangganjanavanich and Cynthia Reynolds

Counseling Theory: Guiding Reflective Practice—Richard D. Parsons and Naijian Zhang

Counselor as Consultant—David A. Scott, Chadwick W. Royal, and Daniel B. Kissinger

Counseling Assessment and Evaluation: Fundamentals of Applied Practice—Joshua C. Watson and Brande Flamez

Counseling Individuals Through the Lifespan—Daniel W. Wong, Kimberly R. Hall, Cheryl A. Justice, and Lucy Wong Hernandez

Becoming a Multiculturally Competent Counselor—Changming Duan and Chris Brown

Career Development and Counseling: Theory and Practice in a Multicultural World—Mei Tang and Jane Goodman

Field Experience: Transitioning From Student to Professional—Naijian Zhang and Richard D. Parsons

Ethical Decision Making for the 21st Century Counselor—Donna S. Sheperis, Stacy L. Henning, and Michael M. Kocet

ETHICAL DECISION MAKING FOR THE 21ST CENTURY COUNSELOR

SAGE was founded in 1965 by Sara Miller McCune to support the dissemination of usable knowledge by publishing innovative and high-quality research and teaching content. Today, we publish more than 850 journals, including those of more than 300 learned societies, more than 800 new books per year, and a growing range of library products including archives, data, case studies, reports, and video. SAGE remains majority-owned by our founder, and after Sara's lifetime will become owned by a charitable trust that secures our continued independence.

Los Angeles | London | New Delhi | Singapore | Washington DC

ETHICAL DECISION MAKING FOR THE 21ST CENTURY COUNSELOR

Donna S. Sheperis

Lamar University

Stacy L. Henning

Webster University

Michael M. Kocet

The Chicago School of Professional Psychology

A book in the series Counseling and Professional Identity

Editors: R. D. Parsons, PhD, and N. Zhang, PhD

Los Angeles | London | New Delhi
Singapore | Washington DC

Los Angeles | London | New Delhi
Singapore | Washington DC

FOR INFORMATION:

SAGE Publications, Inc.
2455 Teller Road
Thousand Oaks, California 91320
E-mail: order@sagepub.com

SAGE Publications Ltd.
1 Oliver's Yard
55 City Road
London EC1Y 1SP
United Kingdom

SAGE Publications India Pvt. Ltd.
B 1/I 1 Mohan Cooperative Industrial Area
Mathura Road, New Delhi 110 044
India

SAGE Publications Asia-Pacific Pte. Ltd.
3 Church Street
#10-04 Samsung Hub
Singapore 049483

Printed in the United States of America

ISBN 978-1-4522-3549-3

Acquisitions Editor: Kassie Graves
Associate Editor: Abbie Rickard
Editorial Assistant: Carrie Montoya
Production Editor: Veronica Stapleton Hooper
Copy Editor: Pam Schroeder
Typesetter: C&M Digitals (P) Ltd.
Proofreader: Ellen Howard
Indexer: Jean Casalegno
Cover Designer: Candice Harman
Marketing Manager: Johanna Swenson

This book is printed on acid-free paper.

15 16 17 18 19 10 9 8 7 6 5 4 3 2 1

BRIEF CONTENTS

DETAILED CONTENTS

List of Guided Practice Exercises

Editors' Preface:
Introduction to the Series

COUNSELING AND PROFESSIONAL IDENTITY IN THE 21ST CENTURY

Ethical Decision Making for the 21st Century Counselor is a text that will introduce you to the basic information and fundamental skills required of all who are beginning their journey toward their development as professional helpers. Obviously, one text, one learning experience, will not be sufficient for the successful formation of your professional identity and practice. The formation of both your professional identity and practice will be a lifelong process—a process that we hope to facilitate through the presentation of this text and the creation of our series: *Counseling and Professional Identity in the 21st Century.*

Counseling and Professional Identity in the 21st Century is a new, fresh, pedagogically sound series of texts targeting counselors in training. This series is not simply a compilation of isolated books matching that which is already in the market. Rather each book, with its targeted knowledge and skills, will be presented as but a part of a larger whole. The focus and content of each text serve as a single lens through which a counselor can view his or her clients, engage in his or her practice, and articulate his or her own professional identity.

Counseling and Professional Identity in the 21st Century is unique not just in the fact that it packages a series of traditional texts but that it provides an integrated curriculum targeting the formation of the reader's professional identity and efficient, ethical practice. Each book within the series is structured to facilitate the ongoing professional formation of the reader. The materials found within each text are organized to move the reader to higher levels of cognitive, affective, and psychomotor functioning, resulting in his or her assimilation of the materials presented into both his or her professional identity and approach to professional practice. While each text targets a specific set of core competencies (cognates and skills), competencies identified by the Council for Accreditation of Counseling & Related Educational Programs (CACREP) as essential to the practice of counseling, each book in the series will emphasize each of the following:

- the assimilation of concepts and constructs provided across the text found within the series thus fostering the reader's ongoing development as a competent professional;
- the blending of contemporary theory with current research and empirical support;
- a focus on the development of procedural knowledge with each text, employing case illustrations and guided practice exercises to facilitate the reader's ability to translate the theory and research discussed into professional decision making and application;
- the emphasis on the need for and means of demonstrating accountability; and
- the fostering of the reader's professional identity and with it the assimilation of the ethics and standards of practice guiding the counseling profession.

We are proud to have served as coeditors of this series, feeling sure that each text will serve as a significant resource to you and your development as a professional counselor.

Richard Parsons, PhD
Naijian Zhang, PhD

AUTHORS' PREFACE

Welcome to the world of ethical practice for counseling professionals! While we have all taken the steps to become a counselor, learning to become an ethical, competent counselor who adheres to relevant laws and stays current on professional issues is a lifelong journey. While students and professors alike sometimes view this as fairly dry content, we beg to disagree. The contemporary ethical dilemmas faced by practicing counselors are some of the most exciting and invigorating topics in our field today!

Ethical Decision Making for the 21st Century Counselor serves as your foundation and guide through the complexities of navigating ethical decisions. We introduce you to the history of ethical decision-making models as well as our unique approach to relational ethical decision making. Because the emphasis is on collaborative relationships with all parties involved, ethical decisions are made in the most conscientious manner, honoring our roles as counselors and emphasizing the relationship.

This text is designed to address specific competencies identified by CACREP as essential to developing an understanding of the processes of ethical, legal, and professional development of a counselor. Specifically the goals of this text are these:

- provide an overview of becoming an ethical, competent counselor;
- assist the reader's identification of his or her own personal values that influence the ethical decision-making process;
- highlight ethical decision-making models that have evolved to address specific considerations;
- introduce a relational model of ethical decision making;
- identify ethical and legal issues related to counseling practice;
- introduce challenges specific to contemporary practice;
- identify steps and processes for resolving ethical dilemmas; and,
- highlight the ethical importance of social justice and advocacy for our clients and our profession.

Chapter	Learning Objective	CACREP Standards
Chapter 1: Introduction to Ethical Decision Making and Ethical Practice	• Describe the foundational ethical principles of autonomy, nonmaleficence, beneficence, justice, and fidelity. • Differentiate between mandatory and aspirational ethics. • Analyze your personal ethics and values using the Counseling Ethics Audit. • Evaluate each step in the ethical decision-making process.	**CACREP Core Standards** **G.1.j.** Ethical standards of professional organizations and credentialing bodies and applications of ethical and legal considerations in professional counseling. **CACREP Clinical Mental Health Standards** **A.2.** Understands the ethical and legal considerations specifically related to the practice of clinical mental health counseling.
Chapter 2: Ethical Decision-Making Models	• Evaluate theory-based ethical decision-making models. • Analyze practice-based ethical decision-making models. • Examine cultural-based ethical decision-making models. • Summarize ethical decision-making models used in crisis counseling and addictions counseling. • Apply ethical decision-making models to a variety of challenging situations.	**CACREP Core Standards** **G.1.j.** Ethical standards of professional organizations and credentialing bodies and applications of ethical and legal considerations in professional counseling. **CACREP Clinical Mental Health Standards** **A.2.** Understands the ethical and legal considerations specifically related to the practice of clinical mental health counseling. **B.1.** Demonstrates the ability to apply and adhere to ethical and legal standards in clinical mental health counseling.
Chapter 3: Cultural Competency and Ethical Decision Making	• Evaluate the importance of creating a purposeful ethical blueprint for effective counseling practice, including the use of formal decision-making models.	**CACREP Core Standards** **G.1.j.** Ethical standards of professional organizations and credentialing bodies and applications of ethical and legal considerations in professional counseling.

Chapter	Learning Objective	CACREP Standards
	• Practice cultural sensitivity in all aspects of the counselor–client relationship. • Utilize the Counselor Value-Based Conflicts Model when faced with cultural values-based conflicts within the counseling relationship. • Differentiate the two main types of consultation and the role that each plays in the ethical decision-making process, especially during cross-cultural therapeutic impasses.	**CACREP Clinical Mental Health Standards** **A.2.** Understands the ethical and legal considerations specifically related to the practice of clinical mental health counseling. **B.1.** Demonstrates the ability to apply and adhere to ethical and legal standards in clinical mental health.
Chapter 4: **Relational Ethical** **Decision-Making**	• Define relational and collaborative ethics. • Describe each of the nine core values that promote ethical practice. • Apply the Relational Ethical Decision-Making Model to resolve ethical dilemmas. • Utilize the Brief Ethical Decision-Making Model to make ethical decisions without consulting others.	**CACREP Core Standards** **G.1.j.** Ethical standards of professional organizations and credentialing bodies and applications of ethical and legal considerations in professional counseling. **CACREP Clinical Mental Health Standards** **A.2.** Understands the ethical and legal considerations specifically related to the practice of clinical mental health counseling. **B.1.** Demonstrates the ability to apply and adhere to ethical and legal standards in clinical mental health counseling.
Chapter 5: Ethics **and the Counseling** **Relationship**	• Examine the advantages and disadvantages of using scientifically based interventions and the ethics surrounding these decisions. • Identify ways to stay up-to-date on professional counseling research. • Describe the difference between empirically supported techniques and unproven or developing techniques. • Identify means of selecting effective interventions. • Explain how to measure counselor competency, and describe the requirements of competency in various specialty areas. • Apply an ethical decision-making approach to determine if a counselor is impaired, and identify when to address impairment.	**CACREP Core Standards** **G.1.d.** Self-care strategies appropriate to the counselor role. **G.5.d.** Counseling theories that provide the student with models to conceptualize client presentation and that help the student select appropriate counseling interventions. Students will be exposed to models of counseling that are consistent with current professional research and practice in the field, so they begin to develop a personal model of counseling. **G.8.e.** The use of research to inform evidence-based practice. **CACREP Clinical Mental Health Standards** **I.1.** Understands how to evaluate critically research relevant to the practice of clinical mental health counseling.

(Continued)

(Continued)

Chapter	Learning Objective	CACREP Standards
Chapter 6: Informed Consent	• Articulate the purpose of informed consent in the client–counselor relationship. • Define best practices for providing informed consent to clients. • Explain the necessary content of informed consent documents. • Develop an informed consent document. • Apply an informed consent process in various counseling settings. • Differentiate the informed consent process when implemented in association with specific practices such as formal assessment, supervision, research, clients lacking the capacity to provide consent, mandated or court-ordered referrals, culture, and technology.	**CACREP Core Standards** **G.1.b.** Professional roles, functions, and relationships with other human service providers, including strategies for interagency and interorganization collaboration and communications. **G.1.j.** Ethical standards of professional organizations and credentialing bodies, and applications of ethical and legal considerations in professional counseling. **CACREP Clinical Mental Health Standards** **A.2.** Understands ethical and legal considerations specifically related to the practice of clinical mental health counseling. **A.7.** Is aware of professional issues that affect clinical mental health counselors (e.g., core provider status, expert witness status, access to and practice privileges within managed care systems). **B.1.** Demonstrates the ability to apply and adhere to ethical and legal standards in clinical mental health counseling. **C.8.** Understands professional issues relevant to the practice of clinical mental health counseling. **D.7.** Applies current record-keeping standards related to clinical mental health counseling.
Chapter 7: Confidentiality and Record Keeping	• Examine the concept of confidentiality and its purposes. • Evaluate occasions when confidentiality can and cannot be broken. • Describe best practice for informing the client.	**CACREP Core Standards** **G.1.b.** Professional roles, functions, and relationships with other human service providers, including strategies for interagency and interorganization collaboration and communications (record keeping).

Chapter	Learning Objective	CACREP Standards
	• Distinguish the requirements of confidentiality among specialized situations including supervision, death, multiple clients, minors and others lacking capacity to give consent, and research and publications. • Assess confidentiality practices in terms of client culture and context. • Describe confidentiality in terms of record keeping.	**CACREP Clinical Mental Health Standards** **A.2.** Understands ethical and legal considerations specifically related to the practice of clinical mental health counseling. **D.7.** Applies current record-keeping standards related to clinical mental health counseling.
Chapter 8: Ethical Decision Making and Managing Professional Boundaries	• Evaluate when dual or multiple relationships are and are not appropriate. • Employ ethical decision-making skills in managing boundaries. • Utilize an ethical decision-making model when considering engaging in boundary extensions. • Apply cultural and contextual considerations to the ethical decision-making process regarding boundary structure.	**CACREP Core Standards** **G.1.j.** Ethical standards of professional organizations and credentialing bodies and applications of ethical and legal considerations in professional counseling. **CACREP Clinical Mental Health Standards** **A.2.** Understands the ethical and legal considerations specifically related to the practice of clinical mental health counseling. **B.1.** Demonstrates the ability to apply and adhere to ethical and legal standards in clinical mental health counseling.
Chapter 9: Minors	• Evaluate the confidentiality rights of minor clients. • Differentiate among confidentiality, privileged communication, and mandated reporting. • Critically analyze a case study involving minor clients and confidentiality using an identified ethical decision-making model.	**CACREP Core Standards** **G.1.b.** Professional roles, functions, and relationships with other human service providers, including strategies for interagency and interorganization collaboration and communications. **G.1.i.** Advocacy processes needed to address institutional and social barriers that impede access, equity, and success for clients.

(Continued)

(Continued)

Chapter	Learning Objective	CACREP Standards
	• Explain how to work with and within a school system with minor clients. • Apply cultural competencies when working with minor clients.	**G.5.d.** Counseling theories that provide the student with models to conceptualize client presentation and that help the student select appropriate counseling interventions. Students will be exposed to models of counseling that are consistent with current professional research and practice in the field, so they begin to develop a personal model of counseling. **G.5.e.** A systems perspective that provides an understanding of family and other systems theories and major models of family and related interventions. **G.6.a.** Developmental stage theories, group members' roles and behaviors, and therapeutic factors of group work. **CACREP Clinical Mental Health Standards** **A.3.** Understands the roles and functions of clinical mental health counselors in various practice settings and the importance of relationships between counselors and other professionals, including interdisciplinary treatment teams. **C.1.** Describes the principles of mental health, including prevention, intervention, consultation, education, and advocacy, as well as the operation of programs and networks that promote mental health in a multicultural society. **C.7.** Recognizes the importance of family, social networks, and community systems in the treatment of mental and emotional disorders. **E.4.** Understands effective strategies to support client advocacy and influence public policy and government relations on local, state, and national levels to enhance equity, increase funding, and promote programs that affect the practice of clinical mental health counseling. **E.6.** Knows public policies on the local, state, and national levels that affect the quality and accessibility of mental health services.

Chapter	Learning Objective	CACREP Standards
Chapter 10: Ethics in Family and Group Counseling	• Apply the specialized practices utilized when counseling a group or family in terms of the counseling relationship, role changes, protection of clients, screening, and termination. • Describe the competencies needed by group and family counselors and the consequences of leading a group without adequate training. • Explain the role of cultural competency in group and family counseling. • Employ ethical confidentiality practices in family and group work. • Examine how to advocate for clients and how to foster their skills to self-advocate.	**CACREP Core Standards** **G.2.d.** Individual, couple, family, group, and community strategies for working with and advocating for diverse populations, including multicultural competencies. **G.2.f.** Counselors' roles in eliminating biases, prejudices, and processes of intentional and unintentional oppression and discrimination. **G.6.a.** Principles of group dynamics, including group process components, developmental stage theories, group members' roles and behaviors, and therapeutic factors of group work. **G.6.b.** Group leadership or facilitation styles and approaches, including characteristics of various types of group leaders and leadership styles. **G.6.c.** Theories of group counseling, including commonalities, distinguishing characteristics, and pertinent research and literature. **G.6.d.** Group counseling methods, including group counselor orientations and behaviors, appropriate selection criteria and methods, and methods of evaluation of effectiveness. **G.6.e.** Direct experiences in which students participate as group members in a small-group activity, approved by the program, for a minimum of 10 clock hours over the course of one academic term. **CACREP Clinical Mental Health Standards** **D.5.** Demonstrates appropriate use of culturally responsive individual, couple, family, group, and systems modalities for initiating, maintaining, and terminating counseling. **E.2.** Understands current literature that outlines theories, approaches, strategies, and techniques shown to be effective when working with specific populations of clients with mental and emotional disorders.

(Continued)

(Continued)

Chapter	Learning Objective	CACREP Standards
Chapter 11: Counselor Education and Supervision	• Analyze the ethical responsibilities of counselor educators related to curriculum, field experience, career development, and their relationships with students. • Analyze the ethical gatekeeping responsibilities of counselor educators related to orientation, evaluation, and remediation of students. • Examine the responsibilities of clinical supervisors and relationships between supervisors and supervisees. • Evaluate the ethical responsibilities of counseling students. • Apply concepts of culture and context to provide effective counseling to individuals with diverse backgrounds.	**CACREP Core Standards** **G.1.b.** Professional roles, functions, and relationships with other human service providers, including strategies for interagency and interorganization collaboration and communications. **G.1.d.** Self-care strategies appropriate to the counselor role. **G.1.e.** Counseling supervision models, practices, and processes. **G.1.f.** Professional organizations, including membership benefits, activities, services to members, and current issues. **G.1.g.** Professional credentialing, including certification, licensure, and accreditation practices and standards, and the effects of public policy on these issues. **G.1.h.** The role and process of the professional counselor advocating on behalf of the profession. **G.1.j.** Ethical standards of professional organizations and credentialing bodies, and applications of ethical and legal considerations in professional counseling.
Chapter 12: Challenges to Ethical Practice in the 21st Century	• Identify personal challenges to wellness and self-care. • Apply research-based strategies to promote self-care. • Describe employer and ethical issues that may arise with outside employment. • Examine policy challenges experienced by practicing counselors including prescription privileges, testing privileges, and licensure reciprocity. • Analyze ethical dilemmas in distance counseling and technology use.	**CACREP Core Standards** **G.1.g.** Professional credentialing, including certification, licensure, and accreditation practices and standards, and the effects of public policy on these issues. **G.1.j.** Ethical standards of professional organizations and credentialing bodies, and applications of ethical and legal considerations in professional counseling. **Clinical Mental Health Counseling (Content Standards)** **A.1.** Understands the history, philosophy, and trends in clinical mental health counseling. **A.2.** Understands ethical and legal considerations specifically related to the practice of clinical mental health counseling.

Chapter	Learning Objective	CACREP Standards
Chapter 13: Resolving Ethical Issues	• Distinguish between ethics and the law. • Examine the ways in which counselors are held to the ethical codes of licensure boards, professional members, and credentialing organizations and licensure boards. • Analyze steps in the adjudication processes in professional organizations and licensure boards. • Describe what to do when counselors are accused of ethical misconduct, and explain risk management strategies to avoid. • Summarize steps to take if you suspect someone of an ethical transgression.	**CACREP Core Standards** **G.1.j.** Ethical standards of professional organizations and credentialing bodies, and applications of ethical and legal considerations in professional counseling. **CACREP Clinical Mental Health Standards** **A.2.** Understands ethical and legal considerations specifically related to the practice of clinical mental health counseling.
Chapter 14: Social Justice and Advocacy	• Define the concept of social justice. • Identify professional organizations related to social justice issues in counseling. • Examine client populations where social justice concerns exist. • Analyze the concept of advocacy, its competencies, and various models. • Describe how to advocate for the counseling profession. • Evaluate personal advocacy practices.	**CACREP Core Standards** **G.1.g.** Professional credentialing, including certification, licensure, and accreditation practices and standards, and the effects of public policy on these issues. **G.1.h.** The role and process of the professional counselor advocating on behalf of the profession. **G.1.i.** Advocacy processes needed to address institutional and social barriers that impede access, equity, and success for clients. **CACREP Clinical Mental Health Standards** **E.2.** Understands the effects of racism, discrimination, sexism, power, privilege, and oppression on one's own life and career and those of the client. **E.4.** Understands effective strategies to support client advocacy and influence public policy and government relations on local, state, and national levels to enhance equity, increase funding, and promote programs that affect the practice of clinical mental health counseling. **E.5.** Understands the implications of concepts such as internalized oppression and institutional racism, as well as the historical and current political climate regarding immigration, poverty, and welfare. **E.6.** Knows public policies on the local, state, and national levels that affect the quality and accessibility of mental health services.

In this text you will find extensive discussion and attention given to ethical decision making as a process. While you will be exposed to common ethical conundrums, we strive to teach you ways to handle any ethical dilemma through the employment of ethical decision-making models. Because there are no persistent right or wrong answers in ethical dilemmas, we invite you to consider each case study through a lens of discovery. Context, culture, and the client–counselor relationship are essential to the process. This text offers you the facts—the hows and whys of ethical and legal issues—and opportunities to practice through case studies and vignettes. Many of these are drawn from the authors' professional experiences and relevant literature. We hope you find them as useful as we do in making ongoing ethical decisions.

MORE THAN JUST BLACK OR WHITE

Training in ethics goes beyond content. To truly understand the material, application is necessary. Knowledge is provided via ethical decision-making models and information about typical ethical challenges. However, the response to these ethical conundrums is never black and white. Instead, we view ethics as shades of grey. You will learn to view the cases in such a way as to identify the complexities including the potential outcomes to each approach. To this end, this book, as with the other books within the series, has been structured in a way to promote the assimilation and personalization of the material presented and the development of higher levels of learning, including the ability to value what is presented.

The chapters in this text include case illustrations and exercises to demonstrate the complexities of ethical decision making. This approach is intentional and allows the reader to explore ethical and legal concepts at multiple levels: the content level, the process level, and the personal level.

- Content. The material presented in this text reflects the most current literature related to ethical constructs, dilemmas, legalities, and the 2014 ACA Code of Ethics. Because ethical challenges and legal precedents are constantly evolving, we view the content as dynamic and expandable within your course discussions.
- Process. Ethical decision making is a highlight of this text with a focus on the process of determining a reasonable solution that protects the client to every extent possible. Because the only perfect solution to an ethical dilemma begins with the words *it depends,* we highlight the process of arriving at that solution. Specifically, this text focuses on the relational elements necessary to practice ethically in our profession.

- Personalization. Finally, as you will discover, ethical dilemmas bring out a range of emotions in counselors and clients. Understanding the impact of personal values and personal ethics on the dilemma is an essential element in ethical decision making. The reader may find some of the ethical dilemmas more challenging than others because of these personal elements. Teasing apart, or bracketing, our personal and professional selves is necessary to ethical behavior as a counselor. We invite you to embrace this challenge as part of professional development.

Ethical Decision Making for the 21st Century Counselor is designed to challenge you—to get you thinking! Case studies are just that: studies. Real people and real ethical dilemmas are more complex than can be presented in the linear format of a case study. Recognize the many layers of complexities contained within each situation as you begin to work toward a better understanding of ethical, legal, and professional issues. We wish you luck upon this journey and are honored to be a part of the process!

ACKNOWLEDGMENTS

A few years ago, three former members and chairs of the ACA Ethics Committee got together at a conference to talk about writing a book together. We discovered a shared passion in advocating to bring greater awareness to our profession on the importance of ethical decision making in our work. Since then, significant research and the development of new and emerging ethics models not found elsewhere have gone into the development of this text. We want to acknowledge our professional peers and clients who have lent their voices to this book. The case studies you read within are based on years of experiences among the authors, who have dedicated our lives to the compassionate care of others. All names and identifying markers of elements of actual cases have been changed to honor confidentiality and protect those involved.

While the three of us are the authors on this work, we would be remiss if we didn't acknowledge all those who have helped us in the process. A special thank you goes to each of the following who so graciously reviewed our project and provided valuable suggestions that made this project something to be proud of. These include the following:

Candace M. McLain
Colorado Christian University

Nicholas Ruiz
St. Mary's University of Minnesota

Rochelle Caroon-Santiago
University of the Incarnate Word

While the aforementioned provided guidance in regard to the content found within this text, it was the special gifts of our developmental editor, Leah Mori, copy editor Pam Schroeder, and cover designer Candice Harman that brought the text from our content to true textbook material.

Our series editors, Rick Parsons and Naijian Zhang, have done a remarkable job developing a comprehensive series for counselor educators and their students. We are so proud to be a part of this series! Thank you especially, Rick, for your speedy reviews and suggestions along the way. You are remarkable!

Finally, we would be remiss if we did not say a very special thank you to Kassie Graves, Senior Acquisition Editor; Abbie Rickard, Associate Editor; and Carrie Montoya, Editorial Assistant, at SAGE Publications who not only kept us focused and on time but provided much-needed support throughout the development of this text. Their grace and generosity were driving forces behind this project, and for that, we are grateful.

This text is dedicated to my five points of light:
Ellis, Jake, Joe Lee, Emily, and Laura Beth. Shine brightly!

Donna S. Sheperis

I dedicate the time and energy involved in this book to
my son Harrison for his matter-of-fact patience throughout and
the presumed expectation that it would complete one day.

Stacy L. Henning

I dedicate this book to the memory of my grandmother, Marie J. Kovacic,
who instilled in me a dedication to learning and higher education.

Michael M. Kocet

About the Authors

Donna S. Sheperis, PhD, is an associate professor in the Department of Counseling and Special Populations at Lamar University. She earned her PhD in Counselor Education from the University of Mississippi. Dr. Sheperis has taught in land-based and fully online programs since 2000. She is a Licensed Professional Counselor in Mississippi and Texas, a National Certified Counselor, a Certified Clinical Mental Health Counselor, and an Approved Clinical Supervisor with more than 20 years of experience in clinical mental health counseling settings.

Dr. Sheperis is active in the counseling profession, holding leadership positions in the Association for Assessment and Research in Counseling and the Association for Humanistic Counseling. She has served as member and cochair of the ACA Ethics Committee. She is active in scholarship and research as well, with multiple articles, books, and chapters in print.

Stacy L. Henning is Associate Chair in the Professional Counseling Department at Webster University. She holds a PhD in Counselor Education from CACREP-accredited doctoral and master's programs and is a Licensed Professional Counselor and an Approved Clinical Supervisor through NBCC. Dr. Henning is an active member in ACA committees, including as a former senior chair to the ACA Ethics Committee and current member of the Public Policy and Legislative Committee; a site team chair for CACREP; active member of university committees including the Graduate Council and Multicultural Committee in addition to multiple department committees; and a practicing professional counselor in St. Louis, Missouri. Current research includes ethics in counselor education, women in life transition, teaching efficacy in counselor education, and neurobiology and counseling efficacy.

Michael M. Kocet is professor and Department Chair of the Counseling Department at the Chicago School of Professional Psychology in Chicago, Illinois. Dr. Kocet most recently served as Department Chair in the Department of Counselor Education at Bridgewater State University in Massachusetts, where he served on faculty from 2002 to 2015 and was awarded the BSU Presidential Award for Diversity, Inclusion, and Social Justice. Dr. Kocet earned his PhD in Counselor Education from the University of Arkansas and completed a graduate certificate in dispute resolution at the University of Massachusetts Boston. He is a Licensed Mental Health Counselor and National Certified Counselor. His professional areas of interest include: ethical issues in counseling; counseling lesbian, gay, bisexual, and transgender (LGBT) clients; and grief counseling. He is the author of numerous journal articles and book chapters on ethics and LGBT and diversity issues. He is the editor of the recently released book *Counseling Gay Men, Adolescents, and Boys: A Guide for Helping Professionals and Educators,* published by Routledge Press. Dr. Kocet served as a member of the ACA Ethics Committee (2001–2007) and chaired the ACA Ethics Code Revision Task Force (2002–2005). He is Past President and current ACA Governing Council Representative of the Association for Lesbian, Gay, Bisexual, and Transgender Issues in Counseling (ALGBTIC). Dr. Kocet currently serves as a board trustee for the Association for Spiritual, Ethical, and Religious Values in Counseling (ASERVIC). He served on the Minority Fellows Program Advisory Council through the National Board of Certified Counselors. Dr. Kocet is active in community service, providing pro bono counseling and clinical supervision for the GLBTQ Domestic Violence Program in Boston, Massachusetts, as well as volunteering as a grief therapist in the role of Healing Circle Leader for Comfort Zone Camp, the nation's largest bereavement camp for children, ages 7 to 17. He has presented at local, state, and national conferences in counseling and student affairs and is sought out as a national speaker and consultant on ethics, diversity, and grief counseling.

Chapter 1

INTRODUCTION TO ETHICAL DECISION MAKING AND ETHICAL PRACTICE

I am a good person, so that will make me a good counselor. I always have had values and morals and know what it takes to live a good life. I shouldn't have any problems, right? I mean, ethical decisions are just taking what I know is right and applying it to the client's situation. So if an adolescent tells me she is thinking about having sex with her boyfriend, I tell her parents. Wait, I mean that I keep her confidence and help her make good choices. Now what do I do?

CHAPTER OVERVIEW

This chapter introduces the reader to the roles and functions of professional codes of ethics. The foundational ethical principles of autonomy, nonmaleficence, beneficence, justice, and fidelity undergird all ethical practice in professional counseling. These principles are manifested in the various codes of ethics developed by professional organizations that counselors join. This chapter helps readers explore their personal values, morals, and ethics that influence how they ethically practice as counselors. These personal considerations have to be integrated into professional considerations, typically through the use of an ethical decision-making model (EDM). As such, the basics of ethical decision making are described. Finally, the intersection between ethics and law is introduced.

LEARNING OBJECTIVES

After reading this chapter you will be able to do the following:

1. Describe the foundational ethical principles of autonomy, nonmaleficence, beneficence, justice, and fidelity.

2. Differentiate between mandatory and aspirational ethics.

3. Analyze your personal ethics and values using the Counseling Ethics Audit (CEA).

4. Evaluate each step in the ethical decision-making process.

5. Examine ethical challenges, and apply ethical codes to each situation.

CACREP STANDARDS

CACREP Core Standards

G.1.j. Ethical standards of professional organizations and credentialing bodies and applications of ethical and legal considerations in professional counseling.

CACREP Clinical Mental Health Standards

A.2. Understands the ethical and legal considerations specifically related to the practice of clinical mental health counseling.

INTRODUCTION

Welcome to the world of ethical decision making and ethical practice in counseling. As counselors, we are reliant on ethical codes and models of decision making that help us serve our clients. This chapter will focus on the foundational purpose of codes of ethics, the principles that guide our practice, how ethical decisions are made, and how ethics works in tandem with law to inform our professional identities.

Being a professional counselor means that we honor the code of ethics put forth by our primary professional organization: the American Counseling Association (ACA). We may find that we also fall under other codes such as those established by the American Mental Health Counselors Association

(AMHCA), the American School Counselors Association (ASCA), and others. Our professional memberships help us determine the codes we fall under, but even if we do not join a professional organization, we are bound to the codes that are considered to be the gold standard of our profession: those of the ACA.

FOUNDATIONAL ETHICAL PRINCIPLES

We will begin our discussion of ethics by talking about some of the foundational principles that underscore an ethical approach to counseling. While various elements of ethics have been discussed, debated, and clarified since the beginning of time, the counseling profession looks to the foundational principles established by Kitchener (1984). Those principles are autonomy, nonmaleficence, beneficence, justice, and fidelity.

Autonomy

Autonomy means to have will or freedom to make independent choices. Essentially, we value autonomy as ethical counselors because we view the clients as having the right and ability to make their own decisions. Autonomy is also reflected in the way we perceive values. The overriding values honored in the session are those of the client. Of course, not all individuals are able to express or even determine their own values, and part of the process of counseling is to assist them in this development (Fisher & Oransky, 2008).

You might be thinking something like this: What do we do if the client's choices are not in their best interests? Of course we may have differing opinions, but we need to remember that is because we have differing values. Our role is to value what the client values. If choices have negative consequences, we help clients see the big picture, so they can adjust their choices accordingly. Overall, we recognize that clients have the right to make their own choices, and we support them in making the best decisions for their situations. If competency is in question, then we may have a different duty, but for the most part, our role is to support the concept of independence in the client.

Nonmaleficence

Most of us have heard of the concept of nonmaleficence, but we have not always heard this formal term. Nonmaleficence simply means to do no harm. You likely have heard of this related to the Hippocratic oath that physicians take. We should never act with malice or intent to harm clients. Rarely, if ever, do counselors intend to harm clients. However, there may be times when we might unintentionally harm clients if we do not thoroughly consider the impact of our decisions (Jennings, Sovereign, Bottorff, Mussell, & Vye, 2005).

In relation to our profession, nonmaleficence also refers to our duty to avoid using ineffective treatments. This becomes important when we select certain theoretical approaches or treatment strategies. We must not use treatments we know to be ineffective (Whitman, Glosoff, Kocet, & Tarvydas, 2006). In addition, our ethical codes require that we share with clients when we are considering new or untested treatment approaches. When considering these approaches, the risks of treatment (harm) must be understood in light of the potential benefits. Ultimately, the previous concept of autonomy comes into play as the client must decide whether the potential benefits outweigh the potential harms.

Beneficence

While doing no harm is certainly important, it seems even more important that as professional counselors we also provide a benefit to clients. Beneficence, in its shortest form, means to do good. Our approaches to treatment should result in an ultimate benefit to the client (Cesta, 2011). We operate from this principle when we work proactively to benefit our clients and help avoid any harm to them. While all principles are important, beneficence seems to direct everything that we do as professional counselors and thus carries significant weight in our decision making.

Justice

The relative equivalent of the word *justice* is fairness. Another synonym is impartiality. But the term justice when applied to counseling ethics does not mean that we always treat clients the same way. As a profession that values the uniqueness of individuals, we recognize that it is impossible to be completely equal with all clients. Rather, justice is a compassionate means of treating all with fairness and integrity in relation to their respective circumstances and inherent context (Forester-Miller & Davis, 1996).

Fidelity

So often when we hear the word *fidelity*, we think of faithful, romantic relationships. There certainly is an element of faithfulness in the word. In relation to counseling, counselors must be mindful to the interests of our clients and keep those in mind first above all others. Fidelity requires that we maintain the trust and confidence of our clients. It further requires that we, as counselors, do what we say we are going to do for our clients (Randall & Biggs, 2008).

In addition to doing what we say we are going to do, fidelity implies that the client is able to trust the counselor. The counselor is responsible for creating a safe environment for clients. One of the core aspects of a safe environment is trust, which is encapsulated in this ethical principle of fidelity. As you can imagine, clients must be able to trust that their counselors will keep their confidences. It is also important that clients trust that their counselors can be helpful. Thus, fidelity is crucial to the relationship.

MANDATORY VERSUS ASPIRATIONAL ETHICS

We have discussed the foundation of ethics, but how do we use ethics? As counselors, we know we are bound by codes of ethics. However, we may not fully understand what it means to be ethical. Most of us believe we are ethical but are unaware that there are different types of ethics.

The basic, fundamental approach to ethics is called mandatory ethics. Following ethical codes from a mandatory perspective means that we are functioning at a letter-of-the-law level. This is the most basic level of ethical behavior and indicates that we are in compliance with the posted ethical regulations of our profession. Mandatory ethics are self-focused. A mandatory approach to ethical practice serves to keep the counselor out of trouble and to provide direction when there is potential for litigation. In other words, counselors who follow a strict mandatory ethics approach are more interested in covering all their bases than serving their clients.

CASE STUDY 1.1

Jocelyn is a counselor at a college counseling center. Keith is a new client who has come in to decide if his current major is the right choice for him. Keith is 19 and a sophomore majoring in math. He is considering a move to accounting and wants you to do a career assessment for him. During your initial intake, you ask about substance use. Keith denies any regular use but does admit to drinking beer a few weeks ago at a fraternity party. In your state, the drinking age is 21.

1. *Do you have a legal obligation to tell someone of Keith's drinking?*

2. *If Keith's mother were to call you, would you be obligated to tell her?*

3. *Could or should you tell Keith's mother that he is considering a major change?*

Aspirational ethics, on the other hand, serve the spirit of the law and have a different focus. Counselors who operate from an aspirational perspective are concerned about client welfare. They demonstrate a measure of respect for the client in all decisions. Such counselors take the time to consider not just how the decision can impact them and their career but also how their actions impact the client, the community, and the profession of counseling as a whole. While the counselor functioning from a mandatory perspective is focused on avoiding malpractice suits, the counselor employing aspirational ethics focuses on what is best for the client.

As you can imagine, you will be advised by others to function from an aspirational perspective. However, only you can be the judge of that. As we move forward in the text and discuss ethical decision making, involving the client, and consulting with others, we hope that you will see the benefit in aspirational ethics.

UNDERSTANDING PERSONAL ETHICS AND VALUES

Beginning counselors in training often believe that the code of ethics will tell us what to do in any given dilemma. In fact, we tend to look to the code as a dynamic document that can apply itself to any situation and give us the correct solution. Unfortunately, ethical dilemmas are not formulas with clear solutions, and ethical codes are not so flexible that they completely wrap around all dilemmas. Counselors must use judgment when executing decisions based on the code, and that judgment is influenced by our values.

It is likely that you feel confident in knowing your values. It is also likely that you feel secure with discerning what is ethical and unethical in most situations. What we find, however, is that ethical dilemmas are complex and rarely as cut-and-dried as we would like. For example, when asked, most people would say that stealing is wrong. But have you ever taken a pen or paper clip from the office? Printed schoolwork on the office computer? Used office time to pay bills or make personal calls? Probably so, yet those are all forms of stealing. These same shades of gray are present in counseling ethics. The cases presented in this text rarely have one right answer. As such, it will be important to understand your values and how they relate to counseling ethics.

Guided Practice Exercise 1.1

What Are My Values?

Counseling Value	How Does This Work in My Personal Life?	What Will This Mean for Me as a Counselor?
• Autonomy—freedom to make independent choices	• Consider a time that you have made a choice all on your own. Remember how risky it felt? What was the outcome? What would you do differently (if anything)?	• How will you allow clients to be the authors of their own stories? What will it be like for you when clients make decisions that you think are not in their best interests?
• Nonmaleficence—avoiding harm	• Consider a time that you have acted to keep someone from being hurt. What motivated you? Did it work?	• Being a counselor means going beyond avoiding harm. However, some treatments are more effective than others. How will you go about finding the best treatment for your clients?
• Beneficence—helping others	• Most counseling students are exceptionally compassionate people. Think about a time that you did something specifically to help another person without expecting any benefit for yourself. How did it work out? How did you feel?	• Clients rely on us to help them. What will you do to make sure clients are being helped? How will you assess and document their growth and change?
• Justice—acting with fairness and integrity	• Consider a time that you had to act based on fairness rather than what you wanted. What were the circumstances? What happened as a result?	• Clients are different and thus cannot all be treated equally. However, we must aim to treat clients in similar situations in similar ways. How will you know you are being fair?
• Fidelity—maintaining trust and confidence	• Most of us learn about trust and confidentiality when it is broken. When has your trust been broken? How did that change your approach to trusting others and being trustworthy to others?	• It is both an ethical and legal requirement to hold client information confidential. However, many clients do not trust this. How can you help them understand your ethical and legal mandates as well as exceptions to those mandates?

Ethical Autobiography

As beginning counselors, we must understand our personal ethics and the ethics of the profession. That way, we can begin to acculturate or blend the two (Bashe, Anderson, Handelsman, & Klevansky, 2007). While there are many books, articles, courses, and seminars to teach us about professional counseling ethics, there is nothing that truly teaches us about our own ethics. One way to approach understanding our own ethics is to reflect on our ethical development. Consider this, how did you develop your personal ethics? Who were your primary influences? What circumstances or events shaped who you are?

CASE STUDY 1.2

Alonzo is a first-year counseling student taking a professionalism and ethics course. As a child, Alonzo had an uncle he could tell anything to. That uncle always held his confidences and was a safe outlet for him to talk to. One day, Alonzo's uncle wasn't around, so he talked with an older cousin about an argument he had with his mother the night before. This cousin was sympathetic but told Alonzo's mother everything he had said!

1. *How do you think these experiences contributed to Alonzo's understanding of trust and confidentiality?*

2. *How might Alonzo use these experiences to better protect confidentiality of his clients?*

It is a useful exercise for beginning counselors to develop an ethical autobiography. This exercise allows you to explore any preexisting beliefs and values that may impact your acculturation into the profession (Bashe et al., 2007). Your history is important. Who you are is important. The way you integrate who you are into the ethical practice of counseling is also important. To facilitate this integration, beginning counselors are encouraged to journal about their development and the influences that have made them who they are.

Developing an ethical autobiography takes you a step beyond simply memorizing the codes of ethics and places your understanding of morals and values within those codes. Begin with an exploration of your upbringing. Who were your primary ethical influences? What events shaped or changed you? When have your ethics ever been challenged, and how did you handle it? Reflecting on these questions allows you to begin understanding yourself as an ethical person and ethical counselor. To build on this experience, write about "the three characteristics, values, motivations, principles, behaviors, or skills that [you] believe will be [your] greatest assets" as a professional ethical counselor (Bashe et al., 2007, p. 64). Follow this by reflecting on how these very same assets could become challenges as a professional ethical counselor. For example, if you say that having a passion for counseling is one of your strengths, you might discuss how this passion will drive you to help others. When looking at how that asset may be a challenge, you also may see that having such passion may lead to over-identification with clients and burnout. By looking at the flip side of this coin, you can begin to appreciate the types of challenges posed by ethical decisions. What seems right can be harmful, and what seems wrong may have benefit.

Counseling Ethics Audit

Learning the codes of ethics for the various professional organizations to which you belong is an initial step in understanding ethical practice. However, we find that many counselors in training or beginning counselors are less certain about how to apply the code to practice. To help you begin to understand how you will practice as an ethical counselor, we invite you to take the CEA. The CEA is a self-exploration tool intended for practicing counselors that was developed by the third author of this text, Dr. Michael M. Kocet. It serves as a way of taking inventory of actual practice and as a guide for reflection on actual practice. Envision yourself as the practicing professional counselor you aspire to be. As you do so, respond to these items. How do you see yourself functioning in this role?

Table 1.1 Counseling Ethics Audit

The Counseling Ethics Audit (CEA)

*The purpose of the CEA is to guide professional counseling practice across settings. It is not intended to be comprehensive in scope but presented as a tool for fostering ethical sensitivity and reflection. Read each statement below. On a scale of 1 to 10, with 1 being **never** and 10 being **always**, rate yourself regarding your professional ethical practice in counseling. Please an X next to the rating that best matches your response.*

(Continued)

Table 1.1 (Continued)

Ethical Awareness and Sensitivity	1	2	3	4	5	6	7	8	9	10
I regularly consult or review the ACA Code of Ethics (2014) as well as other professional codes of ethics I utilize in my counseling practice (minimum of one or two per month) and when dictated by challenging ethical dilemmas.										
I employ a formal model of ethical decision making into my daily professional practice.										
I have a formal professional relationship with a colleague, supervisor, or mentor who provides ongoing ethical guidance and feedback on my professional counseling practice.										
I am aware of how my values and beliefs impact my work with clients and students and take steps to work through conflicts between my personal and professional ethics.										
Informed Consent										
I have a formal, written informed consent statement, which includes my signature and the client's or student's (and legal guardian's) signature and date.										
My written informed consent form has been reviewed by a lawyer or other legal expert.										
I review informed consent procedures and expectations with clients and students verbally and in writing on a regular basis.										
I regularly bring up the issue of informed consent in my sessions with clients.										
Confidentiality										
I do not discuss client issues with friends, family members, or others in my personal life.										
I understand the limitations of confidentiality and explain this to my clients.										
When faced with an ethical situation where confidentiality may have to be broken, I engage in a conversation with my client about the best course of action.										

Ethical Awareness and Sensitivity	1	2	3	4	5	6	7	8	9	10
Record Keeping and Documentation										
I treat clients' files and records with respect in regard to their privacy.										
When using computers or other electronic devices, I use encryption software or other devices to protect client information.										
When having computers or other technology repaired by others, I take active steps to ensure that client information contained on computers or other technologies are maintained in a confidential manner.										
I do have a protocol in place to address client or student requests for access or review of his or her records.										
I ensure that client files are locked and secured at all times.										
I review with administrative staff the ethical and appropriate handling of confidentiality information, such as billing records, social security numbers, and other private information.										
I have left instructions for the handling of client records and confidential information in the event of my incapacitation, illness, or death.										
Boundaries										
I am aware of the importance of maintaining professional boundaries with clients, their families, as well as colleagues and those I work with.										
I have reviewed the ACA (2014) ethical standards on potentially beneficial relationships as well as avoiding inappropriate dual relationships that are harmful to clients.										
When considering engaging in potentially beneficial relationships with clients, I discuss with clients the risks and benefits of such interactions and document in client records such conversations.										

(Continued)

Table 1.1 (Continued)

Ethical Awareness and Sensitivity	1	2	3	4	5	6	7	8	9	10
I understand that it is my responsibility as a counselor to protect the welfare and promote the well-being of clients and students.										
When engaging in potentially beneficial relationships (boundary crossings) with clients, I have ongoing dialogues about such interactions with clients and seek consultation when appropriate regarding any challenges or difficulties.										
I have a formal plan in place (a professional will) regarding how to handle my counseling practice (referral of clients and students to other providers) in the event of my incapacitation, illness, death, or retirement from the profession. I have a professional counseling colleague who will contact my clients (when needed) about my incapacitation, illness, or death and take appropriate steps to ensure an appropriate transition to other counseling services.										
Counseling Setting										
I take steps to ensure that my office or counseling environment is quiet and respects the confidential nature of the therapeutic relationship.										
My office environment uses devices in waiting areas (such as music, sound or static noise devices, or glass partitions) to protect confidential conversations from public areas.										
I ensure that my office environment creates a welcoming and safe environment for clients and students to participate in the counseling process.										
Cultural Sensitivity										
I employ cross-cultural awareness, knowledge, and skills necessary to work competently with clients from diverse backgrounds.										

Ethical Awareness and Sensitivity	1	2	3	4	5	6	7	8	9	10
When working with clients from diverse cultures outside of my area of expertise or competence, I make a referral to a colleague with such expertise or training.										
When referring clients from diverse backgrounds to others, I reflect on the experience and take steps to increase my cultural competency for future work with this cultural population.										
I read professional journal articles, or books addressing multicultural and diversity issues in counseling on a regular basis (a minimum of every 6 to 12 months).										
I attend a workshop or presentation addressing multicultural or diversity issues in counseling a minimum of once every two to three years.										
I am aware of and sensitive to my biases and prejudices regarding clients and students from diverse backgrounds and take active steps to remediate my own cultural insensitivity.										
Continuing Education and Training										
I read professional journal articles, or books addressing ethical issues in counseling on a regular basis (a minimum of every 6 to 12 months).										
I attend a workshop or presentation addressing ethical issues in counseling a minimum of once every two to three years.										
I maintain my professional certificate or licensure renewal requirements as dictated by local, state, or federal policies.										

After completing the CEA, some thoughts and reactions I have to my own ethical practice are these:

STEPS IN THE ETHICAL DECISION-MAKING PROCESS

Clearly, understanding our personal ethical boundaries is part of the process of ethical decision making. However, understanding how to make ethical decisions is also integral to the process. In Chapter 3 of this text, we will introduce you to EDMs that are grounded in specific counseling practices and theories. In Chapter 4, we will cover EDMs used with various client populations. In Chapter 5, we will introduce you to a Relational Ethical Decision-Making Model that will guide you through the remainder of the text. As you can see, understanding EDMs is crucial to ethical practice.

Prior to learning about specific EDMs, we want you to be comfortable with the general ethical decision-making process. To that end, let's take a look at how most counselors make ethical decisions. Our code provides us with some guidelines about ethical decision making. We are reminded in the introduction to the code that we are to use a process to guide our ethical decision making (ACA, 2014).

Ethical Code 1.1

ACA Code of Ethics Purpose.

When counselors are faced with ethical dilemmas that are difficult to resolve, they are expected to engage in a carefully considered ethical decision-making process, consulting available resources as needed.

Source: 2014 American Counseling Association Code of Ethics. Reprinted with permission from American Counseling Association.

So what does an ethical decision look like? First, we have to identify if an ethical challenge even exists. To do so, most of us compare what is happening to our internal moral compass (Johnson, 2012). We may be made aware that there is an ethical challenge by our client, by our colleague, by our supervisor, or by our own sense of right and wrong. We are aware of ethical challenges because we have knowledge of the codes under which we fall.

Ethical Code 1.2

Section H.1.a. Knowledge.

Counselors know and understand the ACA Code of Ethics and other applicable ethics codes from professional organizations or certification and licensure bodies of which they are members. Lack of knowledge or misunderstanding of an ethical responsibility is not a defense against a charge of unethical conduct.

Source: 2014 American Counseling Association Code of Ethics. Reprinted with permission from American Counseling Association.

However, merely having knowledge that a dilemma exists and what the code says about similar dilemmas is not sufficient.

Next, we have to review the ethical code and relevant rules and laws and compare the dilemma to the professional standards. We must be aware of what to do when faced with a circumstance where ethics and laws disagree. As professional counselors, we are not expected to act alone when making ethical decisions.

Ethical Code 1.3

H.1.b. Conflicts Between Ethics and Laws.

If ethical responsibilities conflict with the law, regulations, and/or other governing legal authority, counselors make known their commitment to the ACA Code of Ethics and take steps to resolve the conflict. If the conflict cannot be resolved, counselors, acting in the best interest of the client, may adhere to the requirements of the law, regulations, and/or other governing legal authority.

Source: 2014 American Counseling Association Code of Ethics. Reprinted with permission from American Counseling Association.

Common to most EDMs is the concept of consultation. After identifying the dilemma and checking it against personal and professional standards, it is good practice to consult with someone else in the field and get another counselor's perspective. In fact, our ethical code requires it of us.

Ethical Code 1.4

Section H: Introduction.

Counselors strive to resolve ethical dilemmas with direct and open communication among all parties involved and seek consultation with colleagues and supervisors when necessary.

Source: 2014 American Counseling Association Code of Ethics. Reprinted with permission from American Counseling Association.

Finally, a decision must be made and acted on. Sounds simple, right? As you can imagine, that is rarely the case. Let's take a look at a short case illustration to begin to understand how complex ethical decisions can become.

> *In your newly opened private practice, you receive a call from Alisha, who wants you to see her son Marcus. Marcus is seven years old, and Alisha is worried that his grades are suffering since she and Marcus's father, Donald, divorced earlier this year. Marcus was exposed to his father's rages and frequent drunkenness. Alisha says that Donald is sober now. He lives nearby and sees Marcus every other weekend. Marcus loves both of his parents but is understandably sad that they are not together and that he goes back and forth between the two.*
>
> *You agree to see Marcus and meet with him and Alisha to start working with him. After you see Marcus several times, you receive a call from Donald. Marcus shared with him that he was in counseling with you, and he wants to know what you are working on and how Marcus is doing. What do you do?*

To address this case, we need to consider the steps commonly used in ethical decision making. As you read through the case, you likely had an answer to the question: What do you do? But to answer at this point would be premature. First we must determine if an ethical dilemma exists. The answer to that is probably affirmative. You have entered into a relationship with a child who has parents. Who has the right to the child's information?

It is likely at this point that you have tuned into your own ethical and moral standards. Is it right for Donald to have access to Marcus's information? You may have a different opinion than your peers on this point. Some of you will say that because Alisha initiated the counseling, Alisha is the parent who has the right to access information. Others will say that Donald is a parent too and deserves equal access.

What next? Next we turn to the code of ethics and relevant laws. Specifically, we want to look at ACA Codes B.5.a. and B.5.b.

Ethical Code 1.5

B.5.a. Responsibility to Clients.

When counseling minor clients or adult clients who lack the capacity to give voluntary, informed consent, counselors protect the confidentiality of information received in the counseling relationship as specified by federal and state laws, written policies, and applicable ethical standards.

B.5.b. Parents and Legal Guardians.

Counselors inform parents and legal guardians about the role of counselors and the confidential nature of the counseling relationship. Counselors are sensitive to the cultural diversity of families and respect the inherent rights and responsibilities of parents and guardians over the welfare of their children or charges according to law. Counselors work to establish, as appropriate, collaborative relationships with parents and guardians to best serve clients.

Source: 2014 American Counseling Association Code of Ethics. Reprinted with permission from American Counseling Association.

These codes direct us to protect our clients, even minors, whenever possible. Whenever possible means whenever it does not conflict with policy and law. In addition, we work with parents to understand the confidential nature of the work that we do while respecting the legal right parents have to records.

So where does that leave us? In most states, unless the parent with whom the child does not live (in this case, the father) has lost parental rights, that parent has the legal ability to consent to, or refuse, treatment. In addition, each parent has the right to educational and medical records. When faced with this dilemma, you will want to review your agency policy, consult with your supervisor or another counselor, consult with an attorney if possible, and make and document your decision. Will you involve your minor client in this process? Not likely. Instead, assuming Donald has all parental rights, it is likely that you will share information with him in the same manner that you share information with Alisha.

ETHICAL DECISION-MAKING CHALLENGES

As you can see, there are many elements to consider when making ethical decisions. It is our contention that people enter into the profession of counseling with an innate desire to do good. Consider your own motives. It is likely that you are a counselor or are becoming a counselor because you want to help people. You may have had your own positive experiences with counseling, or you may have lacked access to such care and want to improve options for others. Perhaps you were the go-to person in your peer group and provided lay counseling to your friends. Whatever your motives, chances are that they are driven by good intentions. However, even good people can make bad decisions. How does that happen?

At this stage in your development, ethical transgressions may seem unthinkable. Yet because they happen, we must consider why they happen. First, let's consider where professional counselors make the most missteps. Then we will take a look at how these transgressions may occur. According to data provided by the ACA Ethics Committee (2012), nearly 5,000 ethical inquiries were received during 2011. It is important to add that the number of overall inquiries has increased dramatically. In 2005, there were only 758 inquiries compared to 4,943 in 2012 (Anderson & Freeman, 2006). Of these 4,943 inquiries, 32 percent had to do with confidentiality issues. Concerns in this area include releasing records without permission, responding to subpoenas, and handling expert witness issues. Another 27 percent of the inquiries were related to licensure. Licensure questions include things such as determining if a person who has a license in social work can advertise as a licensed counselor. Finally, 19 percent of the inquiries fall under the category of professional responsibility, which includes soliciting clients through advertising and duty to warn (ACA Ethics Committee, 2012).

Many of these inquiries have easy answers. However, ethical decision making is generally complex. We know that while practicing counselors strive to do good, they may fall into some of the ethical decision-making traps common across many helping professions.

Ethical Traps

As we make an ethical decision, we believe we are doing the right thing for our client and for the profession. We take the context into account and carefully weigh our decisions against ethical best practices. But we are not immune to flawed thinking. Steinman, Richardson, and McEnroe (1998) first identified four potential ethical traps for counselors to consider.

Ethical Trap 1—The Commonsense Objectivity Trap

The first ethical trap is the belief that if the solution makes sense, it is right. Because we are asked to engage in a gut check as part of ethical decision making, we run the risk of using that step as the only litmus test for ethical behavior. What we know is that some ethical decisions do not feel good but are right. Because ethical decisions also are guided by law, they may not pass our gut check but still be the correct course of action. For example, it may feel right to keep a secret for a minor client, but if the secret is contained in the records and a parent requests the records, confidentiality will be broken. Another challenge to this way of thinking is that we are assuming objectivity. The reality is that objectivity is rarely possible in ethical decisions. If we believe we are truly objective, we are probably deluding ourselves! These are our clients, and we care about them. We also have our own opinions, rendering the reaction subjective rather than objective. In other words, because we are human, we cannot be objective in matters that involve us.

Ethical Trap 2—The Values Trap

The second trap is an extension of the first trap and has to do with the distinct differences between our personal values and the values of the profession. When we learn about ethics, we are asked to consider our morals, our values, and even our religious beliefs. While important, these are not professional ethical codes. Decisions based solely on our personal values and convictions may not be ethical. They may feel right, to be sure, but we must acknowledge that the decision is based on our personal influences rather than the edicts of our profession.

Guided Practice Exercise 1.2

Learning About Trust

Many challenging decisions in ethics have to do with minor clients. As such, it is critical to know laws that govern minor clients in your state. Take some time to investigate age of consent laws for your state. At what age can a minor consent to medical (counseling) treatment? Consent to sex? Obtain an abortion?

Ethical Trap 3—The Circumstantiality Trap

The third ethical trap is the idea that there can never be a right or wrong response to an ethical dilemma because of the circumstances under which a behavior occurred. While the response to most ethical dilemmas is initially *it depends*, once the dilemma is fully understood, there is often an explicitly right or wrong response. Clearly, dilemmas are complicated, and context is important. However, there are no circumstances under which a romantic relationship with a current client is an ethically sound decision, for example.

Ethical Trap 4—The Who Will Benefit Trap

The last ethical trap is a bit more challenging to consider. The who will benefit trap describes the implicit or explicit fact that there is a winner and a loser in most ethical decisions. In other words, as counselors, we may find ourselves taking sides and joining forces for and against the parties involved. We talk about breaking confidentiality that inevitably feels like we have violated not just a concept but a person. After all, it wouldn't be breaking confidentiality if they wanted us to share it. As we consider the dilemma, we must not get caught up in winners and losers. Instead, we must work to provide the most ethical outcome. In Chapter 5 we will discuss Relational Ethical Decision Making, which seeks to involve all stakeholders, most importantly the client, in the ultimate decision.

AVOIDING ETHICAL TRAPS

How can we avoid these ethical traps? By avoiding some of the potential rationalizations that may skew our thinking. Some rationalizations that typically get in our way are thoughts such as these:

- If it's necessary, it's ethical.
- If it's legal and permissible, it's proper.
- It's just part of the job.
- It's all for a good cause.
- I was just doing it for you.
- I'm just fighting fire with fire.
- It doesn't hurt anyone.
- Everyone's doing it.
- It's OK if I don't gain personally.
- I've got it coming.
- I can still be objective. (Josephson Institute, 2002, p. 4)

As challenging as ethical decisions may be, there are ways to ensure that you are on the right track. People who go into helping professions such as counseling tend to be kindhearted individuals with a desire to help others. They tend to have some awareness of their own ethics, morals, and values. However, they must follow an EDM to ensure that their personal values assist rather than complicate the process.

What Happens When Unethical Behavior Is Suspected?

We have discussed the concept of ethics and ethical dilemmas. We have considered ethical decision making and common traps we may fall into. We understand that codes of ethics are written to allow professional counselors to keep ourselves in check. In other words, we should apply the codes to ourselves rather than simply using them to evaluate the behavior of others.

However, there will be times when we suspect that someone is behaving unethically. A client may share information about a previous counselor or perhaps someone is engaging in unethical practices in the workplace. What should we do? Consider the following example:

Malana and Geoffrey share an office where they maintain independent private practices. They have worked in this building together for the past three years and occasionally consult with one another. One day, they take a lunch break and walk to the deli down the street. Malana is lamenting her upcoming licensure renewal for the state board saying, "It always makes me so nervous! I am always afraid that I calculated my continuing education wrong or, worse, that I will be subject to a random audit! I attend a lot of conferences and always have enough hours, but for some reason the process makes me nervous." Geoffrey confides, "I don't get nervous—I just make it all up! When the form comes, I write my check for the annual renewal, check the box that says I completed my continuing education, and send it in. Never been audited, so what is the harm? I hate conferences and never attend those. I don't have time to take continuing education classes even if they are online. I'm a good counselor; my clients tell me so and business is good!"

The first thing we need to determine is if there is an ethical transgression and, if so, under which code does it fall? Counselors are obligated by the ACA (2014) Code of Ethics to maintain continuing education.

Ethical Code 1.6

C.2.f. Continuing Education.

Counselors recognize the need for continuing education to acquire and maintain a reasonable level of awareness of current scientific and professional information in their fields of activity. They take steps to maintain competence in the skills they use, are open to new procedures, and keep current with the diverse populations and specific populations with whom they work.

Source: 2014 American Counseling Association Code of Ethics. Reprinted with permission from American Counseling Association.

Counselors should stay informed about the populations they serve and maintain their skills for working with these clients. They keep up-to-date on the latest scientific practices to provide the highest quality services to clients. Because Geoffrey seems uninterested in staying abreast of best practices, Malana has every reason to be concerned. Second, there are legal implications. Geoffrey is misrepresenting himself to their state licensure board, which is illegal. His license could be in jeopardy.

Next, what should Malana do? The last section of the ACA Code of Ethics is Section H: Resolving Ethical Issues. After consulting this section, Malana will find several codes apply under H.2. First, code H.2.a. provides the expectation that some action should be taken.

> ## Ethical Code 1.7
>
> ### H.2.a. Ethical Behavior Expected.
>
> Counselors expect colleagues to adhere to the ACA Code of Ethics. When counselors possess knowledge that raises doubts as to whether another counselor is acting in an ethical manner, they take appropriate action.
>
> *Source:* 2014 American Counseling Association Code of Ethics. Reprinted with permission from American Counseling Association.

However, that action does not immediately translate into a call to the state licensure board. In fact, the code is very clear in H.2.b. that counselors should try to resolve the issue with the other counselor directly, in an informal manner, whenever possible.

> ## Ethical Code 1.8
>
> ### H.2.b. Informal Resolution.
>
> When counselors have reason to believe that another counselor is violating or has violated an ethical standard, they attempt first to resolve the issue informally with the other counselor if feasible, provided such action does not violate confidentiality rights that may be involved.
>
> *Source:* 2014 American Counseling Association Code of Ethics. Reprinted with permission from American Counseling Association.

In this case, Malana can simply bring it up with Geoffrey. She can explain to him that continuing education is a professional responsibility for all counselors and that by not doing so, he is violating both the ACA Code of Ethics and the state licensure board. Hopefully, Geoffrey will recognize the importance of this effort and change his behavior accordingly.

If Malana continues to find that Geoffrey is not obtaining continuing education and is falsifying his licensure renewal, she may have to take additional action. This is when code H.2.c. can be used.

Ethical Code 1.9

H.2.c. Reporting Ethical Violations.

If an apparent violation has harmed substantially, or is likely to harm substantially a person or organization, and is not appropriate for informal resolution, or is not resolved properly, counselors take further action appropriate to the situation. Such action might include referral to state or national committees on professional ethics, voluntary national certification bodies, state licensing boards, or appropriate institutional authorities. This standard does not apply when an intervention would violate confidentiality rights or when counselors have been retained to review the work of another counselor whose professional conduct is in question.

Source: 2014 American Counseling Association Code of Ethics. Reprinted with permission from American Counseling Association.

Ethical violations can and should be reported if there is potential for substantial harm to come to a client and the matter was not resolved after the counselor was informed directly. In this situation, Malana may wish to consult to make sure she is on the right track.

Ethical Code 1.10

H.2.d. Consultation.

When uncertain as to whether a particular situation or course of action may be in violation of the ACA Code of Ethics, counselors consult with other counselors who are knowledgeable about ethics and the ACA Code of Ethics, with colleagues, or with appropriate authorities.

Source: 2014 American Counseling Association Code of Ethics. Reprinted with permission from American Counseling Association.

If her consultants agree, Malana could report what she knows to the state licensure board, ACA, and any other professional organization or credentialing body that apply in Geoffrey's case. These entities may conduct independent investigations resulting in sanctions or even revocation of a license or credentials.

As such, it is in Geoffrey's best interests to follow procedures rather than run the risk of losing his license and practice!

The Intersection of Ethics and Law

Many of the ethical transgressions we discuss are just that, purely ethical transgressions. They do not always have a legal element. However, the astute professional counselor will work hard to minimize any gaps between legal and ethical practice (Stone & Zirkel, 2010). The ACA Code of Ethics actually addresses this in code H.1.b., indicating that when there are conflicts between the law and ethical codes, counselors work to resolve those conflicts.

Ethical Code 1.11

H.1.b. Conflicts Between Ethics and Laws.

If ethical responsibilities conflict with law, regulations, or other governing legal authority, counselors make known their commitment to the ACA Code of Ethics and take steps to resolve the conflict. If the conflict cannot be resolved by such means, counselors may adhere to the requirements of law, regulations, or other governing legal authority.

Source: 2014 American Counseling Association Code of Ethics. Reprinted with permission from American Counseling Association.

As you can see, when no solution is available to bridge the gap between laws and ethics, counselors are advised to follow the law. If a state law is counter to ethical practice, this may be a point of advocacy for counselors in that state.

You may be wondering how laws and ethics can collide if they are both intended to protect clients who are vulnerable in the relationship. In fact, such conflicts are not common, but they do occur. For example, the law does not recognize minor clients. By law, minors cannot enter into contracts and, thus, cannot be clients (Keim & Cobia, 2010). However, as counselors, we offer minor clients many of the ethical rights we offer to adults including involvement in the process and measures of confidentiality. If properly requested, records may be provided to the minor client's parent or guardian (Hermann, 2011). While legal, is it always in the minor client's best interests? That is up to you to decide in conjunction with your client and the parent or guardian. Of course you will want to use an EDM and consult during the process. We are sure you can see how quickly legal and ethical entanglements become complicated!

CONCLUSION

Becoming a professional counselor is a process. Part of the process involves learning the ethical codes and laws that govern our profession. Simply knowing the rules, if you will, is insufficient. Professional counselors who practice ethically also know how to dissect elements of an ethical dilemma and apply an EDM. We understand the importance of consultation, supervision, and documentation. We understand the ethical traps that we may fall prey to, even with the best intentions. And finally, we know how to turn to the code to guide us when faced with a challenge. The remainder of this text will introduce you to the complexities of EDMs and the various dilemmas they help address. It is our hope that through the process, you simply will not learn the material but will begin to apply it as well. Welcome to the beginning of your journey to become an ethical professional counselor!

KEYSTONES

- As counselors, we rely on ethical codes and models of decision making that help us serve our clients. Being a professional counselor means that we honor the ACA Code of Ethics. We also may fall under other codes such as those established by the AMHCA, the ASCA, and others.
- The counseling profession looks to some of the foundational principles that underscore an ethical approach to counseling: autonomy, nonmaleficence, beneficence, justice, and fidelity. Autonomy means to have will or freedom to make independent choices. Nonmaleficence means to do no harm. Beneficence means to do good. Justice is a compassionate means of treating all with fairness and integrity in relation to their respective circumstances and inherent context. Fidelity requires that we maintain the trust and confidences of our clients and do what we say we are going to do for our clients.
- Following ethical codes from a mandatory perspective means that we are functioning at a letter-of-the-law level, while aspirational ethics focus on the spirit of the law and what is best for the client.
- Ethical dilemmas are not formulas with clear solutions.
- Developing an ethical autobiography takes you a step beyond simply memorizing the codes of ethics and places your understanding of morals and values within those codes.
- There are four steps to ethical decision making. The first step is identifying if an ethical challenge even exists. Next, we have to review the ethical code and relevant rules and laws and compare the dilemma to the professional standards. Third, it is important to engage in consultation when making ethical decisions. Finally, we must choose and act on our choice.

- Counselors are not immune to flawed thinking and may fall prey to one of many ethical decision-making traps.
- Ethics and law often intersect but can, at times, collide. When no solution is available to bridge the gap between laws and ethics, counselors are advised to follow the law.

SUGGESTED BEST PRACTICES

- Always keep copies of the most up-to date codes of ethics under which you fall.
- Remember that codes of ethics protect clients and serve as guides for our decisions.
- Make sure that all decisions meet mandatory ethical limits, but strive for aspirational ethical behaviors.
- Keep your focus on the spirit of the law rather than simply the letter of the law.
- Don't look to the code for a list of "Thou Shalts." It isn't in there. Use an EDM.
- Understand your own values, ethics, and morals before you start practice as a counselor so that you can see how they influence your ethical decisions.
- Revisit your ethical autobiography from time to time. We may have been shaped by our childhood, but our adult values, ethics, and morals are our responsibility.
- Talk about ethics and ethical dilemmas with other counselors, so you can keep a sense of how others handle ethical dilemmas.
- Develop a group of trusted colleagues and peers in the profession that you feel comfortable talking about ethical concerns with. Consult with them often.
- Revisit those ethical decision-making traps. Most are slippery slopes that are easy to fall into if you don't stay vigilant.
- Avoid rash decisions when you suspect a colleague is behaving unethically. Chances are that there is no crisis, and you have time to think it through, consult, and talk to the colleague.
- Keep an eye to changes in laws at the state and federal levels. Also, pay attention to case law that sets precedents in the profession.
- Attend ongoing continuing educations related to ethics to maintain awareness of current trends and changes to best practices.

ADDITIONAL RESOURCES

In Print

Sisti, D. A., Caplan, A. L., & Rimon-Greenspan, H. (2013). *Applied ethics in mental health care: An interdisciplinary reader.* Cambridge, MA: MIT Press.

On the Web

Josephson, M. (2014). *The six pillars of character.* Retrieved from http://josephsoninstitute.org/MED/MED-2sixpillars.html

Velasquez, M., Andre, C., Shanks, T., & Meyer, M. J. (2014). *Thinking ethically: A framework for moral decision making.* Retrieved from http://www.scu.edu/ethics/practicing/decision/thinking.html

REFERENCES

ACA Ethics Committee. (2012). *Ethics committee summary—FY 11.* Retrieved from http://counseling.org/Resources/CodeOfEthics/TP/Home/CT2.aspx

American Counseling Association (ACA). (2014). *ACA code of ethics.* Alexandria, VA: Author.

Anderson, D., & Freeman, L. T. (2006). Report of the ACA Ethics Committee: 2004–2005. *Journal of Counseling & Development, 84*(2), 225–227.

Bashe, A., Anderson, S. K., Handelsman, M. M., & Klevansky, R. (2007). An acculturation model for ethics training: The ethics autobiography and beyond. *Professional Psychology: Research and Practice, 38*(1), 60–67. doi:10.1037/0735–7028.38.1.60

Cesta, T. (2011). An ethical dilemma found in a case study. *Hospital Case Management, 19*(8), 119.

Fisher, C. B., & Oransky, M. (2008). Informed consent to psychotherapy: Protecting the dignity and respecting the autonomy of patients. *Journal of Clinical Psychology, 64*(5), 576–588. doi:10.1002/jclp.20472

Forester-Miller, H., & Davis, T. (1996). *A practitioner's guide to ethical decision making.* Retrieved from http://www.counseling.org/counselors/practitionersguide.aspx

Hermann, M. A. (2011). *Law, ethics, and confidentiality.* Alexandria, VA: American School Counselor Association.

Jennings, L., Sovereign, A., Bottorff, N., Mussell, M., & Vye, C. (2005). Nine ethical values of master therapists. *Journal of Mental Health Counseling, 27*(1), 32–47.

Johnson, C. E. (2012). *Organizational ethics: A practical approach* (2nd ed.). Thousand Oaks, CA: Sage.

Josephson Institute. (2002). *Making ethical decisions.* Retrieved from http://josephsoninstitute.org/MED/index.html

Keim, M. A., & Cobia, D. (2010). Legal and ethical implications of working with minors in Alabama: Consent and confidentiality. *Alabama Counseling Association Journal, 35*(2), 28–34.

Kitchener, K. S. (1984). Intuition, critical evaluation and ethical principles: The foundation for ethical decisions in counseling psychology. *Counseling Psychologist, 12*(3), 43–55.

Randall, C., & Biggs, B. (2008). Enhancing therapeutic gains: Examination of fidelity to the model for the intensive mental health program. *Journal of Child and Family Studies, 17*(2), 191–205. doi:10.1007/s10826–007–9159–9

Steinman, S. O., Richardson, N. F., & McEnroe, T. (1998). *Ethical decision-making manual for helping professionals.* Pacific Grove, CA: Brooks Cole.

Stone, C. B., & Zirkel, P. A. (2010). School counselor advocacy: When law and ethics may collide. *Professional School Counseling, 13*(4), 244–247.

Whitman, J. S., Glosoff, H. L., Kocet, M. M. & Tarvydas, V. (2006). *Ethical issues related to conversion or reparative therapy.* Retrieved from http://www.counseling.org/pressroom/newsreleases.aspx?AGuid=b68aba97–2f08–40c2-a400–0630765f72f4

Chapter 2

ETHICAL DECISION-
MAKING MODELS

You sit in your morning worship service enjoying the sermon, the songs, and the fellowship of the congregants. At the end of the service, a woman you have never met before comes up to introduce herself. "I hear you are also a counselor," she says. "I would like to make an appointment with you to work on my recent move to the area. Is it OK if I just give your office a call?" She seems nice enough and would probably make a good client for you. But it seems you are attending the same church. What should you do?

CHAPTER OVERVIEW

This chapter introduces the reader to numerous ethical decision-making models (EDMs). These models are grouped together based on theory, practice, or cultural relevance. Counselors have dozens of EDMs to choose from. The question is which model is the best. Each model has its merits depending on the style of the counselor, the type of client, and the context of the situation. However, as you read through this chapter, you will see a number a commonalities among the models. Most models will suggest investigating relevant codes and laws, engaging in consultation, and considering possible outcomes. However, each model offers a unique lens through which to view the dilemma. Because ethical dilemmas are not black and white, the models in this chapter serve as a reference for evaluating the many shades of gray each dilemma contains.

LEARNING OBJECTIVES

After reading this chapter you will be able to do the following:

1. Evaluate theory-based EDMs.

2. Analyze practice-based EDMs.

3. Examine cultural-based EDMs.

4. Summarize EDMs used in crisis counseling and addictions counseling.

5. Apply EDMs to a variety of challenging situations.

CACREP STANDARDS

CACREP Core Standards

G.1.j. Ethical standards of professional organizations and credentialing bodies and applications of ethical and legal considerations in professional counseling.

CACREP Clinical Mental Health Standards

A.2. Understands the ethical and legal considerations specifically related to the practice of clinical mental health counseling.

B.1. Demonstrates the ability to apply and adhere to ethical and legal standards in clinical mental health counseling.

INTRODUCTION

Now that we know that ethical dilemmas exist, and that there are codes of ethics to guide us in these ethical dilemmas, we need to learn how to make ethical decisions. The ACA Code of Ethics (2014) directs us to use an EDM of our choice.

Ethical Code 2.1

I.1.b. Ethical Decision Making.

When counselors are faced with an ethical dilemma, they use and document, as appropriate, an ethical decision-making model that may include, but is not limited to, consultation; consideration of relevant ethical standards, principles, and laws; generation of potential courses of action; deliberation of risks and benefits; and selection of an objective decision based on the circumstances and welfare of all involved.

Source: 2014 American Counseling Association Code of Ethics. Reprinted with permission from American Counseling Association.

We are directed to ensure that some minimum elements are included in our selected model, but we are not directed to a specific model. In other words, we need to become familiar with models that may prove useful in our practice.

To begin the process, we will take a look at numerous EDMs. This is not meant to overwhelm you with choices but to help you see some common elements in ethical decision making and how specific models are relevant depending on the theoretical orientation of the counselor, the presenting concern of the client, and the context of the dilemma. Counseling is not a one-size-fits-all profession, and making decisions about ethical concerns in counseling is an equally dynamic process.

Ethical decision making occurs when counselors are faced with a dilemma and must develop a solution. It has been defined as being "both legally and morally acceptable to the larger community" (Jones, 1991, p. 387). However, we know that ethics and law are not always in concert with one another. So how do we know that our choices are ethical?

Guided Practice Exercise 2.1

The Decision-Making Process

Think about the last time you made a really difficult decision. Chances are the decision was difficult because there were a number of right answers or no clear-cut wrong answers. How did you go about the process? Did you stew on it in isolation or run it by some trusted friends? Did you consider similar decisions you had made in the past as a guide? In other words, what is your decision-making process?

Because there are no easy answers, the counseling profession suggests that we incorporate an EDM in our work with clients. When we encounter a concern with a client, we first attempt to determine if an ethical problem exists. At times, this may not be clear, and we may benefit from consulting with colleagues to see if there is an ethical concern. If one does exist, we want to consider how best to approach it.

The aim of this chapter is to introduce you to a number of ethical decision-making approaches. The authors of this text do not endorse or recommend one over another. Much like counseling theories, techniques, and interventions, it is important for you as a counselor to determine the best fit model for your work.

THEORY-BASED ETHICAL DECISION-MAKING MODELS

In this section, we will review several EDMs based on theory. Rather than traditional, step-by-step decision-making processes, these approaches are related to principles and virtues needed to make sound ethical decisions. We will begin with one of the foundational theories in our profession, Kitchener's Ethical Justification Model. Then we will discuss EDMs based on theories such as hermeneutics and virtue ethics.

Kitchener's Ethical Justification Model

One of the reasons that we present the Kitchener model first is because it addresses underlying principles or virtues that govern ethical decision making. Rather than being a step-by-step process, Kitchener (1984) asks us to consider the role of four virtues in ethical decision making. These virtues are autonomy, non-maleficence, beneficence, and justice.

Autonomy is foundational to the counseling profession as it supports clients' freedom to make their own decisions, choose their own direction, and be the authors of their own narratives. Of course this reliance on autonomy is based on the supposition that independence is positive and to be valued.

Nonmaleficence means to do no harm. As counselors, we avoid any actions that may hurt our clients or prove ineffective. The challenge with this principle is that some beneficial interventions or decisions carry some risk. The pertinent ethical issue is whether the benefits outweigh the burdens. However, to do no harm is a minimal approach to ethical work with clients. We must also approach our work with the concept of beneficence.

Beneficence in short means to do good. It is insufficient simply to avoid harm, as the concept of nonmaleficence requires. The value of beneficence promotes a responsibility for counselors to help others, especially our clients.

Finally, Kitchener discussed the concept of justice. Justice is not a legal term in this instance; rather, it is the principle of providing equal treatment to people under equal circumstances. It means to treat people fairly.

These principles first outlined by Kitchener have infused the EDMs that follow. Authors of EDMs often use Kitchener's principles as the foundation of their own models or as a way of addressing specific client populations or concerns (Urofsky, Engels, & Engebretson, 2008).

Betan's Hermeneutic Model

While Kitchener outlined the values or principles counselors should use to make ethical decisions, Betan (1997) highlighted the various differences that counselors bring to the table to make those decisions. Counselors approach ethical decision making with a combination of formal training and their own personal values and interests. Hermeneutics is not a word we use frequently, but it is derived from the Greek term for translate or interpret (Schmidt, 2006). Simply put, hermeneutics means interpretation. In terms of ethical decision making, Betan did not espouse a step-by-step approach for making these decisions. Rather, the focus is on the interpretation of existing guides and professional principles as well as personal principles.

As counselors, you bring your own story to your journey with clients. Betan acknowledged that you simply are not making an ethical decision; you are a part of the ethical decision. Counselors must address their own interpretations of the values and principles involved in the decision to make effective decisions that move beyond meeting the minimum standards. In your development as an ethically competent counselor, Betan advises that you must receive training that highlights the limited black-and-white options that are present in ethical dilemmas. This text is one way to address the need to understand the shades of gray and complexities inherent in ethical decisions. In addition, Betan's approach requires that counselors engage in ongoing examination and self-exploration of values and principles to understand our abilities to look fully at our reactions to ethical dilemmas as these reactions are based in our own personal histories. Essentially, Betan's (1997) model asks us to acknowledge our personal reactions to professional issues as we make these ethical decisions.

Guided Practice Exercise 2.2

Continuing Education

When you become licensed, you will have to engage in continuing education. The purpose of ongoing continuing education in ethics is for counselors to stay in touch with emerging trends and their own reactions to these trends. What continuing education does your state require? Specifically, what ethics hours will you be required to pursue and within what time frame to keep your license?

Jordan and Meara (1990) Virtue Ethics

A final underlying theoretical approach to ethical decision making was published by Jordan and Meara (1990). These authors noted that traditional EDMs focused on making decisions that fit all of the rules. In other words, the focus is on what the counselor should do in a situation. By focusing on what the counselor should do, Jordan and Meara argue that the decision is narrow-minded and minimalistic in its approach. Simply by focusing on what should be done, the implication is that the counselor is the person impacted by the decision rather than the client. Jordan and Meara suggested that the ethical decision is an opportunity for the counselor to embody the aspirational virtues of decision making.

Rather than focusing on what the counselor should do, the virtue ethics model focuses on who the counselor should be (Jordan & Meara, 1990). The model suggests that counselors should evolve continually and modify the personal characteristics that influence their professional decisions. In other words, as counselors we need to apply the same principles of self-awareness and growth to ourselves that we ask of our clients. Many counselors follow the philosophy that personal therapy is necessary to provide quality services to our clients. We have to do our own work to do this work well. Jordan and Meara articulated this need in their model by highlighting the opportunities for quality ethical decisions when the counselor is functioning from a self-aware standpoint and interpreting the dilemma from an interpretive perspective.

CASE STUDY 2.1

Virtue Ethics in Action

Keon was first licensed as a professional counselor in 1992. His training and initial clinical work was governed by the 1995 ACA Code of Ethics. It was under the 1995 code that he first learned about the concept of bartering or the exchange of goods or services for counseling services. At the time, the code declared that bartering should be discouraged, although limited exceptions were made available. Keon practices in a working-class neighborhood in a small private practice owned by a colleague. In 2000, Keon had a client who was being seen regularly for outpatient counseling and who unexpectedly lost his job. The client expected this to be temporary, but because he was licensed and bonded as an electrician, he offered to install security lights on the outside of Keon's agency in exchange for a certain number of sessions. If Keon had simply taken the 1995 code at face value, he would not consider this offer. However, from a virtue ethics decision-making model, Keon can interpret this ethical dilemma from different perspectives and consider the values and cultural implications contained within. Of course, consulting with the agency owner is a must as well. It should be noted that during the late 1990s and early 2000s, the profession of counseling was taking this same approach toward bartering. In fact, the 2005 and 2014 codes provide evidence of the evolution of this concept, and bartering has become a more and more acceptable practice.

1. *Why would the American Counseling Association (ACA) alter its stance on bartering?*

2. *Would you feel comfortable engaging in bartering? Why or why not?*

3. *What might be an unacceptable situation for bartering?*

PRACTICE-BASED ETHICAL DECISION-MAKING MODELS

The next types of EDMs we will investigate are those based on practice issues. Practice-based EDMs came on the heels of the theory-based models when counselors expressed a need for more concrete steps to follow. With practice-based models, many of the challenges of the more abstract theoretical approaches are eliminated through step-by-step guides. Ethical decision making is grounded largely in theory-based models, but the actions needed are found more clearly in the practice-based, and thus practical, approaches that follow (Sileo & Kopala, 1993).

Sileo and Kopala (1993) A-B-C-D-E Worksheet

The previous section highlighted theoretical underpinnings that drive quality ethical decision making. While important, these models are not really models in the traditional sense as they do not provide explicit directions for decision making. Sileo and Kopala (1993) evaluated existing models and developed a mnemonic device to help practicing counselors have a more real-world approach to ethical decision making. This model, known as the A-B-C-D-E worksheet, is really an amalgamation of many existing models and is intended to promote the virtue of beneficence (Sileo & Kopala, 1993). The mnemonic with explanations follows.

A—assessment: This includes an examination of all factors leading up to the ethical dilemma. In addition, the counselor must assess his or her own biases and values as well as the strengths and limitations of the client.

B—benefit: What benefits the client while avoiding harm as well as what decision benefits the most parties involved?

C—consequences and consultation: What are the consequences, including legal, ethical, and therapeutic? Counselors may find that these consequences are in conflict with one another. This step is actually a combination step in that it involves consulting with others to determine consequences we may be blind to.

D—duty: Sileo and Kopala suggest counselors ask themselves to whom they owe a duty. Is the duty just to the client, or are there others involved?

E—education: Counselors must be educated about the codes of ethics under which they fall as well as relevant laws and policies.

Clearly, this model is easy for practicing counselors to follow and document. The answers to the steps change based on the dilemma and on the counselor, but the process is uniform. Many counselors find this model to be a practical method for evaluating ethical dilemmas.

CASE STUDY 2.2

Carson is a counselor working in a public mental health agency. One of his clients has been showing signs of regression in his psychiatric condition. The client has been having auditory and visual hallucinations but is taking his medication regularly. Carson and the client agree that hospitalization is necessary. In the client chart, there are a number of records from prior hospitalizations that Carson thinks the hospital would need to best serve his client. However, he is under the impression that he cannot share those records with the hospital.

1. *Using Sileo and Kopala's A-B-C-D-E worksheet, evaluate this ethical dilemma.*

2. *How would Carson check state law about medical records?*

3. *Who might Carson consult with to better address this dilemma?*

Corey, Corey, Corey, and Callahan (2015)

Another practical, step-by-step model was introduced by Corey, Corey, and Callahan in 1998 and revised throughout the years. The current model includes eight steps for the counselor to follow:

1. *Identify the problem.* It may sound simplistic, but if there is not a problem, there is not a problem. Counselors must identify and articulate what the ethical problem is to begin to develop a solution. Putting the dilemma into words is the beginning of working through an ethical decision. If there is a problem, what kind of problem is it? Is it ethical, legal, or both? Are morals and values involved, and if so, how?

2. *Identify the potential issues involved.* Articulating the dilemma allows counselors to look at the problem from multiple perspectives. What will benefit your client? What will benefit other stakeholders? How can you prioritize the concerns? How can you involve your client? These are but a few issues that need to be addressed early in the process.

3. *Review the relevant ethical codes.* This step assumes that the counselor has been educated and is aware of the ethical codes under which the counselor falls. While professional codes of ethics are typically more alike than different, there are times that conflicts arise between codes. In addition, it is rare that codes are specific enough to address the challenge at hand. Thus, the counselor must be aware of the guidance available in the codes.

4. *Know the applicable laws and regulations.* Ethical codes are one thing; state and federal laws are something else entirely. Codes are concepts we as a profession have agreed to, while laws are mandates our society has agreed to live under (Remley & Herlihy, 2009). These don't always go together. We are required to know and understand the laws and policies that may impact our decisions.

5. *Obtain consultation.* Like the previous model, Corey, Corey, and Callahan recognize that counselors do not need to operate in isolation. It is imperative that we reach out to colleagues, supervisors, and others who can effectively weigh in on the ethical dilemma and provide guidance.

6. *Consider possible and probable courses of action.* What could happen during a course of action, and if it did, what would that mean? Find a way to brainstorm the many possibilities before choosing one. In addition, consider if one of those possibilities is involving your client in the solution.

7. *Enumerate the consequences of various decisions.* Do what you can to determine the potential consequences for each of the decisions that were part of Step 6. Consider the ethical principles as you determine these consequences.

8. *Decide on what appears to be the best course of action.* Although there may be many potential solutions, and none may be perfect, at some point a decision must be made. If more consultation needs to occur before this decision is made, then reach out to those people. Despite the advice of consultants, supervisors, and others, the counselor is ultimately responsible for the decision and subsequent action.

The Corey, Corey, and Callahan model is more comprehensive than the Sileo and Kopala model and emphasizes a thoughtful decision-making process. Counselors may need to take these steps in a different order, circle back through steps while working on the same dilemma, or even repeat the process, to arrive at the best possible solution.

Forester-Miller and Davis (1996)

While ACA does not prescribe any one EDM, many counselors are drawn to the model proposed by Forester-Miller and Davis (1996) as it is incorporated in the ACA document "A Practitioner's Guide to Ethical Decision Making" found on the ACA Web site (http://counseling.org/docs/ethics/practitioners_guide.pdf?sfvrsn=2). This document was conceptualized and developed by the ACA Ethics Committee and incorporates many of the principles and steps previously discussed.

1. *Identify the problem.* What is the ethical concern or dilemma? Does a dilemma even exist?

2. *Apply the ACA Code of Ethics.* Go through the ACA code thoroughly and see what, if any, codes apply. If a case were to go to the ACA Ethics Committee, for example, each dilemma must be anchored in a code to be considered by the committee.

3. *Determine the nature and dimensions of the dilemma.* What is the scope of this dilemma? What does the literature say about the dilemma? Consult with colleagues about this dilemma.

4. *Generate possible courses of action.* Consider all of the possible ways this dilemma could end. Some of these endings will be better than others, but they all must be considered so that the best course can be determined.

5. *Consider the potential consequences of all options, and determine a course of action.* Simply determining a possible outcome is not enough. We must also consider the ramifications of the outcome. Acting on an ethical decision creates a ripple effect. Who and what will be impacted besides the client and counselor?

6. *Evaluate the selected course of action.* With a more thorough understanding of all possible outcomes and ramifications, we can select a particular course of action.

7. *Implement the course of action.* Of course, Steps 1 through 6 simply have led up to this step. We must take action to address the ethical dilemma.

Something that Forester-Miller and Davis stress is that different counselors in the same situation may arrive at different conclusions. In addition, they comment that counselors likely are making the most ethical choice if they are honest, operate in the best interest of the client rather than the counselor, and match their decisions to current professional best practice standards.

Tarvydas (2012) Integrative Decision-Making Model of Ethical Behavior

An EDM that incorporates many of the models available to counselors and adds a reflective perspective to address the dilemma from multiple lenses is the Tarvydas Integrative Decision-Making Model of Ethical Behavior. This model strives to seek a balance among all of the issues and the context involved in the decision. Through reflection and collaboration with all stakeholders, the counselor moves beyond the application of ethical codes and laws to include values, prejudices, and biases as well as cultural and societal contexts.

There are four stages in the Tarvydas model:

Stage I. Interpreting the Situation Through Awareness and Fact-Finding

In this stage, counselors attend to their own sensitivity and awareness. In addition, they look beyond the client and counselor to determine all stakeholders in the issue and engage in fact-finding through collaboration with these stakeholders.

Stage II. Formulating an Ethical Decision

In the decision-making stage of the model, counselors must weigh all relevant codes and laws and consider possible actions. As is typical in such models, counselors then play each possibility through and consider both negative and positive impacts. While doing so, it is advised that counselors consult with other professionals who can weigh in on the decision before settling on a final course of action.

Stage III. Selecting an Action By Weighing Competing Nonmoral Values, Personal Blind Spots, or Prejudices

This stage involves the reflective process. Counselors reflect on values, morals, blind spots, and prejudices that have been identified in the decision-making analysis. They also consider the ethical decision in larger contexts, including institutional, cultural, and societal, before determining what is truly the best course of action.

Stage IV. Planning and Executing the Selected Course of Action

Finally, counselors make a plan to follow through on the selected course of action. They consider potential barriers and develop plans in advance to address these. In the end, they must document and evaluate the action they determined to inform future ethical decision making.

With an emphasis on a studious approach that includes reflection on the counselor's prejudices and the social and cultural ramifications, the Tarvydas model presents counselors with a unique opportunity to integrate traditional ethical decision making with a reflective approach to determine the best course of action.

 Kocet, McCauley, and Thompson (2009)
Ethical Decision Making for Student Affairs

The Kocet, McCauley, and Thompson model was developed by one of the coauthors of this text and was developed specifically for use in student affairs. However, the elements in the model are applicable across disciplines of counseling practice.

There are 12 specific steps in this model:

1. Develop an ethical worldview.

2. Identify the ethical dilemma or problem.

3. Weigh competing ethical principles.

4. Select relevant ethical guidelines and professional standards.

5. Examine potential cultural and contextual issues impacting the ethical dilemma.

6. Investigate applicable laws, campus regulations, policies, procedures, handbooks, Web sites, and so on.

7. Search for ethical, legal, and professional precedence.

8. Engage in collaborative consultation and brainstorming.

9. Evaluate possible consequences and options of action or inaction.

10. Choose a course of action.

11. Implement the selected course of action.

12. Reflect on the experience as it relates to future ethical decisions.

CULTURAL-BASED ETHICAL DECISION-MAKING MODELS

While the majority of the previous models imply taking culture into consideration when making an ethical decision, and at least one model, the Tarvydas model, relies on reflection on the culture involved, there are several models that make culture a primary focus of ethical decision making.

Cottone's (2004) Social Constructivism Model

When counselors make ethical decisions, they typically view the client as an individual. The Social Constructivism Model makes the relationships between individuals of primary importance. "Social constructivism is founded on ideas that allow for all conclusions about human functioning to be understood based on the biological and social factors that affect behavior" (Cottone, 2004, p. 5). Social constructivism posits that our understanding of an individual is based on relationships.

The Social Constructivism Model is an interactive process best defined in this fashion:

1. Obtain information from all involved.

2. Assess the nature of the relationships among all involved. Are they harmonious? Conflictual? Adversarial?

3. Consult colleagues, experts, ethical codes, laws, and other regulations.

4. Negotiate among these first three concepts to arrive at a consensual decision.

5. Engage in interactive reflection throughout the process.

Using the Social Constructivism Model means that instead of making an ethical decision for the client and other stakeholders, the decision is made with these parties. As such, the client's culture is intertwined in the decision-making process.

The following case analysis shows the Social Constructivism Model in action:

Janie is a mental health counselor assigned by her agency to work in the local high school. Because she works for the agency, rather than the school district, she is not considered to be a school counselor. One of her clients, Esme, is a senior due to graduate in June. She initially was referred for depression because she was staying home from school and complaining about the work. Janie discovers that Esme's parents want her to go to college, but Esme wants to go to cosmetology school and work in a salon. Esme's school counselor placed her in the college prep track years ago, but Esme is sure that she does not wish to go to college. However, she feels pressured by her parents, the school counselor, and the school principal to take the college route rather than go to a technical school.

Because she is under 18, Esme's parents often check in with Janie about her progress in counseling. Specifically, they want to know that their daughter is doing what she needs to do to get into college. Janie currently is avoiding their calls to decide what to do next. To use the Social Constructivism Model, Janie first would gather information from more than just her client. She should get Esme's parents' perspective as well as the perspective of the stakeholders at Esme's school. Following the model, Janie must evaluate the nature of the relationships among stakeholders. In addition, she will want to consult with colleagues and mentors as well as any applicable ethical codes and laws. Ideally, Janie will be able to build a bridge between stakeholders to benefit her client. It also is suggested that she engage in a reflective process, so journaling about these challenges may benefit Janie's ethical decision-making practice.

Garcia, Cartwright, Winston, and Borzuchowska (2003) Transcultural Integrative Model

Another EDM that places great importance on the culture of the client and the counseling practice is the Transcultural Integrative Model. This model borrows heavily from the Social Constructivism Model and also adds elements of the Tarvydas model discussed in the section on practice-based models. The authors of the Transcultural Integrative Model assert that as we have learned more about the importance of culture and developed counseling theories to address this importance, so too should we place great emphasis on culture when making ethical decisions. We share the belief that a culturally competent counselor should make culturally responsive ethical decisions (Garcia et al., 2003).

The model consists of the following steps:

1. *Interpret the situation through awareness and fact-finding.* This step includes becoming culturally sensitive, determining the presence of an ethical dilemma, defining the stakeholders involved, and gathering the information needed to make an informed decision.

2. *Formulate an ethical decision.* This step includes taking a close look at the ethical dilemma, reviewing relevant codes and laws, developing a list of potential actions and outcomes, consulting with others, and deciding on the best choice.

3. *Weigh competing, nonmoral values, and affirm the course of action.* The goal of this step is to consider personal and cultural values that may impact the decision. Thus, this step involves looking at our own personal biases as well as those ingrained at the institutional and societal levels.

4. *Plan and execute the selected course of action.* Finally, in Step 4, we act on the ethical dilemma. We determine what the action will be, anticipate and resolve barriers to this action, implement the action, and document our choice.

x missing prioritizing guiding principles

The Transcultural Integrative Model combines what many believe to be the best of the best in terms of elements of ethical decision making. It has been used in research, and there are multiple articles outlining its use (see Garcia et al., 1999; Garcia, Forrester, & Jacob, 1998). It has been used to address specific issues such as HIV/AIDS disclosure. However, this is not the only model with applications for specialty practice. In this next and final section of EDMs, we will look at models used in specific specialty areas of practice.

ETHICAL DECISION-MAKING MODELS FOR SPECIALTY PRACTICE

The previous models presented in this chapter were either general in nature, related to particular counseling theories, or aligned with practice models. One lesson we can take from what we have learned so far is that there is no single model that fits all counselors, clients, or contexts. In this section, we will discuss EDMs that are useful in specific counseling settings such as crises, family counseling, and addictions counseling.

Crisis Counseling

Crisis work is, by nature of crises, a systemic approach. There are multiple levels of people, families, institutions, organizations, and societies impacted. Consider a crisis such as Superstorm Sandy or Hurricane Katrina. Individuals, families, communities, and our nation as a whole were impacted. As such, the decisions and ethical dilemmas crisis counselors face have a far-reaching impact. Jordan (2010) proposed that crisis ethical decision making should come from "an eco systemic perspective" (p. 1). What this means is that crisis counseling decisions impact multiple layers of clients and the systems in which they operate. There are 10 steps for ethical decision making in crisis situations:

1. Identify the ethical concern within the context of the disaster.

2. Consider personal (the crisis counselor's) self, beliefs and values, skills, and knowledge.

3. Identify the code(s) of ethics involved.

4. Determine possible ethical traps.

5. Frame a preliminary response.

6. Consider the consequences.

7. Prepare an ethical resolution.

8. Get feedback and consultation from other crisis counselor(s).

9. Take action.

10. Review the outcome.

Addictions Counseling

Work in addictions counseling is fraught with ethical difficulties ranging from informed consent to managing group confidentiality. As such, the Center for Education and Drug Abuse Research (CEDAR), a National Institute on Drug Abuse–funded center at the University of Pittsburgh, published an EDM specific for addictions professionals (Coleman, 2013). Relying heavily on the work of Kitchener (1984) and Rest (1984), five steps are outlined in this model.

1. *Increase ethical sensitivity.* Similar to empathy, increasing ethical sensitivity requires counselors to see the dilemma through the eyes of clients.

2. *Identify and prioritize guiding principles.* What are the priorities (e.g., justice, beneficence, autonomy) in the dilemma?

3. *Develop an ethical plan of action.* Generate a strategy based on the desired outcomes.

4. *Implement ethical action.* This is the action step and one in which counselors recognize that they are willing to take any consequences that follow.

5. *Evaluate the outcome.* Coleman (2013) indicates that most models stop before this step. However, it is crucial that counselors reflect back on the dilemma so that it becomes a source of learning. Could the dilemma have been prevented? If so, how? If not, what could have been handled differently? Every ethical dilemma becomes an opportunity to become a more ethical counselor.

APPLICATION OF ETHICAL DECISION-MAKING MODELS

We have covered a lot of models in this chapter. The challenge now is to learn how to apply the models. Let's take a case example and walk through how we might apply a model.

Case Example

LaShauna is a school-based counselor in a small town working in an elementary setting. She attended a school team meeting with administrators, teachers, and a school psychologist about Karl, a student who has become increasingly disruptive in the classroom. Karl's behavior is interfering with his ability to learn as well as the learning environment of his classmates. A school team meeting was scheduled to develop an appropriate plan or intervention to meet Karl's educational needs. LaShauna has been working with Karl, who has experienced severe sexual abuse within the last six months, as well as working with the Department of Human Services (DHS). Prior to the school team meeting, the principal let LaShauna know that he was expecting her to explain to the team what has been happening to Karl to help the other professionals in attendance better understand his disruptive behavior.

Applying the Corey, Corey, and Callahan Model

LaShauna is a clinical mental health counselor but works in a school environment with minor clients. Because of the type of clients she sees as well as the type of ethical dilemmas she commonly faces, LaShauna has chosen the Corey, Corey, and Callahan practice-based model as it provides her with a step-by-step guide for making a decision.

1. *Identify the problem.* LaShauna feels trapped when asked by the principal to be prepared to discuss all of Karl's case in the team meeting. Her gut check tells her that there is a problem. Upon closer inspection, she realizes that the problem she has identified is whether or not to break Karl's confidentiality with the treatment team.

2. *Identify the potential issues involved.* LaShauna recognizes several issues involved. First, she is the only counselor on the team and thus the only person held to the codes of ethics that she follows. Second, she is concerned that if the entire team knows of Karl's abuse, they will change how they work with Karl. Finally, she worries that her own working relationship with Karl will be compromised if he learns that she has been talking about him behind his back.

3. *Review the relevant ethical codes.* LaShauna goes to her ACA Code of Ethics to see what applies to this situation. She identifies the following:

   A.1.a. Primary Responsibility. The primary responsibility of counselors is to respect the dignity and to promote the welfare of clients.

   A.2.b. Types of Information Needed (Partial). Clients have the right to confidentiality and to be provided with an explanation of its limitations (including how supervisors and treatment team professionals are involved).

   B.1.c. Respect for Confidentiality. Counselors do not share confidential information without client consent or without sound legal or ethical justification.

B.2.d. Minimal Disclosure. To the extent possible, clients are informed before confidential information is disclosed and are involved in the disclosure decision-making process. When circumstances require the disclosure of confidential information, only essential information is revealed.

B.5.a. Responsibility to Clients. When counseling minor clients or adult clients who lack the capacity to give voluntary informed consent, counselors protect the confidentiality of information received in the counseling relationship as specified by federal and state laws, written policies, and applicable ethical standards.

4. *Know the applicable laws and regulations.* LaShauna has to research state and federal laws. Because the child abuse has been reported, and Karl is working with DHS, there are no additional reporting issues. In their state, Karl is considered a minor, making him subject to ethical codes written for minor clients. In addition, LaShauna looks at her agency policy and contract with the school district. In it she discovers only that school-based counselors serve as active members of treatment teams.

5. *Obtain consultation.* LaShauna is still unclear on how much to share with the team, so she seeks consultation from colleagues. First, she consults with another agency counselor who advises her to participate in the team meeting and share behavioral observations of Karl. Further, she advises LaShauna not to discuss the sexual abuse as it is not integral to his current school performance and may adversely impact his treatment by other team members. LaShauna also consults with a colleague who is a retired educator. He tells LaShauna that everyone on the team should be aware of everything she is aware of to best help Karl. Finally, LaShauna reaches out to a former professor and mentor from her counseling program. From her LaShauna receives the advice to remind Karl's mother of the scope and limitations of confidentiality before the meeting and to offer only information necessary to the educational goals of Karl's treatment team.

6. *Consider possible and probable courses of action.* After consulting, LaShauna realizes she simply could tell the team everything she knows, which would allow everyone to be on the same page and prevent her from having to decide what information is important. Conversely, LaShauna recognizes that minimal disclosure is also an option.

7. *Enumerate the consequences of various decisions.* LaShauna realizes that if she simply shares all with the team, the burden of decision making will be off her shoulders. She will not have to keep secrets, and she can hope that the team can

hold the confidence. If they do not, LaShauna recognizes, Karl may become the subject of gossip in the school and community. LaShauna further concludes that all information may not be necessary to provide the treatment team with what they need to best support Karl's educational plan. However, she worries that she may leave out information that would be critical to the team.

8. *Decide on what appears to be the best course of action.* Ultimately, LaShauna chooses to involve Karl's mother in the process. She meets with her prior to the team meeting to let her know that she will be offering only the information necessary to benefit his educational plan. LaShauna documents her decision-making process, her meeting with Karl's mother and his team, and the outcome.

CONCLUSION

Understanding multiple EDMs is not necessary to ethical practice. However, finding the model that best suits you as a counselor as well as your client population is the responsibility of ethical counselors. This chapter walked you through numerous EDMs based on theory, client population, and general practice considerations. As you can see, most models contain similar components, and it really does come down to finding the best fit for each counselor, client, and context. You will want to refer back to this chapter as you evaluate the many cases presented throughout this text.

KEYSTONES

- Ethical decision making occurs when counselors are faced with a dilemma and must develop a solution. The profession of counseling suggests that we incorporate an EDM when working with clients.
- Theory-based EDMs relate to principles and virtues needed to make sound ethical decisions, rather than presenting a step-by-step decision-making process. These models include Kitchener's Ethical Justification Model, the hermeneutics model, and virtue ethics.
- Kitchener's model asks counselors to consider the role of four virtues in ethical decision making: autonomy, nonmaleficence, beneficence, and justice. Autonomy is foundational to the counseling profession as it supports the freedom of clients to make their own decisions, choose their own direction, and be the authors of their own narratives. Nonmaleficence means to do no harm. Beneficence means to do good. Justice is the principle of providing equal treatment to people under equal circumstances.

- In the hermeneutic model, counselors are not simply making an ethical decision, they are a part of the ethical decision.
- The virtue ethics model focuses on who the counselor should be rather than focusing on what the counselor should do.
- Practice-based EDMs serve as step-by-step guides to help counselors make ethical decisions. These include the A-B-C-D-E worksheet; the Corey, Corey, and Callahan model; Forester-Miller and Davis model; Tarvydas Integrative Decision-Making Model of Ethical Behavior; and the Kocet, McCauley, and Thompson model.
- The A-B-C-D-E worksheet is an amalgamation of many existing models and is intended to promote the virtue of beneficence.
- A culturally competent counselor should make culturally responsive ethical decisions. While a majority of the theory-based and practice-based EDMs imply that counselors should take culture into consideration when making an ethical decision, there are several models that make this a primary focus. These models include the Tarvydas model, Cottone's Social Constructivism Model, and the Transcultural Integrative Model.

SUGGESTED BEST PRACTICES

- Read through many EDMs before deciding which ones are best for your practice.
- Keep this chapter handy so that you can reference multiple decision-making models when faced with a dilemma.
- Know your theoretical orientation, and know it well. Match your EDM to your theoretical approach. Chances are they will dovetail nicely for you in this fashion.
- Read literature on the efficacy of using certain EDMs.
- Be flexible. You may have a go-to EDM but need to try something new in certain situations.
- Note that a common thread to ethical decision making is consultation. Regardless of the model that you use, discuss the dilemma with others, and get their input.
- Document the ethical dilemma, the decision-making model you used, who you consulted with, and the outcome.
- Remember that ACA posted the Forester-Miller and Davis model on its Web site as a sample model considered as a best practice in the profession.
- If you practice in a specific discipline, such as student affairs or hospice care, look for EDMs that fit your discipline.
- Include culture and context in all ethical decision-making processes.
- Practice ethical decision making through the use of case studies.
- Attend continuing education workshops that focus on how to make ethical decisions in addition to presenting ethical dilemmas.

ADDITIONAL RESOURCES

In Print

Hecker, L., & Associates. (2010). *Ethics and professional issues in couple and family therapy.* New York: Taylor & Francis.

Pope, K., & Vasquez, M. (2011). *Ethics in psychotherapy and counseling* (4th ed.). San Francisco, CA: Jossey-Bass.

On the Web

Dobrin, A. (2012). *Am I right? How to live ethically*. Retrieved from http://www.scu.edu/ethics/practicing/decision/thinking.html

Games

Quandary: An Ethical Decision-Making Game. http://www.quandarygame.org/

Apps

Markkula Center for Applied Ethics. (2014). The ethical decision-making assistant: Making an ethical decision app (Version 1.0). [Mobile application software]. Retrieved from http://www.scu.edu/ethics/ethical-decision/

REFERENCES

American Counseling Association (ACA). (2014). *ACA code of ethics.* Alexandria, VA: Author.

Betan, E. J. (1997). Toward a hermeneutic model of ethical decision making in clinical practice. *Ethics & Behavior, 7*(4), 347–365.

Coleman, A. K. (2013). *The drug and alcohol forum: An ethical decision-making model for practitioners*. Center for Education and Drug Abuse Research, University of Pittsburgh. Retrieved from http://www.pitt.edu/~cedar/forum/coleman.html

Corey, G., Corey, M. S., & Callahan, P. (1998). *Issues and ethics in the helping professions*. Pacific Grove, CA: Brooks/Cole.

Corey, G., Corey, M., Corey, C., & Callahan, P. (2015). *Issues and ethics in the helping professions* (9th ed.). Stamford, CT: Cengage.

Cottone R. R. (2004). Displacing the psychology of the individual in ethical decision making: The social constructivism model. *Canadian Journal of Counselling, 38*(1), 5–13.

Forester-Miller, H., & Davis, T. (1996). *A practitioner's guide to ethical decision making.* American Counseling Association.

Garcia, J., Cartwright, B., Winston, S., & Borzuchowska, B. (2003). A transcultural integrative model for ethical decision making in counseling. *Journal of Counseling & Development, 81*(3), 268.

Garcia, J., Forrester, L., & Jacob, A. (1998). Ethical dilemma resolution in HIV/AIDS counseling: Why an integrative model? *International Journal of Rehabilitation & Health, 4*(3), 167–181.

Garcia, J. G., Froehlich, R. J., Cartwright, B., Letiecq, D., Forrester, L. E., & Mueller, R. O. (1999). Ethical dilemmas related to counseling clients living with HIV/AIDS. *Rehabilitation Counseling Bulletin, 43*(1), 41–50.

Jones, T. M. (1991). Ethical decision making by individuals in organizations: An issue-contingent model. *Academy of Management Review, 16*(2), 366–395.

Jordan, A. E., & Meara, N. M. (1990). Ethics and the professional practice of psychologists: The role of virtues and principles. *Professional Psychology: Research and Practice, 21*(2), 107–114. doi:10.1037/0735–7028.21.2.107

Jordan, K. (2010). *An ethical decision-making model for crisis counselors.* Retrieved from http://counselingoutfitters.com/vistas/vistas10/Article_89.pdf

Kitchener, K. S. (1984). Intuition, critical evaluation, and ethical principles: The foundation for ethical decisions in counseling psychology. *The Counseling Psychologist, 12,* 43–55.

Kocet, M. M., McCauley, J., & Thompson, L. (2009). *Ethical decision-making model for student affairs.* Retrieved from http://ebookbrowse.com/kocet-mccauley-thompson-ethical-decision-making-model-sa-revised-doc-d370114178

Remley, T. P., & Herlihy, B. P. (2009). *Ethical, legal, and professional issues in counseling* (3rd ed.). Upper Saddle River, NJ: Pearson Education.

Rest, J. (1984). Research on moral development: Implications for training psychologists. *The Counseling Psychologist, 12*(19), 18–27.

Schmidt, L. K. (2006). *Understanding hermeneutics.* [Electronic resource]. Durham, UK: Acumen.

Sileo, F., & Kopala, M. (1993). An A-B-C-D-E worksheet for promoting beneficence when considering ethical issues. *Counseling and Values, 37,* 89–95.

Tarvydas, V. M. (2012). Ethics and ethics decision making. In D. R. Maki & V. M. Tarvydas (Eds.), *The professional practice of rehabilitation counseling* (pp. 339–370). New York: Springer.

Urofsky, R. I., Engels, D. W., & Engebretson, K. (2008). Kitchener's principle ethics: Implications for counseling practice and research. *Counseling and Values, 53*(1), 67–78.

Chapter 3

Cultural Competency and Ethical Decision Making

Michante is a 29-year-old male from the Sioux tribe who comes to counseling at his town's mental health agency. He grew up on the reservation and lived there until six months ago. He barely graduated from high school and has held short-term manual labor jobs over the past 10 years but nothing long-term. Michante and his siblings were raised by their mother and maternal grandmother—his father left the family when Michante was four years old. Michante is randomly assigned to Janice, a licensed mental health counselor who has worked at this agency for eight years. Janice is Caucasian and grew up in a traditional family with two parents, siblings, and family dog. She was raised in an upper-middle-class neighborhood and attended private schools and well-known universities.

During the first session, Michante explains that he has never been to counseling before and is anxious about the process. He informs Janice that he left the reservation and moved to town to find a better paying job but feels increasingly lonely and misses his family and community on the reservation. He indicates that he has begun drinking every day, sometimes even in the morning, to cope with not having a job and not being near his family. While Michante's impression is that Janice is a kind, respectful person, he is not sure that he made the right decision to speak with her. Michante looks around the room and sees Janice's diplomas from Yale University and New York University and photos of Janice and her husband and children on family vacations in Europe and Disney World. He also notices her expensive clothing and jewelry and comments, "I don't know why I even came here. I am not sure if counseling is for me." How should Janice respond to Michante?

CHAPTER OVERVIEW

This chapter introduces the reader to the importance of demonstrating cultural competency in any ethical decision-making process. As Kocet (2009) stated, every counseling relationship should be considered a cross-cultural therapeutic relationship. It is important for counseling professionals to recognize that cultural and ethical competencies are interwoven to ensure the welfare of each and every client. This chapter helps readers explore how to view ethical issues through a multicultural lens, not only taking into account the unique aspects of each ethical dilemma at hand but also considering the cultural context and factors that shape how we as counselors view an ethical dilemma as well as how cultural factors influence how we make ethical decisions.

LEARNING OBJECTIVES

After reading this chapter you will be able to do the following:

1. Evaluate the importance of creating a purposeful, ethical blueprint for effective counseling practice, including the use of formal decision-making models.

2. Practice cultural sensitivity in all aspects of the counselor–client relationship.

3. Utilize the Counselor Value-Based Conflicts Model when faced with cultural values-based conflicts within the counseling relationship.

4. Differentiate the two main types of consultation and the role that each plays in the ethical decision-making process, especially during cross-cultural therapeutic impasses.

CACREP STANDARDS

CACREP Core Standards

G.1.j. Ethical standards of professional organizations and credentialing bodies and applications of ethical and legal considerations in professional counseling.

CACREP Clinical Mental Health Standards

A.2. Understands the ethical and legal considerations specifically related to the practice of clinical mental health counseling.

B.1. Demonstrates the ability to apply and adhere to ethical and legal standards in clinical mental health counseling.

INTRODUCTION

By the nature of our work, regardless of the setting or the population with whom we choose to work, counselors make many ethical judgments throughout the day. As you are starting to learn, some ethical issues may appear commonplace or clear-cut, while others may be very complex and contain intricate shades of gray (Dolgoff, Harrington, & Loewenberg, 2012). Regardless of the complexity of the issue, we must have an organized, purposeful way of approaching each ethical situation and strive to demonstrate not only ethical competency in our work but cross-cultural competency as well. To aid us in this process, ethics scholars have created various ethical decision-making models (EDMs) to serve as frameworks for how to think through and approach ethical challenges as they arise (Corey, Corey, Corey, & Callahan, 2015; Cottone, 2011; Jungers & Gregoire, 2013; Welfel, 2013). Many of these EDMs were presented in Chapter 2. In this chapter, we will examine the process of ethical decision making but through the cultural worldview of our clients and ourselves.

Ethical decision making, in most circumstances, is an intentional and purposeful process that involves identifying key ethical issues, reviewing relevant standards from professional codes of ethics, determining potential legal issues, consulting with supervisors and colleagues, reviewing the professional literature, and weighing core ethical principles (Kitchener & Anderson, 2011; Welfel, 2013). In addition to reviewing a professional code of ethics and speaking with supervisors, we as counselors are obligated to use an EDM to help structure and organize our approach to the dilemma, taking into account any cultural factors that can impact the outcome or action to be undertaken. Professional codes of ethics also have their limitations. Codes of ethics are not revised annually, but updated versions often are crafted every 7 to 10 years, which means that codes of ethics can become outdated the moment new standards are released. New ethical issues emerge in the in-between times when codes and revisions of those codes are completed (Herlihy & Dufrene, 2011). Without utilizing a decision-making model, we may approach a dilemma feeling directionless and unsure of how best to proceed.

Most ethical challenges trigger both a cognitive and an affective or emotional response in counselors—what we like to call *a head and heart process.* Formal EDMs can offer a step-by-step ordering to your thoughts, especially when you may be trying to address the emotional impact that a dilemma has created in either your personal or professional life (Houser & Thoma, 2013; Kitchener & Anderson, 2011). While most EDMs are comprehensive and detailed, many lack any direct reference to cultural considerations. This is a clear deficit in the ethics canon and is deserving of further research and clinical attention. Let's take a look at how culture intersects all of the ethical decisions we make.

PURPOSEFUL, CULTURAL, ETHICAL DECISION MAKING

As it is stated throughout this text, ethical decision making is an intentional practice; it is not done in a haphazard manner. Anecdotally, if on a national scale professional counselors were surveyed regarding their use of formal EDMs in their daily practices, our assumption is that most practitioners would likely quietly admit that (a) they don't know of any specific EDMs, except ones they may have heard about in graduate school, and (b) they don't use a model in their day-to-day decision-making practices. Even though the ACA Code of Ethics has a clear standard requiring that professional counselors employ a formal decision-making model in ethical situations, we fear that this critical ethical practice may not be happening within the profession on a consistent basis.

Ethical Code 3.1

I.1.b. Ethical Decision Making.

When counselors are faced with an ethical dilemma, they use and document, as appropriate, an ethical decision-making model that may include, but is not limited to, consultation; consideration of relevant ethical standards, principles, and laws; generation of potential courses of action; deliberation of risks and benefits; and selection of an objective decision based on the circumstances and welfare of all involved.

Source: 2014 American Counseling Association Code of Ethics. Reprinted with permission from American Counseling Association.

Such formal models should not only be utilized when faced with significant ethical dilemmas but should be read and reviewed regularly to foster ethical development and reflection no matter how major (or minor) the ethical issue (Houser & Thoma, 2013).

Seven-Step Ethical Assessment Screen

While ethics scholars have presented us with numerous frameworks for ethical consideration, Dolgoff and colleagues (2012) present an ethical assessment screen originally designed with social workers in mind but that also can be a useful tool for professional counselors. They present a seven-step ethical assessment screening for professional reflection that can be useful when facing a cross-cultural ethical dilemma, which we summarize here:

1. Identify the relevant professional values and ethics, your own relevant values, and any societal values relevant to the ethical decision to be made in relation to this ethical dilemma.

2. Determine what you can do to minimize conflicts among personal, societal, and professional values.

3. Identify alternative ethical options that you may take.

4. Determine which of the alternative ethical options will minimize conflicts between your client's and others' rights and welfare and society's rights and interests.

5. Decide which alternative action will be most efficient, effective, and ethical as well as result in doing the least harm possible.

6. Consider and weigh both short- and long-term ethical consequences.

7. Complete a final check: Is the planned action impartial, generalizable, and justifiable?

Creating a Culturally Competent Ethical Foundation

Consider this: Before a building is constructed, an architect is needed to draft plans and sketches of what the structure will look like. The architect considers heights, dimensions, widths, and other important considerations. The architect must also reflect on additional factors, including environmental issues that may impact the building's construction prior to actually building the structure. All of the formal blueprints for a new building are created before any construction begins, ensuring that the right tools are used to provide a strong, solid foundation. This preplanning ensures a structure is built according to local, state, and national regulations and is constructed in a manner in which everyone who enters or occupies the building is safe.

This same notion of preplanning applies to being a culturally competent and ethical counselor. Our profession has an ethical foundation to the work that is done with a goal of assessing the unique cultural needs of our clients. This foundation, comprised of the core ethical principles, is discussed in Chapter 2. How ethical decisions are made and the thought processes behind the action that will be taken integrate this ethical foundation into each step of the process. The ethical decision-making processes we engage in and utilize, including formal decision-making models, can be viewed as the ethical blueprint for effective counseling practice. Exercising a formal ethical decision-making process while taking into account the unique aspects of our client's culture demonstrates to stakeholders, clients, and society as a whole that we in the counseling profession take our responsibility to protect clients and the public from harm seriously, and we work to prevent professionals from making erroneous and premature decisions.

DEMONSTRATING CULTURAL SENSITIVITY

The values held by counselors often work to assist the therapeutic relationship. This sensitivity can also cause challenges. As counselors, we have a professional obligation to monitor ourselves and seek out consultation, supervision, personal counseling, or other appropriate steps when working through dilemmas that are especially challenging. One essential component of our education and training is in the area of cultural competence. All counselors, regardless of the type of setting, population, or clinical focus, must be able to demonstrate consistently multicultural sensitivity. Imbedded throughout many of our professional codes of ethics is the concept of integrating cultural awareness and practice in all aspects of our work (Arredondo et al., 1996).

We must actively show cultural sensitivity in all aspects of the therapeutic relationship, including the following:

1. The role that a support network can play in helping to provide support to clients

Ethical Code 3.2

A.1.d. Support Network Involvement.

Counselors recognize that support networks hold various meanings in the lives of clients and consider enlisting the support, understanding, and involvement of others (e.g., religious/spiritual/community leaders, family members, friends) as positive resources, when appropriate, with client consent.

Source: 2014 American Counseling Association Code of Ethics. Reprinted with permission from American Counseling Association.

2. The informed consent process and awareness of the role that language differences can play in the counseling relationship

Ethical Code 3.3

A.2.c. Developmental and Cultural Sensitivity.

Counselors communicate information in ways that are both developmentally and culturally appropriate. Counselors use clear and understandable language when discussing issues related to informed consent. When clients have difficulty understanding the language that counselors use, counselors provide necessary services (e.g., arranging for a qualified interpreter or translator) to ensure comprehension by clients. In collaboration with clients, counselors consider cultural implications of informed consent procedures and, where possible, counselors adjust their practices accordingly.

Source: 2014 American Counseling Association Code of Ethics. Reprinted with permission from American Counseling Association.

3. The various ways to view confidentiality and privacy from a cultural perspective

Ethical Code 3.4

B.1.a. Multicultural and Diversity Considerations.

Counselors maintain awareness and sensitivity regarding cultural meanings of confidentiality and privacy. Counselors respect differing views toward disclosure of information. Counselors hold ongoing discussions with clients as to how, when, and with whom information is to be shared.

Source: 2014 American Counseling Association Code of Ethics. Reprinted with permission from American Counseling Association.

4. The importance of not discriminating against clients in any form (ACA Standard C.5.)

5. Cultural sensitivity in the process of diagnosis and assessment (ACA Standards E.5.b., E.5.c., E.8.)

6. Multicultural inclusiveness in supervision, teaching, and training (ACA Standards F.2.b., F.7.c., F.11.a., F.11.b., and F.11.c.)

7. The importance of being considerate of multicultural and disability issues when using social media and technology (ACA Standard H.5.d.)

Those are many elements to consider. Threaded throughout all of our interactions with clients, we must strive to demonstrate respect and uphold the dignity of each client and his or her cultural traditions and not engage in cultural tunnel vision (Corey et al., 2015). Culturally and ethically competent practitioners must view the entire code of ethics and ethical scholarship and research through the lens of cultural context (Corey et al., 2015; Houser & Thoma, 2013). We must strive to understand that the culture of both the counselor and the client impacts the therapeutic relationship and everything the relationship encompasses. The counseling relationship includes the assessment process; theories and techniques used in counseling practice; and how issues of communication, trust, and mutual understanding are fostered (or in some cases hindered). We must be comfortable asking clients questions to learn more about their cultural values, traditions, and beliefs but also recognize that at times, we must engage in our own professional research to better understand the cultural worldview of our clients.

We should assume that every counselor–client interaction could potentially be a multicultural interaction (Kocet, 2009). We also must understand that it is nearly impossible to have the awareness, knowledge, and skills necessary to work effectively with each and every cultural population that exists. However, when unsure or lacking in the experience and education about a particular client population, we must take active steps to increase personal awareness, gather necessary knowledge and research about the cultural population, and through consultation and supervision, increase our skill set to practice empathically and sensitively according to the cultural needs of our client. We cover this topic in more detail in Chapter 12 in our discussion of competence.

Guided Practice Exercise 3.1

The Culturally Sensitive Intake

Contact a local mental health agency, and ask to see a copy of the intake assessment form. Examine the form from both an ethical competency lens and a cross-cultural competency lens. What aspects of a client's cultural identity may be missing from the intake form? If you could revise the form to make it more culturally sensitive and inclusive, what would you add and why?

COUNSELOR VALUE-BASED CONFLICTS MODEL (CVCM)

Counselors will sometimes face issues within their clinical work that create internal value conflicts. Sometimes these conflicts are based on cultural differences that exist between a counselor and a client. While the goal of counseling is not for professionals to be neutral or value free, it is our ethical obligation not to impose our values onto clients.

Ethical Code 3.5

A.4.b. Personal Values.

Counselors are aware of—and avoid imposing—their own values, attitudes, beliefs, and behaviors. Counselors respect the diversity of clients, trainees, and research participants and seek training in areas in which they are at risk of imposing their values onto clients, especially when the counselor's values are inconsistent with the client's goals or are discriminatory in nature.

Source: 2014 American Counseling Association Code of Ethics. Reprinted with permission from American Counseling Association.

Kocet and Herlihy (2014) created a working model that is slightly different than a traditional EDM. The Counselor Value-Based Conflicts Model (CVCM) is designed to assist counselors when faced with a conflict involving a potential personal or professional value conflict between themselves and a client or another stakeholder such as a colleague or supervisor. This model covers an array of opportunities, including situations that deal with cultural issues. The CVCM contains five steps that encourage mental health professionals to reflect on how to navigate through the ethical conundrum.

The first step of the CVCM involves determining what the source or nature is of the value conflict within the counseling relationship: *Is the value conflict of a personal nature, or is it a professional conflict?* The second step challenges the practitioner to explore the central issue that could prevent him or her from practicing effectively with the client. On a personal level, a counselor's morals, religious biases, or cultural viewpoints may impede negatively the effective delivery of a professional standard of care to the client. If the issue is a professional one, it could surface within the counselor as countertransference or could be a deficiency in a clinician's skills, training, or expertise. For example, consider the case of a counselor who has developed a strong rapport with a client. After a few sessions, the client reveals an eating disorder, but the counselor has no formal training in eating disorders. This may cause the counselor to experience a professional value conflict—the conflict involves wanting to help the client, but this desire conflicts with his or her lack of training or expertise needed to offer an appropriate standard of care to the client.

The third step of the CVCM encourages the professional counselor to seek guidance and assistance to ensure that a quality standard of care is being given to the client. On both the personal and the professional level, the provider should consult the professional code of ethics as well as with supervisors or colleagues on the matter. The counselor may need to determine if further multicultural education or training is needed to rectify the conflict or, if it involves a personal conflict, the counselor may need to seek personal counseling or participate in self-care strategies to work through a personal, religious, or moral value conflict while still providing effective counseling services.

In the fourth step of the CVCM, the counselor needs to determine the course of action to be taken and evaluate its appropriateness to the situation. If a referral is needed, the counselor must determine what is prompting such a necessary referral. Does the issue involve an unconscious or unexamined cultural bias or interpersonal conflict that is impeding the counselor's ability to work with the client? An example would be a case in which a client believes in a traditional, patriarchal hierarchy in a marriage, while the counselor believes in a more egalitarian model of romantic partnerships where both men and women have an equal voice. Conversely, is the reason for a referral due to a counselor's lack of appropriate education, training, or skill deficiency in a certain area, such as eating disorders, and not because of a personal bias against the client? The effectiveness of any potential plan to remediate one's own deficits as a counselor should be assessed in an ongoing manner.

The fifth and final step of the CVCM works to ensure that whatever formal action the counselor has chosen promotes the dignity and welfare of the client. This includes demonstrating unconditional positive regard for the client's cultural identity.

The CVCM can be used along with a traditional EDM. One aspect that the CVCM and other models share is their emphasis on personal reflection and its overarching role in reaching an ethical solution that promotes best practices. Let's take a look at how that might apply in a case study.

CASE STUDY 3.1

Colin received his degree in pastoral counseling and has strong personal values related to abortion. He is doing his internship in a public mental health agency when his adult client, Arlene, tells him she is pregnant and pursuing an abortion. She is ready to start college and cannot imagine having a baby at the same time. Fortunately, she says, her state allows legal abortions. She doesn't ask Colin's opinion or advice; she simply states it as a decision she has made.

(Continued)

(Continued)

1. *How might Colin's values influence his response to Arlene?*

2. *What should his response be?*

3. *Using the CVCM, how can Colin determine the best way to overlook his personal values and be present for the client?*

As you can imagine, values are fluid rather than static in nature. We begin to develop our professional values often in our graduate training, and these values go through further transformation in our professional practice. Forming an ethical identity is shaped by personal morals and principled ideology, what Schlenker calls an ethical ideology (as cited in Houser & Thoma, 2013). An ethical ideology exists when a person forms an integrated framework of beliefs, values, standards, and self-images that influences how a counselor assesses what is "right" or "wrong." As we maneuver through ethical challenges involving cross-cultural differences with clients, an important step is seeking out ethical wisdom from others in the profession. This process is known as consultation. In the next section we will delve into what consultation is and ways to practice it.

To invite you to further reflect on the role that your personal values may play in your professional ethical decisions, you are encouraged to complete the Ethics and Values-Based Conflicts Exercise. This exercise can be done independently or discussed in small or large groups in class.

Guided Practice Exercise 3.2

Ethics and Values-Based Conflicts

Examining Ethical Issues and Personal Values in the Counseling Relationship

Rate yourself on a scale of 1 to 10, identifying the level of conflict between personal and professional values in the following scenarios (with 1 being minimally conflicted and 10 being extremely conflicted).

Scenarios	Self-Score
1. A client who reports selling drugs to high school students.	6
2. Accepting a Facebook friend request from a former client.	
3. A female client who believes that a man is the head of the household and the sole decision maker in the family.	
4. A client who is highly religious and often shares his or her passionate beliefs about her or his faith during sessions, which differ significantly from your personal beliefs—the client requests you pray with him or her at the start of your sessions.	
5. A client who engages in prostitution (including having customers who she has served in her home while her children are in the other room) to earn money to pay rent and feed her children.	
6. A gay client who is very religious and indicates he no longer wants to be gay and instead wants to marry a woman—he has begun dating a woman from his local church.	
7. A client who is considering terminating a pregnancy because of her career aspirations and inconvenient timing—she terminated another pregnancy two years ago for similar reasons.	
8. A supervisor who instructs the counselors at the agency to provide whatever diagnosis is necessary to the insurance company to extend services to clients and provide them with more counseling sessions.	
9. A college student who is considering dropping out of college and working at a local convenience store—the client is highly intelligent.	
10. A client who has been diagnosed with a sexually transmitted disease and continues to engage in unprotected sex with multiple partners.	
11. A client coming to counseling for work on anger management issues who continually uses racist, sexist, or homo-prejudiced comments in sessions.	
12. A six-year-old child who was born a boy biologically and now identifies as a transgender girl—the girl's parents are supportive of their daughter, who fully dresses and identifies as a girl, but the girl's school doesn't know which bathroom the child should use and relegates the child to use the school nurse's bathroom.	
13. A parent who believes the best way to discipline his or her children is through corporal punishment.	
14. A client who is into swinging or group sex as a way to express his or her sexual freedom.	

ROLES AND TYPES OF CONSULTATION

Counselors should consult or seek advice and information from others when they encounter cultural populations with whom they have limited knowledge or skill. There are two main types of consultation: relational consultation and scholarship and research consultation.

Relational Consultation

One type of consultation that counselors typically engage in is referred to as a *relational consultation*—this involves reaching out to a supervisor, a colleague, a former counseling professor, or an expert in the field to discuss (either through e-mail, chat, videoconferencing, in person, or phone call) the ethical dilemma in question. The people we often call in a consultation provide us with their professional perspectives and may share stories about similar ethical experiences they have had in their own professional practices working with clients from similar cultural backgrounds. An ethics consultant may ask you questions about the ethical situation and ask you reflective questions relevant to the cultural nuances of the professional relationship for you to consider. Consulting with one or more counseling colleagues about an ethical or a cross-cultural dilemma you are facing has several advantages: (a) Consultation provides a variety of clinical viewpoints and perspectives you may not otherwise have considered; (b) it helps you organize your thoughts and gives you new insights into examining the dilemma; and (c) it provides a formal mechanism to document your ethical decision-making process, especially in the case of legal issues.

When you consult on an ethical issue, you always should do your best to document that you engaged in an ethics consultation. You also need to document with whom you consulted, the role and purpose of the consultation, and the outcome of the consultation. For example, you will want to make note of how the consultation aided you in the decision-making process and what steps you are taking in the future. Consulting with other counselors or supervisors is well supported in the ACA Code of Ethics (2014).

Ethical Code 3.6

B.7. Case Consultation.

Information shared in a consulting relationship is discussed for professional purposes only. Written and oral reports present only data germane to the purposes of the consultation, and every effort is made to protect client identity and to avoid undue invasion of privacy.

Source: 2014 American Counseling Association Code of Ethics. Reprinted with permission from American Counseling Association.

Further, ACA (2014) Code of Ethics Standard B.7.b. focuses on limiting the scope of information disseminated to other colleagues.

Ethical Code 3.7

B.7.b. Disclosure of Confidential Information.

When consulting with colleagues, counselors do not disclose confidential information that reasonably could lead to the identification of a client or other person or organization with whom they have a confidential relationship unless they have obtained the prior consent of the person or organization or the disclosure cannot be avoided. They disclose information only to the extent necessary to achieve the purposes of the consultation.

Source: 2014 American Counseling Association Code of Ethics. Reprinted with permission from American Counseling Association.

In other words, consultation is not gossip. If a counselor finds him- or herself discussing intimate, personal details of what a client shared in session that is not relevant to resolving the ethical dilemma, then the conversation is more gossip in nature and is not a true professional consultation. Counselors should share only the most basic and pertinent information about the case, including aspects of the client's cultural identity, in a way that respects the client and still aids in reaching a successful resolution to the ethical dilemma.

CASE STUDY 3.2

Esther is a member of the local Mennonite church and lives and works within the community. She has worked with her elders on issues related to depression off and on for most of her adult life. The elders decide that Esther should seek outside help and contact you to work with her. Your only real knowledge of the community is the types of work they do about town, but you are willing to see the Esther to determine if it is a good fit. When Esther arrives, she is accompanied by church elders. Although she is an adult, she is adamant that they are involved in her treatment and care and are consulted regularly.

1. *Read standard A.1.b. from the 2014 ACA Code of Ethics. How might this code relate to Esther's stance that her church elders be involved in her care?*

2. *What does it mean to involve a support network?*

(Continued)

(Continued)

3. *Consider the steps you would take to have a religious or spiritual leader or another important person from the client's culture be a part of one or more counseling sessions.*

4. *How do you feel about this taking place?*

5. *How should client confidentiality be addressed, especially when outside individuals are present in a therapeutic session?*

Scholarship and Research Consultation

In the scenario presented at the start of this chapter, Michante shares with Janice, the counselor, his apprehension about beginning the counseling process. It is critical for Janice to recognize that there could be significant cultural issues at play that may be impacting Michante's desire to terminate counseling services. Janice should use her training in multicultural competence to recognize her own limitations. It is necessary, and ethical, for us to recognize when we lack awareness, knowledge, or skills to work with certain cultural populations. Because we may not be the best at seeing our own deficiencies, we should seek the perspectives of others. Then we should take active steps to rectify our professional or personal deficiencies that impede our work as counselors.

In this ethical dilemma, Janice recognizes that she has limited knowledge of Native American clients, particularly of the Sioux tribe. Through her own level of self-awareness, she recognizes there are multiple cultural differences that exist between herself and Michante, including gender, racial or ethnic, and socioeconomic status. Because of the multicultural training she received in her graduate training, as well as continuing education workshops she has attended, Janice knows to validate Michante's apprehension and asks him open-ended questions to explore what may be impacting his hesitancy for beginning counseling. Janice normalizes and validates his feelings. Janice also speaks to Michante and openly raises the issue of some of the cultural differences she recognizes and asks him if those differences are also weighing on his mind.

Michante begins to relax and recognizes that maybe Janice does understand some of the reasons why he is hesitant to enter a counseling relationship with her. Rather than trying to coerce Michante to remain in counseling, she validates the cultural differences between them, which reduces his anxiety and apprehension. Janice is up front with Michante about not having detailed knowledge about the Sioux tribe, but she tells him that she has a former colleague living out of state who is a Native American psychologist who does have extensive experience counseling Native Americans. She says that with Michante's permission, she could contact her colleague to increase her knowledge so that she can better support Michante. Janice also tells Michante that if there is anyone from his tribe that he would like to join him in a future counseling session, that that could be arranged. Michante appreciated Janice's steps to reach out to her colleague as well as offering him the opportunity to bring someone from his tribe to future counseling sessions. By Janice taking those initial steps, Michante felt she was conveying her respect for him. He said he would be open to coming back for a second counseling session.

A second type of consultation, often underutilized, is *scholarship and research consultation.* This second type of consultation often is not considered by most counselors. When most counselors hear the word *consultation,* they primarily think of speaking to another counselor or supervisor, yet consulting the counseling literature or literature from similar fields can be a significant part of the ethical decision-making process. We find scholarship and research consultation especially beneficial when the counselor may have little knowledge or information about the unique cultural attributes of the client. Scholarship and research consultation involves conducting a search of a library database and reviewing journal articles, books, or other scholarly publications most relevant to the ethical dilemma. In other words, after you leave graduate school, you will still investigate the literature when faced with a topic about which you have little information.

For example, if a counselor is facing an ethical dilemma involving competency in a particular area, then he or she may search out information on that topic or information relevant to that area of specialization. There is no specific type of information a counselor has to research, but the act of seeking out formal scholarship may offer a new perspective.

Let's reexamine the scenario presented at the beginning of this chapter. In addition to consulting with her colleague, Janice also takes steps to research the literature that focuses on counseling Native American individuals. She reviews her local library database and discovers two books and three articles that appear to offer some useful cultural information. Over the next few months, Janice pores over the literature. She discovers information about Native American culture that is useful in her work with Michante, including what to say and what not to say. Janice understands that she cannot nor should not apply everything she reads in the literature to her work with Michante. As a culturally trained counselor, Janice recognizes that while literature on diverse populations is meaningful to her work and growth as a counselor, she cannot use the information in a cookie-cutter fashion, applying the information gleaned from the counseling literature equally to every single client.

Imagine what would happen if Janice gave referrals to everyone who was culturally different from herself—chances are she would not have a practice. Engaging in sensitive consultation and collaboration allows counselors to work effectively with new populations while maintaining a sense of competency. In addition, we hope you noticed how transparent Janice was with Michante about the process and how she involved him in the discussion. She didn't simply consult and research in isolation; she engaged in a relational decision-making process that we will discuss more in Chapter 4.

Scholarship and research consultation can help us in an ethical dilemma in a variety of ways: (a) it helps us identify best practices based on empirical or qualitative data that can give strength to a specific action we take; (b) it demonstrates that we are engaging in steps within the ethical decision-making process that are sound and based on a high quality of care for our clients; and (c) the counseling literature may provide for a richer and more in-depth examination of an issue compared to that of an informal conversation with a colleague or supervisor. Again, most counselors may not have considered that reading a journal article, book, or Web site constitutes an ethics consultation, but we are advocating to include scholarship and research consultation as a viable option.

Counselors who engage in scholarship and research consultation also should document in client case notes or other appropriate venue the title and author of the publication or URL of the source of consultation and how the information is relevant and useful to resolving the ethical dilemma.

CONCLUSION

As we have learned in this chapter, ethical decision making can be a multilayered process. There are multiple considerations to take into account, including, but not limited to, the client's (or counselor's) cultural background and the impact on the counseling relationship, the use of a formal versus informal EDM, the role that values play when sorting out the nuances of an ethical dilemma, and finally, the two main types of ethical consultation that may be useful to work through ethical challenges in cultural encounters.

Counselors in training (CITs), as well as seasoned practitioners, are encouraged to engage in actively ongoing self-reflection and not treat ethical issues as only those times when major ethical bombs are dropped in our laps. Rather, developing and utilizing ethical sensitivity throughout all of our professional interactions can lead to a greater rewarding practice.

KEYSTONES

- Counselors must be aware of their own cultural biases, prejudices, and other hindrances that take away from effective counseling practice.
- When making ethical decisions, counselors should utilize a decision-making process that can include reviewing professional codes of ethics, consulting with others, and reviewing relevant literature.
- Dolgoff and colleagues (2012) have presented a seven-step ethical assessment screen to be used when facing cross-cultural ethical dilemmas. The steps include: identifying professional, personal, and societal values that are relevant to the ethical dilemma; determining how to minimize conflicts among these values; identifying alternative ethical options; determining which alternative minimizes conflicts between the client's and others' rights welfare and society's rights and interests; deciding which alternative is most efficient, effective, and ethical and results in the least harm; considering short- and long-term consequences; and asking if the planned action is impartial, generalizable, and justifiable.
- An essential component of counselor education and training is in the area of cultural competence. All counselors consistently must demonstrate multicultural sensitivity and should assume that every counselor–client interaction could be a multicultural interaction (Kocet, 2009).
- Counselors must be comfortable asking clients questions to learn more about their cultural values, traditions, and beliefs but also recognize that at times, counselors must engage in their own professional research to better understand the cultural worldview of clients.
- The CVCM assists counselors who are faced with a potential personal or professional value conflict between themselves and a client or another stakeholder, which can be utilized with cultural issues. Counselors must consult with supervisors and colleagues when they encounter cultural populations with whom they have limited awareness, knowledge, or skill.
- Relational consultation involves reaching out to a supervisor, colleague, former professor, or expert in the field to discuss an ethical dilemma.
- Scholarship and research consultation occurs when a counselor consults counseling literature or literature from similar fields to help with the ethical decision-making process.

SUGGESTED BEST PRACTICES

- Approach ethical decision making purposefully and with intention. Now is not the time to wing it!
- Be gentle with yourself if you find that the ethical dilemma triggers an emotional response. That is typical, and you can use the gut check as part of the ethical decision-making process.

- Break the mold. Don't relegate EDMs to a graduate school experience.
- Use the ethical assessment screening to help your reflection process when facing an ethical dilemma, particularly when cultural elements are involved.
- Create a strong ethical foundation in graduate school, and continue to build on it throughout your professional career.
- Avoid resting on your laurels. There is never a time in our careers when we don't need to keep learning and sharpening our ethical decision-making practices.
- Always attend to the impact of culture on the counseling process. This includes both the culture of the client and the counselor.
- Remember that your values will change, and as they change, the way you approach ethical decisions will change.
- Whenever possible, involve your client in the decision-making process. It's just the right thing to do.
- Keep reading the literature, even when you are out of school and may not feel that you have to.
- Go out of your way to learn about other cultures and increase the limits of your cultural competency.
- Keep your focus on best practices in all that you do as a professional counselor, including ethical decision making.

ADDITIONAL RESOURCES

In Print

Elliot, G. R. (2011). When values and ethics conflict: The counselor's role and responsibility. *Alabama Counseling Association Journal, 37*(1), 39–45.

Levitt, D. H., & Hartwig Moorhead, H. J. (Eds.). (2013). *When values and ethics collide: Real-life ethical decision making.* New York: Routledge/Taylor & Francis.

On the Web

Cross-cultural counseling: How to be more effective. (2010). *HPSO Risk Adviser.* Retrieved from http://www.hpso.com/pdfs/db/newsletters/HPS008v2_coun.pdf?fileName=HPS008v2_coun .pdf&folder=pdfs/db/newsletters&isLiveStr=Y

Shallcross, L. (2010). Putting clients ahead of personal values. *Counseling Today.* Retrieved from http://ct.counseling.org/2010/11/putting-clients-ahead-of-personal-values/

REFERENCES

American Counseling Association (ACA). (2014). *ACA code of ethics.* Alexandria, VA: Author.

Arredondo, P., Toporek, R., Brown, S., Sanchez, J., Locke, D., Sanchez, J., & Stadler, H. (1996). Operationalization of the multicultural counseling competencies. *Journal of Multicultural Counseling and Development, 24*(1), 42–78.

Corey, G., Corey, M., Corey, C., & Callahan, P. (2015). *Issues and ethics in the helping professions* (9th ed.). Stamford, CT: Cengage.

Cottone, R. R. (2001). A social constructivism model of ethical decision making. *Journal of Counseling & Development, 79,* 39–45.

Dolgoff, R., Harrington, D., & Loewenberg, F. (2012). *Ethical decisions for social work practice* (9th ed.). Belmont, CA: Brooks Cole.

Herlihy, B., & Dufrene, R. (2011). Current and emerging ethical issues in counseling: A delphi study of expert opinions. *Counseling and Values, 56*(1–2), 10–24.

Houser, R., & Thoma, S. J. (2013). *Ethics in counseling and therapy: Developing an ethical identity.* Los Angeles: Sage.

Jungers, C., & Gregoire, J. (Eds.). (2013). *Counseling ethics: Philosophical and professional foundations.* New York: Springer.

Kitchener, K. S., & Anderson, S. (2011). *Foundations of ethical practice, research, and teaching in psychology and counseling* (2nd ed.). New York: Routledge.

Kocet, M. (2009). Multicultural ethical perspectives. In C. Lee, D. Burnhill, A. Butler, C. Hipolito-Delgado, M. Humphrey, O. Munoz, & H. J. Shin (Eds.), *Elements of culture in counseling: Theory and practice* (pp.193–210). Upper Saddle River, NJ: Pearson.

Kocet, M., & Herlihy, B. (April 2014). Addressing value-based conflicts within the counseling relationship: A decision-making model. *Journal of Counseling & Development, 92*(2), 180–186. doi:10.1002/j.1556–6676.2014.00146.x

Welfel, E. R. (2013). *Ethics in counseling and psychotherapy* (5th ed.). Pacific Grove, CA: Brooks/Cole.

Chapter 4

RELATIONAL ETHICAL DECISION MAKING

Your 9 a.m. client walks into your office for her regularly scheduled session. She has a bright smile on her face. She hands you a fresh, steaming cup of coffee from your favorite coffee shop around the corner and says, "I've noticed that each week during our session, you have a caramel macchiato coffee on your desk. I know that you're not a morning person, so I just thought I would pick you up your favorite." That particular morning was hectic. You didn't have time to grab your morning ritual cup of coffee and are craving some right now. While you know the cup of coffee is only worth about $5.79, you don't know what to say to the client. You don't have time to run down the hall to speak to your supervisor or to make a phone call to your former counseling ethics professor to consult—you need to make an ethical decision in the moment. You are not even sure if it is an ethical dilemma. How do you respond to the client? Do you accept the coffee or decline it? Is it just a cup of coffee or a slippery slope of a boundary crossing just waiting to happen?

CHAPTER OVERVIEW

This chapter introduces the reader to the importance of the relationship, particularly the client–counselor relationship, in ethical decision making. The importance of counselor self-reflection and self-awareness is highlighted. This chapter also introduces a relational ethical decision-making model (EDM) that builds on these essential components of relationship, self-reflection, and self-awareness. The model is presented through the lens of a case study that explores the ethical decision-making dynamics involved.

LEARNING OBJECTIVES

After reading this chapter you will be able to do the following:

1. Define relational and collaborative ethics.

2. Describe each of the nine core values that promote ethical practice.

3. Apply the Relational Ethical Decision-Making Model to resolve ethical dilemmas.

4. Utilize the Brief Ethical Decision-Making Model to make ethical decisions without consulting others.

CACREP STANDARDS

CACREP Core Standards

G.1.j. Ethical standards of professional organizations and credentialing bodies and applications of ethical and legal considerations in professional counseling.

CACREP Clinical Mental Health Standards

A.2. Understands the ethical and legal considerations specifically related to the practice of clinical mental health counseling.

B.1. Demonstrates the ability to apply and adhere to ethical and legal standards in clinical mental health counseling.

INTRODUCTION

Most existing EDMs share common elements and tend to focus on the counselor–supervisor relationship and the current reporting hierarchy (Cottone & Tarvydas, 2007). In most cases, the models refer to counselors being faced with an ethical dilemma and consulting a supervisor or senior colleague on the issue to strategize an approach to reach an ethical resolution. In these instances, counselors then return to the client to inform him or her of how the ethical dilemma will be resolved (Sperry, 2007; Welfel, 2013). Rarely is the client directly involved with the counselor in reaching an appropriate ethical resolution.

In this chapter, we propose a model that is based on *relational ethics,* also known as *collaborative ethics,* which focuses on the ethics of care model within the therapeutic relationship and takes a collaborative approach to reaching ethical decisions (Davis, 1997). Compared to traditional EDMs addressed in this book that focus on a more linear approach to reaching ethical conclusions and taking steps to resolve dilemmas (Sperry, 2007), the model we present offers a nuanced perspective that actively involves clients, students, families, and other stakeholders when appropriate.

NINE CORE VALUES PROMOTING ETHICAL PRACTICE

We will start this chapter by looking at values that promote our ethical practice. In a study involving core ethical values of master therapists, Jennings and colleagues (2005) identified nine core values that promote ethical practice. These values are organized into two categories: (1) building and maintaining interpersonal attachments and (2) building and maintaining expertise.

Building and Maintaining Interpersonal Attachments

The first category, building and maintaining interpersonal attachments, includes the values of relational connection, autonomy, beneficence, and nonmaleficence. Because the foundation of the counseling profession is the therapeutic relationship, connecting with clients, supervisors, and colleagues is the keystone and foundation of all that we do. As professional counselors, we are relational beings—our work is centered on human interaction. We believe that through the professional relationship, communication, and interaction between counselor and client, well-being and growth can be fostered.

The other three values in this first category speak to the core ethical principles of the profession, which have been mentioned in other parts of this book. Autonomy speaks to the ability and right of clients and others to make decisions that best serve them and ensures that clients are not coerced into doing certain things. Autonomy advocates for client choice.

CASE STUDY 4.1

Priscilla is a licensed counselor who specializes in working with children. She has a popular parenting guide in print that is sold at the local bookstore. When Priscilla takes on a new client, she requires that the parents purchase her parenting book, so they can incorporate the strategies she is using in session with the child at home.

1. *Do you think this is ethical practice? Why or why not?*

2. *How does this relate to the concept of autonomy?*

3. *What impact might this requirement have on the relationship with the parents?*

Beneficence means that we promote safety and well-being in all our interactions and interventions used with and for clients. Caring is at the center of beneficence. The opposite of beneficence is doing harm and is where the principle of nonmaleficence comes into play. This principle states that we must avoid harming clients, whether physically, emotionally, or psychologically.

Building and Maintaining Expertise

The second category, building and maintaining expertise, includes the values of competence, humility, professional growth, openness to complexity and ambiguity, and self-awareness. Competence means that professionals are skilled in the art and science of counseling. We must have the necessary education, training, and skills to practice effectively with clients and stakeholders. Part of being competent also means learning new approaches, theories, methods, and treatment modalities. Given the nature of the discipline, the counseling profession must not remain static. We must be equipped to increase our skill sets and participate in continuing education. Humility helps us recognize our own limitations—not in a negative way but in a humanistic manner. We cannot be everything to all clients, and we must recognize when we have reached our limitations and seek counsel and support from trusted colleagues and supervisors.

Guided Practice Exercise 4.1

Involving the Client in Ethical Decisions

Here is a question for reflection: What types of ethical situations would you be most comfortable collaborating with clients about? What ethical situations or issues would you find most challenging in discussing with clients? What makes those issues most difficult for you? What kind of support would you need to work through the dilemma?

The next value is professional growth. This relates to the value of competence. Counselors actively seek out new training experiences, both formal and informal, to broaden our skills and capacity to assist others. We are energized by identifying as lifelong learners and always see ourselves as having the role of student. We never stop growing. The next ethical value is openness to complexity and ambiguity. Oftentimes, new counselors want to find the "right" answer or will turn to the most expedient solution to resolve an ethical dilemma. However, the quickest available solution may not be in the best interest of the client or other individuals involved. Sometimes it is critical to examine the nuances and facets of each ethical conundrum. We must learn to become comfortable with the fact that straightforward solutions are not always readily available or may not exist at all. Because we work with human beings, we must recognize that a cookie-cutter approach may not be appropriate or helpful. Rather than examining ethics from a black-and-white perspective, counselors must strive to practice *counseling in gray*—learning to embrace the struggle of weighing competing ethical principles and obligations. Being an ethical counselor means bringing flexibility to your work and not making sudden decisions but employing a thoughtful response when situations call for such steps.

The final ethical value is self-awareness. Compared to most professions, the field of counseling prides itself on the promotion of self-reflection and self-awareness, especially during one's graduate training program. Not only must we be conscious of our professional strengths and limitations, but we also must be aware of our personal biases, perceptions, vulnerabilities, prejudices, and worldview, which may impact the counseling relationship. We only can help people walk on their journeys of self-awareness and growth if we have begun the work of walking our own paths of self-awareness and working through the struggle of making those necessary life discoveries about ourselves.

Guided Practice Exercise 4.2

Ethical Decisions in Practice

Interview a professional mental health counselor in your community. Discuss the process he or she uses to make ethical decisions. Does the professional use a formal EDM? Why or why not? What are the benefits of using an EDM in his or her counseling practice? Ask the counselor to discuss her or his view of the most pressing ethical issues she or he has faced in his or her professional career.

As you can see, these ethical values may be useful when examining ethical decision making collaboratively with clients and other stakeholders. Now, we will present a Relational Ethical Decision-Making Model for you to consider.

THE RELATIONAL ETHICAL DECISION-MAKING MODEL

The Relational Ethical Decision-Making Model is designed to create an intentional, collaborative way for counselors and clients to work together to reach a successful resolution to an ethical dilemma. Using an ethical relational approach in counseling practice necessitates that we diligently work to help clients understand our professional and ethical obligations and engage clients in reflecting on ethical decisions that we need to undertake. While it is unnecessary to hand out copies of the ACA Code of Ethics to each and every client at the start of the counseling relationship or to review a specific EDM, all counselors should include a clear description on their informed consent form of what codes of ethics are abided by and how clients can address any ethical concerns regarding their counselor's conduct, including recourse for filing an ethical complaint against a professional counselor. We should establish an ethical foundation for our counseling practice and discuss the overarching topic of ethics in counseling with our clients on a consistent basis.

Relational ethics takes the position that we should collaborate with our clients, based on the bedrock of the professional relationship, to work through sensitive issues together. In contrast, traditional EDMs place the power and control on our shoulders as the counselor or a supervisor often dictates the outcome of ethical issues. In a relational approach, the wisdom and insight of the client also enter the dialogue. The client is viewed as an important part of the process to resolve an ethical conundrum. This relational model may be useful when we need to directly involve a client, family member, or other stakeholder in the ethical decision-making process.

Figure 4.1 Relational Ethical Decision-Making Model

1. Continually examine the role that ethics play within the therapeutic relationship.
2. Identify the ethical dilemma or problem, including various contextual layers, cultural considerations, and ethical ambiguity, seeking consultation and supervision as warranted.
3. Discuss with the client the professional ethical obligations of counselors and the ethical dilemma, and address how the dilemma impacts the counseling relationship.
4. Working with the client, examine the core ethical principles that are most prominent within this ethical dilemma.
5. Consider the ethical dilemma, including perceptions, values, biases, and beliefs from both the counselor's and client's points of view.

(Continued)

Figure 4.1 (Continued)

6. Examine how boundaries within the therapeutic relationship are impacted as a result of the ethical conundrum, including the counselor's and client's affective and cognitive domains.
7. Look into applicable laws; campus, agency, or department regulations; policies; procedures; handbooks; Web sites; and so on that may inform your decision.
8. Consult professional literature, as well as professional colleagues and experts (with client consent), regarding best practices in similar ethical dilemmas.
9. Collaborate with the client in brainstorming potential resolutions to the dilemma, and evaluate possible consequences and outcomes of action or inaction.
10. Choose a course of action, working through any challenges that may exist within the therapeutic relationship about the ethical issue.
11. Implement a selected course of action, addressing client concerns in a mutually supportive environment.
12. Evaluate how the ethical decision will impact the counseling relationship currently, as well as in the future.

Source: ©2013 Michael M. Kocet, PhD.

For the purposes of following each step of the decision-making model, a case example is presented, which will be discussed within the context of the model.

Case Example

Rebecca is a 34-year-old Latina woman who has been seeing you for professional counseling for the past six months. She came to counseling for help with self-esteem, body-image issues, and finding a romantic relationship. This is Rebecca's first time seeking out a professional counselor, due in part to pressure from her family not to do so. Because of their cultural and religious views, Rebecca's family believed she should seek guidance from her parish priest instead of a stranger. Rebecca sought out a professional counselor because she did not want to talk to her priest about romantic relationship issues, especially those of a sexual nature. For the past few months, Rebecca repeatedly mentions in session her family's disapproval of her seeing you for counseling. Over the past six months you have worked diligently to foster a strong therapeutic relationship with Rebecca. You went over your informed consent form and talked about the risks and benefits of counseling, issues related to confidentiality, record keeping, billing, and so on. Even though she is fairly new to the counseling process, Rebecca seems to have a solid grasp of what the counseling relationship is about and how it can help her.

During your most recent counseling session with Rebecca, she mentions that her eight-year-old niece is having her First Holy Communion in three weeks and invites you to her family's home for the First Holy Communion party. Rebecca has a large, extended, and close-knit family, and she explains that this party would be attended by almost everyone, including aunts, cousins, siblings, parents, and grandparents. Rebecca feels that if you attend the party and meet her family, they would get to know you and be more open to Rebecca seeing you for counseling. She is the first person in her immediate family to attend professional counseling, and she often has to talk to her family about what happens in session.

Your initial reaction is one of panic and apprehension. A client never has invited you to his or her home before. In your graduate training, you took a course on ethical and legal issues in counseling, and your professors constantly talked about maintaining professional boundaries with clients. You restrict the amount of personal information you share with clients and have never considered meeting a client anywhere other than your office.

Applying the Relational Ethical Decision-Making Model

1. Continually examine the role that ethics play within the therapeutic relationship.

As some ethics scholars assert, developing ethical sensitivity and awareness is an important component of being a competent and ethically intentional counseling professional (Sperry, 2007; Welfel, 2013). Fostering a mind-set of ethical sensitivity in all aspects of your professional practice is designed to take a proactive, rather than reactive, step in working with clients. Ethics not only should be considered in the midst of a crisis or major ethical concern with a client or stakeholder but should be integrated into every interaction, session, meeting, phone call, e-mail correspondence, text message, or social media posting you make.

Fundamental to ethical sensitivity is the question: *Is what I am doing, saying, or writing in my role as a professional counselor promoting what is in the best interest and well-being of those I serve as well as my colleagues, supervisors, the general public, and myself?* Being an ethically sensitive counselor means that we continually grow and challenge ourselves to view our everyday practice through an ethical lens. For example, how often should we review and reflect on our professional codes of ethics? We speculate that most counselors look at professional codes of ethics only out of obligation when faced with a major ethical situation with a client or supervisee where it warrants being pulled from a folder and consulted. In a relational approach to ethics, ethical practice is based on the premise that good counseling practice is ethical practice. We must become socialized within our profession to make ethical decision making an active and daily part of our professional practice and not something done on rare occasions or only out of necessity. Ethical sensitivity becomes more of a lifestyle in our professional development.

Regarding the case example, because of your ethical sensitivity, you are aware that Rebecca has brought a significant ethical issue for you both to consider. You listen thoughtfully to her invitation to attend the First Holy Communion party at her family's home. You also are aware of your personal thoughts and feelings about the invitation, but you convey unconditional positive regard to Rebecca and her invitation.

2. Identify the ethical dilemma or problem, including various contextual layers, cultural considerations, and ethical ambiguity, seeking consultation and supervision as warranted.

This step is very similar to other existing decision-making models. An important aspect of examining any potential ethical dilemma is understanding what the problem actually is. We must then grapple with the nuances and complex challenges that exist within the dilemma. For example, are there cultural issues that are impacting the counseling relationship and how the ethical issue is viewed, either by the counselor or the client? Cultural issues, such as gender or gender identity, age, race, sexual orientation, religion or spirituality, and other factors impact not only the client's worldview and how he or she frames issues but ours as well. At this early stage of the model, it may be helpful to speak with colleagues or supervisors to obtain an initial grasp of what ethical issues may exist. It is not an appropriate time to make a decision, but speaking with others may clarify what issues must be considered. This second step calls upon the counselor to be flexible with ambiguous parts of the problem or dilemma. Not everything will be clear-cut, which can be frustrating, and we must be mindful of our emotions while tackling the dilemma to think things through clearly and responsibly.

Regarding Rebecca's invitation to her family's home, you identify that the ethical dilemma pertains to dual or multiple relationships and her desire for you to meet her family, so they may become more open to supporting Rebecca's attendance in counseling. You also take into account Rebecca's culture and family traditions and worldviews. You respect the fact that family is important to the Latino culture, and you cannot unilaterally make a decision not to attend the party. You also understand the reasons why Rebecca's family may be hesitant for her to seek out professional counseling. You learned in your multicultural counseling training that many Latino families are close-knit and believe it is disrespectful to share personal family issues with a stranger.

You have an initial conversation with your supervisor, apprising her of Rebecca's invitation. There is not a clear, formal policy at your agency that prohibits you from attending the party. However, you have a close professional relationship with your supervisor, and she encourages you to think through the nuances of the dilemma and identify potential options. You choose to think it through and involve Rebecca in the decision-making process.

3. Discuss with the client the professional ethical obligations of counselors and the ethical dilemma, and address how the dilemma impacts the counseling relationship.

In this important stage of the model, counselors discuss with clients their professional and ethical obligations. Depending on the complexity of the ethical issues, it may be helpful for you to show your clients a copy of the professional code of ethics that you use and talk about the role that it plays in your training, education, and growth as a counselor.

In this scenario, you speak with Rebecca during your next session and thank her for the gracious invitation to her family's home. You discuss how, as a licensed professional counselor, you are obligated to follow the professional code of ethics written by the American Counseling Association. You explain the purpose of a code of ethics and how the ethical guidelines help you to reflect on the best way to provide counseling services to all of your clients. You invite Rebecca to join you in having a more in-depth conversation about the invitation to the party, and she is glad to do so.

4. Working with the client, examine the core ethical principles that are most prominent within this ethical dilemma.

As mentioned previously, the core ethical principles are the bedrock of the counseling relationship (Corey, Corey, & Callahan, 2011; Horner & Kelly, 2007; Jennings et al., 2005; Welfel, 2013). In every ethical dilemma, we must examine the ethical principles to see which take precedence. While ethics scholars do not contend that any single ethical principle plays a greater role in the counseling relationship, our worldview, values, and training may impact how we view the principles and which principle plays a more prominent role in a particular ethical situation. Therefore, the order of the core principles, from most relevant to least relevant, may change according to each ethical conundrum.

In the scenario, you discuss the core principles of autonomy, beneficence, and nonmaleficence with Rebecca so that she understands your professional obligation. You explain the view of each ethical principle and have Rebecca identify the principles that she believes have the utmost importance to her and her invitation. You also discuss any similarities or disagreements you both may have regarding your view of the most essential principles impacting this ethical situation. Through your discussion, you identify the core ethical principles, and you both believe that autonomy and beneficence play a central role in Rebecca's family situation. You support Rebecca's autonomy for inviting you to the family event, and you both recognize that Rebecca views your presence at the family gathering as potentially beneficial to her work in therapy.

5. Consider the ethical dilemma, including perceptions, values, biases, and beliefs from both the counselor's and client's points of view.

During this step, you discuss your concerns with Rebecca and the fact that you have never been to a client's home before or met a client outside of your office. You express your concerns regarding confidentiality and how other information discussed between the two of you might come under question by members of Rebecca's family. You recognize that your cultural worldview of the counseling relationship is very different than Rebecca's tradition. Rebecca places a great emphasis on family, and she understands that for her counseling to be successful, she needs support from her extended family and to know that she is not shaming them by talking to a stranger about family business. Rebecca explains that getting to know her family members and sharing a meal together is a sign of respect and mutual caring. From Rebecca's perspective, by getting to know the family members, you would earn their trust, which in turn may permit her to continue seeing you in the counseling relationship.

6. Examine how boundaries within the therapeutic relationship are impacted as a result of the ethical conundrum, including the counselor's and client's affective and cognitive domains.

One way to safeguard the boundaries of your counseling relationship with Rebecca is to continue discussing your concerns and potential issues that would negatively impact the counseling relationship by your attendance at the family gathering. You discuss your thoughts with Rebecca as well as the feelings and apprehension you feel about attending the party. You tell Rebecca about your graduate training and your worldview about the role of boundaries within the counseling relationship and that you take it very seriously. You express reservations about not wanting to disrupt or cause harm to the therapeutic relationship that you have built together over the past six months. You also ask Rebecca about her thoughts and feelings of you possibly meeting her family members and what the dynamic might be like at the party.

**7. Look into applicable laws; campus, agency, or
department regulations; policies; procedures; handbooks;
Web sites; and so on that may inform your decision.**

You and Rebecca review your professional code of ethics together, and with
Rebecca's input, you identify the key ethical standards that you believe are most
applicable to the issue of attending the family event. The standards in the American
Counseling Code of Ethics that are most relevant to this situation are these:

Ethical Code 4.1

A.6.b. Extending Counseling Boundaries.

Counselors consider the risks and benefits of extending current counseling relationships beyond conventional parameters. Examples include attending a client's
formal ceremony (e.g., a wedding or commitment ceremony or graduation), purchasing a service or product provided by a client (excepting unrestricted bartering),
and visiting a client's ill family member in the hospital. In extending these boundaries,
counselors take appropriate professional precautions such as informed consent, consultation, supervision, and documentation to ensure that judgment is not impaired and
no harm occurs.

A.6.c. Documenting Boundary Extensions.

If counselors extend boundaries as described in A.6.a. and A.6.b., they must
officially document, prior to the interaction (when feasible) the rationale for such an
interaction, the potential benefit, and anticipated consequences for the client or former client and other individuals significantly involved with the client or former client.
When unintentional harm occurs to the client or former client, or to an individual
significantly involved with the client or former client, the counselor must show
evidence of an attempt to remedy such harm.

I.1.b. Ethical Decision Making. When counselors are faced with an ethical dilemma,
they use and document, as appropriate, an ethical decision-making model that may
include, but is not limited to, consultation; consideration of relevant ethical standards, principles, and laws; generation of potential courses of action; deliberation of
risks and benefits; and selection of an objective decision based on the circumstances
and welfare of all involved.

Source: 2014 American Counseling Association Code of Ethics. Reprinted with permission from American
Counseling Association.

You examine the counseling staff-hiring manual and discover there is currently no policy on visiting clients' homes. You also check the state licensure regulations, and there is nothing prohibiting or even addressing home visits. You do some research online and uncover that three mental health agencies similar to yours throughout the country have developed policies on visiting clients in their home. One agency bans counselors from making home visits, while the other two have policies that permit counselors to visit clients' homes and include the protocol for such visits to take place. You decide to print these sample policies to share with your supervisor.

8. Consult professional literature, as well as professional colleagues and experts (with client consent), regarding best practices in similar ethical dilemmas.

You consult with your supervisor about agency policy and regulations governing visits to clients' homes and agree that there is no current policy; however, you share with your supervisor the policies of other agencies across the country that were developed for situations that are similar to yours. Your supervisor believes that your situation with Rebecca is an important issue that all counselors at the agency should discuss. She indicates that without revealing your client's information, she will place the topic on the agenda for the next staff meeting because other counselors may grapple with this type of dilemma in the future and a formal agency policy is warranted. Your supervisor is also appreciative of the fact that you have involved your client actively in the decision-making process. You share that based on the conversations you have had with Rebecca concerning the ethical dilemma, you can already see the trust level between you becoming deeper, and as a result, Rebecca is more invested in the counseling process.

9. Collaborate with the client in brainstorming potential resolutions to the dilemma, and evaluate possible consequences and outcomes of action or inaction.

In this next step of the model, you and Rebecca work jointly to identify the costs and benefits of your attendance at the family gathering. The two of you carefully weigh all of the factors, and you feel that you have worked together to identify potential issues that might arise—both potentially helpful issues as well as those that may be negative or harmful to Rebecca's continuation in counseling. For example, you and Rebecca talk about what to do if her family members want to know what is discussed in her counseling sessions and how to approach the topic of confidentiality with her family in a way that is respectful but also supports Rebecca's autonomy regarding what is and is not shared with her extended family. You discuss the potential for family members to pressure you to reveal personal information shared by Rebecca. Rebecca responds by stating how she would prefer that you handle confidentiality with her family and what she feels comfortable being shared.

You also speak to the concern that Rebecca or her family may want you to return for additional family functions. You discuss with Rebecca that this would be the only family event you will attend and explain that you cannot have an ongoing relationship with her family. The sole purpose of your attendance at the party would be to earn the family's trust for Rebecca to continue seeking counseling. It also would benefit you to see Rebecca interact with her family and would illuminate some of the family dynamics that Rebecca has mentioned in the counseling relationship. Rebecca then shares why it is important to her that you attend the First Communion party. After hearing her perspective, you have a stronger sense of the potential benefit of attending the party. You also discuss with Rebecca that another potential benefit is that the anxiety and stress she is currently experiencing because of family pressure to stop going to counseling may cease if her family trusts her counselor and is more comfortable with the situation. This would result in Rebecca being able to focus more intently on her therapeutic goals that you established together during her initial counseling appointments.

By the end of the session with Rebecca, the two of you have identified the various concerns, risks, and benefits of attending the party, and you both feel good about the selected outcome.

10. Choose a course of action, working through any challenges that may exist within the therapeutic relationship about the ethical issue.

You and Rebecca make the decision together that you will attend the First Holy Communion party, with clear guidance from Rebecca on what to share and what not to share concerning private information disclosed in the counseling relationship. You also make it clear and Rebecca understands that this visit is a one-time occurrence, and you will not attend future family events. Rebecca is prepared to discuss this with her family if they press her on it. You jointly write out the goals of the visit and what Rebecca hopes to accomplish with your presence at the family gathering. You both sign the goals sheet. You give a copy to Rebecca and place a copy in her counseling record. You and Rebecca agree to revisit the issue if the counseling relationship changes in a negative way as a result of the party. You discuss this with your supervisor and explain the rationale and how it fits with the therapeutic goals you and Rebecca have established. Your supervisor supports this decision and asks that you set up a follow-up supervision meeting with her following the family event.

11. Implement a selected course of action, addressing client concerns in a mutually supportive environment.

You attend the First Holy Communion party at Rebecca's family's home. You are introduced to her parents, siblings, nieces, nephews, aunts, cousins, and neighbors. At one point, one of Rebecca's aunts begins inquiring about the information that Rebecca shares with you, and based on your prior conversation with Rebecca and her consent, you give her aunt a minimal but respectful response and then continue to mingle and get to know the other family members. After hearing family members' stories about Rebecca growing up, you gain a very strong sense of the role of family in Rebecca's life and how concerned her family is about her well-being and happiness. Over the course of the party, you can see that the family members trust you more and have a better understanding of why Rebecca is seeking your help as her counselor.

By the end of the party, in front of Rebecca, Rebecca's father gives you his blessing to provide counseling to his daughter. You see the huge smile on Rebecca's face, and you can tell how pleased she is that she can continue seeing you for counseling. As you prepare to leave, Rebecca's parents thank you for helping their daughter and for the guidance you are providing.

12. Evaluate how the ethical decision will impact the counseling relationship currently as well as in the future.

At the session following the party, you process with Rebecca how she feels and how her family members responded to your presence at the family gathering. Rebecca reports that her parents were appreciative of the respect that you showed them and everyone in the family, and they enjoyed watching you try the traditional foods of the family. They told Rebecca that they liked your sense of humor and love of their cultural music. Rebecca becomes very animated and thanks you profusely for attending the party. She indicates that the conversations you had prior to the party were helpful in thinking everything through. She feels it was an extremely positive outcome and has no concerns about your visit with her family. From Rebecca's perspective, although there are some extended family members who disapprove of her attending counseling, receiving her parents' approval was the most important part of the day for her.

You also discuss your thoughts and feelings about attending the party. You debrief with Rebecca about some of the family dynamics and roles that you observed during your time at the party. You tell Rebecca that while you had initial concerns regarding the ethical decision to attend the party, you now realize that it was an appropriate choice to attend. Over the next few sessions, you and Rebecca continue to work on her therapeutic goals. The anxiety and stress she was experiencing because of her family's earlier pressure to terminate counseling has been eliminated, and she can now focus on other pertinent therapeutic issues. You also follow up with your supervisor on what the family visit was like and what you learned. Because the event went so well, your supervisor asks for your assistance in crafting a policy for the agency.

Guided Practice Exercise 4.3

Comparing EDMs

Examine two or three EDMs found in the literature or Chapter 2. How do they compare to the Relational Ethical Decision-Making Model found in this chapter? What are the similarities and differences?

Now that you have seen the relational model in action, what are your thoughts? Can you see the benefit of involving the client in the decision-making process? While most EDMs suggest consultation and some even suggest consulting with the client, rarely is the client seen as a primary stakeholder from an ethical decision-making standpoint. We view that as a deficiency of many models and ask that you maintain a willingness to engage in relational decision making throughout your career.

THE BRIEF ETHICAL DECISION-MAKING MODEL

Following the relational model, along with other formal EDMs, takes some time. As mentioned, counselors may not always have the time or ability to consult a formal EDM or to consult with a supervisor or colleague prior to making an ethical decision. In those moments, it may be helpful to have a simpler model that can be memorized. We present a Brief Ethical Decision-Making Model (BEM).

ETHICS

BEM follows the acronym ETHICS:

E—*Examine ethical principles.* Ask the following questions: Does it promote the client's choices (autonomy)? Is it helpful (beneficence) or harmful (nonmaleficence)? Are you being faithful (fidelity) and fair (justice)?

T—*Trust* your clinical judgment and experiences. If the situation isn't safe for the client, for others, or for yourself, take necessary precautions.

H—*Have a conversation* with the client about your ethical responsibilities. Discuss this directly with the client when feasible. Speak about the dilemma you are facing.

I—*Instigate a safety plan* for the client and for yourself. Can a final decision about the ethical dilemma be made later? What is the immediate ethical issue that needs to be resolved right away?

C—*Code of ethics.* Can you review it in the here and now with the client?

S—*Self-reflect.* What would your ethical role models say about the action or step that you are about to take?

CASE STUDY 4.2

Quentin has been seeing his client, Jennifer, for about two months when he runs into her in a social setting. They are both members of the local United Way, which often holds community gatherings that members attend. While at this recent event, Quentin took pains to avoid Jennifer. However, Jennifer approaches him during the cocktail hour to say hello. While they are chatting, Jennifer's husband approaches. He innocently asks how they know each other. Quentin knows that her counseling is a secret from her husband. Quickly, Quentin runs through the steps of the BEM he learned in graduate school.

1. *How is the client's autonomy impacted?*

2. *Are there any safety needs to address?*

3. *What is the best choice of action for the here and now?*

4. *What could Quentin have done prior to this encounter to prepare himself and his client?*

Applying the BEM

To better understand ethical decision making, it helps to apply the model to a case example. Let's apply the BEM to the scenario presented at the beginning of this chapter.

E—*Examine ethical principles.* Ask: Which ethical principles apply to this morning coffee dilemma? Does your client have the freedom to buy coffee for you? Is the client expressing her appreciation for your value and work in counseling with this gesture? What would be helpful in this situation? Would accepting the cup of coffee help the therapeutic relationship? Could it, for example, help the client's self-esteem knowing she did a nice gesture for you? Or is accepting the cup of coffee potentially harmful to the therapeutic relationship? What if you accepted the coffee and then the client, to gain your approval, begins bringing you a cup of coffee for each weekly session? If you refuse to accept the cup of coffee, could it be harmful to the client because she would feel rejected? Are you staying true to your professional boundaries? Are you being true to yourself? Are you being true to your code of ethics? Finally, are you being fair? If you accept the cup of coffee, would you have to accept similar gestures from all clients? If you don't accept the cup of coffee, are you treating the client justly? What if the client did not have many financial resources, so buying the cup of coffee was a significant financial gesture? Should you throw the cup of coffee in the garbage in front of the client? Should you let it sit on your desk getting cold and allow the client to wonder why you are not drinking it?

T—*Trust* your clinical judgment and experiences. In this situation, there does not seem to be any apparent risk factors for either you or the client. In this step, examine your inner compass: What is your inner wisdom advising you to do? How have you handled other similar situations?

H—*Have a conversation* with the client about the ethics of accepting or declining the morning coffee. How does this one moment impact the counseling relationship? Is it a one-time gift? Does one cup of coffee even constitute a gift according to the code of ethics? What is the client's intention of giving the cup of coffee—a small thank-you? Is it a way to manipulate you in some way? Is it a potential boundary slippery slope waiting to happen? What does the client say about the dilemma?

I—*Instigate a safety plan* for the client and for yourself. There does not appear to be a safety issue in this particular dilemma. While it may appear to be viewed as a lower-level ethical dilemma, whether or not you accept the cup of coffee from the client could impact the therapeutic relationship and either help or hinder trust in the counseling process between you and the client.

C—*Code of ethics.* In this situation, it may be helpful to consult the code of ethics, particularly the standard about accepting gifts from clients. Does a cup of coffee constitute as a gift? The client may benefit from reviewing the ethical standard together with you and discussing its impact on your professional relationship.

S—*Self-reflect.* What would your supervisor, mentor, or parent say if they could observe how you handled the coffee dilemma in the session with the client?

Would they be proud of your actions and how you discussed it with your client? Would they have concerns over how you handled the situation? What have you learned from resolving other ethical issues that could help you reflect on this current situation with the morning coffee?

Having a thorough understanding of theory and practice-based EDMs from Chapter 2, an emphasis on relational ethical decision making as presented in this chapter, and finally, a brief model with a simple mnemonic (ETHICS) to follow should put you in a good place to begin to address ethical cases and make ethical decisions.

Guided Practice Exercise 4.4

Developing Your Own Approach

What is your plan for integrating a formal EDM into your counseling practice? What ethical situations do you think would benefit more from using the BEM?

CONCLUSION

In traditional ethical decision-making processes, counselors typically remove the client from the ethical equation, often turning directly to supervisors or colleagues in the field to garner insight into how to work through the dilemma. Involving clients in the ethical decision-making process may appear an unusual step; however, as demonstrated in the case example, when we take a thoughtful and proactive approach to reaching ethical decision making that is mutually determined between us and our clients, there is the potential for many positive outcomes to be achieved. This chapter addressed such benefits of using a Relational Ethical Decision-Making Model.

KEYSTONES

- Most existing EDMs share common elements and tend to focus on the counselor–supervisor relationship. The client rarely is involved directly with the counselor in reaching an appropriate ethical resolution.
- Relational ethics offers a nuanced perspective that actively involves clients, students, families, and other stakeholders when appropriate.
- The core ethical values of relational connection, autonomy, beneficence, and nonmaleficence are categorized as those building and maintaining personal attachments.

- The core ethical values of competence, humility, professional growth, openness to complexity and ambiguity, and self-awareness are categorized as those that involve building and maintaining expertise.
- The Relational Ethical Decision-Making Model is designed to create an intentional, collaborative way for counselors and clients to work together to successfully resolve an ethical dilemma.
- The Relational Ethical Decision-Making Model is made up of 12 steps.
- The Relational Ethical Decision-Making Model places great emphasis on counselors and clients working together to discuss the ethical dilemma, core ethical principles, and potential resolutions and their outcomes.
- The BEM can be utilized when a counselor does not have time or the ability to consult a supervisor or review a formal EDM. This model involves examining ethical principles, trusting your clinical judgment and experiences, having a conversation with the client about your ethical responsibilities, instigating a safety plan, reviewing your code of ethics, and self-reflecting.

SUGGESTED BEST PRACTICES

- Keep a focus on the involvement of the client in the ethical decision-making process.
- Consider that ethical decisions are not linear. Instead, they are a reflexive process with many twists and turns.
- Pay attention to how you build and maintain relationships in your personal and professional life. Likely there are parallels and strengths to draw from.
- As a relational being, use your talents to meet your clients where they are.
- Consider how you build and maintain expertise outside of formal course work. How will you continue to grow as an ethical counselor?
- Get comfortable with ambiguity. Human lives and ethical dilemmas are inherently ambiguous.
- Push yourself to become more and more self-aware.
- Consider seeking your own counseling to become more aware. It is important to do your own work if you are going to work as a counselor.
- Talk with clients about how you make ethical decisions before there is an ethical dilemma.
- Treat ethics as an integrated part of your practice, not simply something to be brought out when there is a problem.
- Rather than having stock answers to how you will handle challenges, be willing to weigh each dilemma based on the context.
- When an ethical dilemma does arise, talk with clients throughout the process. Invite them into the decision making.
- Use the front-page test to evaluate your actions—would you be comfortable if the outcome of your ethical decision was on the front page of the newspaper?

ADDITIONAL RESOURCES

In Print

Austin, W. (2008). Relational ethics. In L. Given (Ed.), *The SAGE encyclopedia of qualitative research methods* (pp. 749–750). Thousand Oaks, CA: Sage doi:http://dx.doi.org/10.4135/9781412963909.n378

Henderson, K. L., & Malone, S. L. (2012). Ethical fairy tales: Using fairy tales as illustrative ethical dilemmas with counseling students. *Journal of Creativity in Mental Health, 7*(1), 64–82. doi:10.1080/15401383.2012.660128

Keskin, M. O. (2013). "What should I do?" Making ethical decisions in certain hypothctical cases. *International Journal of Academic Research, 5*(6), 87–98. doi:10.7813/2075–4124.2013/5–6/B.16

Pergert, P., & Lützén, K. (2012). Balancing truth-telling in the preservation of hope: A relational ethics approach. *Nursing Ethics, 19*(1), 21–29. doi:10.1177/0969733011418551

On the Web

Baker, B. (2009). *Deal with clients you don't like.* Retrieved from http://www.apa.org/monitor/2009/02/clients.aspx

Gabriel, L. (2008*). Relational ethics, boundary riders and process sentinels: Allies for ethical practice.* Retrieved from http://www.counseling.org/docs/default-source/vistas/vistas_2008_gabriel.pdf?sfvrsn=9

REFERENCES

American Counseling Association (ACA). (2014). *ACA code of ethics.* Alexandria, VA: Author.

Corey, G., Corey, M. & Callahan, P. (2011). *Issues and ethics in the helping professions* (8th ed.). Belmont, CA: Brooks/Cole.

Cottone, R. R. & Tarvydas, V. M. (2007). *Counseling ethics and decision making* (3rd ed.). Upper Saddle River, NJ: Pearson.

Davis, A. (1997). The ethics of caring: A collaborative approach to resolving ethical dilemmas. *Journal of Applied Rehabilitation Counseling, 28*(1), 36–41.

Horner, R., & Kelly, T. B. (2007). Ethical decision making in the helping profession: A contextual and caring approach. *Journal of Religion & Spirituality in Social Work, 26*(1), 71–88.

Jennings, L., Sovereign, A., Bottorff, N., Mussell, M., Pederson, M. & Vye, C. (2005). Nine ethical values of master therapists. *Journal of Mental Health Counseling, 27*(1), 32–47.

Sperry, L. (2007). *The ethical and professional practice of counseling and psychotherapy.* Boston: Pearson.

Welfel, E. R. (2013). *Ethics in counseling and psychotherapy: Standards, research and emerging issues* (5th ed.). Belmont, CA: Brooks/Cole.

Chapter 5

ETHICS AND THE COUNSELING RELATIONSHIP

Erica has been working for the same state mental health agency for more than 10 years. Her caseload of 60 to 75 clients rotates frequently, and she typically sees five or more clients daily in addition to running groups, managing a day treatment program, and attending staff meetings. Erica's mother, who has early stages of dementia, has been living with Erica and her family for the past 18 months. Recently, Erica's daughter, who is a high school junior, found out she was pregnant. In addition, Erica and her husband have been fighting frequently and are talking about divorce. Daily, Erica wonders, "How can I keep going?" She feels like work is the only place where she has some peace. She is tired, and her clients can see that. Her colleagues are worried about her. What should she do? Is she competent to continue to work with clients? What does it mean to be an impaired professional?

CHAPTER OVERVIEW

This chapter reviews the connection between ethics and the overall counseling relationship. At its core, the ACA Code of Ethics (2014) was written to provide a foundation for a quality relationship between the client and a counselor. Multiple areas are addressed within the code that serve as building blocks for this foundation. For example, ethical counselors are expected to practice using scientifically proven methods. This ensures that counselors understand why the techniques they choose are the best fit for the clients they serve. In addition, ethical counselors are expected to be competent. However, there are no true litmus tests for competency. Similarly, ethical counselors are not impaired counselors. Yet impairment is often a slippery slope that may not be noticed until it is too late. Finally, ethical counselors are expected to be a part of the larger profession and to collaborate and consult with colleagues. In this chapter, we will discuss ethical codes and choices that impact your role as a professional counselor. Key ACA ethical codes and the related CACREP (2009) standards are also denoted for your use.

LEARNING OBJECTIVES

After reading this chapter you will be able to do the following:

1. Examine the advantages and disadvantages of using scientifically based interventions and the ethics surrounding these decisions.

2. Identify ways to stay up-to-date on professional counseling research.

3. Describe the difference between empirically supported techniques and unproven or developing techniques.

4. Identify means of selecting effective interventions.

5. Explain how to measure counselor competency, and describe the requirements of competency in various specialty areas.

6. Apply an ethical decision-making approach to determine if a counselor is impaired, and identify when to address impairment.

CACREP STANDARDS

CACREP Core Standards

G.1.d. Self-care strategies appropriate to the counselor role.

G.5.d. Counseling theories that provide the student with models to conceptualize client presentation and that help the student select appropriate counseling interventions. Students will be exposed to models of counseling that are consistent with current professional research and practice in the field, so they begin to develop a personal model of counseling.

G.8.e. The use of research to inform evidence-based practice.

CACREP Clinical Mental Health Standards

I.1. Understands how to evaluate critically research relevant to the practice of clinical mental health counseling.

INTRODUCTION

When we begin our journey to become professional counselors, we typically envision all of the great work we will do with our clients. Rarely do we think about the steps we must take to continue to do great work with clients. However, as practicing counselors, the authors of this text are acutely aware of how important it is to stay on our ethical toes, so to speak.

Counselors must stay current on the treatment strategies and techniques best suited for our clients. There are numerous methods used to do so, and we will discuss some of these options in this chapter. Staying current with treatment strategies is not the only way counselors maintain competence. This chapter also will discuss ways to become competent in different areas. Finally, counselors must avoid impairment, and we will look at ways to determine and prevent impairment, including the use of consultation with colleagues. All of the practices in this chapter are part of the fundamental building blocks to an ethical foundation of the counseling relationship.

SCIENTIFIC BASES FOR TREATMENT

It is likely that you are dreaming of the day that you finish your degree program and become a professional counselor. You can envision your office, your clients, and your typical workday. In this vision, you enjoy your work and are a successful counselor. This success may be partially the demand for your services as a counselor but also hopefully will be because you are effective at helping your clients. We certainly hope this dream comes true for each of you!

But we have questions. . . . How exactly do you help your clients? How do you know that what you are doing with clients will be effective? What will you use to guide your interventions? The answers to these questions lie in counseling research.

Counseling Research

You may have read the words *counseling research* and thought "Nooooooo!" Some students and new professionals run away from the word *research.* In this case, we ask that you consider that as helping professionals, we have an ethical responsibility to read and review research related to the work we do with clients. It is not required that we become researchers, although many of us do, but that we become informed consumers of relevant research.

Ethical Code 5.1

C.7.a. Scientific Basis for Treatment.

When providing services, counselors use techniques/procedures/modalities that are grounded in theory and/or have an empirical or scientific foundation.

Source: 2014 American Counseling Association Code of Ethics. Reprinted with permission from American Counseling Association.

The ACA Code of Ethics reminds counselors to use interventions that are empirically sound (Standard C.7.a.). Empirically sound interventions are those that have been tested, or proven, usually in an experimental fashion. Imagine going to a physician when you have a cold. The physician may offer a remedy of cough syrup, fluids, and rest because that is what researchers have found to be effective. That would probably be a treatment plan you could understand and would follow. Conversely, the physician may suggest running a marathon in cold weather and running the cold right out of your system. Some of you may follow that suggestion, but most of us would not! We would want to know how it works. That is what our clients deserve as well. The ACA Code of Ethics addresses this fundamental right of clients in Standards C.7.b. and C.7.c., which allow clients to know about techniques that are under development and protect clients from harm.

Ethical Code 5.2

C.7.b. Development and Innovation.

When counselors use developing or innovative techniques/procedures/ modalities, they explain the potential risks, benefits, and ethical considerations of using such techniques/procedures/modalities. Counselors work to minimize any potential risks or harm when using these techniques/procedures/modalities.

C.7.c. Harmful Practices.

Counselors do not use techniques/procedures/modalities when substantial evidence suggests harm, even if such services are requested.

Source: 2014 American Counseling Association Code of Ethics. Reprinted with permission from American Counseling Association.

Key to these ethical codes is the fact that the code does not tell counselors what techniques to use; it simply directs us to ensure there is relevant research to support the interventions we choose and a communication of that information to clients.

HOW TO REVIEW PROFESSIONAL RESEARCH RELATED TO COUNSELING

The profession of counseling has developed a large body of literature to help support and direct the work that we do with clients. Due to the ease of researching cognitive behavioral therapy (CBT), this particular approach has some of the most research related to empirically proven interventions (Kaplan, 2006). But CBT is not the only theory with an empirical basis. There are a number of ways counselors can learn about empirically supported theories and interventions.

The first place professional counselors learn about such interventions is in counselor education preparation programs. Typically, theories courses provide an introductory understanding of the literature, and research courses teach students how to evaluate critically the information that they will encounter as counselors. But what do you do after your training program? Researchers have found numerous strategies to help maintain awareness of current best practices, including attending continuing education workshops (Martino, 2010). Professional counselors engage in ongoing continuing education that allows us to encounter the most current practices in the profession. It is critical to look for the research in any presentation we attend to determine if the technique being presented is supported empirically or is simply the presenter's opinion.

Another way that professional counselors stay up-to-date with research is to belong to professional organizations that publish research journals. We learn in our counselor preparation programs to look toward peer-reviewed, scholarly literature, such as that published by ACA divisions, to inform our practice. The articles published in journals such as the *Journal of Counseling & Development* go through a rigorous review process before being accepted for publication and dissemination to professional counselors. When reading articles about interventions in these journals, professional counselors can trust that they are supported. It then becomes the counselor's responsibility to determine if the proven technique fits the clients they are treating.

UNPROVEN OR DEVELOPING TECHNIQUES

Not all techniques used in counseling have empirical support. The ACA Code of Ethics allows counselors to move beyond empirically tested techniques if they are honest with clients about their use. Remember our example of going to the physician with a cold and receiving the cold-weather marathon treatment plan? In this case, the physician shares that there is no research study to support this plan, but experience with recent patients has found it to be effective. In other words, the treatment strategy is unproven or developing. This allows the patients to decide if the marathon approach is a good choice for them. Assuming they understand the risks, they may agree to give it a try. Or they may ask for a more scientifically proven treatment choice such as the cough syrup, fluids, and bed rest. Provided this an informed choice, the physician has acted ethically. The same is true with counseling.

Oftentimes counselors will attend a continuing education workshop and learn new and developing interventions. These interventions may seem like a good fit for certain clients with whom they are working. To offer clients these options, the ACA Code of Ethics requires that counselors share the risks and ethical considerations. In addition, counselors must discuss with clients ways that they are protecting the clients from harm. With this form of informed consent, the counselor and client may agree to a particular intervention. The counseling profession values an integrative and technically eclectic approach but asks that these decisions be made with the client's welfare in mind (Kaplan, 2006).

Selecting Effective Interventions

When the ACA Code of Ethics was revised in 2005, a new ethical mandate related to scientific bases for interventions was added and retained in the 2014 revision.

Ethical Code 5.3

C.7.a. Scientific Basis for Treatment.

When providing services, counselors use techniques/procedures/modalities that are grounded in theory and/or have an empirical or scientific foundation.

Source: 2014 American Counseling Association Code of Ethics. Reprinted with permission from American Counseling Association.

Many medical and helping professions have addressed the need for empirically based intervention, but this was the first time that the counseling profession had an ethical code that spoke specifically to this aspect of counseling. What criteria does an intervention have to meet to qualify under this code?

Counseling and related literature refers to scientific bases for interventions, empirically based interventions, and evidence-based practices. These three terms are virtually interchangeable. A good definition for these practices is "treatments that have been shown through clinical research to produce positive outcomes" (National Alliance on Mental Illness, 2007, p. 4). Ideally, these results are shown in two or more studies performed by different research groups. In other words, these are interventions that work. For empirically based interventions, there is substantiated research to support their effectiveness. Counselors can choose an empirically based intervention and have reason to believe that the work they do with clients will be beneficial. Likewise, clients can feel confident when counselors use empirically based interventions.

An empirically based intervention should show improvement in presenting symptoms. For example, clients would expect to see symptom reduction such as fewer panic attacks or outbursts of anger. In addition, using an empirically based intervention should result in improved functioning. This may include improved mood, more compliant behavior, or better grades in school. Finally, empirically based outpatient interventions should result in less need for inpatient treatment (National Alliance on Mental Illness, 2007).

With all of these advantages, why wouldn't we always use scientifically based interventions? According to Chorpita, Becker, and Daleiden (2007), some counselors fear such a manualized approach does not allow for creativity with clients. To combat this, counselors are encouraged to take the practice methods that fit best with their work to avoid feeling locked in to a manualized protocol. Chorpita and colleagues (2007) also cite that counselors may find the researched intervention too complex to incorporate or even is incompatible with the type of work that they do. As such, counselors may be resistant to their use. Finally, because there are not empirically based interventions for all types of clients or disorders, counselors may not be able to use interventions with a scientific basis at all times. Just because an intervention is not empirically based does not mean that it won't be effective. However it is up to the counselor to inform the client that an unproven technique is being used (see ACA Standard C.7.b.).

The counseling profession has determined that it is in the best interests of our clients to strive to use interventions with a scientific basis. We know that our clients are often well informed and educated about the process of counseling. In addition, it is part of our ethical foundation to promote the autonomy of clients by involving them in their treatment planning. The following case example showcases how critical it is to attend to ethical codes related to empirically based interventions.

Case Example

Counselor Joe Schmo, LPC, has a private practice in an urban area. He provides outpatient individual counseling to adults and often receives referrals for aftercare counseling from area inpatient psychiatric facilities. He has built a strong outpatient practice on the basis of these referrals.

Many of the clients he sees are women with anxiety disorders. One day, while seeing a new patient referred after a hospital stay, Joe explains to her that he will be doing some anxiety reduction work. His client finds that reasonable as her severe stress coupled with awareness of childhood trauma caused her to seek intensive help in the first place. She is feeling much calmer now that she has been discharged but wants to be able to handle life stressors more successfully.

> *Joe explains to her that he will be doing a stress test at the beginning and end of each session with guided imagery as part of the session. He tells her that the goal is to reduce her stress during the session so that she leaves feeling better than she did when she arrived. His client readily agrees because clearly he is a professional and will be able to help her.*
>
> *Joe's method of stress test is to do a manual chest wall assessment. He places his hands on her chest and lightly massages the muscle, he says, to determine how tight her muscles are. At the end of the session he repeats this action to make a comparison. During the first session, he tells her that he will gather a baseline for this information and compare her progress to that baseline.*
>
> *While his client is impressed that he is using a measure of assessment, she is uncomfortable with the touching and does not return. Later, she discovers that other clients filed complaints against Joe for this behavior. When summoned to a hearing with the LPC board, Joe was asked the following:*
>
> *Is this a scientifically proven method of stress assessment?*
>
> *If not, does he inform his clients that this is an unproven method?*
>
> *Where was he trained in this assessment?*
>
> *Do all clients receive this same assessment?*
>
> *The board learned that not only was this an unproven method, but Joe never discussed the risks and benefits with his client. He could cite no formal training of this technique. Finally, it was discovered that this was a method offered to female clients only. Subsequently, Joe was sanctioned by the state LPC board and lost his license.*

While such a case may be surprising to a beginning counselor, these things do happen in our profession. All counselors receive some training in ethics as part of their graduate program, and all licenses require ongoing continuing education in training. So why do cases like Joe's happen? Largely, counselors who violate the codes of ethics are not using an EDM. Imagine how many of these violations could be prevented if a counselor simply took the time to consult the codes, consult with colleagues, and use an EDM.

COUNSELOR COMPETENCE

The previous section addressed the effectiveness of an intervention. Another area addressed in the ACA Code of Ethics has to do with the effectiveness of a counselor, or counselor competence. The introduction to Section C of the code reminds us that counselors must "practice in a nondiscriminatory manner within the boundaries of professional and personal competence" (ACA, 2014, p. 8). But what does that really mean? Competence refers to an attribute held by the counselor, not the treatment method, and is "the extent to which a therapist has the knowledge and skill required to deliver a treatment to the standard needed for it to achieve its expected effects" (Fairbum & Cooper, 2011, para. 6).

The ACA Code of Ethics states that competence is based on a number of factors, including education, experience, and certification.

Ethical Code 5.4

C.2.c. Qualified for Employment.

Counselors accept employment only for positions for which they are qualified given their education, training, supervised experience, state and national professional credentials, and appropriate professional experience. Counselors hire for professional counseling positions only individuals who are qualified and competent for those positions.

Source: 2014 American Counseling Association Code of Ethics. Reprinted with permission from American Counseling Association.

Each of these factors provides a brick in the foundation of competence, but taken singly, each one is insufficient. As you can imagine, education contributes to our clinical experiences, which allows us the opportunity to be licensed or certified. However, no one counselor is completely competent in all areas.

Measuring Competency

Competency often is used synonymously with capability. If a counselor possesses the competency to work with a particular population of presenting problem, then that counselor is presumed capable. But how do we measure competency? A search of the Mental Measurements Yearbook and Tests in Print, a database of assessment instruments used in counseling, education, and business, finds there are no tests that measure counselor competence. The measurement of competency in graduate counseling programs is built largely on clinical skill aptitude (Erikson & McAuliffe, 2003). However, new literature is supporting the evaluation of student competency on the basis of skills, behaviors, and professional dispositions (Swank, Lambie, & Witta, 2012). Unfortunately, these measures are for students only. Once a student is granted a degree and joins the ranks of professional counselors, there is no way to measure competency.

As a professional, competency typically is demonstrated via experience and credentialing or licensure. Experiences in specific clinical populations allow us to share with clients our history of success in treating clients in similar situations. Certifications and licensure say to the public that we have met some minimum standards as established by the state or accrediting body. Many of us are licensed by the state, which demonstrates meeting expected levels of general competency. Further, many counselors choose to develop competency in specialty areas.

CASE STUDY 5.1

Grace recently started seeing clients in her college counseling clinic. She is assigned Surinder, a young woman from India who is worried about an upcoming visit by her parents. Surinder comes in for her first appointment and tells Grace that she lives off campus with her boyfriend of two years but has not told her parents. During the visit, her boyfriend will stay with some of his friends, so they can keep the true nature of their relationship secret. Surinder tells Grace that she and her boyfriend, who is also Indian, plan to marry after graduate school. Her parents approve of her dating this young man but would not approve of them living together. Grace has never worked with an Indian client before and wonders if she is culturally competent to do so.

1. *How would Grace know if she was competent to see Surinder?*

2. *What does Grace need to know to provide ethical counseling services to Surinder?*

3. *What steps could Grace take if she chooses to work with Surinder?*

Competency in Specialty Areas

Consider your graduate program. What type of counselor is it training you to be? It is likely that you are getting a degree in a generalist profession such as school, career, or clinical mental health counseling. If you become licensed, does that generalist degree mean you cannot see families or couples unless you are in a marriage, couple, and family counseling program? Of course not. Your program is probably preparing you well for basic relational work. However, you may wish to become proficient in forensic analysis or trauma counseling. To do so, you would want to obtain additional training and certification.

Take for instance the school counselor who learns a lot about working with children of all ages. She takes the required course work and exam and engages in the necessary number of supervised clinical hours to be licensed in her state. Perhaps what she really wants to do is have a part-time private practice working with children who have trauma histories. More specifically, she wants to engage these children in play therapy. She had one course in play therapy in her graduate program and wants to pursue greater competency. Rather than conducting play therapy with children on the basis of one graduate-level course, she takes additional training and engages in additional supervised hours to become a registered play therapist. With this credential as evidence of her additional training and clinical work, she can be reasonably secure in her competence as a play therapist.

We also often hear the term *cultural competence*. According to the National Center for Cultural Competence (2014), there is no single definition of cultural competence. The definition has evolved over the last 25 years, with culture implying a cohesive set of thoughts, attitudes, and behaviors and competence suggesting the ability to be effective in treatment. A beginning counselor reasonably may be expected to understand the culture in which he was raised, but what does it take to become multiculturally competent?

The Association for Multicultural Counseling and Development (AMCD) is the ACA division most closely tied to multicultural competence. AMCD "seeks to develop programs specifically to improve ethnic and racial empathy and understanding. Its activities are designed to advance and sustain personal growth and improve educational opportunities for members from diverse cultural backgrounds" (AMCD, 2014, para. 1). AMCD defines multicultural competence as being comprised of knowledge, skills, and awareness in three areas: the counselor's understanding of his or her own values and biases, counselor's understanding of the client's worldview, and culturally appropriate intervention strategies. While there are numerous opportunities to enhance our cultural competence through continuing education, clinical experiences, and personal growth activities, there is no end to cultural competence. In other words, maintaining cultural competence is a lifelong responsibility of ethical counselors.

In addition to cultural competence, we have the opportunity to become competent in specific areas of professional activity. Similar to the example of the school counselor receiving endorsement as a play therapist, counselors can gain competence in specialty areas. Many counselors receive some training in substance abuse counseling, for example. However, to be truly competent as a substance abuse counselor, more training and experience is needed. The code addresses this specifically related to new specialty areas of practice.

Ethical Code 5.5

C.2.b. New Specialty Areas of Practice.

Counselors practice in specialty areas new to them only after appropriate education, training, and supervised experience. While developing skills in new specialty areas, counselors take steps to ensure the competence of their work and to protect others from possible harm.

Source: 2014 American Counseling Association Code of Ethics. Reprinted with permission from American Counseling Association.

To practice as an ethical counselor, the code reminds counselors to take positions only for which they are qualified.

Ethical Code 5.6

C.2.c. Qualified for Employment.

Counselors accept employment only for positions for which they are qualified given their education, training, supervised experience, state and national professional credentials, and appropriate professional experience. Counselors hire for professional counseling positions only individuals who are qualified and competent for those positions.

Source: 2014 American Counseling Association Code of Ethics. Reprinted with permission from American Counseling Association.

Although a new position, title, and salary may be tempting, counselors need to make sure they are qualified to serve the clients they are hired to serve. In addition, competent counselors are asked to engage in ongoing continuing education and to monitor their effectiveness when working with clients.

Ethical Code 5.7

C.2.f. Continuing Education.

Counselors recognize the need for continuing education to acquire and maintain a reasonable level of awareness of current scientific and professional information in their fields of activity. Counselors maintain their competence in the skills they use, are open to new procedures, and remain informed regarding best practices for working with diverse populations.

Source: 2014 American Counseling Association Code of Ethics. Reprinted with permission from American Counseling Association.

Ethical Code 5.8

C.2.d. Monitor Effectiveness.

Counselors continually monitor their effectiveness as professionals and take steps to improve when necessary. Counselors take reasonable steps to seek peer supervision to evaluate their efficacy as counselors.

Source: 2014 American Counseling Association Code of Ethics. Reprinted with permission from American Counseling Association.

Reading professional journals, attending conferences, and engaging in research are ways to continue to strive for competence.

Guided Practice Exercise 5.1

I'm In Over My Head!

Think about a time that you felt like you were in over your head. What was going on? What skills, knowledge, and experience did you lack that contributed to the feeling? Finally, what did you do about it?

COUNSELOR IMPAIRMENT

One of the biggest challenges to competence is impairment. Counselors can experience impairment on a continuum that includes a range from burnout to impairment. You may hear of compassion fatigue, vicarious trauma, or secondary traumatic stress. These are terms used to describe the effects of hearing the traumas of others but not directly experiencing the trauma ourselves (Simpson & Starkey, 2006). Everyone experiences a bit of burnout, right? If you are a graduate student juggling work, family, and a busy life, you probably feel a bit burned out from time to time yourself. What does it take to reach the level of impairment? The ACA Code of Ethics says that ethical counselors should be alert to signs of impairment and seek help rather than continue to provide services to clients.

Ethical Code 5.9

C.2.g. Impairment.

Counselors monitor themselves for signs of impairment from their own physical, mental, or emotional problems and refrain from offering or providing professional services when impaired. They seek assistance for problems that reach the level of professional impairment, and if necessary, they limit, suspend, or terminate their professional responsibilities until it is determined that they may safely resume their work. Counselors assist colleagues or supervisors in recognizing their own professional impairment and provide consultation and assistance when warranted with colleagues or supervisors showing signs of impairment and intervene as appropriate to prevent imminent harm to clients.

Source: 2014 American Counseling Association Code of Ethics. Reprinted with permission from American Counseling Association.

However, it has been the experience of the authors that counselors who are becoming impaired often don't have the insight to evaluate their level of impairment objectively. As counselors, and humans, we tend to see impairment in others before we see it in ourselves.

The ACA Task Force on Counselor Wellness and Impairment

In 2003, ACA created the Task Force on Impaired Counselors, which later became the ACA Task Force on Counselor Wellness and Impairment. This task force was charged with developing ways to identify, intervene with, and assist impaired counselors. Specifically, ACA developed the task force to educate counselors in hopes of preventing impairment and, if not prevent, provide opportunities for intervention and treatment (ACA, n.d.).

The task force established the working definitions of counselor impairment for our field, including the following:

> Therapeutic impairment occurs when there is a significant negative impact on a counselor's professional functioning which compromises client care or poses the potential for harm to the client. Impairment may be due to substance abuse or chemical dependency; mental illness; personal crisis (traumatic events or vicarious trauma, burnout, life crisis); and physical illness or debilitation. (Lawson & Venart, 2005, p. 243)

These definitions laid the foundation for ethical codes related to impairment.

In addition, the task force went a step further in defining impairment from an ethical perspective, saying, "Impairment in and of itself does not imply unethical behavior. Such behavior may occur as a symptom of impairment, or may occur in counselors who are not impaired" (Lawson & Venart, 2005, p. 243). In other words, it is not possible to set a single standard for impairment in counselors. An ethical decision-making approach must be used to determine if a counselor is indeed impaired.

Guided Practice Exercise 5.2

Personal Wellness

The ACA Task Force on Impaired Counselors later became the ACA Task Force on Counselor Wellness and Impairment. Why do you think the name change occurred? What does the focus on wellness mean to you? Ask around; how do people you look up to manage wellness? What personal approaches to wellness do you employ now? What wellness activities do you think you need to consider for your professional career?

Recognizing Personal Impairment

What causes impairment in counselors? As helping professionals, we have a tendency to take on the burdens of others. When working with clients, counselors must set aside their own problems to focus on others. Consider the brief vignette at the start of the chapter. Erica cannot be fully present for her clients if she is thinking about her mother, daughter, and husband. Of course, we are not fully able to compartmentalize and ignore what is happening in our own lives. Likewise, our client stories may remind us of our own stories.

The majority of the literature focuses on recognizing impairment in others. Because of this, it is critical to rely on consultation, supervision, and peer review to check for personal impairment. When counselors find themselves heavily burdened, as in the story of Erica, work performance may suffer. Talking this through with a supervisor, trusted colleague, or personal therapist may be the best way to recognize personal impairment.

CASE STUDY 5.2

Kelly is a licensed counselor in group practice. She has been with this group for several years and has a thriving practice. Kelly is also close to several of the counselors in the practice and knows that two of them are in recovery for alcohol dependence. These two colleagues have many years of sobriety and are regular members of Alcoholics Anonymous (AA).

From time to time, Kelly believes that she also has a problem with alcohol. She has discussed this with her colleagues, and they have introduced her to the AA program of recovery. Kelly attended a few meetings and decided that she, too, is an alcoholic. The AA program requires total abstinence from alcohol, and this is something Kelly struggles with. She can get a few months of sobriety but always relapses. She does not come to work under the influence but binge drinks after work and on the weekends.

Kelly is embarrassed that she wants to stay sober but cannot. She works with many clients who are making changes in their lives and feels like she does a good job helping them through a variety of life issues. There is concern in her office as to whether Kelly should see clients if she continues to struggle with alcohol.

1. *Is Kelly an alcoholic? Is she impaired?*

2. *Should Kelly continue to see clients?*

3. *What would you do if you were one of Kelly's coworkers?*

Intervening When a Colleague Is Impaired

While it may be less subjective to define impairment in others rather than in ourselves, addressing impairment can still be challenging. The ACA Code of Ethics tells us that when we suspect any ethical violation, including impairment in others, our first step is an informal resolution with the counselor in question.

Ethical Code 5.10

I.2.a. Informal Resolution.

When counselors have reason to believe that another counselor is violating or has violated an ethical standard and substantial harm has not occurred, they attempt to first resolve the issue informally with the other counselor if feasible, provided such action does not violate confidentiality rights that may be involved.

Source: 2014 American Counseling Association Code of Ethics. Reprinted with permission from American Counseling Association.

Specific to impairment, our colleagues in psychology have published a model for intervention that includes evaluating the information, determining who should talk to the person in question, taking time to prepare for the meeting, balancing empathy and compassion with clarity and facts, being prepared for discussion, and being sure to follow up (O'Conner, n.d.). When approaching your colleague, recognize that some of the facts may be misconstrued. It is important to be prepared to listen without taking on the role of the counselor. Encouraging your colleague to seek help and protect clients can benefit all parties involved. While confronting a colleague is never easy, protecting the public is a priority of the profession and the counselors involved.

CONCLUSION

As counselors, one of our primary responsibilities is to the counseling relationship. While it is expected that licensed counselors have some generally accepted skills as a helping professional, it is critical to move beyond the mandatory level of ethical practice to a more aspirational level. Counselors must understand the research related to empirically supported treatment strategies and their ethical use. In addition, counselors must attend to levels of competence with an ever-broadening array of specialty areas of counseling. Finally, counselors must be attuned to the potential for impairment and strategies for mitigating impairment. By attending to these elements of ethical practice, we are best suited to protect the helping relationship with the clients we serve.

KEYSTONES

- Though the ACA Code of Ethics does not tell counselors what techniques to use, it reminds us to use interventions that are empirically sound. Empirically sound interventions have been tested or proven, usually in an experimental fashion. Clients should be informed if the intervention is not empirically based.
- It is important to stay current on research and new practices in the field. Professional counselors engage in ongoing continuing education and seek out peer-reviewed, scholarly literature to do so.
- The terms scientific bases for interventions, empirically based interventions, and evidence-based practices are virtually interchangeable. One definition for these practices is "treatments that have been shown through clinical research to produce positive outcomes" (NAMI, 2007, p. 4).
- Competence refers to an attribute held by the counselor, not the treatment method. It is based on factors such as education, experience, and credentialing or licensure.
- One area of competence is cultural competence. AMCD defines multicultural competence as being comprised of knowledge, skills, and awareness in three areas: counselors' understanding of their own values and biases, counselor's understanding of the client's worldview, and culturally appropriate intervention strategies.
- A counselor can choose to become competent in specific areas of professional activity, such as substance abuse counseling.
- One of the biggest challenges to competence is impairment. Therapeutic impairment occurs when there is a significant negative impact on a counselor's professional functioning that compromises client care or poses the potential for harm to the client. Impairment may be due to substance abuse or chemical dependency; mental illness; personal crisis (traumatic events or vicarious trauma, burnout, or life crisis); and physical illness or debilitation.
- When we suspect any ethical violation, including impairment in others, our first step is an informal resolution with the counselor in question.

SUGGESTED BEST PRACTICES

- Constantly ask yourself, "How do I know what I am doing is working?"
- Read about new interventions, attend workshops on new interventions, and assess these ideas based on their empirical support.
- Share your rationale for why you are doing what you are doing with your clients. Let them know the process and anticipated outcome.
- Don't fear research. Research is your friend.
- Never assume you are competent. Never assume you are not. Competence is on a continuum.

(margin handwritten note: ? . for future employer)

- Seek competency in specialty areas through training and certifications. Visit the National Board for Certified Counselors (NBCC) Web site to see the types of credentials they offer.
- Seek to increase your cultural competence in all that you do.
- Choose jobs that may challenge you but not those for which you are neither qualified nor competent.
- Widen your definition of impairment. What we cannot see, we cannot address.
- Don't be a superhero. Take the cape off some days and take care of yourself.
- Involve yourself in ongoing self-care and wellness activities.
- Be cautious if you suspect a colleague is impaired. Because impairment is hard to see in ourselves, your colleague may react defensively to any discussion. Approach the situation with evidence and an action plan. Be supportive.

ADDITIONAL RESOURCES

In Print

Raines, J. C. (2008). *Evidence-based practice in school mental health.* New York: Oxford University Press.

On the Web

Self-Care Assessment Worksheet. (n.d.). http://www.creating-joy.com/taskforce/PDF/ACA_task force_assessment.pdf

Self-Care Strategies Worksheet. (n.d.). http://www.creating-joy.com/taskforce/PDF/ACA_task force_selfcare.pdf

Shallcross, L. (2011). Taking care of yourself as a counselor. *Counseling Today.* Retrieved from http://ct.counseling.org/2011/01/taking-care-of-yourself-as-a-counselor/

Williams, R. (2011). The importance of self-care. *ASCA School Counselor.* Retrieved from https://www.schoolcounselor.org/magazine/blogs/january-february-2011/the-importance-of-self-care

REFERENCES

American Counseling Association (ACA). (2014). *ACA code of ethics.* Alexandria, VA: Author.

American Counseling Association. (n.d.). *ACA's task force on counselor wellness and impairment.* Retrieved from http://www.counseling.org/knowledge-center/counselor-wellness

Association for Multicultural Counseling and Development (AMCD). (2014). *About AMCD.* Retrieved from http://www.multiculturalcounseling.org/index.php?option=com_content &view= article&id=62&Itemid=82

Chorpita, B. F., Becker, K. D., & Daleiden, E. L. (2007). Understanding the common elements of evidence-based practice: Misconceptions and clinical examples. *American Academy of Child and Adolescent Psychiatry, 46*(5), 647–652.

Council for Accreditation of Counseling & Related Educational Programs (CACREP). (2009). *CACREP 2009 standards.* Retrieved from http://www.cacrep.org/doc/2009%20Standards%20 with%20cover.pdf

Erikson, K., & McAuliffe, G. (2003). A measure of counselor competency. *Counselor Education and Supervision, 43*(2), 120–133.

Fairbum, C. G., & Cooper, Z. (2011). Therapist competence, therapy quality, and therapist training. *Behaviour Research and Therapy, 49*(6–7), 373–378. Retrieved from http://www.ncbi .nlm.nih.gov/pmc/articles/PMC3112491/

Kaplan, D. (2006). New mandates for selecting interventions. *Counseling Today.* Retrieved from http://ct.counseling.org/2006/06/ct-online-ethics-update-8/

Lawson, G., & Venart, B. (2005). Preventing counselor impairment: Vulnerability, wellness, and resilience. In G. R. Waltz & R. K. Yep (Eds.), *VISTAS: Compelling perspectives on counseling, 2005* (pp. 243–246). Alexandria, VA: American Counseling Association.

Martino, S. (2010). Strategies for training counselors in evidence-based treatments. *Addiction Science and Clinical Practice, 5*(2), 30–39.

National Alliance on Mental Illness (NAMI). (2007).*Choosing the right treatment: What families need to know about evidence-based practices.* Author: Arlington, VA.

National Center for Cultural Competence. (2014). *Definitions of cultural competence.* Retrieved from http://www.ncccurricula.info/culturalcompetence.html

O'Connor, M. F. (n.d.). Intervening with an impaired colleague. Retrieved from http://www .apapracticecentral.org/ce/self-care/intervening.aspx

Simpson, L. R., & Starkey, D. S. (2006). Secondary traumatic stress, compassion fatigue, and counselor spirituality: Implications for counselors working with trauma. *VISTAS 2006 Online Library.* Retrieved from http://www.counseling.org/resources/library/vistas/vistas06_online-only/Simpson.pdf

Swank, J. M., Lambie, G. W., & Witta, E. (2012). An exploratory investigation of the Counseling Competencies Scale: A measure of counseling skills, dispositions, and behaviors. *Counselor Education & Supervision, 51*(3), 189–206. doi:10.1002/j.1556–6978.2012.00014.x

Chapter 6

INFORMED CONSENT

Jeanine, a graduate student, sat across from her faculty supervisor and stared down at her lap. "I didn't remember—I forgot. I forgot to mention that if he told me about harming another—the beating of his child—that I would have to report it by law. I forgot to tell him also that much of what he said to me in confidence would be shared with you, my faculty supervisor. I forgot to provide informed consent. I forgot. I'm new at this. I know I am supposed to cover all of this in my introductory session, but I just blanked—now what!"

CHAPTER OVERVIEW

This chapter reviews the multiple ethical codes and related practices of informed consent in professional counseling. Informed consent is so critical to the practice of counseling that it makes up one of the largest sections of the American Counseling Association (ACA, 2014) Code of Ethics. The code delineates various aspects of informed consent that impact our practice. As a developing counselor, you must be aware of the different components that the informed consent process can include. Informed consent is highly dependent on the setting in which you will practice and must include the integration of related cultural aspects. As counselors, we take an overarching approach to informed consent as an ongoing and living process. In this chapter, we will review practice applications and components to assist you in creating consent forms. The role of client collaboration and consultation with professional colleagues, a listing of related ACA ethical codes, and the related Council for Accreditation of Counseling & Related Educational Programs (CACREP, 2009) standards are also denoted for your use.

LEARNING OBJECTIVES

After reading this chapter you will be able to do the following:

1. Articulate the purpose of informed consent in the client–counselor relationship.

2. Define best practices for providing informed consent to clients.

3. Explain the necessary content of informed consent documents.

4. Develop an informed consent document.

5. Apply an informed consent process in various counseling settings.

6. Differentiate the informed consent process when implemented in association with specific practices such as formal assessment, supervision, research, clients lacking the capacity to provide consent, mandated or court-ordered referrals, culture, and technology.

CACREP STANDARDS

CACREP Core Standards

G.1.b. Professional roles, functions, and relationships with other human service providers, including strategies for interagency or interorganization collaboration and communications.

G.1.j. Ethical standards of professional organizations and credentialing bodies, and applications of ethical and legal considerations in professional counseling.

CACREP Clinical Mental Health Standards

A.2. Understands ethical and legal considerations specifically related to the practice of clinical mental health counseling.

A.7. Is aware of professional issues that affect clinical mental health counselors (e.g., core provider status, expert witness status, and access to and practice privileges within managed care systems).

B.1. Demonstrates the ability to apply and adhere to ethical and legal standards in clinical mental health counseling.

C.8. Understands professional issues relevant to the practice of clinical mental health counseling.

D.7. Applies current record-keeping standards related to clinical mental health counseling.

INTRODUCTION

Informed consent pertains to a client's right to be provided with enough information to make decisions regarding his or her treatment in counseling.

Ethical Code 6.1

A.2.a. Informed Consent.

Clients have the freedom to choose whether to enter into or remain in a counseling relationship and need adequate information about the counseling process and the counselor. Counselors have an obligation to review in writing and verbally with clients the rights and responsibilities of both counselors and clients. Informed consent is an ongoing part of the counseling process, and counselors appropriately document discussions of informed consent throughout the counseling relationship.

Source: 2014 American Counseling Association Code of Ethics. Reprinted with permission from American Counseling Association.

As counselors, we promote client autonomy and have the privilege to be able to empower the client early in our relationship through the use of informed consent. The term *informed* refers to the action by the counselor to provide adequate and pertinent information about the counseling process and procedures to the client, so the client can make a knowledgeable decision regarding the choice to participate in counseling. The action of consent belongs to the client and is provided to the counselor. It relates to the ethical principle of autonomy, one of the four principles of ethical practice asserted by Kitchener (1984). You may recall other concepts from our discussion in Chapter 2, including beneficence, the counselor's responsibility to make decisions based on the good of the client; nonmaleficence, the counselor's responsibility to not do harm; and justice, the counselor's responsibility to ensure counseling decisions and actions are fair to the client. Informed consent is a client right.

As practicing counselors, it is important that we understand that all codes of professional counseling ethics require an informed consent process, and most state practice laws mandate it. The ethical codes of ACA (2014), the National Board for Certified Counselors (NBCC, n.d.), the Center for Credentialing and Education's (CCE, 2008) approved clinical supervisors, and the Association for Counselor Education and Supervision (ACES, 2011) all require their members to use an informed consent process. The American Psychological Association (APA, 2010) and the National Association of Social Workers (NASW, 2008) also require an informed consent procedure to be part of a counseling process. Informed consent is considered a critical component to counseling relationships by professional guilds, and counselors should understand the why and how of implementing it.

PURPOSE OF INFORMED CONSENT

Why do we have informed consent? The why of informed consent pertains to providing enough information about treatment and process for clients to make their own decisions about pursuing services under our care. The concept originated in the medical field at the turn of the 20th century, after a judge's ruling on a court case determined that patients have a right to be provided enough information by the physician to make their own decisions regarding treatment (see *Schloendorf v. Society of New York Hospital,* as cited in Pope & Vasquez, 1991*).* Before informed consent, the physician made all decisions related to patient care without consultation with the patient. Can you imagine not knowing why you were receiving the treatment you needed? At that time, this practice was accepted by the general public, who considered medical treatment (and doctors) to be something they followed rather blindly. The addition of informed consent brought the patient (and now client) into the decision-making process regarding treatment and, in effect, strengthened the healing relationship.

As counselors, we know that trust adds to and builds the healing relationship. It becomes a natural part of the consent process when clients are encouraged to ask questions during and throughout the counseling process (Fisher & Oransky, 2008). Trust is increased when informed consent occurs on a consistent basis (Cook, 2009). This is what we mean when we say that informed consent is a living, changing, dynamic entity. It is not a one-time event. Maintaining this dialogue and ensuring trust in your counseling relationships may serve to protect you from inappropriate accusations or grievances related to lack of information or understanding on the part of the client. Informed consent provides the dual advantage of creating trust and strengthening the therapeutic alliance while providing necessary information to the client that may protect you from ending up in court.

CASE STUDY 6.1

As a full-time faculty member, licensed professional counselor (LPC), and certified clinical hypnotherapist, I sometimes supplement our counseling services by providing relaxation therapy for students who have test anxiety or other issues that may benefit from this type of therapy. A colleague of mine who referred a student to me was so impressed with the improvement in her student's phobia that she referred another colleague to me whose husband was having some issues that she thought might be best served by the therapeutic approach I use.

(Continued)

(Continued)

The mission of our department and counseling services is to serve the entire university community, so I felt that extended to my colleague's spouse. I met with him as a professional courtesy and dispensed with the usual intake interview but verbally explained the limits of confidentiality and obtained his verbal agreement to receive treatment. At the end of the first session, the client expressed surprise at how much insight he gained from the process and asked to continue treatment. After our second hypnotherapeutic session, he again expressed surprise at how much relief and resolve he felt and expressed an interest to continue our work together. At this point I realized that this would be an ongoing counseling relationship and decided to request that he sign informed consent and receive the statement of client rights and responsibilities. I have kept very brief notes on his issues and progress and will continue to work with him.

1. *What ethical dilemmas are found in this scenario?*

2. *What standards of documentation are appropriate for this client's case?*

3. *How would you have managed this situation?*

4. *How does professional courtesy manifest itself in counseling settings? How does that differ from medical settings and why?*

Contributed by Janice Munro, EdD, associate professor and assistant dean, Department of Counseling, Lindenwood University.

Best Practices

We have discussed the why of informed consent; now let's look at the how. The how of informed consent includes implementing best practices and procedures. These practices include being clear in your language of informed consent and paying special attention to multicultural aspects (Recupero & Rainey, 2005). In addition, it is best practice to provide both verbal and written forms of consent (Wheeler & Bertram, 2008). The informed consent process should be ongoing (Goddard, Murray, & Simpson, 2008), which makes this a dynamic procedure for you and your client. Finally, counselors provide best practice when they know their state statutes and ethical codes. Health Providers Service Organization (HPSO), a leading supplier of mental health providers' liability insurance, warns counselors to attend to something known as health literacy, stating that "only 12% of U.S. adults have proficient health literacy" (2012, p. 1). Health literacy is actually informed consent; it involves ensuring that your client understands his or her rights in relation to your counseling work, including what will happen in counseling sessions and if and when counseling typically works or helps a client. In general, your client's health literacy means ensuring that he or she understands counseling and the work with you.

When developing an informed consent, it generally is expected that counselors provide the proposed process and procedures on a written form that requires the client's signature. Written informed consent forms should be explained and signed prior to the first session or in the initial part of a new client session and must occur prior to any recording of the session. While it might seem convenient to have the client sign the document along with other presession documents or with an administrative staff member, it is up to you to review this document thoroughly in a way your client can understand. The written document provides verification that you engaged with the client in an informed consent process and provides the client with something to reference (Mitchell, 2007). It is part of the start of your therapeutic alliance.

When you are verbally explaining the content of the form, it is important to use clear language that is developmentally appropriate for the client and that takes the client's cultural aspects into consideration. As counselors see clients of all ages, cultures, and abilities, how do we do this?

- Directly ask the client if he or she understands the information. Just as we discussed in Chapter 4, involving the client in decision making is important. Ultimately, you will experience clients with cognitive impairment and some who do not use English as their primary language. Take special care to ensure that each client understands your process and procedures.
- Follow your direct question regarding the client's understanding by inviting the client to ask questions regarding the process (Fisher & Oransky, 2008). Again, you are building on the relationship to develop a richer therapeutic alliance. Inviting the client into the decision-making process will help to close any gaps in understanding.
- Another suggestion is to ask clients how they prefer to receive educational information; that is, is the information better understood when read, heard, or viewed on a screen (HPSO, 2012)? In other words, tailor the way you provide the consent to the client to allow for comprehension, a primary goal of informed consent (Cook, 2009), and to document client understanding of information and consent of treatment (Bernstein & Hartsell, 2004).

Informed consent that uses both written and verbal modes of communication helps each client understand the process and their rights.

After you have successfully completed the informed consent process and have retained the client's signature on the written consent form, remind your client that he or she may ask questions now and throughout the counseling process. It is also important to share with the client that you will also ask for consent if and when treatment shifts. This is the time to seek consent and understanding on the client's part.

Guided Practice Exercise 6.1

The Process of Consent

Forming an alliance with the client in the first session is critical. This is also the time when you provide informed consent. Break into groups of three, and practice providing a verbal informed consent procedure from a written form while maintaining plenty of eye contact and attending to forming an alliance with the client. One person is the counselor, one is the client, and one writes observations of the counselor and then provides feedback afterward. Shift roles until all have had the opportunity to be the counselor. Process how it was to attempt to create an alliance while also providing an informed consent, a process than can be perceived as clinical and cold if not done with attention to the relationship.

CASE STUDY 6.2

Christina, age 21, was brought to counseling by her mother (and legal guardian), Marie. Marie described Christina as "very smart, but very different." Christina had not done well in school, was socially awkward, and was academically delayed. She was unable to gain meaningful employment and had worked only occasionally at a vocational rehabilitation program. Marie signed the original informed consent yet made it clear to the counselor that "to do or not do counseling is Christina's choice."

The counselor conducted an evaluation in conjunction with Christina's primary care physician. Christina was diagnosed with autism. She had gone undiagnosed her entire life.

Christina eagerly engaged in the counseling process. After 28 weeks of therapy, Marie contacted the counselor and said Christina would have to discontinue counseling due to the cost. Marie explained that her husband recently was laid off from his job, and they didn't have the money to continue the sessions. The counselor could hear Christina in the background demanding to continue counseling. In an attempt to assist the family, the counselor offered to continue sessions for one month at a rate of $10 per session. Marie thanked the counselor but remained firm in her decision to end the counseling sessions.

The following week Christina made an appointment herself and came with $10 in hand. Christina reminded the counselor, "My mom said it was my choice to do or not do counseling—and I want to do it." The counselor felt trapped. Christina was 21, and her guardian initially had made it very clear that it was Christina's choice to participate in counseling.

1. Could Christina ethically be turned away?

2. Did the counselor have a duty to inform Marie?

3. Who, in this situation, is the client, and to whom is the counselor responsible?

4. Which statement is to be honored: Marie's first statement authorizing Christina to make the choice about counseling or Marie's second statement ending counseling?

5. What are some next steps for the counselor?

Contributed by Daniel Blash, PhD, LPC, NCC, clinical counselor and adjunct faculty at Webster University.

A client providing consent to informed treatment is always a voluntary process (Barnett & Johnson, 2010). Because consent belongs to the client, a counselor cannot force a client to consent to treatment. Even in mandatory or court-ordered treatment, the client's participation is a choice. You may find this statement surprising, but it is only the client's attendance that is mandatory. You have probably seen the movie *Good Will Hunting,* in which Matt Damon's character is required to see Robin Williams's character for therapy. Many of the initial sessions are spent in total silence, while Matt Damon's character meets the minimum standard of attendance only.

Just because the client does not agree to the consent doesn't mean the counselor is off the hook. The voluntary aspect to consent should not be confused with the counselor's requirement to provide informed consent. In other words, our responsibility to provide adequate information to receive consent from the client is required, but the client's consent to treatment is voluntary. Clients are not required to give consent—it is something they independently choose to do once they have enough information to make a decision (Younggren, Foote, Fisher, & Hjelt, 2011). Hence, informed consent involves the process of providing enough information to our client for the client to choose the best treatment independently.

Best practice includes an understanding by the counselor and the client that informed consent is ongoing and renegotiable (Abrahams, 2007). Too often, we get in the habit of mentally checking off the box with informed consent: we practice informed consent as a one-time occurrence, explaining a form of general information and never again verifying client understanding of a technique or checking in with the client on his or her understanding of the progression of treatment. Without ongoing check-in, the informed consent process is not complete.

Counseling is a process wherein diagnoses may change, and practiced techniques and approaches likely also will change depending on what best heals the client. The practice of occasionally checking in with clients will provide supportive evidence if a client files a grievance against you related to lack of information. To comply with ethical practice and the law in most states, counselors utilize the practice of informed consent as a regular check-in with clients to verify that the client understands the process in which the counselor and client are engaging. Hence, an important element to the practice of informed consent is the regularity of it: checking in with your client to confirm that he or she understands the techniques or approaches you are using and then documenting his or her understanding. If the client does not understand the approach, technique, or process, this is the time to collaborate, educate, and seek consent. Documented, regularly informed consent will help to position your practice ethically and, equally important, ensure that the client is collaborating in his or her growth and development in counseling.

One final best practice involves the professional obligation to know your state statutes, professional ethical codes, and agency procedures and policies (HPSO, 2012) related to professional counseling. Note that we are not simply recommending, and we are not saying "be familiar with." To practice ethically and keep your clients (and yourself) safe, know your state's legal statutes around professional counseling, the ACA Code of Ethics, any other specialty ethical codes under which you practice (e.g., American School Counselors Association [ASCA] or ACES), and the rules and protocols of the agency or practice within which you work. Being unfamiliar with ethical codes and counselor practice laws is one way that professional counselors get involved in wrongdoing. Obviously, learning the codes and laws after violating them is inappropriate timing. Take the time now to familiarize yourself with the Web sites that provide this information. A good guideline practice is to learn the ACA Code of Ethics and your state laws well enough to be the preferred choice among your colleagues to provide consultation. Remember that ignorance of ethical codes is not an excuse for unethical practice and will bring you no relief should a client sue over breach of ethics.

In sum, here is the how of informed consent:

1. Tell the client what you are going to do and how you are going to do it.

2. Ensure that the client understands.

3. Seek voluntary agreement to treatment via signature in your presence.

4. Make a copy of the signed form, and provide it to the client.

5. Continually check in when treatment shifts.

These general practices will help develop trust in the therapeutic relationship and involve the client in the treatment process.

Important Content of Consent Documents

Recommended information to be included on a consent form should include the following items provided in Table 6.1—believe it or not, this list is not exhaustive!

Additional information that is important to discuss and seek consent for follows. This content should be provided in written format, explained verbally, and then followed up with an invitation for the client to ask questions.

- Permission to seek information from participating treatment professionals
- Consent for treatment of minors or clients lacking the capacity to provide consent, requiring a guardian's signature
- Health Insurance Portability and Accountability Act (HIPAA) compliance forms
- Support system names and contact information
- Client contact information and history of counseling
- Intake mental health status exam
- Approval to tape (for clinical supervision or if needed)

Now you can see how involved the process is! Informed consent is your client's first impression of you, your practice, and the counseling process. It is important that the documents and process are warm and inviting (Bernstein & Hartsell, 2004). As you know by now, without developing an alliance with your client early on, the client will not trust you enough to raise the painful issues that will enable him or her to heal. Informed consent works well when you collaboratively set an agenda for each session followed by eliciting and responding to feedback. While this section has covered the general process of informed consent, informed consent must be tailored in specific circumstances, settings, and with specific populations. A more thorough discussion of such follows.

Guided Practice Exercise 6.2

The Protocol of Consent

Develop an informed consent form for your practice. Create the form as if you will actually use it; this is, make it appealing, easy to read, culturally sensitive, and comprehensive. Make sure to include content that addresses all populations discussed in this chapter and is appropriate for all cultures. Save it for your counseling practice upon graduation.

Table 6.1   Components of a Written Informed Consent

- Purposes and goals of your treatment approach
- Techniques and procedures you may use
- The relationship between you and the client (roles and nontherapeutic contact)
- Anticipated duration of treatment (this may shift after treatment has started; hence, an item that will need to be renegotiated or reviewed at a later date if it becomes apparent that treatment ends at a different time than initially discussed)
- Length of time that written records will be kept
- Limitations, potential risks, and what could happen if a client refuses services
- Implications of diagnosis, that is, third-party knowledge, including insurance companies and potential legal constituents
- Protocol regarding how the client may submit a complaint about your services
- Client's right to refuse treatment
- Benefits of services and alternative approaches
- The counselor's qualifications, including experience, credentials, and degrees
- The counselor's values and theoretical approach
- Transfer plan or how services will be provided upon your death or incapacitation
- If others will participate in providing services (e.g., supervisors, interns, physicians)
- Who will have access to files (e.g., counselor, assistants, or supervisors)
- Emergency contact information, for example, 911 and your cell phone number (if you will be providing it); also a definition of what constitutes an emergency
- Client's preferred approach to chance meetings outside of session
- Fees and billing arrangements, including how, when, and what to pay; amount due at time of service; if you charge interest on late payments or unpaid balances; if you will bill third parties
- Your policy on cancellation, missed appointments, and being late
- How assessments will occur (administration, interpretation, and feedback) if used
- Mention of the client's right to access records
- Limits of confidentiality, that is, who will be contacted and what will be stated if a client states harm to self or others
- If client is involuntary and counseling is mandated, then the specific terms of the mandated sessions
- If conducting distance counseling (via the Internet), a list of limitations and benefits specific to technology, including confidentiality concerns, third-party payers' perspective of distance counseling, related laws, emergency procedures and referral contacts specific to seeing someone long distance, and reasons for referral or requiring that the client transition to face-to-face counseling (see "Technology," this chapter, p. 130)

INFORMED CONSENT AND SPECIFIC PRACTICES

There are a number of specific practices in which informed consent is needed, and the process will differ among them. In this section, we will guide you through the processes in which assessments are given, supervision of the counselor is required, research is conducted, clients lack the capacity to give consent, counseling is involuntary or mandated, cultural context is necessary, and technology is used.

Assessment

Counselors often use assessment instruments in the process of treating our clients and to support them in their decision making and development. Assessments also are used to support the accurate diagnosis of clients and as tools to help clients address their concerns. Examples include using personality inventories to help couples understand one another's characteristics, using achievement inventories to help educational teams develop suitable course requirements for individual students, and offering interest inventories to assist clients in selecting pertinent occupations and careers. Assessments are helpful tools for counseling but must be used appropriately.

Ethical practice in the use of assessment inventories in counseling requires adequate informed consent regarding all components of the assessment including the administration, delivery, and feedback parts of the process.

Ethical Code 6.2

E.3.a. Explanation to Clients.

Prior to assessment, counselors explain the nature and purposes of assessment and the specific use of results by potential recipients. The explanation will be given in the language the client (or other legally authorized person on behalf of the client) can understand.

Source: 2014 American Counseling Association Code of Ethics. Reprinted with permission from American Counseling Association.

The process includes receiving client consent to initiate the assessment and ensuring that the client understands the assessment and its purpose. As with other approaches to informed consent, we should consider the client's cultural background and how that culture may interpret the use of assessments and use language that the client understands. Ethical processing of assessments means that as the counselor, you verify client understanding of the reason for the assessment, method, how the assessment will be administered, and results of the assessment and the ensuing effects on your client's welfare (Barnett & Johnson, 2010). Counselors do not administer assessments that are not in the best interests of our clients.

Ethical Code 6.3

E.3.b. Recipients of Results.

Counselors consider the client's and/or examinee's welfare, explicit understandings, and prior agreements in determining who receives the assessment results. Counselors include accurate and appropriate interpretations with any release of individual or group assessment results.

Source: 2014 American Counseling Association Code of Ethics. Reprinted with permission from American Counseling Association.

Another form of assessment, forensic assessment, involves counselors providing professional assessment of an individual's psychological well-being to courts or other entities. This involves our professional judgment, often combined with the use of assessment inventories. These types of assessment relationships may be classified under professional consultation, forensic counseling, and mediation. When this form of assessment occurs, it is our ethical responsibility to ensure that the individual being assessed understands that the client–counselor relationship is one of measurement only and that counseling per se (e.g., multiple sessions) will not occur. Ethical practice also calls for counselors to verify that the individual being assessed understands the process and who will receive the results. If you are assessing minors or court-ordered clients, you must be clear in your explanations to the client as well as the guardian (or courts). They need to understand that their consent to the assessment means others will have access to the results, which may or may not support what the client believes to be accurate. It is especially important that this type of informed consent should be provided in writing and requires the client's signature.

Ethical Code 6.4

E.13.b. Consent for Evaluation.

Individuals being evaluated are informed in writing that the relationship is for the purposes of an evaluation and is not therapeutic in nature, and entities or individuals who will receive the evaluation report are identified. Counselors who perform forensic evaluations obtain written consent from those being evaluated or from their legal representative unless a court orders evaluations to be conducted without the written consent of the individuals being evaluated. When children or adults who lack the capacity to give voluntary consent are being evaluated, informed written consent is obtained from a parent or guardian.

Source: 2014 American Counseling Association Code of Ethics. Reprinted with permission from American Counseling Association.

Supervision

Informed consent in the supervision setting is parallel to informed consent in a clinical setting. The only difference is that the client is actually a counselor, who is the supervisee. A counselor in training must be given an informed consent that mirrors the ones we have discussed already with one added component: counselors in training are required to tell the client that they are under supervision and with whom they will share the contents of the counseling session(s). In other words, the supervisee's clients have to know that the supervisor will be privy to session content.

In addition, ethical practice guides trainees to explain to a client that they are required to share session content with their supervisors, treatment teams, course professors, and peers to advance their skills. It is the client's right to be provided this information prior to any counseling or any taping device being activated and to reject working with a counselor who is in training or to the use of taping in sessions. This information should be provided during the informed consent process when exceptions to confidentiality are discussed, and the informed consent between the supervisor and supervisee should contain that requirement.

Ethical Code 6.5

F.1.c. Informed Consent and Client Rights.

Supervisors make supervisees aware of client rights, including the protection of client privacy and confidentiality in the counseling relationship. Supervisees provide clients with professional disclosure information and inform them of how the supervision process influences the limits of confidentiality. Supervisees make clients aware of who will have access to records of the counseling relationship and how these records will be stored, transmitted, or otherwise reviewed.

Source: 2014 American Counseling Association Code of Ethics. Reprinted with permission from American Counseling Association.

CASE STUDY 6.3

A 13-year-old girl is being counseled by a doctoral intern at a local mental health clinic. In the course of counseling, the child's grandmother asks for information about the girl's expressed concerns. The grandmother signed the informed consent form as the legal guardian of the child. The counselor relays to the girl that her grandmother has requested information about the content of their discussions and that as a counselor she is, by law, required to answer the grandmother's questions because she is the legal guardian. The 13-year-old then tells the counselor that the grandmother isn't her legal guardian and that her mother has official custody. The counselor is now faced with an ethical dilemma. The counselor has been treating a minor client without parental consent.

The counselor consults her supervisor at the clinic, an LPC. The supervisor states that an effort should be made to contact the mother and to get her consent (informed consent) to treat the 13-year-old. Both agree that they need to continue seeing the client as she has some serious emotional concerns. The counselor and the supervisor consult with the agency administrator (who holds a master's of business administration degree and is a noncounselor), who directs them to cease counseling until consent is obtained from the mother as services are being provided on a contract that could be in jeopardy if ethical or legal concerns arise. Without consent, no treatment is to be given, according to the administrator. The counselor and the supervisor then agree to seek the mother's consent. Contact is made with the mother by a phone number provided by the client. The mother cannot come to the clinic but agrees to meet the counselor at a local restaurant in her hometown to sign the papers. The counselor drives to the agreed-upon site, but the mother does not show up for the meeting. Follow-up contact is attempted, with no response from the mother.

The counselor and supervisor then agree to meet with the grandmother to explain the situation and to enlist her support in getting the mother's consent. The grandmother agrees. Later it is learned that the grandmother threatened the mother with parental rights termination based on child abandonment, and she obtained the mother's consent under the threat. A signed and notarized copy of the consent form is presented to the clinic with the mother's signature. Another form is presented to the clinic that indicates the mother has signed over parental rights to the grandmother, who also signs a counseling consent form.

The counselor, under the supervisor's direction, reinitiates counseling with the 13-year-old but informs the client that her grandmother has the right to know the information that is discussed in counseling (should the grandmother request information). The client acknowledges that she understands.

1. What could have been done differently in this case?

2. Did the counselor or the agency make errors?

3. What ethical standards apply?

4. Is there enough information to ensure that counseling can be ethically reinitiated in this case?

Contributed by R. Rocco Cottone, PhD, professor and coordinator of the Doctoral Programs Department of Counseling and Family Therapy, University of Missouri–St. Louis.

Research Participants

Informed consent is also a required component to any research being carried out by counselors. It is the counselor-researcher's responsibility to ensure that our research participants understand their rights in the research process. We must verify participants' understanding of the study; this requirement is especially important when the population being studied is vulnerable, such as those identified as substance abusers, minors, or the cognitively impaired. In a study by Rounsaville, Hunkele, Easton, Nich, and Carroll (2008), only a few more than half of the study participants indicated understanding of the contents of the informed consent component of the study, while 20 percent did not understand that they had the right to refuse participation. The Rounsaville and colleagues study underscored the significance of confirming that study participants understand their rights related to participating in the study and, specifically, to the informed consent.

Counselors conducting research also should include client debriefing as part of the research protocol. Debriefing involves working with the participants to process their experience in the related study. It also can include discussing any future steps related to the research, such as publication and how the clients are protected and how the clients may feel when they see their story as part of a research project and in writing. Keeping communication open and clear with a client study participant is critical ethical practice and also maintains the therapeutic relationship. As a final consideration in research, the participants' cultural contexts always should be considered, and the consent process must be delivered in a language that is understood by the participant.

The related ethical code lists the participants' rights, making the process of developing the written document clearer for practitioners (ACA, 2014).

Ethical Code 6.6

G.2.a. Informed Consent in Research.

Individuals have the right to decline requests to become research participants. In seeking consent, counselors use language that

1. accurately explains the purpose and procedures to be followed;

2. identifies any procedures that are experimental or relatively untried;

3. describes any attendant discomforts, risks, and potential power differentials between researchers and participants;

4. describes any benefits or changes in individuals or organizations that might reasonably be expected;

5. discloses appropriate alternative procedures that would be advantageous for participants;

6. offers to answer any inquiries concerning the procedures;

7. describes any limitations on confidentiality;

8. describes the format and potential target audiences for the dissemination of research findings; and

9. instructs participants that they are free to withdraw their consent and discontinue participation in the project at any time, without penalty.

Source: 2014 American Counseling Association Code of Ethics. Reprinted with permission from American Counseling Association.

Research that includes a detailed informed consent is one step closer to being ethically sound. This can be tedious for the researcher and the potential participant, and therefore researchers may fear the lengthy informed consent may drive away potential participants. But the reality is that ethical practice as well as the institutional review boards that monitor research require a detailed consent form. By developing a form that meets the ACA Code of Ethics, you will be more protected as a researcher.

Clients Lacking Capacity to Give Consent

It is not surprising that at the heart of informed consent are the concepts of client comprehension and autonomy: whether or not the client understands the content of the informed consent and as it relates to the freedom to choose treatment. But what do professional counselors do when clients may not comprehend the consent process or do not have the capacity to make a decision on treatment? These are known as clients who lack the capacity to provide consent and, therefore, require special attention. As you know, we are required ethically to include clients in the decision-making process, attain their consent to treatment, and encourage them to discuss services with family members or guardians (Remley & Herlihy, 2007).

Ethical Code 6.7

A.2.d. Inability to Give Consent.

When counseling minors, incapacitated adults, or other persons unable to give voluntary consent, counselors seek the assent of clients to services and include them in decision making as appropriate. Counselors recognize the need to balance the ethical rights of clients to make choices, their capacity to give consent or assent to receive services, and parental or familial legal rights and responsibilities to protect these clients and make decisions on their behalf.

Source: 2014 American Counseling Association Code of Ethics. Reprinted with permission from American Counseling Association.

When it is not possible to include clients in the decision-making process, we work to attain something known as *assent*. For example, when a minor is seen in counseling, the minor has no legal ability to give consent. Instead, the legal guardian provides consent. The counselor then works to gain the client's assent, which is an agreement to treatment. We seek to establish a collaborative relationship with the guardian to best serve the client while acknowledging the guardian's responsibility to protect the client. In addition, we work to empower the minor or otherwise incapacitated client by gaining their assent to the process.

Some clients may have abilities that have not been acknowledged in previous diagnoses. Counselors are cautioned to not take for granted or automatically assume a diagnosis is correct when the client's cognitive abilities do not match the formerly stated diagnosis (Fisher & Oransky, 2008). It is important to take steps to diagnose the client correctly with assessment instruments that measure an individual's cognitive capacity, so you may determine consent capacity. When appropriate, reevaluating a client diagnosis is a more humane and acceptable form of client care, which is necessary when working with those who may lack the capacity to give consent. As in all cases, we must tailor the informed consent process to fit the needs or cognitive capacity of each client (Laidlaw, 1999).

The bridge between assent from the client and consent from the guardian can be a delicate one for counselors to walk. Informed consent requires that the client be competent to understand and provide voluntary consent regarding services (Commons et al., 2006). When clients do not fit this definition, we must be true to our profession and seek equality and positive regard for all persons. Seek understanding and consent from the guardians of such clients, yet always advocate for the client's needs that you have assessed as necessary for effective treatment. Advocacy for all clients is something that competent counselors engage in regularly, but we are especially attentive to advocacy and client rights with those who lack the capacity to provide consent.

Involuntary or Mandatory Counseling

Other clients who may not fit neatly into our established informed consent procedures are those who are required to participate in mandatory professional counseling. These clients can range from those court ordered to attend an anger management class to the employee sent to you for a mandatory substance abuse screening. These clients also are afforded the right to informed consent. However, as with clients lacking capacity to provide consent, the process of informed consent may feel somewhat incongruent to the counselor when it is provided to clients who are mandated to participate in counseling. You now know that informed consent requires the counselor to provide information regarding services, explain the benefits and limitations of those services, and seek client understanding and voluntary consent to services. That said, how do you seek voluntary consent when the counseling is mandated by a judge and a client may be unwilling to cooperate?

Remember that ethical practice requires counselors to practice from a position of beneficence and nonmaleficence of the client (Beauchamp & Childress, 1979). This means always making decisions and practicing from the perspective of doing what is best for the client. We should make every effort for client consent to treatment even when the treatment is mandated. Imagine being a counselor in a correctional facility. You may have to work harder to develop and maintain a therapeutic relationship with this client population than others. Strategies such as inviting the client into the process of informed consent, acknowledging the difficulty of the mandated situation, providing informed consent in an ongoing manner, and involving the client in any report that is shared with others or the courts may help to cultivate a therapeutic relationship and assist with garnering consent (Barnett & Johnson, 2010).

Counselors outside of correctional facilities are, at times, required to report counseling progress to the courts. Including your clients in determining that part of session content that will be reported to the courts may help to strengthen the client–counselor relationship. Limit the information released to outside parties to only that which is necessary. Involving your client in the consent and reporting process will integrate our profession's spirit of informed consent and concern for our clients' rights more adequately.

Ethical Code 6.8

B.2.d. Court-Ordered Disclosure.

When ordered by a court to release confidential or privileged information without a client's permission, counselors seek to obtain written, informed consent from the client or take steps to prohibit the disclosure or have it limited as narrowly as possible because of potential harm to the client or counseling relationship.

Source: 2014 American Counseling Association Code of Ethics. Reprinted with permission from American Counseling Association.

Culture and Context

Quality counseling includes a focus on culture threaded throughout the process. This includes special attention during the informed consent process. Because this is our first genuine connection with the client, we need to consider potential variations in how the client may perceive the informed consent process (HPSO, 2012). The HPSO, an organization providing insurance for counselors and counseling students alike, recommends that we consider several cultural contexts when providing informed consent:

- Who typically makes decisions in the family?
- Are the decisions of elders or authoritative figures in the family unquestioned, and therefore they retain all decision-making power?
- Are there some family members who should not be included in treatment?
- Who should be contacted in case of emergency intervention with the client?

These questions will alert you to the cultural context within which informed consent should be delivered to any client and especially those of a different culture. When possible, it is best to be familiar with a client's culture before beginning counseling. You even may need to retain a translator if the client's spoken language is different than your own. Remain open to and able to hear the client's perception of his or her cultural values, traditions, and related choices when you are taking the client through the informed consent process. Remember, they may not match yours.

Ethical Code 6.9

A.2.c. Developmental and Cultural Sensitivity.

Counselors communicate information in ways that are both developmentally and culturally appropriate. Counselors use clear and understandable language when discussing issues related to informed consent. When clients have difficulty understanding the language used by counselors, they provide necessary services (e.g., arranging for a qualified interpreter or translator) to ensure comprehension by clients. In collaboration with clients, counselors consider cultural implications of informed consent procedures, and where possible, counselors adjust their practices accordingly.

Source: 2014 American Counseling Association Code of Ethics. Reprinted with permission from American Counseling Association.

Technology

The informed consent process requires special attention when counseling services or initiation of services are performed electronically (more on technology and counseling in Chapter 12). Ethical codes suggest that informed consent be provided verbally and in writing. But how does this occur when counseling is conducted from a distance and via electronic sources? Should there be added inclusions in the consent process? How do you check for understanding, that is, consent?

In many ways, informed consent integrates the same components when applied to clients being treated via electronic format as when treating the client in a face-to-face venue. Informed consent must still include all of the components listed in Table 6.1 plus a few additional components. As with face-to-face clients, informed consent via technology must be approached as an ongoing and evolving process (Rudd et al., 2009). In most situations, but always in distance situations, counselors are required to address issues related to HIPAA. HIPAA pertains to communications—specifically, electronically transmitted communications—concerning the health care of an individual.

Guided Practice Exercise 6.3

Protecting Client Privacy

Review the HIPAA regulations, and highlight those that pertain to counseling practice. Develop a written form that covers the HIPAA regulations and is written in a client-friendly format. Save it for your counseling practice upon graduation.

When we use computers in the counseling process (such as for scheduling, intake interviews, and actual counseling), we are required to ensure the confidentiality of all communications. This means placing appropriate and adequate firewalls on computers utilized in the counseling process and communicating specific confidentiality risks associated with the use of computers. Ethical codes mandate that counselors include in their informed consent the possibility of others who may have access to their computer. This includes employees or individuals who have access to the computer, such as IT technicians and administrative staff. In addition, counselors should discuss with the client the fact that those who have access to the client's computer, such as family members or employment personnel if an employer-owned computer, also have the potential to gain access to written communications. As an ethical counselor, you have an obligation to remind clients of these potential risks to their confidential information.

Ethical Code 6.10

H.3. Client Verification.

Counselors who engage in the use of distance counseling, technology or social media to interact with clients take steps to verify the client's identity at the beginning and throughout the therapeutic process. Verification can include, but is not limited to, using code words, numbers, graphics, or other nondescript identifiers.

Source: 2014 American Counseling Association Code of Ethics. Reprinted with permission from American Counseling Association.

Counselors who practice distantly (counseling via the Internet) are responsible for knowing and sharing with clients the laws that pertain to counseling from a distance in their particular state. States differ in how they permit counselors to practice from a distance. Some require the practicing counselor be licensed in the state in which the client resides and the state in which the counselor resides; some require the counselor be licensed only in the state in which the counselor resides. If you are intending to conduct professional counseling from a distance, you must be trained appropriately and be aware of your state's laws regarding distance counseling as well as those of any state in which a potential client may reside. Then communicate those laws to your client as part of your informed consent.

Practicing ethically from a distance also includes confirming that clients understand how to proceed if electronic connection is lost during a session and what to do in the event of an emergency (Barnett & Johnson, 2010). This is critical information to include in the informed consent process. It is also important to confirm in writing, as well as verbally, that the client understands the process. It is helpful to provide a backup emergency contact source for the client. You should ensure that all clients have a list of appropriate referral sources in case they decide they need a face-to-face counseling approach or they come to need a more direct type of care. Discuss referral options with your client and opportunities when it is appropriate to reach out to a referral source.

Relatedly, good practice also includes defining the term *emergency* in your informed consent process. Clients may have different perceptions of what an emergency is and may unwittingly cross boundaries as a result. Some clients may assume a family conflict is an emergency and, therefore, deserving of an impromptu session with you via the Internet. Likewise, others may become conflicted and even suicidal yet may not be in the frame of mind to reach out to their counselor or follow previously agreed-upon emergency steps if the situation has not been addressed as an emergency in the informed consent process. If you participate in distance counseling, ensure that your informed consent process is clear and detailed.

Finally, counseling in a distance format requires that you also obtain written consent from those who care for minors or clients who are considered incompetent. It is our responsibility to verify a client's status in regard to age and or competency and then to pursue written consent from the appropriate legal authority or parent. This is the same consent component as in face-to-face counseling, yet when counseling is conducted via electronic means, obvious visual cues may not be present for the counselor to have a more accurate assessment of the client's age and or abilities. Nonetheless, written consent must be procured by the legal guardian.

Best practice in informed consent as applied in a distance counseling relationship includes adapting your informed consent process to meet ethical codes and state laws and regulations. And remember that regardless of where you practice counseling, distant or not, informed consent is ongoing and evolving. Like face-to-face counseling, consent about these and all consent components should be discussed each time the counseling shifts to a new approach or new techniques, and in general, any time new information is discovered that pertains to the counselor–client relationship.

Ethical Code 6.11

H.2.a. Informed Consent and Disclosure.

Clients have the freedom to choose whether to use distance counseling, social media, or technology within the counseling process. In addition to the usual and customary protocol of informed consent between counselor and client for face-to-face counseling, the following issues, unique to the use of distance counseling, technology, or social media, are addressed in the informed consent process:

- distance counseling credentials, physical location of practice, and contact information;
- risks and benefits of engaging in the use of distance counseling, technology, or social media;
- possibility of technology failure and alternate methods of service delivery;
- anticipated response time;
- emergency procedures to follow when the counselor is not available;
- time zone differences;
- cultural or language differences that may affect delivery of services;
- possible denial of insurance benefits; and
- social media policy.

Source: 2014 American Counseling Association Code of Ethics. Reprinted with permission from American Counseling Association.

Guided Practice Exercise 6.4

Counseling From a Distance

The literature on distance counseling is in its early stages. Professional counseling literature could use more research and information on this quickly growing topic of interest and practice. Conduct a literature review on distance counseling and ethical practice, and develop a manuscript for potential publication.

CONCLUSION

Counselors and our clients typically are aware that the concept of informed consent exists—we are all used to signing some documents before we see a new health care provider. However, clients rarely are aware of the extent of informed consent in the counseling profession. We are responsible for thoroughly understanding limits and exceptions to confidentiality and sharing those with clients in a way that they can understand. To do so, we must keep up with the changing climate of counseling, the use of supervision and technology, continually evolving laws and policies, and methods of protecting the client whenever possible. Using this chapter as a foundation, beginning counselors can start their own process of developing a thorough informed consent for the clients they will serve.

KEYSTONES

- Informed consent pertains to a client's right to be provided with enough information to make decisions regarding his or her treatment in counseling. The action of consent belongs to the client and is provided to the counselor. The why of informed consent pertains to providing enough information about treatment and process for the client to make his or her own decisions about pursuing services under the counselor's care. The how of informed consent includes implementing best practices and procedures.

- All codes of professional counseling ethics require an informed consent process, and most state practice laws mandate it. Informed consent provides the advantage of creating trust and a therapeutic alliance and potentially may protect a counselor from ending up in court. Informed consent should be provided in written and verbal forms. When verbally explaining the content of the form, we must use clear language that is developmentally appropriate for the client and that takes the client's cultural background into consideration.

- Informed consent is an ongoing process, continually evolving with the therapy process.

- Ethical practice in the use of assessment inventories requires adequate informed consent regarding all components of the assessment, including the administration, delivery, and feedback parts of the process.

- Counselors in training must obtain informed consent and, in doing so, are required to tell clients that they are counselors in training and with whom they will share the contents of the counseling session(s).

- Informed consent is also a required component to any research being carried out by counselors.

- Ethically, counselors are required to include our clients in the decision-making process, obtain their consent to treatment, and encourage them to discuss services with family members or guardians. When that is not possible, we work to attain the client's assent (agreement) to treatment and then provide informed consent to the legal guardian.

- Counselors should make every effort for client consent to treatment even when the treatment is mandated.

- Informed consent integrates the same components when applied to clients being treated via electronic format as when treating the client in a face-to-face venue. When we use computers in the counseling process (such as for scheduling, intake interviews, and actual counseling), we are required to ensure confidentiality of all communications. Counselors who practice distantly (counseling via the Internet) are responsible for knowing and informing their clients of the laws that pertain to counseling from a distance in their particular state.

SUGGESTED BEST PRACTICES

- Just as you expect informed consent when you see your primary care physician, know that your clients expect it from you.
- Remember that informed consent is what allows us to make decisions about our care.
- Informed consent is not a form to be run through but a process we provide to our clients.
- Think of informed consent as an extension of that trust building that counselors are constantly engaged in.
- Have good documentation of informed consent, but be willing to personalize the process.
- Use clear language in your documents that is easily understood by most clients in the populations you treat.
- Get assent from clients who are not able to give consent, such as minors and individuals who are impaired.
- Remember that informed consent is a process, not a product. More than a one-time signature, informed consent flows throughout the counseling relationship.
- Stay up-to-date on state laws related to informed consent. They are ever changing.
- Look to the literature and other professionals in your area to develop informed consent documents that are best practices.
- Have informed consent documents for each area of specialty that you practice. The informed consent for family counseling is different from the informed consent for an assessment, for example.
- Distance counseling still requires informed consent. This process is even more important when practicing using technology, as the regulations are constantly developing.

ADDITIONAL RESOURCES

In Print

Bridges, N. (2010). Clinical writing about clients: Seeking consent and negotiating the impact on clients and their treatments. *Counseling and Values, 54*(2), 103–116. doi:10.1002/j.2161–007X .2010.tb00009.x

Daniels, J. (2001). Managed care, ethics, and counseling. *Journal of Counseling & Development, 79*(1), 119–122. doi:10.1002/j.1556–6676.2001.tb01950.x

Hohmann-Marriott, B. E. (2001). Marriage and family therapy research: Ethical issues and guidelines. *The American Journal of Family Therapy, 29*(1), 1–11. doi:10.1080/01926180126081

Kress, V. E., Hoffman, R. M., & Eriksen, K. (2010). Ethical dimensions of diagnosing: Considerations for clinical mental health counselors. *Counseling and Values, 55*(1), 101–112. doi:10.1002/j2161–007X.2010.tb00024.x

Tucker, K. L. (2009). Ensuring informed end-of-life decisions. *Journal of Palliative Medicine, 12*(2), 119–120. doi:10.1089/jpm.2009.9675

On the Web

The Center for Ethical Practice. (n.d.). Retrieved from http://www.centerforethicalpractice.org/

Health Information Privacy. (n.d.). HIPPA government site. Retrieved from http://www.hhs.gov/ocr/privacy/index.html

HIPPA.com. (n.d.). HIPPA nongovernment site. Retrieved from http://www.hipaa.com/

REFERENCES

Abrahams, H. (2007). Ethics in counselling research fieldwork. *Counselling & Psychotherapy Research, 7*(4), 240–244. doi:10.1080/14733140701707068

American Counseling Association (ACE). (2014). *ACA code of ethics.* Alexandria, VA: Author.

American Psychological Association (APA). (2010). *APA code of ethics.* Retrieved from http://www.apa.org/ethics/code/index.aspx?item=1

Association of Counselor Education and Supervision (ACES). (2011). *Best practices in clinical supervision.* Retrieved from http://www.acesonline.net/wp-content/uploads/2011/10/ACES-Best-Practices-in-clinical-supervision-document-FINAL.pdf

Barnett, J. E., & Johnson, W. B. (2010). *Ethics desk reference for counselors.* Alexandria, VA: American Counseling Association.

Beauchamp, T. L., & Childress, J. F. (1979). *Principles of biomedical ethics.* Oxford, UK: Oxford University Press.

Bernstein, B. E., & Hartsell, T. L. (2004). *The portable lawyer for mental health professionals: An A-Z guide to protecting your clients, your practice, and yourself* (2nd ed.). Hoboken, NJ: John Wiley & Sons, Inc.

Center for Credentialing and Education (CCE). (2008). *CCE code of ethics.* Retrieved from http://cce-global.org/Downloads/Ethics/ACScodeofethics.pdf

Commons, M. L., Rodriquez, J. A., Adams, K. M., Goodheart, E. A., Gutheil, T. G., & Cyr, E. D. (2006). Informed consent: Do you know it when you see it? Evaluating the adequacy of patient consent and the value of a lawsuit. *Psychiatric Annals, 36*(6), 430–435.

Cook, D. A. (2009). Thorough informed consent: A developing clinical intervention with suicidal clients. *Psychotherapy: Theory, Research, Practice, Training, 46*(4), 469–471. doi:10.1037/a0017903

Council for Accreditation of Counseling & Related Educational Programs (CACREP). (2009). *CACREP 2009 standards.* Retrieved from http://www.cacrep.org/doc/2009%20Standards%20with%20cover.pdf

Fisher, C. B., & Oransky, M. (2008). Informed consent to psychotherapy: Protecting the dignity and respecting the autonomy of patients. *Journal of Clinical Psychology, 64*(5), 576–588. doi:10.1002/jclp.20472

Goddard, A., Murray, C. D., & Simpson, J. (2008). Informed consent and psychotherapy: An interpretative phenomenological analysis of therapists views. *Psychology and Psychotherapy: Theory, Research, and Practice, 81*(2), 177–191. doi:10.1348/147608307X266587

Health Providers Service Organization (HPSO). (2012). Improving health literacy improves client outcomes. *Risk Advisor for Counselors.* Retrieved from http://www.hpso.com/pdfs/db/newsletters/2012-Counselor-Risk-Advisor.pdf?fileName=2012-Counselor-Risk-Advisor.pdf&folder=pdfs/db/newsletters&isLiveStr=Y

Kitchener, K. S. (1984). Intuition, critical evaluation, and ethical principles: The foundation for ethical decisions in counseling psychology. *The Counseling Psychologist, 12*(3), 43–55.

Laidlaw, T. S. (1999, August). Review of *Negotiating Consent in Psychotherapy.* [Review of the book *Negotiating consent in psychotherapy,* by P. O'Neill]. *Canadian Psychology/Psychologie canadienne, 40*(3), 275–277. doi:10.1037/h0092514

Mitchell, R. W. (2007). *Documentation in counseling records: An overview of ethical, legal, and clinical issues* (3rd ed.). Alexandria, VA: American Counseling Association.

National Association of Social Workers (NASW). (2008). *Code of ethics.* Retrieved from http://www.socialworkers.org/pubs/code/code.asp

National Board for Certified Counselors (NBCC). (n.d.). *Code of ethics.* Retrieved from http://nbcc.org/code_of_ethics/

Pope, K. S., & Vasquez, M. J. (1991). *Ethics in psychotherapy and counseling: A practical guide for psychologists.* San Francisco, CA: Jossey-Bass.

Recupero, P. R., & Rainey, S. E. (2005). Informed consent to E-therapy. *American Journal of Psychotherapy, 59*(4), 319–331.

Remley, T. P., & Herlihy, B. (2007). *Ethical, legal, and professional issues in counseling* (2nd ed.). Upper Saddle River, NJ: Pearson/Merrill Prentice Hall.

Rounsaville, D. B., Hunkele, K., Easton, C. J., Nich, C., & Carroll, K. M. (2008). Making informed consent more informed: Preliminary results from a multiple-choice test among probation-referred marijuana users entering a randomized clinical trial. *Journal of the American Academy of Psychiatry and the Law, 36*(3), 354–359. Retrieved from http://www.jaapl.org.library3.webster.edu/content/36/3/354.full?%3f

Rudd, M. D., Joiner, T., Brown, G. K., Cukrowicz, K., Jobes, D. A., Silverman, M., & Cordero, L. (2009). Informed consent with suicidal patients: Rethinking risks in (and out of) treatment. *Psychotherapy: Theory, Research, Practice, Training, 46*(4), 459–468. doi:10.1037/a0017902

Wheeler, A. M. N., & Bertram, B. (2008). *The counselor and the law: A guide to legal and ethical practice* (5th ed.). Alexandria, VA: American Counseling Association.

Younggren, J. N., Foote, W. E., Fisher, M. A., & Hjelt, S. E. (2011). A legal and ethical review of patient responsibilities and psychotherapist duties. *Professional Psychology: Research and Practice, 42*(2), 160–168. doi:10.1037/a0023142

Chapter 7

CONFIDENTIALITY AND RECORD KEEPING

Sedef was working on progress notes one day when a process server came by with a subpoena. Sedef sighed; she had been expecting this to happen. She consulted with her colleagues, who told her she was stuck. There was nothing to do but comply. She responded to the subpoena as her colleagues had recommended. Sedef provided all the information that the attorney requested in the subpoena. After all, once a subpoena is delivered, a mental health professional has to turn over the corresponding document, right?

CHAPTER OVERVIEW

This chapter reviews the ethical codes and related practices of confidentiality and record keeping. Expanding on the concept of informed consent, confidentiality across your practice, including record keeping, is highlighted in the American Counseling Association (ACA, 2014) Code of Ethics. Understanding when confidentiality can and should be broken is critical to all counselors. Specific scenarios related to confidentiality and record keeping, a listing of related ACA ethical codes, and the related Council for Accreditation of Counseling & Related Educational Programs (CACREP, 2009) standards are also denoted for your use.

LEARNING OBJECTIVES

After reading this chapter you will be able to do the following:

1. Examine the concept of confidentiality and its purposes.

2. Evaluate occasions when confidentiality can and cannot be broken.

3. Describe best practices for informing the client.

4. Distinguish the requirements of confidentiality among specialized situations including supervision, death, multiple clients, minors and others lacking capacity to give consent; and research and publications.

5. Assess confidentiality practices in terms of client culture and context.

6. Describe confidentiality in terms of record keeping.

CACREP STANDARDS

CACREP Core Standards

G.1.b. Professional roles, functions, and relationships with other human service providers, including strategies for interagency/interorganization collaboration and communications *(record keeping).*

CACREP Clinical Mental Health Standards

A.2. Understands ethical and legal considerations specifically related to the practice of clinical mental health counseling.

D.7. Applies current record-keeping standards related to clinical mental health counseling.

INTRODUCTION

If counselors were not required to maintain confidentiality, would clients disclose the depths of their consciences and their related troubles and fears in a counseling session? Why would they disclose if there was no promise or presumption of their secrets, hurts, and fears remaining private? How would trust exist between us and our clients? And without trust, how would alliance develop and, ultimately, healing occur?

Confidentiality is an integral and expected component of any healthy and successful counseling relationship (Welfel, 1998). Confidentiality must be present for clients to feel protected and for the potential of trust to develop in the client–counselor relationship. However, there are limitations as to when the contents of a session are kept private. Although it is tempting to say, "What is said here, stays here," it is simply not true at all times. It is vital to the therapeutic relationship that those occasions when confidentiality must be broken are discussed with the client in the initial interview, the informed consent. Remember from Chapter 6 that informed consent is ongoing and, therefore, when our clients are talking about a topic that must be reported outside of the counseling relationship, we are to remind them of that requirement. Confidentiality is a client's right.

Confidentiality is a detailed concept that is complex and multifaceted in practice yet is not always recognized as such. This chapter reviews the characteristics of confidentiality in addition to when it must be broken and maintained, who has rights or access to confidential information, and precautions associated with when a counselor must breach it. The chapter also reviews ways in which technology impacts confidentiality and how confidentiality impacts record keeping. Case illustrations and exercises are provided to help transition your reading to application.

ELEMENTS OF CONFIDENTIALITY

As noted, confidentiality is a critical component to the action of counseling, without which, why would anyone see a counselor? It is an absolute necessity of our profession. Confidentiality occurs between the counselor and the client. It is our promise to the client that generally what is said in session stays in session, and it is a key factor to building trust and therefore session depth. Clients own their stories, and when confidentiality is in place, they are assured their stories remain private.

Ethical Code 7.1

B.1.b. Respect for Privacy.

Counselors respect the privacy of prospective and current clients. Counselors request private information from clients only when it is beneficial to the counseling process.

Source: 2014 American Counseling Association Code of Ethics. Reprinted with permission from American Counseling Association.

CASE STUDY 7.1

Sarah, who works as substance abuse counselor at a counseling agency, was out for coffee and ran into Tiffany, a client she had seen for an agency intake. Tiffany recognized Sarah and approached her. "Sarah, how are you doing?" Sarah responded, "Great! How are you doing?" Speaking loud enough for neighboring people to hear, Tiffany said, "I have been doing OK. I can't seem to stop using. I do want to say that I really appreciated the way we connected and how you understood what I was going through during my assessment. After my intake, I was assigned to Mark, and I did not find him very helpful. He just did not understand me and made me feel uncomfortable. I decided not to continue seeing him and have been struggling to get control of my life and to kick my habit." Sarah responded, "I am sorry to hear that. I hope that you are able to find another counselor who you feel can help you." Tiffany continued, "Is Mark even qualified to be a counselor?"

Sarah thought to herself that Tiffany was right; Mark was an inexperienced counselor. He should only be conducting intake assessments, and many female clients have talked about how he makes them feel uncomfortable. Sarah smiled and said to Tiffany, "Maybe finding a counselor that you feel more comfortable with is best." Tiffany erupted, "I knew it! I knew Mark was not a good counselor. I knew that Mark was not helping me. Can I switch to you? What do you think I should do?" Feeling uncomfortable about where the conversation was heading and the lack of privacy, Sarah quickly grabbed her coffee and told Tiffany that she had to get going. Tiffany continued talking to Sarah and following her out of the coffee shop, "Oh . . . my friend Tricia is seeing you, and she said you are great. Do you know Tricia? She's a tall gal, long blonde hair, and super skinny. She really likes you a lot. Do want me to tell her you said, 'Hi'?"

1. How should Sarah respond to Tiffany mentioning that Sarah is counseling Tricia?

2. Is this conversation appropriate to have in a public setting, when Sarah is not Tiffany's counselor?

3. Discuss how to draw boundaries with potential and current clients when coincidentally meeting them in public locations.

Contributed by Erika Raissa Nash Cameron, PhD, assistant professor, University of San Diego.

Strongly supported by ethical codes, confidentiality is considered by the field to be necessary for an appropriate, adequate, and healing counseling experience. *Privilege* is a legal concept or term that refers to state law granting a right (or privilege) to a counselor (or other professional) to maintain confidentiality. *Privileged communication* pertains to those communications (or session content) that are permitted (and, in fact, required in some cases) to remain confidential based on who the law grants the privilege to. If your state grants privileged communication to licensed professional or mental health counselors, you may keep client information confidential. Not all states grant privilege to counselors; in fact, privilege is granted to medical doctors and psychologists on a federal level but not to psychotherapists in general (Remley & Herlihy, 2014). Hence, professional counselors, marriage and family therapists, and social workers are granted privilege only per state (Corey, Corey, & Callahan, 2011).

Privacy also can be a legal term and refers to the client's right to nondisclosure of content that is discussed in session. Our clients have the right to determine what—if any—of their private information we may share with others. Privacy is a legal term that is granted by law but is our responsibility to maintain. In other words, while the law defines privacy, we must work to ensure it is part of the counseling process. It is critical that we are familiar with our state's laws pertaining to confidentiality, privilege, and privacy.

Guided Practice Exercise 7.1

Ever-Changing State Law

Students often ask why certain texts don't mention the "obvious" state laws such as which states provide privileged communications statutes for licensed professional counselors (LPCs). The response to this inquiry is important to understand: State laws change routinely. Counselors in training and licensed counselors must be familiar with current law and stay abreast of proposed changes in the legislature to practice ethically and to limit their professional liability. The excuse of lack of familiarity with changing laws will not protect a counselor in court.

Exercise: Search your state's LPC web page, and locate the state regulations pertaining to LPCs. Print the laws, and bring them to class for a discussion around privileged communications, confidentiality, and privacy in your state.

The primary purposes of confidentiality are to provide privacy for the clients and to place control of the shared information in their hands. Confidentiality, like consent and privilege, is, in most cases, the client's to own. With certain exceptions, confidentiality and privileged communication mean the client decides who gets to know what and when. Clients often seek out counseling for the opportunity to talk about difficult situations and times in their lives that may have left feelings of shame and defeat. One of the tenets of professional counseling presumes that we will provide a safe-enough environment that the client feels free enough to talk about anything. If we disclose something that a client stated in session to a third party without his or her permission to disclose the information, we are in violation of ethical codes and, in some cases, state law pertaining to confidentiality. Privacy (in regard to the client's concerns) and confidentiality (or control of who hears what) are the client's rights in counseling. The presumption is that what is said in session stays in session. However, there are times when breaking confidentiality is the appropriate and safe action.

Ethical Code 7.2

B.1.c. Respect for Confidentiality.

Counselors protect the confidential information of prospective and current clients. Counselors disclose information only with appropriate consent or with sound legal or ethical justification.

Source: 2014 American Counseling Association Code of Ethics. Reprinted with permission from American Counseling Association.

BREACHING CONFIDENTIALITY

Before breaching confidentiality, counselors should take precautionary steps to help ensure ethical practice. First, we should always seek consultation from other professionals who have expertise in the area of concern if we are uncertain about breaking confidentiality. We have talked a great deal about consultation in this book, and in cases where confidentiality may need to be broken, outside consultation should be made with a colleague or an attorney. If with a colleague, you should inform him or her that your inquiry is an official consultation. Remember that a professional consultation may be used as support of ethical decisions, so it is important that the person with whom you are consulting is aware that the question is an official consultation that may come up later.

Second, you will need to implement procedures, including ethical decision-making models (EDMs) that are common practice in the field of professional counseling. This is known as practicing the standard of care and will be expected should a situation devolve into a legal case. Finally, document all steps and the rationale behind each step (Bernstein & Hartsell, 2004). Remember, if it isn't documented, it doesn't exist. Taking the actions outlined in this section will show evidence that serious consideration and necessary precautions occurred prior to breaking confidentiality, which may help to assuage the potential for litigious behavior.

Guided Practice Exercise 7.2

The Good Old-Fashioned Rolodex

Years ago, counselors used something known as a Rolodex. This handy little box that spun at the flick of a wrist provided a way to maintain a list of contact information for referral sources and other important parties. Today, counselors keep this list on

(Continued)

(Continued)

smartphones, computers, and other technological aids. Yet maintaining some form of an address book is critical for the mental health counselor. We need referrals for ourselves as well as our clients.

Exercise: Go onto the Internet and locate the names of attorneys who have training in mental health care law or confidentiality and who are local to your practice. Next, locate and record the contact information for colleagues in your field whom you know and respect. This will be the beginning of your present-day version of the Rolodex. Whether you keep them on a device that fits in your pocket or in a little box on your desk, being proactive by having the contact information of important professional colleagues is the intelligent way to begin practice.

Informing the Client

Determining when confidentiality may be breached is challenging. However, a discussion of this must occur in the initial informed consent with clients and throughout additional sessions if something that needs to be disclosed arises. Reasons for potential disclosure also should be listed on the written informed consent that the client signs. Remember to check for client understanding when providing informed consent as the courts view client comprehension as the counselor's responsibility (Wheeler & Bertram, 2012). Counselors who do not inform clients of occasions when confidentiality may be broken are practicing unethically and potentially breaking the law.

Ethical Code 7.3

B.1.d. Explanation of Limitations.

At initiation and throughout the counseling process, counselors inform clients of the limitations of confidentiality and seek to identify situations in which confidentiality must be breached.

Source: 2014 American Counseling Association Code of Ethics. Reprinted with permission from American Counseling Association.

When confidentiality must be broken, it is best done by discussing related reasons and the process that will occur with our clients (Daniels, 2001). Whenever possible, we recommend involving your clients in the sharing of their information.

You can discuss with them the possible outcomes of disclosing information or making mandated reports to appropriate authorities and also help the clients prepare for potential aftermath related to the reporting. Having this discussion may help them to prepare psychologically and even physically and could serve to maintain trust in the client–counselor relationship.

Why should you involve the client? In certain situations, it can be therapeutic to involve the client's participation in the reporting or disclosure of information. For example, in instances of past sexual abuse, it may be helpful for the client to be involved in the reporting phone call to the appropriate entities. In some situations, they may make the reporting call while you are present and in support, or the reverse may be more appropriate where they are present while you make the reporting call. It is not unusual for clients to be uncomfortable with the suggestion to participate in a reporting call. You should discuss the reporting process and the potentially therapeutic effects that participation may have for that particular client as well as discuss any possible negative effects. For some clients, participation is too difficult. When this occurs, you can report the incident after the client leaves the session and discuss the call in the next session. With all clients, the counselor is required to ensure that the clients understand what is happening, why it is happening, and that they can exercise their rights to participate or not.

In some cases where breach of confidentiality is required, counselors may be required to warn or protect the general public. Some states require counselors to warn and protect potential victims named by a client, while others do not; some states will support counselors in protecting their clients' privacy, while others will not. It is vital to know your state law. As a practicing counselor in Mississippi, one of your text authors has warned third parties of an imminent threat by a client. Those reports were not only ethical; they were required by state law. However this same counselor, now practicing in the state of Texas, is not allowed to report imminent threats by her clients to third parties. Knowing each state law under which you fall helps guide your ethical decision making. The following section delineates the significance of the duty to warn and protect.

Duty to Warn and Protect

Duty to warn was named as one of the top 10 ethics issues among ACA members in 2012 (Henning et al., 2012). Concern with how and when to implement duty to warn was requested for consultation commonly. Duty to warn was established from the now-famous 1974 case of *Tarasoff v. Regents of University of California.* This case was the result of a psychotherapeutic relationship in which a psychologist was told by a male client that he intended to kill a fellow

Table 7.1   Circumstances Related to Breaking Client Confidentiality

1. When a client discloses harm to self

ACA ethical code B.2.a. Danger and Legal Requirements

The general requirement that counselors keep information confidential does not apply when disclosure is required to protect clients or identified others from serious and foreseeable harm or when legal requirements demand that confidential information must be revealed. Counselors consult with other professionals when in doubt as to the validity of an exception. Additional considerations apply when addressing end-of-life issues.

2. When providing a guardian access to records as in the cases of minors and adults who are incompetent

3. When providing records to managed health care organizations

ACA ethical code B.3.d. Third-Party Payers

Counselors disclose information to third-party payers only when clients have authorized such disclosure.

4. When a client pursues litigation against a counselor

5. When a court orders a subpoena for records and there are no state statutes around privileged communications for counselors

ACA ethical code, B.2.c. Court-Ordered Disclosure

When subpoenaed to release confidential or privileged information without a client's permission, counselors obtain written, informed consent from the client or take steps to prohibit the disclosure or have it limited as narrowly as possible due to potential harm to the client or counseling relationship.

6. When the client records are related to forensic counseling

7. Counseling that occurs in an electronic environment or data is sent electronically (clients are to be informed of the risk related to family members, employers, or others gaining access to shared counseling communications)

8. Counseling that occurs in a group setting or sessions in which the client is a family or more than one individual

9. Counseling or related assessments that are court ordered (note this differs from a court-ordered subpoena for counseling session documents)

10. Data related to research in which the client openly participated

11. Information provided to allied health professionals (when the client agrees with written release)

12. Clinical supervision

ACA ethical code B.3.b. Treatment Teams

When client treatment involves a continued review or participation by a treatment team, the client will be informed of the team's existence and composition, information being shared, and the purposes of sharing such information.

Circumstances that require the counselor report to a stated authority and also notify other persons (or authorities) of the potential of harm by their client.

13. Disclosure of harm to another

ACA ethical code B.2.a. Danger and Legal Requirements

The general requirement that counselors keep information confidential does not apply when disclosure is required to protect clients or identified others from serious and foreseeable harm or when legal requirements demand that confidential information must be revealed. Counselors consult with other professionals when in doubt as to the validity of an exception. Additional considerations apply when addressing end-of-life issues.

14. Disclosure of neglect of another

ACA ethical code B.2.a. Danger and Legal Requirements

15. Disclosure of having a contagious disease

ACA ethical code B.2.b. Contagious, Life-Threatening Diseases

When clients disclose that they have a disease commonly known to be both communicable and life threatening, counselors may be justified in disclosing information to identifiable third parties if they are known to be at demonstrable and high risk of contracting the disease. Prior to making a disclosure, counselors confirm that there is such a diagnosis and assess the intent of clients to inform the third parties about their disease or to engage in any behaviors that may be harmful to an identifiable third party.

female student who had rebuffed his requests for attention and love. The psychologist requested the campus police pick up the student-client, which occurred. The psychologist also recommended the student-client be committed on a psychiatric hold and diagnosed the client with severe and acute schizophrenia and as harmful. However, before hospitalization could take place, the police released the client because he appeared rational and the supervisor of the treating psychologist overrode the recommendation to commit. The psychologist did what he was supposed to do, right? A few months later, the client stopped seeing the psychologist and killed the woman whom he told the psychologist he would kill. No warning was ever provided to the woman. Her family then successfully sued the psychologist and other university employees. In 1974, the case resulted in the statute that is now known as *duty to warn*.

In 1976, the *Tarasoff* ruling was amended to include the duty to protect in addition to warn. Simply warning a potential target is not considered enough action on the part of the professional when a client discloses intent to harm in states that follow the *Tarasoff* precedent. The professional also must enact protection of the client, which is typically accomplished by calling the police and informing them of the disclosure, but also can be achieved by making contact with the intended target to warn him or her and then notifying the police. As an example, one of your text authors has called the sheriffs office to inform them that a third party was threatened as well as directly calling the person who was threatened. As you can imagine, these are not easy calls to make. It is important to remember that not all states have adopted *Tarasoff* case law or require a duty to warn and protect. this reason, counselors must verify the stance held by their state to ensure confidentiality is not broken unknowingly and potentially illegally.

Table 7.2   Preventative Considerations for Counselors Concerning Duty to Warn

Barnett and Johnson (2010) delineate suggested practices related to a counselor and duty to warn and duty to protect in their guide, *Ethics Desk Reference for Counselors.* This guide delineates each code in the ACA (2005) Code of Ethics and provides preventive tips and considerations that are related to each code. The following are those practices suggested for counselors to pursue when treating clients who may be a threat to others:

1. Accept the obligation to intervene when a client poses a threat to self or identifiable others.

2. At times, protecting the client and others may involve providing more intensive treatment to protect the client from acting on impulse; at other times, fulfilling this obligation may necessitate a breach of confidentiality and contact with authorities.

3. Know your own jurisdiction's legal requirements when it comes to exceptions to confidentiality.

4. Clearly inform clients of the limits of confidentiality in these circumstances in advance.

5. Routinely seek consultation with knowledgeable colleagues when deciding whether to violate confidentiality for the purpose of protecting someone from harm.

6. When a terminally ill client is considering hastening his or her own death, review state and federal guidelines, review ethical considerations, and seek consultation.

Source: Barnett & Johnson, 2010, p. 36.

CASE STUDY 7.2

One morning I walked into my waiting room to discover Luigi, the man responsible for the cleaning services, sitting in a chair, agitated, wringing his hands, looking very distraught. He pleaded for me to see him as soon as possible. Noting his distress, I made space for him that afternoon.

When he came to my office, he explained the source of his distress. Recently, he discovered his wife sitting up late at night communicating with another man on the computer. He believed this man was interested romantically in his "beautiful" wife and feared she was interested in him. This greatly upset Luigi. He had been unable to sleep, eat, or work. He ranted on and on about this man taking away his beautiful wife. He stated that she denied any involvement with this man, but he remained convinced he was right. Luigi's plan to control his wife's behavior and win her back was to have sex with her three to four times a day.

Unfortunately, he was not as successful as he would have liked to have been with this plan. He wanted to send "his boys" to "take care of him." He said he wasn't going to have him killed, just send him to the hospital. Because Luigi had a history of drug running and other criminal activities and he was involved in "bloody clean-ups" (cleaning up murder and suicide scenes), I believed his statement to be a credible threat. I explained to him my duty to warn, and he told me he would give me the man's name and a two-day warning before he sent his boys to harm the man. We shook on his promise, and he agreed to return the next afternoon.

Being a bit taken aback by his threat, I called a lawyer who specialized in mental health issues. He stated that I did not need to call the police but that I should use my best clinical judgment in determining the strength of the client's word. I documented the phone consultation and also documented our handshake agreement. I truly believed Luigi would keep his word.

A few days later, Luigi and his wife came for a session. His beautiful wife was missing several teeth, had long, straight, greasy hair, and looked very tired. She assured me that Luigi did not have enough money to have the man killed, but he did have enough to have his limbs broken. I renewed my two-day warning handshake agreement with Luigi and left for vacation.

When I returned, I saw Luigi and his wife. The relationship appeared a lot less troubled, and she looked much more rested. Luigi reported that he had sent "his boys" to visit the man on the computer. As per our agreement, there was no physical contact. However, it appears that the man on the computer was so impressed by the visit that he acknowledged his romantic intentions and agreed to stop contacting Luigi's wife completely. I'm not sure what was said, but apparently the man received the message loud and clear. It appeared all was well with Luigi and his wife.

1. What are the ethical codes that are related to this client situation?

2. Would you have contacted the police to warn and protect?

3. Is there an alternative to the handshake agreement that you prefer?

Provided by Pam Nickels, PhD, LPC, private practitioner and adjunct professor, Webster University.

Duty to Warn Regarding Contagious and Life-Threatening Diseases

In the same category as duty to warn, counselors may also have a responsibility to the public when a client discloses having a life-threatening communicable disease. It is critical to recognize that the ethical code requires the disease be both communicable and life threatening. For example, syphilis is communicable but not traditionally considered life threatening in this day and age. In addition to what you can warn about, the act of duty to warn about a life-threatening disease is defined differently from state to state. Again, being familiar with your state's legal statutes is important. Once you understand your state laws around disclosure related to life-threatening diseases, ethical codes require that counselors attempt to verify that the client has the disease and assess the client's potential to spread it. You should seek to gain evidence of the client's contagion or disease and discuss with him or her ways to safeguard others from contracting the disease.

If the client commits to you that he or she will practice taking precautions around protecting others from contracting their disease seriously (and your state law permits it), the counselor does not have to break confidentiality related to the contagious disease. For example, a client may have tuberculosis but is being treated and avoiding vulnerable people. Or, a client has HIV and is not in a current sexual relationship. Furthermore, if the client has no names of potential victims (e.g., the client with HIV tells you that he or she has a habit of having unprotected sex with one-night stands and does not have names or contact information of those individuals), the counselor cannot break confidentiality. That said, it is the counselor's responsibility to attempt to persuade the client to protect others. Enacting duty to warn when it comes to life-threatening and contagious diseases is dependent on the law, the client's commitment to protect others from the disease, and the availability of a named target.

Ethical Code 7.4

B.2.c. Contagious, Life-Threatening Diseases.

When clients disclose that they have a disease commonly known to be both communicable and life threatening, counselors may be justified in disclosing information to identified third parties if the parties are known to be at serious and foreseeable risk of contracting the disease. Prior to making a disclosure, counselors assess the intent of clients to inform the third parties about their disease or to engage in any behaviors that may be harmful to an identified third party. Counselors adhere to relevant state laws concerning disclosure about disease status.

Source: 2014 American Counseling Association Code of Ethics. Reprinted with permission from American Counseling Association.

Professional "Sharing" (aka the Office Water-Cooler or Dinner-Table Discussion)

Who else is information shared with? Who do you de-stress with at the end of the day? Think about it. We come home from work, or we are out with our friends, and most of us want to engage in a little venting about the challenges of our work-day. While it is human nature to want to do this, it is important that counselors learn early the distinction of not sharing detailed client information (Welfel, 1998). Sharing parts of your day is normal. Talking about those events or items that impacted your day without providing any type of identifying information is acceptable. However, sharing details of client sessions and your resulting feelings, thoughts, dilemmas, or conclusions is unprofessional, inappropriate, and unfair to your client.

Of course, you have the outlet of a supervisor or treatment team to assist with those feelings, thoughts, and dilemmas. Your partner's or friends' responses could unduly influence your future actions with the client, and most partners or friends likely are not qualified to respond to your comments and concerns about your client; those who are should understand that any information you glean from your chat could be considered an official consultation. Most nonclinical professionals do not share the same interest in client details as the practicing counselor and are not qualified to be the consultant even if they do. Welfel (1998) has recommended more research in this area to determine how counselors can maintain intimacy and connection with their families regarding work events that may keep them late, distract them, or simply make up their day. After all, you are a person first then a counselor. However, communications and conversations regarding client session content should remain with other mental health professionals and in a setting that provides privacy.

Ethical Code 7.5

B.1.b. Respect for Privacy.

Counselors respect the privacy of prospective and current clients. Counselors request private information from clients only when it is beneficial to the counseling process.

Source: 2014 American Counseling Association Code of Ethics. Reprinted with permission from American Counseling Association.

Professional consultation with other clinical counseling professionals provides opportunities for us to share client issues and receive feedback. Treatment teams and regular clinical supervision are standard formats for consultation. Treatment teams typically occur in large practice or agency settings, while clinical supervision by a qualified expert is required for licensure. It is also a wise practice postlicensure, so we remain in the habit of receiving feedback on our treatment approaches and have a regularly scheduled opportunity to share client concerns. Consultation, treatment teams, and supervision should occur in a private setting out of the way of clients, hallway traffic, and other employees.

Ethical Code 7.6

B.3.b. Interdisciplinary Teams.

When services provided to the client involve participation by an interdisciplinary or treatment team, the client will be informed of the team's existence and composition, information being shared, and the purposes of sharing such information.

Source: 2014 American Counseling Association Code of Ethics. Reprinted with permission from American Counseling Association.

As you can imagine, there are occasions when nonclinical employees need to access confidential client records. In larger practice settings, for example, office staff often are required to maintain filing systems, organization, and office management. As a result, these individuals have the potential to view private client information. Administrators of such settings and counselors have the responsibility to regularly train staff on confidentiality practices of client information and then document the training (Barnett & Johnson, 2010). If staff breach confidentiality, the practice is responsible. While you cannot guarantee the behavior of every person who works in your practice, you can ensure that they are made aware of the expectations. Documented evidence of staff training on confidentiality practices will help to keep a practice ethical.

Ethical Code 7.7

B.3.a. Subordinates.

Counselors make every effort to ensure that privacy and confidentiality of clients are maintained by subordinates, including employees, supervisees, students, clerical assistants, and volunteers.

Source: 2014 American Counseling Association Code of Ethics. Reprinted with permission from American Counseling Association.

Ethical Code 7.8

B.3.c. Confidential Settings.

Counselors discuss confidential information only in settings in which they can reasonably ensure client privacy.

Source: 2014 American Counseling Association Code of Ethics. Reprinted with permission from American Counseling Association.

Practices Related to Minimal Disclosure

Ethical codes and state statutes concerning confidentiality require something known as minimal disclosure. Minimal disclosure means that counselors take precautions to provide only the information that is necessary to any inquiring authority or individual. There are exceptions to confidentiality, and counselors can breach it only when appropriate and in a manner that is ethical and acceptable per their state's laws. Not all states share the same confidentiality or privileged communications laws. When legal authorities such as courts require information and release of that information is appropriate in that state, counselors are cautioned by the ACA (2005) Code of Ethics to release only the content that is specific to the authority's request.

Ethical Code 7.9

B.2.e. Minimal Disclosure.

To the extent possible, clients are informed before confidential information is disclosed and are involved in the disclosure decision-making process. When circumstances require the disclosure of confidential information, only essential information is revealed.

Source: 2014 American Counseling Association Code of Ethics. Reprinted with permission from American Counseling Association.

But what should you do when you are required by law to share information? When required to disclose client information, the ethical code again advises that counselors disclose only the information that is necessary and only to approved recipients. Approved recipients often include judges, law officials, and specific allied health professionals working with the client. Counselors should not release records automatically just because a legal authority (attorney or police) has requested the information. They should make every attempt to retain a written release of information from the client when possible before releasing information (Barnett & Johnson, 2010; Bernstein & Hartsell, 2004; Welfel, 1998). Further, in the spirit of minimal disclosure, do not assume that a client's complete file must be released—only the information that is pertinent to the request and the situation should be released. Spontaneously turning over copies of complete files is unethical. It does not have the client's best interest in mind and could lead to a lawsuit for breach of contract (confidentiality) on the part of the counselor.

Consult with your attorney regarding the documents that have been served, even when you are served with a subpoena for information. States have varying and changing laws on disclosure. In some states, mental health counselors can be sued for disclosing information even when a subpoena has been issued. Cases that involve double reporting of child abuse, such as reporting suspected abuse to the authorities and then releasing information pursuant to a court order, could violate client confidentiality in some states (Pope & Vasquez, 1991). Counselors must understand the laws surrounding confidentiality and privilege in their state and use caution when agreeing to release information if they are to protect their clients and themselves.

As always, make sure you are working with your client whenever possible. Keeping the client informed of the process when records are ordered to be turned over is important for maintaining trust and the therapeutic relationship (Barnett & Johnson, 2010). Explaining the court order, related laws, and the information that is to be released and discussing the potential consequences of related actions with the client will keep him or her updated and involved in the process and communications with the authorities. This may help to strengthen the therapeutic relationship by providing the opportunity to counsel the client about the mandated disclosure. Keeping clients tied into the reporting process is part of a healthy counseling relationship.

Ethical Code 7.10

B.2.d. Court-Ordered Disclosure.

When ordered by a court to release confidential or privileged information without a client's permission, counselors seek to obtain written, informed consent from the client or take steps to prohibit the disclosure or have it limited as narrowly as possible because of potential harm to the client or counseling relationship.

Source: 2014 American Counseling Association Code of Ethics. Reprinted with permission from American Counseling Association.

Ethical Code 7.11

B.1.c. Respect for Confidentiality.

Counselors protect the confidential information of prospective and current clients. Counselors disclose information only with appropriate consent or with sound legal or ethical justification.

Source: 2014 American Counseling Association Code of Ethics. Reprinted with permission from American Counseling Association.

CONFIDENTIALITY AND SPECIFIC PRACTICES

As you have seen, confidentiality is imperative in a counselor's work with clients. However, the ways in which we maintain or break client confidentiality depend upon the situation. Specific practices that we will discuss in this section include supervision, death of the client or counselor, multiple individuals as the client, minors and those lacking capacity, research, and culture.

Under Supervision

Confidentiality pertains to clinical supervision. When the process of supervision requires that the supervisee's client information be shared with one or more professionals, how is confidentiality maintained in the clinical supervision process?

Critical to the concept of confidentiality in supervision is the process of informed consent regarding supervisee training. Supervisees are required by law in most states and by ethical code to disclose to the client during the informed consent process those persons with whom they will share client session content and that they are in training. Clients must understand that by the very nature of clinical supervision, the supervisee has to share sometimes very detailed client information that has been discussed in session. The sharing is with at least one supervisor (often two for the student in training) in weekly individual supervision (Blackwell, Strohmer, Belcas, & Burton, 2002; CACREP, 2009). Supervisees must make clear to the client that information also may be shared with a treatment team or up to 12 peer supervisees in group supervision when the supervisee is required to present cases via tape, case notes, treatment plans, and other points of learning. Clients can misunderstand the initial informed consent wherein the supervisees state that they are in training and therefore required to share important session information. Signed releases in the form of a written informed consent and permission to tape must be obtained from each client.

Ethical Code 7.12

F.1.a. Client Welfare.

A primary obligation of counseling supervisors is to monitor the services provided by supervisees. Counseling supervisors monitor client welfare and supervisee performance and professional development. To fulfill these obligations, supervisors meet regularly with supervisees to review the supervisees' work and help them become prepared to serve a range of diverse clients. Supervisees have a responsibility to understand and follow the ACA Code of Ethics.

Source: 2014 American Counseling Association Code of Ethics. Reprinted with permission from American Counseling Association.

Ethical Code 7.13

F.1.c. Informed Consent and Client Rights.

Supervisors make supervisees aware of client rights, including the protection of client privacy and confidentiality in the counseling relationship. Supervisees provide clients with professional disclosure information and inform them of how the supervision process influences the limits of confidentiality. Supervisees make clients aware of who will have access to records of the counseling relationship and how these records will be stored, transmitted, or otherwise reviewed.

Source: 2014 American Counseling Association Code of Ethics. Reprinted with permission from American Counseling Association.

Ethical Code 7.14

B.6.c. Permission to Record.

Counselors obtain permission from clients prior to recording sessions through electronic or other means.

Source: 2014 American Counseling Association Code of Ethics. Reprinted with permission from American Counseling Association.

Ethical Code 7.15

B.6.d. Permission to Observe.

Counselors obtain permission from clients prior to allowing any person to observe counseling sessions, review session transcripts, or view recordings of sessions with supervisors, faculty, peers, or others within the training environment.

Source: 2014 American Counseling Association Code of Ethics. Reprinted with permission from American Counseling Association.

When working with counselors under supervision, clients do not have a right to request that their information not be shared with a supervisor. However, the client does have the right to request a counselor who is not under supervision and not required to share information or receive a referral to an agency with available trained counselors. For the protection of the client, confidentiality cannot be exclusive to the client–counselor relationship when the counselor is in training. Nonetheless, sharing of information is required when consultation is necessary, and clients should be helped to understand that confidentiality cannot ever be guaranteed.

Death of Client or Counselor

Maintaining confidentiality extends past the death of the client or the counselor. Let's first look at the death of a client. Counselors have an ethical and, in most states, legal obligation to maintain confidentiality of a client's records after the client has passed away. Specifically, the rules that applied when the client was alive still apply after the client's death (Kaplan, 2006). Bernstein and Hartsell (2004) recommend that when facing the death of a client, a counselor should request that the court provide a ruling regarding who will have access to the client's records. This can take time, so counselors are advised to move quickly after a client passes or even before if the counselor is working with a terminally ill client.

Ethical Code 7.16

B.3.f. Deceased Clients.

Counselors protect the confidentiality of deceased clients consistently with legal requirements and the documented preferences of the client.

Source: 2014 American Counseling Association Code of Ethics. Reprinted with permission from American Counseling Association.

Now let's shift to the death of the counselor. Did you know you still are responsible for client confidentiality after your death? As hard as that may be to conceive, it is true! As mentioned in Chapter 6, counselors are advised to include content on the intake form regarding transfer of client files upon the death of the counselor (Bernstein & Hartsell, 2004; Wheeler & Bertram, 2012). In general, the counselor's executor or administrator has rights to all things owned by the counselor or that are disclosed in the counselor's will. However, most clients do not want a stranger (the executor or administrator) having access to their counseling files. Therefore, counselors should include on the intake form provisions for the distribution of client files in the case of the counselor's passing. This can include other counselors who are in a position to resume counseling with the client, such as a practice partner. Counselors may also choose to list recipients of client files in their will. Well-prepared counselors include on their intake form who will have access to client files in the case of the death of a client or the counselor and who will resume counseling in the case of the counselor passing.

Ethical Code 7.17

B.6.i. Reasonable Precautions.

Counselors take reasonable precautions to protect client confidentiality in the event of the counselor's termination of practice, incapacity, or death and appoint a records custodian when identified as appropriate.

Source: 2014 American Counseling Association Code of Ethics. Reprinted with permission from American Counseling Association.

A note on clients who wish to hasten their own deaths: In the recent edition of the ACA (2014) Code of Ethics, codes regarding hastening one's own death were eliminated due to strong professional opinions on both sides of the discussion. Trust is at the heart of the client–counselor relationship. When a counselor is considering maintaining or breaking confidentiality over a client's discussions of death, initial discussions should be with the client. Counselors are advised to seek consultation with legal experts to review local law related to right to die and confidentiality and to consult with other mental health professionals to examine related mental health ethical codes and the counselor's professional opinion regarding why they are choosing to break or maintain confidentiality. The right to hasten one's own death is a legal concept in most states, and the experienced counselor will consult with the client, legal, and professional experts.

When More Than One Person Is the Client

Counseling couples, families, and groups along with counseling that occurs over the Internet are situations that provide less-than-perfect settings for confidentiality. Clients need to be informed of who may have access to the notes and the primary ways in which confidentiality may not be kept (Berg, Landreth, & Fall, 2013; Wilcoxon, Remley, Gladding, & Huber, 2007). When the client is more than one person, for example, a group, family, or couple, it is important that the counselor make it clear to all members that confidentiality cannot be guaranteed. While we can guarantee that we will keep content private (within legal limits), we cannot make the same claim for others in the room. When counseling groups, it is important to enlist group thoughts regarding consequences for group members who break confidentiality. A group may want to permit a member who breaks confidentiality to remain in the group but to respond to confrontation regarding the breach. Conversely, the group may want the member dismissed from the group. Group leaders also will want to remind members at the start of each meeting of the limits to confidentiality (Berg et al., 2003).

Similarly, when counseling couples, we must discuss the nature of confidentiality with both partners. You may want to maintain separate files with a couple: one for the couple and one for each partner (Corey et al., 2011). At the very least, you should avoid mentioning counseling content related only to one partner in the other's file. Remember that these files may be subpoenaed years after counseling ends and that individuals should have access only to their content, not the content of another family member. Minimizing what is kept in case notes is always important and becomes emphasized when working with couples. As you can imagine, content that can be incriminating to one partner should be avoided.

Ethical Code 7.18

B.6.e. Client Access.

Counselors provide reasonable access to records and copies of records when requested by competent clients. Counselors limit the access of clients to their records, or portions of their records, only when there is compelling evidence that such access would cause harm to the client. Counselors document the request of clients and the rationale for withholding some or all of the record in the files of clients. In situations involving multiple clients, counselors provide individual clients with only those parts of records that relate directly to them and do not include confidential information related to any other client.

Source: 2014 American Counseling Association Code of Ethics. Reprinted with permission from American Counseling Association.

Counseling that occurs over the Internet has multiple opportunities for the loss of confidentiality. Anyone other than the client who has access to the client's computer may be able to view conversations between the counselor and client. The potential for hackers and for the client or counselor to send information to the wrong e-mail address is always a risk. Who hasn't sent the accidental, hopefully non-incriminating, text to the wrong person? The same mistakes can happen with e-mail. The Health Insurance Portability and Accountability Act (HIPAA, 2010) contains regulations pertaining to the privacy of electronically stored and retrieved client health care information. The rules change regularly, and counselors are cautioned to stay abreast of HIPAA, retain appropriate forms, and keep computer software and systems in compliance.

When more than one individual participates in a counseling session, the counselor cannot guarantee confidentiality and should regularly remind client members of that.

Minors and Those Lacking Capacity

There are basic protocols that apply when addressing confidentiality and minors and those who lack the capacity to provide consent. Much of this was covered in our discussion in Chapter 6. In general, all rights that protect children also protect those who have been declared as incompetent by the courts (Remley & Herlihy, 2014). When working with children and those lacking capacity, counselors should enlist the cooperation of the parents or guardian and collaborate with them. It is critical that we explain the roles and rights of those involved in the counseling process in the initial session and in written informed consent. Parents and guardians should be helped to understand the importance of confidentiality in the counseling relationship and process to understand the significance of taking a backseat to the counseling process of the minor when appropriate. We can help parents and guardians to understand and to trust that we will share information with the parent or guardian when we believe sharing will assist in the client's progress.

Ethical Code 7.19

B.6.f. Assistance With Records.

When clients request access to their records, counselors provide assistance and consultation in interpreting counseling records.

Source: 2014 American Counseling Association Code of Ethics. Reprinted with permission from American Counseling Association.

If session content must be shared with parents, it may be therapeutic for the minor to assist in the sharing of the information. At the very least, minors should be made aware that information will be shared. Counselors can brainstorm options with minors for sharing the information. Remley and Herlihy (2014) mention several options, including the counselor sharing the information with the minor in the room, the minor sharing the information with the counselor in the room, or the minor or the counselor sharing the information when the other is not in the room or when not in session. Regardless of method, minors should be part of the decision to break confidentiality.

As we have discussed, counselors always have a responsibility to consider the cultural context of a client. This responsibility is emphasized with minors because of the parent–child relationship. These relationships differ depending on culture. For example, families from collectivist cultures value interdependence within the family. As such, these parents and guardians may not value confidentiality in the counseling process and may seek to be involved heavily in treatment and decision making of their children and relatives. We must collaborate with these families and work with the client's assent and preferences while balancing the family's requests and the law.

Ethical Code 7.20

B.5.b. Responsibility to Parents and Legal Guardians.

Counselors inform parents and legal guardians about the role of counselors and the confidential nature of the counseling relationship. Counselors are sensitive to the cultural diversity of families and respect the inherent rights and responsibilities of parents/guardians over the welfare of their children/charges according to law. Counselors work to establish, as appropriate, collaborative relationships with parents/guardians to best serve clients.

Source: 2014 American Counseling Association Code of Ethics. Reprinted with permission from American Counseling Association.

When determining when to break confidentiality of minor clients, counselors have to consider several factors. When does one break confidentiality? With whom is the information shared? What if the parents are separated and in a custody battle? What if a parent demands information that the counselor deems it unnecessary to share or even potentially harmful to the client to share? What if the client derives from a more collectivist culture that disregards confidentiality of the individual? Who should sign the release of information form?

For these and other concerns related to the confidentiality of a minor or client lacking capacity, we must be familiar with the related laws and statutes in the state in which treatment is occurring. State laws pertaining to the mental health care of children vary widely. The age that is considered minor also varies. Although minors and those lacking capacity are not able to provide consent to treatment in most cases, at all times these special clients should be provided the opportunity to assent to treatment (Recupero & Rainey, 2005). Competent counselors will integrate these clients' preferences and best interests into the treatment plan (Fisher & Oransky, 2008), and informed consent should be provided at a level that the client can comprehend. We have a responsibility to involve all clients in their treatment. Every decision must have the autonomy and beneficence of the client in mind.

Ethical Code 7.21

B.5.a. Responsibility to Clients.

When counseling minor clients or adult clients who lack the capacity to give voluntary, informed consent, counselors protect the confidentiality of information received—in any medium—in the counseling relationship as specified by federal and state laws, written policies, and applicable ethical standards.

Source: 2014 American Counseling Association Code of Ethics. Reprinted with permission from American Counseling Association.

Ethical Code 7.22

B.5.c. Release of Confidential Information.

When counseling minor clients or adult clients who lack the capacity to give voluntary consent to release confidential information, counselors seek permission from an appropriate third party to disclose information. In such instances, counselors inform clients consistent with their level of understanding and take culturally appropriate measures to safeguard client confidentiality.

Source: 2014 American Counseling Association Code of Ethics. Reprinted with permission from American Counseling Association.

Research and Publications

There are a number of ethical codes that relate to research and publications, but certainly those regarding confidentiality deserve our scrutiny. Many of you have been in classes and heard stories or read case studies—such as those in this text—that are rooted in real client stories. Counselors and counselor educators who share their clients' stories in published manuscripts have an ethical obligation to receive written permission from the client to disclose their story or change enough of the details of the client's story to protect their identity (Bridges, 2010; Welfel, 1998; Woodhouse, 2012).

Woodhouse discusses three potential negative side effects of using client stories in our writing as a factor of research or method of education. First, how does a clinician-researcher disguise information enough that clients cannot identify themselves while simultaneously not disrupting the integrity of the story or lesson? Second, if clients read their stories as written by their counselor, how does it impact the client–counselor relationship? Finally, how does the act of writing about a client affect the public's perception of counseling and confidentiality?

What we have learned is that, for the most part, seeking client consent prior to including his or her story in a manuscript, enabling the client to read the manuscript, and then processing the story with the client prior to publication actually can provide a therapeutic tool when attended to carefully (Bridges, 2010). Working through the story from the counselor's perspective may help clients to hear a perspective that they do not hear in session. Recent research in neuroscience also points to catharsis and healing being more apt to occur when clients process information on a cognitive level while also writing, reading, and discussing it (Berg et al., 2013). Benefits aside, it is critical to change enough identifying information of the client that the client cannot be identified by readers or audience members of a presentation regardless of how cathartic the telling of the story is (Bernstein & Hartsell, 2004). The counselor must change enough information to maintain the confidentiality of the client without losing the point of the shared story.

Ethical Code 7.23

G.2.d. Confidentiality of Information.

Information obtained about research participants during the course of research is confidential. Procedures are implemented to protect confidentiality.

Source: 2014 American Counseling Association Code of Ethics. Reprinted with permission from American Counseling Association.

Ethical Code 7.24

G.l.e. Precautions to Avoid Injury.

Counselors who conduct research with human participants are responsible for the welfare of participants throughout the research process and should take reasonable precautions to avoid causing emotional, physical, or social harm to participants.

Source: 2014 American Counseling Association Code of Ethics. Reprinted with permission from American Counseling Association.

When data collection and the development of a manuscript are completed and the study or story is published, the researcher has the ethical responsibility to destroy all records. Students, educators, and clinicians participating in writing that includes information from counseling sessions or related confidential information are required by code and typically also by their institutions to destroy all data that may be considered of a private nature. Cleaning off computer drives is also important and sometimes forgotten. Students must ensure that their digital recorders are erased. An appropriate time frame for destroying confidential records and data is approximately 1 to 14 days following acceptance for publication.

Ethical Code 7.25

B.l.a. Multicultural/Diversity Considerations.

Counselors maintain awareness and sensitivity regarding cultural meanings of confidentiality and privacy. Counselors respect differing views toward disclosure of information. Counselors hold ongoing discussions with clients as to how, when, and with whom information is to be shared.

Source: 2014 American Counseling Association Code of Ethics. Reprinted with permission from American Counseling Association.

CONFIDENTIALITY, CULTURE, AND CONTEXT

As discussed in the section about confidentiality with minors, a client's culture must be attended to when addressing confidentiality. Some cultures prefer that family be involved in any decision making or goal of therapy. Latino and Asian cultures tend to be collectivist in lifestyle, meaning that they value decisions being made by the family or those who are close to the client (Robinson Wood, 2012). They often view the immediate family, and sometimes extended family, as being part of the decision-making process (McGoldrick, Giordano, & Garcia-Preto, 2005). The client may expect the counselor to invite family members to participate in some sessions, and the family may expect to be involved in some sessions. In these instances, confidentiality is still present. Yet, the definition of the client may have shifted from the individual who initially arrived for treatment to the family who supports that individual. The family is viewed as the client, and confidentiality is maintained among members. Nevertheless, counselors should use an approach similar to that of informed consent and check for client understanding around inviting in family members and sharing of information and the session.

Confidentiality among family members can become complicated for a counselor. All members involved in counseling that involves more than one individual are expected to maintain others' confidentiality. Just like with counseling groups, we no longer have ultimate control over shared information in family counseling because we do not have control over members of the family and the information they may expose. The risk for loss of confidentiality is increased when family members become involved. Therefore it is helpful to remind members regularly of the importance of confidentiality to the success of counseling with their loved one.

RECORD KEEPING

Confidentiality also pertains to the protection of written client records and to keeping those records out of the reach of unauthorized individuals. Bernstein and Hartsell (2004) recommend that counselors protect client records by maintaining documents under two different methods of lock. As an example, counselors can place their records in a locked filing drawer (method 1) that is kept in a locked office (method 2). Keeping records locked also ensures no one walks off with a record unintentionally. It is essential that only individuals who need access to client records have such. When we are talking about records, we are not just talking about case notes. Any written information about the client, including scheduling and billing, are considered client records and are to be protected.

It is good business for counseling agencies and practices to have a written policy delineating who may access client records. While most staff need to view client records at different times, not all staff will need to have open access to records. For example, volunteer staff likely will not require access to records. Clerical staff may assist in record storage, but they typically do not need access to client session notes. Supervisees, students, and counselors will maintain the records and need to review them but only of the clients they serve. Ultimately, conscientious care of the client record is critical.

Agencies and counseling practices also have a duty to provide ongoing training to staff on the protection of client records (Barnett & Johnson, 2010). Vigilance about how records are cared for is important and is another step to safeguarding the practice. Noticing how staff treat records—even simply retrieving from and replacing back into file drawers—should be managed. Client records should not be left out to be filed later or left on a counter for the next staff who needs to review the record. You may have noticed that at your physician's office, for example, patient records are placed on the door for the doctor to retrieve on the way into the room. That would not be acceptable in a counseling practice where anyone could wander by and read a confidential record. Ensuring that all employees of a counseling site understand the concept of confidentiality and the components of good record keeping is paramount to ethical practice.

Ethical Code 7.26

B.3.a. Subordinates.

Counselors make every effort to ensure that privacy and confidentiality of clients are maintained by subordinates, including employees, supervisees, students, clerical assistants, and volunteers.

Source: 2014 American Counseling Association Code of Ethics. Reprinted with permission from American Counseling Association.

Ethical Code 7.27

B.6. Creating and Maintaining Records and Documentation.

Counselors create and maintain records and documentation necessary for rendering professional services.

Source: 2014 American Counseling Association Code of Ethics. Reprinted with permission from American Counseling Association.

Ethical Code 7.28

B.6.b. Confidentiality of Records.

Counselors ensure that records and documentation kept in any medium are secure and that only authorized persons have access to them.

Source: 2014 American Counseling Association Code of Ethics. Reprinted with permission from American Counseling Association.

Because this chapter contains so many practical tips related to confidentiality and record keeping, we are including a suggested practices section for your reference. This list includes recommended practices gathered from this chapter. You may use it as a checklist and summarization of the application steps of the information provided in this chapter.

CONCLUSION

Having been introduced to informed consent in the previous chapter, you now have been informed of the importance of confidentiality and the protection of client welfare. Decisions about confidentiality and record keeping are some of the most common challenges to counselors throughout their careers. It will be important to refer to the concepts and suggested best practices presented in this chapter as you approach these challenging decisions in your own practice.

KEYSTONES

- Confidentiality is an assumed component of any healthy and efficacious counseling relationship.
- Because there are limitations as to when the content of a session is kept private, counselors should become familiar with their state's laws pertaining to confidentiality, privilege, and privacy.
- If a counselor discloses something that a client stated in session to a third party without receiving permission from the client to disclose the information, the counselor is in violation of ethical codes and, in some cases, state law pertaining to confidentiality.
- Before breaking confidentiality, seek consultation from other professionals who have expertise in the area of concern if you are uncertain regarding whether to break confidentiality. Implement procedures that are common practice in the field of professional counseling. Document all steps and the rationale behind each step.
- Delineating those occasions when confidentiality may be breached must occur in the initial informed consent with clients and throughout additional sessions if something that needs to be disclosed arises.
- When confidentiality must be broken, it is best done by discussing related reasons and the process that will occur with clients.
- When legal authorities such as courts require information, and release of that information is appropriate in that state, counselors are cautioned by the ACA (2014) Code of Ethics to release only the content that is specific to the authority's request.

- Counseling couples, families, and groups and counseling that occurs over the Internet are situations that provide less-than-perfect settings for confidentiality. Clients need to be informed of who may have access to the notes and the primary ways in which confidentiality may not be kept.
- Confidentiality also applies to written client records. Client records must be protected from all unauthorized individuals.

SUGGESTED BEST PRACTICES

- Develop an address book (electronic or in print) with contacts in various counseling specialties, including counselors who have expertise in working with specialized types of clients for referral and consultation purposes. Specialties may include those who treat violent clients, clients from particular cultures, clergy, and any other type of client that may not be considered typical in practice.
- Know the duty to warn and protect laws in your state.
- When requesting a professional consult from a colleague, ensure you have stated up front that this is a professional consult, so they understand the information could be subpoenaed.
- Know your state laws around confidentiality, privileged communication, and privacy.
- Learn and use an actual EDM delineated in the literature.
- Document all consultations.
- Document each action and the reason why you took it.
- Protect client information in all possible situations except when harm of self or another is imminent (or other limits of confidentiality listed in Table 7.1).
- Include in your informed consent regarding when client information is shared and to whom.
- Be clear with clients about the limits of confidentiality when the client numbers more than one individual, for example, groups, families, or couples.
- Include in your practices and actions those practices that are common among mental health professionals in your field (standard of care).
- Attend risk management seminars frequently enough to keep up with changing laws, HIPAA, and ethical codes related to technology and confidentiality.
- Understand laws and ethical practice regarding documentation.
- Train staff on your practice's record-keeping policies.

ADDITIONAL RESOURCES

In Print

Hartsell, T. L., Jr., & Bernstein, B. E. (2008). *The portable ethicist for mental health professionals: A complete guide to responsible practice* (2nd ed.). Hoboken, NJ: John Wiley & Sons.

On the Web

Child Welfare Information Gateway. (n.d.). *U.S. Department of Health and Human Services.* Retrieved from https://www.childwelfare.gov/topics/systemwide/laws-policies/state/

Health Providers Service Organization (HSPO). (n.d.). Retrieved from http://www.hpso.com/newsletter12

Risk Management. (n.d.). ACA. Retrieved from http://www.counseling.org/knowledge-center/ethics/risk-management

REFERENCES

American Counseling Association (ACA). (2005). *ACA code of ethics.* Retrieved from http://www.counseling.org/resources/codeofethics/TP/home/ct2.aspx

ACA. (2014). *ACA code of ethics.* Alexandria, VA: Author.

Barnett, J. E., & Johnson, W. B. (2010). *Ethics desk reference for counselors.* Alexandria, VA: American Counseling Association.

Berg, R. C., Landreth, G. L., & Fall, K. A. (2013). *Group counseling: Concepts and procedures* (5th ed.). New York: Routledge.

Bernstein, B. E., Hartsell, T. L., Jr. (2004). *The portable lawyer for mental health professionals: An A-Z guide to protecting your clients, your practice and yourself* (2nd ed.). Hoboken, NJ: John Wiley & Sons.

Blackwell, T. L., Strohmer, D. C., Belcas, E. M., & Burton, K. A. (2002). Ethics in rehabilitation counselor supervision. *Rehabilitation Counseling Bulletin, 45*(4), 240–247. doi:10.1177/00343552020450040701

Bridges, N. A. (2010). Clinical writing about clients: Seeking consent and negotiating the impact on clients and their treatments. *Counseling and Values, 54,* 103–116. doi:10.1002/j.2161–007X.2010.tb00009.x

Corey, G., Corey, M. S., & Callahan, P. (2011). *Issues and ethics in the helping professions* (8th ed.). Belmont, CA: Brooks/Cole.

Council for the Accreditation of Counseling & Related Educational Programs (CACREP). (2009). *CACREP Standards, 2009.* Retrieved from http://www.cacrep.org/wp-content/uploads/2013/12/2009-Standards.pdf

Daniels, J. (2001). Managed care, ethics, and counseling. *Journal of Counseling & Development, 79*(1), 119–122. doi:10.1002/j.1556–6676.2001.tb01950.x

Fisher, C. B., & Oransky, M. (2008). Informed consent to psychotherapy: Protecting the dignity and respecting the autonomy of patients. *Journal of Clinical Psychology, 64*(5), 576–588. doi:10.1002/jclp.20472

Health Insurance Portability and Accountability Act of 1996, 42 U.S.C. § 1320d-9 (2010).

Henning, S. L., Martz, E., Walsh, M., Henderson, K., Perkins, G., & Bonfini, J. (2012, March). *Current trends in ethics: A discussion with the ACA Ethics Committee.* Paper presented at the American Counseling Association Conference, San Francisco.

Kaplan, D. (2006). *Obligations for protecting the confidentiality of the deceased.* Retrieved from http://ct.counseling.org/2006/10/ct-online-ethics-update-5/

McGoldrick, M., Giordano, J., & Garcia-Preto, N. (Eds.). (2005). *Ethnicity and family therapy* (3rd ed.). New York: Guilford.

Pope, K. S., & Vasquez, M. J. (1991). *Ethics in psychotherapy and counseling: A practical guide for psychologists.* San Francisco: Jossey-Bass.

Recupero, P. R., & Rainey, S. E. (2005). Informed consent to E-therapy. *American Journal of Psychotherapy, 59*(4), 319–331. Retrieved from http://search.ebscohost.com/login.aspx?direct=true&db=psyh&09701–003&site=ehost-live

Remley, T. P., & Herlihy, B. (2014). *Ethical, legal, and professional issues in counseling* (4th ed.). Upper Saddle River, NJ: Pearson/Merrill Prentice Hall.

Robinson Wood, T. (2012). *The convergence of race, ethnicity, and gender* (4th ed.). Upper Saddle River, NJ: Pearson Merrill Prentice Hall.

Sutton. (2001). Tarasoff v. Regents of University of California, 131 Cal. Rptr. 14 (1976).

Welfel, E. R. (1998). *Ethics in counseling and psychotherapy: Standards, research, and emerging issues.* Pacific Grove, CA: Brooks/Cole.

Wheeler, A. M. N., & Bertram, B. (2012). *The counselor and the law: A guide to legal and ethical practice* (6th ed.). Alexandria, VA: American Counseling Association.

Wilcoxon, S. A., Remley, T. P., Jr., Gladding, S. T., & Huber, C. H. (2007). *Ethical, legal, and professional issues in the practice of marriage and family therapy* (4th ed.). Upper Saddle River, NJ: Pearson/Merrill Prentice Hall.

Woodhouse, S. S. (2012). *Clinical writing: Additional ethical and practical issues. Psychotherapy, 49(*1), 22–25. doi:10.1037/a0026965

Chapter 8

ETHICAL DECISION MAKING AND MANAGING PROFESSIONAL BOUNDARIES

James is a math teacher for the local high school and has been a client in Daniel's private practice for two years. James and Daniel have a strong, professional therapeutic relationship. Due to James's recent divorce and child support payments, he is struggling to make ends meet and is having difficulty affording his $45 per session co-pay for counseling. With all of the transitions in his life, James recognizes how urgently he needs to remain in counseling. He remembers that Daniel's son Jonathan attends the local junior high. At a recent session, James discloses to Daniel his struggle with finances and offers math tutoring to Daniel's son in exchange for counseling sessions. Even though Daniel has not shared this with James, his son Jonathan is struggling with math and could benefit greatly from additional tutoring. Daniel recognizes that he would save quite a bit of money by not having to pay an outside tutor to help his son. Daniel considers his client's offer to barter services. What should Daniel do?

CHAPTER OVERVIEW

This chapter will help the reader examine the challenges that are presented with what is commonly known as dual relationships, multiple relationships, or managing professional boundaries. Boundaries foster trust and maintain the integrity of the counseling relationship. This chapter will review the benefits and risks involved when extending the role of the counselor. Regardless of counseling experience or the setting in which a professional works, all counselors will face ethical conundrums related to maintaining professionalism while encountering challenges to how we form and maintain boundaries with clients, supervisees, and other stakeholders. Counselors have varying perspectives about when and if to engage in a multiple relationship with a client or former client.

LEARNING OBJECTIVES

After reading this chapter you will be able to do the following:

1. Evaluate when dual or multiple relationships are and are not appropriate.

2. Employ ethical decision-making skills in managing boundaries.

3. Utilize an ethical decision-making model (EDM) when considering engaging in boundary extensions.

4. Apply cultural and contextual considerations to the ethical decision-making process regarding boundary structure.

CACREP STANDARDS

CACREP Core Standards

G.1.j. Ethical standards of professional organizations and credentialing bodies, and applications of ethical and legal considerations in professional counseling.

CACREP Clinical Mental Health Standards

A.2. Understands the ethical and legal considerations specifically related to the practice of clinical mental health counseling.

B.1. Demonstrates the ability to apply and adhere to ethical and legal standards in clinical mental health counseling.

INTRODUCTION

Almost every aspect of our daily lives is structured by boundaries. Imagine a world where no boundaries existed and the implications that might have. Let's consider driving, for example. There are numerous boundaries that exist when it comes to driving a car. There are typically lines on the road indicating which side of the road to drive on. There are stop signs and traffic signals that drivers must obey. These markers, signs, and signals are forms of boundaries. They guide us in moving our vehicles from place to place, promote safety on the road, and ensure that order is maintained and that people are not harmed. All of that seems perfectly normal, right?

Now consider this: What if there were no boundaries in driving—no signals, stop signs, lines on the road, or speed limits? Things would become pretty chaotic to say the least, and most likely, there would be many crashes and injuries on the road because drivers would not follow the same rules and expectations—everyone would drive however and wherever they wanted.

Another example of boundaries is social etiquette. There are unwritten and unspoken rules and boundaries that people maintain. For example, it would be an inappropriate boundary violation for a stranger to walk up to someone else's table at a restaurant and begin eating his or her food. We also find it inappropriate to hug people we don't know or are not introduced to. Not conforming to societal boundaries or managing our relationships with strangers, as well as friends, family members, and coworkers, could result in hurt feelings, discomfort, as well as potential harm.

As vital as it is to have boundaries on the road and in social interactions, it is equally important to have boundaries in our professional relationships. In the following section we will explore the boundaries that exist between clients and counselors and how to manage them ethically and appropriately.

PROFESSIONAL BOUNDARIES

The ethics literature stresses the importance of knowing the various terms that are used in understanding professional boundaries in counseling as well as the nuances and perspectives each term carries with it (Herlihy & Corey, 2015; Jungers & Gregoire, 2013). The following are some of the terms you may encounter when considering this topic: dual relationships, multiple relationships, boundary crossings, and boundary extensions. A dual or multiple relationship occurs when a counselor engages in a professional counseling–related relationship with a client, student, supervisee, research participant, or other professional stakeholder while simultaneously engaging in a nonprofessional relationship with the same person (Corey, Corey, Corey, & Callahan, 2015; Kitchener & Anderson, 2011). In other words, multiple or dual relationships occur when we hold two or more roles with an individual at the same time. The overlap also can be between two professional roles, such as instructor and counselor. Many counselors traditionally have been wary about engaging in multiple relationships with clients because of the potential for the appearance of abuse of power that is inherent in the role of the professional counselor.

Types of Boundaries

Houser and Thoma (2013) outline four types of boundaries related to being a professional counselor: counselor social boundaries, psychological boundaries, financial boundaries, and counselor physical boundaries. Counselor social boundaries involve relationships that may occur in a social context, such as casual contact outside of the professional counseling office. Technology and social media are other examples where a counselor may post personal information about family members, vacations, and so on, that can be visible to clients. Clearly, social boundaries could be crossed through these means. Psychological boundaries include issues of counselor self-disclosure and how much information, if any, we should ethically share with a client within the therapeutic relationship. Financial boundaries involve how we structure things like establishing fees and payments for counseling services, decisions on a sliding fee scale process, engaging in bartering or not, and handling client nonpayment of services. The next boundary for consideration is counselor physical boundaries. Examples of these include a counselor having a sexual or intimate relationship with a client or other forms of physical contact between them, such as hugging and other forms of nonsexual touch. Physical boundaries also can involve home-based therapy or having a counseling session outside of the traditional counseling office.

We would like to add a fifth boundary for consideration—emotional boundaries. Emotional boundaries revolve around ways counselors manage the sensitive range of emotions we experience in and out of sessions about clients and clients' experiences. As empathic humans, we are impacted by the relationship with the client. For example, an emotional boundary may involve having protective feelings toward a client, which may be healthy in situations where the client needs protection. However these feelings also could be a form of unresolved countertransference and be more about us as counselors than about the client.

There is also what is referred to as the "slippery slope" of dual or multiple relationships (Corey et al., 2015; Jungers & Gregoire, 2013). The premise of the slippery slope is that once a counselor dips a proverbial toe into the water of blurring professional boundaries, even on what may appear to be an insignificant level, there is a strong potential for serious breaches of ethical conduct. These breaches potentially could bring harm to the counseling relationship. It is incumbent on us as professional counselors to monitor ourselves and maintain boundaries that reflect a high standard of ethical practice and uphold the welfare and dignity of our clients (Corey et al., 2015; Kitchener & Anderson, 2011). All of these issues are important considerations when it comes to managing boundaries in professional counseling.

Managing Boundaries

At times, having a multiple relationship with a client may be unplanned and spontaneous, such as running into a client unexpectedly at a party or other social gathering. Other times, engaging in a multiple relationship with a client may be an intentional, purposeful decision that aids the client in meeting therapeutic goals, such as a mental health counselor who also serves as a basketball coach for the same student–basketball player at a local high school. Some counselors may take the professional stance of "once a client, always a client," meaning that they choose never to engage in a social or personal relationship with a client or former client outside of the counseling relationship. Other professionals, recognizing the unique circumstances that exist when counseling certain cultural populations or counseling clients in rural or other geographic locations, need to display therapeutic flexibility in their understanding of how to frame professional boundaries and may choose to engage in a simultaneous relationship with a current or former client. What might be a healthy, professional, and ethical boundary extension in one case may be extremely unethical and unwarranted in another case. In other words, there are no perfectly right choices for every occasion. The client, the counselor, and the context weigh heavily in the decision making.

When determining if it is appropriate to engage in a boundary extension with a client, counselors should consult the professional codes of ethics, examine current legal considerations and precedence, review relevant counseling scholarship on the subject, and consult with supervisors or colleagues who have experience managing multiple boundaries in a professional setting. We also must reflect on the motivation for engaging in a multiple relationship or boundary extension. Why do you think it is a good idea? The primary goal should remain what is in the best interest of the client, not what may be self-serving or beneficial to you as a professional counselor (Gutheil & Brodksy, 2008).

We must recognize the various levels of complexity when it comes to managing professional boundaries. For example, when developing an informed consent form for clients or guardians, it is important not to have rigid rules and expectations that leave little room for therapeutic flexibility. To explore your approach to the levels of ethical complexity, you are encouraged to complete the Guided Practice Exercise 8.1 and discuss it with your peers and, if in a class, your instructor. Discuss what influences your self-ranking and what clinical situations might change your rating.

Guided Practice Exercise 8.1

Managing Professional Boundaries Reflection

Rate yourself on a scale of 1 to 10, identifying the level of comfort you self-identify in the following scenarios (with 1 being extremely uncomfortable and 10 being extremely comfortable).

Item	Self-Score
Accepting a cup of coffee from a client at the start of an early-morning session (you haven't had your morning coffee yet).	
Purchasing Girl Scout cookies from a minor client.	
Taking a walk outside with a client during a counseling session.	
Attending a wedding of a client.	
Attending the funeral of a client.	
Visiting a client in the hospital.	
Hugging a grieving client in a counseling session who is sobbing after experiencing the death of a parent.	
Being Facebook friends with a former client.	
Self-disclosing to a client about personal struggles with anxiety and depression as a way to normalize those issues for the client.	
Being invited to a one-time family celebration at a client's home.	
Attending the same church, synagogue, or mosque as a client.	
Having a social relationship or friendship with a parent of a student in the school where you are a school adjustment counselor.	
Hiring a former client (who is an out-of-work carpenter) to build a bookcase for your office.	
Accompanying a client who is dealing with agoraphobia to a concert. (It is the client's first public event in a decade.)	
Giving a client from your therapy group a ride home because his or her car broke down.	
Attending the same dance club as a client (you know the client frequents this same club, and you will see him or her often).	
You live in a small town; there is only one mechanic. The mechanic requests that you provide counseling to his or her child. (You are the only counselor in the town who works with children.)	

Section A.6. in the American Counseling Association (ACA,2014) Code of Ethics provides specific ethical guidance when it comes to managing and maintaining boundaries and professional relationships in counseling. As counselors we have an obligation to reflect on the nature of our past relationships when considering taking on new clients or engaging in any type of formal, professional role with individuals we have had more personal, social, or even casual or distant relationships with, including shared memberships in clubs or organizations.

Ethical Code 8.1

A.6.a. Previous Relationships.

Counselors consider the risks and benefits of accepting as clients those with whom they have had a previous relationship. These potential clients may include individuals with whom the counselor has had a casual, distant, or past relationship. Examples include mutual or past membership in a professional association, organization, or community. When counselors accept these clients, they take appropriate professional precautions such as informed consent, consultation, supervision, and documentation to ensure that judgment is not impaired and no exploitation occurs.

Source: 2014 American Counseling Association Code of Ethics. Reprinted with permission from American Counseling Association.

The ethical standards in the ACA Code of Ethics repeatedly state in Section A.6. that counselors examine both the risks and benefits of engaging in boundary extensions. Note that the standard focuses on the risks and areas of concern but also states that it is equally critical for counselors to examine the potential benefits to the client when engaging in boundary extensions. If the risks outweigh the benefits, the choice should begin to become clearer.

CASE STUDY 8.1

Julie, age 47, is a mental health counselor who has held a private practice in her community for the past seven years. Julie purposely has worked to create a private practice that specializes in serving the lesbian, gay, bisexual, and transgender (LGBT) community. She enjoys her work with clients and strives to create a healthy balance between her therapy work and her personal life. She devotes time to her family, volunteers for a local literacy program with at-risk youth, and is very active

(Continued)

(Continued)

in the local chapter of the Human Rights Campaign (HRC), a national LGBT political organization. She holds the position of fund-raising and developments cochair in her city for the local HRC chapter.

Julie has been working with her client Meghan, age 42, for a little longer than a year. Meghan recently is divorced (with no children) and has moved to the area as a way to begin a new life as an out lesbian. Meghan has experienced some depression as a result of the divorce and is coming out of a physically and emotionally abusive relationship. She has been isolating herself and is not getting to know her neighbors. She also has been hesitant to get involved in her community. Through their work together, Julie has tried to help Meghan work on her goal of reaching out and creating a strong support system for herself in the lesbian community. Julie has not shared with Meghan about her personal community involvement in HRC, although they briefly (and appropriately) have discussed her family (due to the fact that Julie has pictures of her partner and kids in her office). Julie has talked with Meghan over the past few months about ways to ease her depression through engagement in some type of group or community event.

A few weeks later, Julie is facilitating a meeting of the fund-raising committee for the HRC. It is the first committee meeting of the fall, focusing on an upcoming fund-raising event. New members were encouraged to join the fund-raising committee. Julie arrives early to help organize information and welcome old friends back to the committee when Meghan walks in the room. Both look a bit surprised and caught off guard. Julie does not approach Meghan but briefly smiles at her, welcoming other new members and encouraging everyone to pick up a name tag. Meghan begins talking to other members of the fund-raising committee. While Julie is a bit flustered by Meghan's appearance at the meeting, as cochair of the committee, she continues with her leadership role throughout the meeting. It is evident that Meghan has already made some connections with new group members and returning members. Julie and Meghan do not speak at all before, during, or after the committee meeting.

Julie is preparing for her upcoming session with Meghan. This will be the first session since seeing one another at the meeting.

1. *How should Julie prepare for her next session with Meghan? What should Julie address in her next counseling appointment?*

2. *What are the ethical issues in this scenario? What ethical standards from the code of ethics apply to this case?*

3. *What are the risks and benefits of Julie and Meghan both being a part of the same organization?*

In older versions of the ACA Code of Ethics, dual relationships, which is sometimes still seen in the ethics literature, was viewed as something to avoid at all costs. However, due to issues faced regularly by counselors practicing in rural areas, as well as those who specialize in working with certain cultural populations, avoiding these boundary crossings is next to impossible. Even the language found in the ethics literature, as well as our professional code of ethics has evolved. For example, language that previously instructed us to avoid dual relationships has changed to the term *boundary extension,* which places greater emphasis on the way in which we examine professional boundaries. Let's further explore this with a case example.

Case Example

Phil is a licensed professional counselor at a mental health–counseling agency in his small town where he has been practicing for 13 years. His primary clinical focus is working with children and adolescents. He is also a volunteer basketball coach for the local high school. He has been volunteering as a coach for the past five years. Recently, Phil started counseling Brad, a 14-year-old sophomore at the same high school where Phil coaches. Brad has been struggling with depression for the past six months due to the sudden death of his father, who suffered a fatal heart attack. Brad is the oldest of three children and is afraid to discuss his grief with his mother because he believes he needs to be the "man of the house" and take care of his mom and younger siblings. Brad reports to Phil that he does not want to burden his mom with his own grief and instead, focuses on getting good grades and working a part-time job to help the family make ends meet.

However, over the past few weeks Phil notices that Brad's depression is worsening due in part to stifling his emotions, especially around his family members. Brad played freshman basketball last year but stopped after his dad's death. Phil recently encouraged Brad to get back on the team as a way to cope more positively with his grief and loss. Brad took Phil's suggestion and rejoined the team; however, it means that Phil will now be his basketball coach and his counselor. What should Phil do?

Phil recognizes the boundary extension that now exists due to being Brad's counselor and his coach simultaneously. To practice ethically, Phil discusses the potential ethical issues with Brad, especially respecting Brad's confidentiality. Phil indicates to Brad that he has an ethical obligation to care for Brad's well-being, and they can engage in a counselor-coach relationship only if (a) Brad and his mom consent to this dual role, (b) it has a clear therapeutic goal, and (c) Phil protects Brad's privacy and confidentiality. Phil also talks with the director of the mental health agency where he works and explains the rationale for potentially establishing this dual relationship with his minor client and how this boundary extension could enhance the therapeutic relationship.

Ethical Code 8.2

A.6.b. Extending Counseling Boundaries.

Counselors consider the risks and benefits of extending current counseling relationships beyond conventional parameters. Examples include attending a client's formal ceremony (e.g., a wedding/commitment ceremony, graduation), purchasing a service or product provided by a client (excepting unrestricted bartering), and visiting a client's ill family member in the hospital. In extending these boundaries, counselors take appropriate professional precautions, such as informed consent, consultation, supervision, and documentation to ensure that judgment is not impaired and no harm occurs.

Source: 2014 American Counseling Association Code of Ethics. Reprinted with permission from American Counseling Association.

CASE STUDY 8.2

Phil explains to Brad that when he is acting in the role of basketball coach, he cannot discuss in public issues that Brad has brought up in their counseling sessions. However, Phil tells Brad that he is free to discuss anything that takes place on the basketball court in their counseling sessions. Phil explains that the other players and coaching staff will not know that Brad is seeing Phil for counseling. Phil explains that having the opportunity to coach and work with Brad as a basketball coach might offer unique insights, and things that he can learn about Brad may be helpful in their counseling work together.

Phil also reviews potential risks with Brad. For example, Phil indicates to Brad that if he is struggling in his performance as a player, it could mean that he would be benched. Phil talks with Brad about how that might impact their counseling relationship. As a coach, Phil explains, he has a position of authority and has the ability to have Brad play a lead role on the team or bench him. Brad understands but indicates that having Phil as both a coach and counselor could help him, especially in his struggle with his dad's death. Phil creates a special informed consent form for him and Brad (and Brad's mom) to review and sign in accordance with the ACA Code of Ethics.

Phil also explains to Brad that once they engage in the counselor-coach relationship and it becomes awkward or uncomfortable for either of them at any point, they will revisit it, discuss it together, and make a decision to terminate one of the professional roles, most likely, finding another coach to work with the basketball team.

After a few weeks of having the boundary extension, Phil sees improvement in Brad. In a recent session, Phil and Brad discuss Brad's difficulty in expressing his grief in front of his mom and feeling that he cannot talk openly with her. Brad believes that if he talks about his dad with his mom, it would cause her pain and make her very upset. Phil then reminds Brad about the work they did on the basketball court when Brad was struggling to make his free throws. During practice, Brad continually expressed negative thoughts and had major self-doubt about his ability to improve his free throw shot. In his role as basketball coach, Phil was able to talk Brad through it and challenge his negative thought process. Over the course of a few practices and Phil's coaching techniques, Brad overcame his negative self-talk about his performance on the court, and he improved his free throws.

Phil reminded Brad of this in their recent counseling session. He also challenged Brad that if he could overcome his negative thoughts about his basketball skills, then is it possible that he could use a similar approach in overcoming his negative thoughts about talking to his mom? Brad agreed, and over the next few weeks, he spoke with his mom about the grief he was experiencing about his dad's death. Brad's mom shared her own struggle with grief, and Brad felt closer to her as a result of openly sharing his feelings. Brad's mom reassured him that he can cry and express his grief openly with her and his siblings and still be the man of the house.

Ethical Code 8.3

A.6.c. Documenting Boundary Extensions.

If counselors extend boundaries as described in A.6.a., they must officially document, prior to the interaction (when feasible), the rationale for such an interaction, the potential benefit, and anticipated consequences for the client or former client and other individuals significantly involved with the client or former client. When unintentional harm occurs to the client or former client, or to an individual significantly involved with the client or former client, the counselor must show evidence of an attempt to remedy such harm.

Source: 2014 American Counseling Association Code of Ethics. Reprinted with permission from American Counseling Association.

In this example, there was an important benefit that resulted in Phil serving as Brad's counselor as well as his coach. Phil had the unique perspective of being able to see Brad interact and perform on the basketball court, which informed their work in the counseling setting. This is an example of when a boundary extension can benefit the client immensely as long as the counselor consults with supervisors and colleagues, discusses the risks and benefits with the client, and documents the boundary extension via a revised informed consent and in the clinical notes.

Guided Practice Exercise 8.2

Phil's Philosophy on Boundary Extensions

In small groups, discuss the steps Phil took in his work with Brad. Do you agree with the boundary extension that Phil created with Brad by being both his counselor and his coach? Are there other considerations that Phil should think about concerning this overlap? What other issues can you identify that may raise an ethical concern? What other benefits of the dual relationship do you see?

EMPLOYING AN ETHICAL DECISION-MAKING MODEL

As was noted in Chapter 2, there are often no easy answers to most ethical situations, but utilizing an ethical decision-making process can help solidify our ethical steps and ensure that the welfare of our clients remains at the forefront. Chapter 2 introduced numerous examples of EDMs we can choose from, including theory-based models and practice-based models. Regardless of the EDM we choose, the central point is to actively use the framework of a model to guide the decision-making process at each and every step. Kitchener and Anderson (2011) and Welfel (2013) discuss the importance of mental health professionals being reflective about ethical practice, including the use of sound reasoning. Kitchener and Anderson (2011) provide a useful model that can help us consider whether or not to engage in an extension of professional boundaries with a client or former client. We summarize their steps here for your use:

1. Pause and think about your response. Think about the implications on the therapeutic relationship if you were to engage in a boundary extension or multiple relationship with a client. How would the counseling relationship improve? How does this boundary extension help the client meet the established therapeutic goals? If the change in relationship does not, then you should not be engaged in a boundary crossing. How might the change in relationship potentially harm the client, cause confusion, or cause a significant power differential?

2. Review the available information. Review the facts of the decision to embark on a dual or multiple relationship. Are you treating this situation in a similar way you would with other clients?

3. Identify possible options. Review the risks and benefits of engaging in such a multiple relationship. The client should be involved in the conversation and option exploration, including the risks and benefits.

4. Consult the ethics code. What ethical standards from the codes of ethics can guide the decision?

5. Assess the foundational ethical issues. What are the core ethical issues at stake? What ethical principles (autonomy, beneficence, nonmaleficence, fidelity, or justice) apply in this situation?

6. Identify legal issues and agency policy. It is important to do your homework when it comes to ethical decisions. Have other counselors or mental health professionals in an ethical conundrum had successful outcomes by engaging in similar boundary crossings? What were any legal issues that arose as a result of these similar situations?

7. Reassess options, and identify a plan. Consult with a colleague or supervisor before embarking on a boundary extension. An outside perspective may aid you in examining a new avenue or a new concern that you had not considered before.

8. Implement the plan, and document the process. Document each step of the process, particularly why you are choosing to engage in a dual or multiple relationship. Document which specific therapeutic goal is supported by such action.

9. Reflect on the outcome of your decision. If you and your client decide together to engage in a boundary extension, you should have ongoing conversations about how the overlap is working and impacting the counseling relationship. Do any adjustments or clarifications need to be made? Is either individual uncomfortable or feeling uneasy about the current structure of the professional relationship? Is this new role negatively impacting the counseling process? If so, you should work with the client to find an appropriate resolution to the situation, including the possibility of having to end the outside role or relationship to preserve the sanctity of the counseling process.

BOUNDARIES AND CONTEXTUAL CONSIDERATIONS

As stated earlier in this chapter, counselors are encouraged not to make black-and-white decisions when engaging in boundary extensions with clients or former clients. Houser and Thoma (2013) encourage us to examine our motivation to act ethically, which also is called our ethical identity or ethical ideology. Also, cultural and contextual considerations should play an important role when reasoning through to a decision of whether or not to engage in a multiple relationship or to alter a current boundary structure within the counseling relationship.

Let's examine some examples to illustrate this more clearly. Many times, clients want to bring gifts to their counselors. The issue of receiving gifts from clients, especially around certain holidays throughout the year or other special occasions, may cause a boundary concern to enter the therapeutic relationship. On the surface, especially to a new counselor, the response to this may seem clear-cut—the counselor should establish a no gift policy and have a standard statement about not being able to accept any gifts from any clients at any time. While that may appear to be a clear-cut solution, is it the best? It is important for us to be aware that making such a policy decision may in fact unintentionally be engaging in unethical conduct. The ACA Code of Ethics should be consulted for guidance.

Ethical Code 8.4

A.10.f. Receiving Gifts.

Counselors understand the challenges of accepting gifts from clients and recognize that in some cultures, small gifts are a token of respect and gratitude. When determining whether or not to accept a gift from clients, counselors take into account the therapeutic relationship, the monetary value of the gift, the client's motivation for giving the gift, and the counselor's motivation for wanting to accept or decline the gift.

Source: 2014 American Counseling Association Code of Ethics. Reprinted with permission from American Counseling Association.

Standard A.10.f. provides additional guidance for us to consider. It is reasonable for a counselor to refuse a client's gift if the client's motivation is to influence the counseling process, such as a gift for the counselor to give a favorable report to a court about a mandated client's participation in therapy. This is a straightforward example of when it likely would be warranted to refuse a gift. However, there are other situations when it could be detrimental to the client's welfare to refuse a gift.

Standard A.10.f. encourages us to be mindful of cultural issues that influence gift giving. If a client comes from a cultural tradition where giving a small gift (a monetary value of under $25) is a sign of care and respect, then a counselor refusing the gift outright actually may harm the client by offending his or her cultural beliefs and unintentionally may hamper the therapeutic process. Because the counselor refused the token gift, the client may feel disrespected and not feel unconditional positive regard from the counselor. In addition to the cultural context and monetary value of the gift, the stage of the therapeutic relationship is an integral part of knowing what action should be taken. A client giving a gift during the second session likely will be handled differently than a client giving a gift to the counselor at the last session of their counseling relationship as a token of gratitude after two years of therapeutic work together.

This same idea of making decisions based on client, culture, context, and so on, also can be applied to a variety of other issues impacting the counselor–client relationship: counselor self-disclosure, touch in therapy, and having a therapy session outside of the counseling office. There are numerous considerations and complexities that must be taken into account. For example, it likely would be highly inappropriate and a poor boundary crossing for a counselor to reach over during a session to touch the knee of a client and squeeze it. This could be an emotional or psychological trigger to the client, especially a client who may have experienced trauma related to physical or sexual abuse. However, it may be appropriate for a counselor to place his or her hand on the shoulder of a client as he or she leaves the office after a particularly challenging session. Therefore, where a counselor touches the client and the context can play significant roles in determining the rightness or wrongness of one's actions.

In the course of a professional counselor's career, she or he may encounter a client who makes flirtatious or sexual advances or comments to the counselor. A client commenting about a counselor's outfit may appear minor in nature, but as we have been discussing, assessing the context of the situation is critical. What specifically a client says about the counselor's clothing and the tone and manner in which it is said can be either a passing and simple compliment ("Those are great shoes you have on") or a serious ethical situation ("That blouse really accentuates your figure"). When it comes to sexual or physical attraction, counselors are encouraged to seek out supervision and consultation actively in those types of matters because the slippery slope phenomenon discussed earlier certainly can be applied to those types of incidents.

As you can see, having a blanket policy, whether about receiving gifts or attending a function outside of the counseling setting with a client, may be tempting but also may become a therapeutic hindrance. Moving from a rigid posture to a more inclusive, reasoned approach is warranted. As counselors, we learn that black and white is rare and that we live in shades of gray. Becoming flexible and being comfortable with ambiguity is a hallmark of an ethical counselor.

CONCLUSION

Boundary issues are rampant in counseling. Because we practice a relational discipline, there are inherent challenges in the boundaries of those relationships. Knowing how to make decisions that are in the best interest of your client, as the vulnerable party in the relationship, and yourself is the focus of this chapter. By using the ethical decision-making tips provided, beginning counselors should be able to move forward in establishing and maintaining appropriate boundaries. In addition, counselors can better understand how to manage boundary crossings when they arise.

KEYSTONES

- There are a variety of terms used within the counseling profession to describe the counselor taking on additional roles outside of the counselor–client relationship: dual relationships, multiple relationships, boundary crossings, and boundary extensions.
- Types of boundaries that counselors face include counselor social boundaries, psychological boundaries, financial boundaries, counselor physical boundaries, and emotional boundaries.
- Boundary extensions can involve a wide range of issues, such as touch in therapy, counselor self-disclosure to clients, attending an outside function of a client, having the counselor and client participate in the same outside organization, and simultaneously serving as a coach and counselor.
- The therapeutic goals and welfare of the client always should be at the forefront of whether or not to engage in a boundary extension. Other considerations include codes of ethics, legal considerations, counseling literature, and the opinions of other professionals with experience in managing boundaries.
- Practitioners and ethics scholars have a wide range of views about engaging in multiple relationships.
- Counselors must consider issues such as cultural context and geography (rural areas) and may find it impossible to avoid multiple relationships.
- Counselors must consult with supervisors and colleagues prior to engaging in any boundary extension and document the process used to find a workable solution that benefits the client.
- Kitchener and Anderson (2011) have created a model to help counselors consider engaging in an extension of professional boundaries, which involves reviewing the available information, identifying possible options and assessing their ethical and legal issues, choosing a plan and implementing and documenting the process, and reflecting on the outcome.

SUGGESTED BEST PRACTICES

- Consider what you feel like when people don't respect your boundaries. That is how clients feel as well.
- Attend to how you handle the multiple relationships already present in your life: your child's teacher who is also your friend, the babysitter who is the daughter of a colleague, or the neighbor who is your banker. These relationships can help you understand boundaries better.

- Whenever you are tempted to self-disclose in session, pause. See if it can wait until next session. Then check your motives. Many of us have a me-too response to client stories. We think that information may help them, but is it possible that it would diminish their own story or cause them to be concerned about you?
- Be aware of the emotional impact seeing clients has on you. You are not made of Teflon. What do you do with that impact?
- Talk with your clients while they are in your office about how you will handle seeing them outside of the office. Make this part of your informed consent.
- When considering extending a boundary, engage in an ethical decision-making process. Consult with another professional and the client before proceeding.
- Remember why ACA moved away from language admonishing us to avoid dual relationships to managing boundary extensions. Sometimes it is in the best interest of the client.
- Pay attention to ethics in the news. Many problems are the result of engaging in multiple relationships without consideration for how it would create a therapeutic benefit for the client.
- Consider each boundary extension within its context and through the lens of the relevant culture.
- Rather than having stock responses or rules about boundary issues, be willing to evaluate each based on benefit to the client.
- Although it has been discussed before in this text, don't forget to document your decision.
- Always involve the client and process any unintentional boundary crossings, such as running into a client in a social setting, in the following session.

ADDITIONAL RESOURCES

In Print

Allan, J., Liston-Smith, J., & Whybrow, A. (2010). Effective boundary management—the signature of professionalism? *Coaching Psychologist, 6*(1), 48–53.

Barnett, J. E. (2014). Sexual feelings and behaviors in the psychotherapy relationship: An ethics perspective. *Journal of Clinical Psychology, 70*(2), 170–181. doi:10.1002/jclp.22068

Calmes, S. A., Piazza, N. J., & Laux, J. M. (2013). The use of touch in counseling: An ethical decision-making model. *Counseling & Values, 58*(1), 59–68. doi:10.1002/j.2161–007X.2013.00025.x

Pope, K. S., & Keith-Spiegel, P. (2008). A practical approach to boundaries in psychotherapy: making decisions, bypassing blunders, and mending fences. *Journal of Clinical Psychology, 64*(5), 638–652. doi:10.1002/jclp.20477

On the Web

Stone, C. (2011). *Boundary crossing: The slippery slope.* Retrieved from http://schoolcounselor .org/magazine/blogs/july-august-2011/boundary-crossing-the-slippery-slope

Zur, O. (2015). *Dual relationships, multiple relationships, boundaries, boundary crossings & boundary violations in psychotherapy, counseling & mental health.* Retrieved from http:// www.zurinstitute.com/dualrelationships.html

REFERENCES

American Counseling Association (ACA). (2014). *ACA code of ethics.* Alexandria, VA: Author.

Corey, G., Corey, M., Corey, C., & Callahan, P. (2015). *Issues and ethics in the helping professions* (9th ed.). Stamford, CT: Cengage.

Gutheil, T., & Brodsky, A. (2008). *Preventing boundary violations in clinical practice.* New York: Guilford.

Herlihy, B., & Corey, G. (2015). *ACA ethical standards casebook* (7th ed.). Alexandria, VA: American Counselor Association.

Houser, R., & Thoma, S. (2013). *Ethics in counseling and therapy: Developing an ethical identity.* Los Angeles, CA: Sage.

Jungers, C., & Gregoire, J. (Eds.). (2013). *Counseling ethics: Philosophical and professional foundations.* New York: Springer.

Kitchener, K. S., & Anderson, S. (2011). *Foundations of ethical practice, research, and teaching in psychology and counseling* (2nd ed.). New York: Routledge.

Welfel, E. R. (2013). *Ethics in counseling and psychotherapy: Standards, research, and emerging issues* (5th ed.). Belmont, CA: Brooks/Cole.

Chapter 9

MINORS

You love your job as a middle school counselor. The kids are changing so rapidly at this stage of development, and you get to be a part of it! Many of them confide in you in ways you never imagined. JoEllen, one of your 8th graders, drops by to tell you she has a new boyfriend. She just turned 14 and is sure he is "the one." She has known him for years even though he is 16 and in 10th grade. You suspect she is thinking of having sex with him, and when you bring this up, she doesn't deny it. The age of consent in your state is 15. What should you do?

CHAPTER OVERVIEW

This chapter introduces the reader to the many opportunities and challenges inherent in working with minor clients. Because so many counselors find working with children and adolescents to be their calling, this chapter brings some of the ethical realities to the forefront. The basics of negotiating confidentiality, duty to warn, and other ethical dilemmas are presented. In addition, the involvement of relevant family is discussed. Finally, relevant codes from the American Counseling Association (ACA, 2014) Code of Ethics are presented.

LEARNING OBJECTIVES

After reading this chapter you will be able to do the following:

1. Evaluate the confidentiality rights of minor clients.

2. Differentiate between confidentiality, privileged communication, and mandated reporting.

3. Critically analyze a case study involving minor clients and confidentiality using an identified ethical decision-making model (EDM).

4. Explain how to work with and within a school system with minor clients.

5. Apply cultural competencies when working with minor clients.

CACREP STANDARDS

CACREP Core Standards

G.1.b. Professional roles, functions, and relationships with other human service providers, including strategies for interagency or interorganization collaboration and communications.

G.1.i. Advocacy processes needed to address institutional and social barriers that impede access, equity, and success for clients.

G.5.d. Counseling theories that provide the student with models to conceptualize client presentation and that help the student select appropriate counseling interventions. Students will be exposed to models of counseling that are consistent with current professional research and practice in the field, so they begin to develop a personal model of counseling.

G.5.e. A systems perspective that provides an understanding of family and other systems theories and major models of family and related interventions.

G.6.a. Developmental stage theories, group members' roles and behaviors, and therapeutic factors of group work.

CACREP Clinical Mental Health Standards

A.3. Understands the roles and functions of clinical mental health counselors in various practice settings and the importance of relationships between counselors and other professionals, including interdisciplinary treatment teams.

C.1. Describes the principles of mental health, including prevention, intervention, consultation, education, and advocacy, as well as the operation of programs and networks that promote mental health in a multicultural society.

C.7. Recognizes the importance of family, social networks, and community systems in the treatment of mental and emotional disorders.

E.4. Understands effective strategies to support client advocacy and influence public policy and government relations on local, state, and national levels to enhance equity, increase funding, and promote programs that affect the practice of clinical mental health counseling.

E.6. Knows public policies on the local, state, and national levels that affect the quality and accessibility of mental health services.

INTRODUCTION

This chapter addresses the ethical codes and varying practices used when working with minor clients. Counseling minors requires multicultural competence; a strong understanding of your state law, health care, and local school systems regulations; and practice with how a treatment approach varies with a minor versus when applied with an adult, even with the same diagnosis.

Interpersonal skills are critical for counselors and even more so for those working with minor clients. This special population potentially includes several other constituents or family members who may want to be involved heavily in the treatment planning and goal setting for the minor client. Yet, if the minor client is capable of good decision making, the counselor will want to build trust with that client (and the related constituents and family) and include that minor in his or her treatment planning. Working with minors is a unique practice that takes specific training with special attention to human growth and development and psychological theory, law and local regulations, and cultural competence.

CONFIDENTIALITY

The rights of minor clients have evolved over the course of history. Children were once considered the property of their fathers, with no legal rights or obligations. In the United States, children were not considered from a legal perspective until the first legal decisions related to minors and the creation of the first juvenile court in the late 1800s (National Association of Counsel for Children, 2014). Minor clients continue to have few legal rights, especially as they relate to mental health treatment.

Counselors are charged with the duty to safeguard the confidentiality of the client.

Ethical Code 9.1

B.5.a. Responsibility to Clients.

When counseling minor clients or adult clients who lack the capacity to give voluntary, informed consent, counselors protect the confidentiality of information received in the counseling relationship as specified by federal and state laws, written policies, and applicable ethical standards.

Source: 2014 American Counseling Association Code of Ethics. Reprinted with permission from American Counseling Association.

Ethically, the minor is our client. However, in the eyes of the law, the parent or guardian is the only party legally recognized. What does this mean in practice? For most of our work with children, it means that we offer a form of confidentiality to our minor client that includes the legal reality that their parent or guardian has a right to request information about sessions. In addition, counselors have ethical responsibilities to safeguard the release of confidential information about clients to third parties.

Ethical Code 9.2

B.5.c. Release of Confidential Information.

When counseling minor clients or adult clients who lack the capacity to give voluntary consent to release confidential information, counselors seek permission from an appropriate third party to disclose information. In such instances, counselors inform clients consistent with their level of understanding and take culturally appropriate measures to safeguard client confidentiality.

Source: 2014 American Counseling Association Code of Ethics. Reprinted with permission from American Counseling Association.

In all cases, counselors are best served by consulting their state laws.

Managing confidentiality with minor clients can be difficult. On one hand, children and adolescents are some of the most underserved clients in terms of receiving mental health care (Sherman, Moscou, & Dang-Vu, 2009). On the other hand, minor clients lack the ability to give legal consent for treatment, and the parent or guardian has legal rights to the content of their sessions. Younger clients may not have much in terms of privacy needs, but as you can imagine, adolescents would be extremely reluctant to share with a counselor if they thought everything they discussed would go straight to their parents. Counselors often strike a compromise with minors and guardians. Sessions with older children may be held in confidence if the counselor agrees to adhere to the legal mandates of reporting harm, discussed further in this chapter. In these situations, the safety of the client should rule the decision to share information with parents and guardians.

Privileged Communication

Clearly, confidentiality is an ethical consideration that becomes complicated when working with minor clients. As previously discussed in Chapter 7, privacy is the right of the client to decide what is shared with whom, while confidentiality

is the ethical concept outlining the obligation of the counselor to protect information. Privileged communication, unlike confidentiality, is actually a legal concept.
It is defined as the legal right that protects clients from disclosing information
during legal proceedings without informed consent (Krueger & Labbe, 2012) In
fact, counselors are offered privileged communication as an option for clients only
if it is clearly outlined in state law.

For example, Mississippi state law § 73–30–17 Nondisclosure of Information:
Exceptions (Mississippi State Code, 2013, 73–30–17) affords licensed counselors
privileged communication. In other words, counselors who have not yet achieved
licensure status, have lost or lapsed their license, or never pursue licensure do not
have privileged communication to offer clients regardless of age. Texas law is less
clear. Texas state law Family Code, § 6.705 offers marriage counselors some
privilege in which files, records, and work products are not admissible as evidence
in a court (Texas Office of the Attorney General, 2000). However, this law does
not address what qualifies someone to be a marriage counselor; for example, does
it require being a licensed professional counselor (LPC) or a licensed marriage and
family therapist (LMFT)?. What does this mean for minor clients? While there are
many laws that do impact disclosure of information related to minors (e.g., the
Family Educational Rights and Privacy Act [FERPA]), privileged communication
is not one of them. In the case of the legal option of privileged communication,
minors are held to the legal construct that they cannot enter into contracts and thus
have no right to privileged communication.

But what about the parent or legal guardian? Technically, the counselor could
call for privileged communication using the parent's or legal guardian's rights if
asked to testify in court. Because privileged communication is not guaranteed, a
judge can overrule this right depending on the legal case, and the information may
still be disclosed. This potential is closely tied to precautions counselors take
while documenting events, which are discussed in Chapter 7.

Mandated Reporting

A crucial element of working with minor clients is the concept of mandated
reporting. Mandated reporting refers to those individuals and circumstances that
require a breach of the minor's confidentiality regardless of whether the client or
parents want the information disclosed (U.S. Department of Health and Human
Services, 2014). Clients often report behaviors that may be dangerous to self or
others and require the counselor to use professional judgment to determine if a
report is warranted. Mandated reporting often is legislated in state law. For example,
Mississippi state law indicates that any adult who has reason to suspect that a
child is being abused is considered a mandated reporter (Mississippi State Code,

2013, 97–5–51). Similarly, Texas has a specific mandated reporting law for professionals but adds that any person with reason to suspect abuse or neglect must make a report (Texas Family Code 2013, 261.101). Other states, such as West Virginia, place limitations on nonprofessionals making reports (see https://www .childwelfare.gov/systemwide/laws_policies/statutes/manda.pdf). As with all legal-related decisions, checking state and federal law is crucial to ethical decision-making practice.

While the code of ethics places the autonomy of client choice at the forefront of decision making about confidentiality, the law overrides this ethical right to autonomy when a minor client is in danger of harm by others, of harm to others, or of harm to self. These issues become more complicated as counselors are faced with knowing what constitutes abuse, self-harm, and threats to others.

CASE STUDY 9.1

Malia is a 13-year-old middle school student who was asked to see the school counselor when the teacher noticed that she was listless in class, not interacting with others, and increasingly irritable. The teacher reported seeing this behavior first appear about three weeks ago and is concerned that Malia is falling behind because she is not attending to her classwork. The school counselor, Justin, initiates a counseling relationship with Malia and covers informed consent from the outset.

During the course of their work together, Justin learns that Malia's parents are getting a divorce and that Malia has been increasingly isolating herself at home. At night, she often goes to her room, listens to music, and cuts herself on her upper arm. She describes the cutting as "helpful," saying "it just feels good to feel that pain and not the pain in my heart." Malia denies being suicidal and has no previous history of suicide ideation, attempts, depression, or treatment. Justin informs parents when he initiates an ongoing counseling relationship with a student. Malia's parents are aware that she is seeing the counselor but have not asked for information about the sessions. Justin wonders if he should report Malia's cutting behavior to her parents.

When presented with a scenario like Malia's, counselors often differ in their approaches to mandated reporting. Some counselors view cutting as "harm to self" and find that disclosure is warranted. Others view this behavior as "non-suicidal self-mutilation" (Baetens et al., 2014; Gonzales & Bergstrom, 2013; Young, Sproeber, Groschwitz, Preiss, & Plener, 2014) and elect not to disclose. Because there is no uniform standard for approaching this dilemma, what should beginning counselors do?

If we follow the Relational Ethical Decision-Making Model presented in Chapter 4, we could analyze this case as follows:

1. Continually examine the role that ethics play within the therapeutic relationship.

Justin has started the relationship well by initiating a formal counseling relationship with Malia. By reviewing informed consent from the beginning, he has a foundation to fall back on and refer to throughout the process.

2. Identify the ethical dilemma or problem, including various contextual layers, cultural considerations, and ethical ambiguity, seeking consultation and supervision as warranted.

When Justin becomes aware of Malia's self-injury, it is in her best interest to consider the cultural context within which the behavior occurs. The self-injury started with her parents' talk of divorce and seems tied to that process. It is important for Justin to perform a thorough suicide assessment before continuing. At this point, the situation is best served if Justin reaches out to his counseling supervisor and appropriate colleagues for consultation about his process and decisions with Malia.

3. Discuss with the client the professional ethical obligations of counselors and the ethical dilemma, and address how the dilemma impacts the counseling relationship.

Justin needs to discuss this ethical dilemma with Malia. Although she is 13, there is no reason to believe that she is not cognitively capable of appreciating the ethical dilemmas related to self-harm and informed consent. Justin is likely concerned that disclosure to her parents would disrupt his therapeutic relationship with Malia. Involving her in the decision making does not guarantee preservation of the counseling relationship, but it is an ethical first step.

4. Working with the client, examine the core ethical principles that are most prominent within this ethical dilemma.

In addition to ethical codes related to minors and informed consent, Justin may also consider the following ethical principles from the 2014 ACA Code of Ethics:

A.1.a. Primary Responsibility: Justin's main responsibility is to Malia, his client.

Ethical Code 9.3

A.1.a. Primary Responsibility.

The primary responsibility of counselor is to respect the dignity and promote the welfare of clients.

Source: 2014 American Counseling Association Code of Ethics. Reprinted with permission from American Counseling Association.

A.2.d. Inability to Give Consent: Because Malia is a minor, Justin can seek her assent only to services and the process of counseling.

Ethical Code 9.4

A.2.d. Inability to Give Consent.

When counseling minors, incapacitated adults, or other persons unable to give voluntary consent, counselors seek the assent of clients to services and include them in decision making as appropriate. Counselors recognize the need to balance the ethical rights of clients to make choices, their capacity to give consent or assent to receive services, and parental or familial legal rights and responsibilities to protect these clients and make decisions on their behalf.

Source: 2014 American Counseling Association Code of Ethics. Reprinted with permission from American Counseling Association.

B.2.e. Minimal Disclosure: When sharing information with Malia's parents, Justin would be wise to consider this standard, which asks counselors to share only the information necessary to provide appropriate treatment.

Ethical Code 9.5

B.2.e. Minimal Disclosure.

To the extent possible, clients are informed before confidential information is disclosed and are involved in the disclosure decision-making process. When circumstances require the disclosure of confidential information, only essential information is revealed.

Source: 2014 American Counseling Association Code of Ethics. Reprinted with permission from American Counseling Association.

Justin is charged with balancing the ethical principle of autonomy, the client's right to make choices about treatment, with the principle of beneficence, the imperative to do good in the counseling relationship so that the client benefits.

5. Consider the ethical dilemma, including perceptions, values, biases, and beliefs from both the counselor's and the client's points of view.

Justin may have some of his own values about self-harm that are not necessarily in line with the literature. If so, he will consider ACA Standard A.4.b. to avoid imposing his own values.

Ethical Code 9.6

A.4.b. Personal Values.

Counselors are aware of—and avoid imposing—their own values, attitudes, beliefs, and behaviors. Counselor respect the diversity of clients, trainees, and research participants and seek training in areas in which they are at risk of imposing their values onto clients, especially when the counselor's values are inconsistent with the client's goals or are discriminatory in nature.

Source: 2014 American Counseling Association Code of Ethics. Reprinted with permission from American Counseling Association.

Justin also needs to consider Malia's perceptions. In her peer group, the practice of cutting is not uncommon, nor is it considered life threatening.

6. Examine how boundaries within the therapeutic relationship are impacted as a result of the ethical conundrum, including the counselor's and client's affective and cognitive domains.

Justin is aware that bringing Malia's family into the situation could have both negative and positive impacts. He is concerned that he will lose her trust and perhaps make life at home tenser for Malia if he discloses her behavior. Conversely, he wonders if bringing her parents into the situation may help them see the impact they are having on their child. He also must take Malia's concerns and fears about breaking confidentiality into account and how it would impact their therapeutic relationship. During this examination, Justin may elect to discuss these concerns with Malia.

*7. Look into applicable laws; campus, agency,
department regulations, policies; procedures; handbooks;
Web sites; and so on that may inform your decision.*

Justin reviews his state law and finds that for minor clients, mandated reporting is related to instances of abuse or neglect. Because self-mutilation does not fall under either category, he does not find much direction in state law. Additionally, his school has no policy on how teachers, counselors, or administrators are to handle self-harm behaviors. Because there is no clear direction, he turns to the literature to help inform his choice.

*8. Consult professional literature, as well as professional
colleagues and experts (with client consent), regarding
best practices in similar ethical dilemmas.*

Justin reviews the current literature on adolescent self-injury, family dynamics, the impact of divorce on adolescents, and other topics.

*9. Collaborate with the client in brainstorming potential
resolutions to the dilemma, and evaluate possible
consequences and outcomes of action or inaction.*

After this thorough review of ethics, law, culture, context, and the literature and after consultation with colleagues, supervisors, and other professionals, Justin sits with Malia to discuss the possible outcomes.

*10. Choose a course of action, working through
any challenges that may exist within the therapeutic
relationship about the ethical issue.*

Together, they decide that Justin will call Malia's parents in for a session in which Malia will share her fears and the behaviors that have come as a consequence of those fears.

*11. Implement selected a course of action, addressing
client concerns in a mutually supportive environment.*

Justin and Malia plan for the meeting with Malia's parents in a way that allows her to feel supported and empowered. Following the session, they process the outcome together. Malia retains her role as someone who is part of the treatment plan, not just the object of the plan.

12. Evaluate how the ethical decision will impact the counseling relationship currently as well as in the future.

Because Justin involved Malia in this process from the beginning, the evaluation of how the ethical decision will impact the counseling relationship has begun. It is now up to Justin to continue to assess this decision, as well as others, on the counseling relationship and to be open with Malia about this assessment.

Through the use of the Relational Ethical Decision-Making Model, Justin is able to address what might be a confusing and emotionally draining decision in a straightforward fashion. This case provides us with a clear way to conceptualize ethical decision making with minors. As you can see, the process is similar for minors and adult clients. Following an EDM is our best strategy for making these decisions. Because ethical dilemmas arise in more areas than mandated reporting for minor clients, let's look at some other ethical considerations.

Informed Consent

Informed consent is the foundation of the client–counselor relationship. It defines the basis of trust between the parties (Gümüş & Gümüş, 2009). When best applied, it begins with the intake and continues as an ongoing part of the client–counselor relationship. Informed consent is considered a legal agreement and must be documented according to state law in all 50 states (Zur, 2014). Elements of informed consent were previously covered in Chapter 6. With minor informed consent, it is necessary that counselors review not only the codes of ethics under which they fall but also state and federal law.

As you have no doubt learned throughout this textbook, laws about counseling practice differ from state to state. The same is true for minor consent laws. For example, in the state of Texas, minor clients are not allowed legally to provide consent for their own medical or psychological treatment in most cases. A parent, guardian, or another adult relation, such as a sibling, aunt, or uncle, may be allowed to provide consent (Texas Family Code, 2013, Chapter 32). However, there are occasions when a minor client may consent to his or her own treatment. Children over the age of 16 who live independently and manage their own financial affairs are able to seek their own treatment. Additionally, minors of any age are allowed to seek treatment, under Texas law, for issues related to infectious, contagious, or communicable diseases; pregnancy; or alcohol and drug treatment. In fact, federal law complements any state law that allows minors to seek treatment for drug or alcohol concerns without consent if the treatment provider received federal funding for such treatment.

Federal regulations were issued to protect minor clients' information and ensure access to treatment. In many states, the minor client can provide his or her own consent to treatment without parental knowledge. In states where parental knowledge and consent is required, Title 42 of the Code of Federal Regulations (C.F.R.), Public Health, protects their records from disclosure (2014). While these provisions apply only when the treatment provider receives some federal assistance, the vast majority of treatment providers fall into this category. What does this mean for you? If you work in an alcohol and drug facility, the informed consent rules for minors are likely different than for those who work solely with mental health concerns. As you have read many times throughout this text, it is essential to review and stay up-to-date on all codes and laws under which you may practice.

Guided Practice Exercise 9.1

The Legalities of Counseling Minors

Work with a team of three peer student counselors in training, and look up all the laws in your state that pertain to counseling minors. Make a brief presentation to class peers about the laws, and provide a handout delineating all laws.

WORKING WITH SCHOOL SYSTEMS

Working with school systems can be complicated for counselors and counselors in training. There are multiple parties who are involved and participate in the treatment of the student-client identified by a school system. Teachers, guidance counselors, and principals from the school side; parents or guardians, an outside (the school) clinical counselor, and the client from the client side; and possibly a representative from the medical field such as a psychiatrist all may be involved in the client's care. This group must consider local laws and specific behaviors permitted in regard to services provided to students when working with student-clients in a state-funded school system. They must collaborate and work toward the best interest of the client, which can be difficult when working with so many individuals with differing needs.

When many individuals are involved in the treatment planning of one student-client, differing goals and needs can become intertwined and the focus on the student-client can be lost. School employees such as principals and teachers may feel a responsibility to see that the school's needs are heavily considered. When this occurs, the school system's needs can become confused with the client's needs. The counselor has the responsibility to work with this group to ensure that the client's needs are the focus of treatment planning and that treatment is appropriate. The focus must remain on the client's best interests in these collaborations, and secondary concerns such as school funding or a school's related reputation should not become the driving force behind the treatment planning. The clinical counselor will participate and at times lead these discussions, so the focus remains on the best interests of the client.

Practices related to the treatment of the student-client also can be multilayered. Confidentiality and determining who in the school system is appropriate to access and potentially be involved with client information can be complex. Those who have not had adequate and regular training in student mental health records may not understand when information is to remain confidential and how much information should be shared with others, when appropriate. Counselors working with school systems need to ensure that the staff are educated regularly on the practices of sharing minimal information about a client and providing access to confidential information only to those who truly need it. There is no need for all staff in an office to have access to confidential records when one individual can be available at all times to access the information. There is no need for an entire student file to be copied for a meeting when only specific sessions or actions are to be discussed by the team. Not all parties related to the student-client need to have access to all information. Counselors may have to train school systems that they work with on confidentiality and practices related to the mental health of students.

Ethical Code 9.7

B.2.e. Minimal Disclosure.

To the extent possible, clients are informed before confidential information is disclosed and are involved in the disclosure decision-making process. When circumstances require the disclosure of confidential information, only essential information is revealed.

Source: 2014 American Counseling Association Code of Ethics. Reprinted with permission from American Counseling Association.

Ethical Code 9.8

B.5.c. Release of Confidential Information.

When counseling minor clients or adult clients who lack the capacity to give voluntary consent to release confidential information, counselors seek permission from an appropriate third party to disclose information. In such instances, counselors inform clients consistent with their level of understanding and take culturally appropriate measures to safeguard client confidentiality.

Source: 2014 American Counseling Association Code of Ethics. Reprinted with permission from American Counseling Association.

Minimization also should be practiced when determining a treatment group. Teachers, principals, and guidance counselors all do not have to be involved directly in the treatment of each student-client case. The school guidance counselor or clinical counselor can help determine who should be involved in the client's treatment. More parties may need to be involved when the student-client has a dual or complicated diagnosis or uninvolved parents or guardians or requires several supportive services. Fewer parties may need to be involved when the student situation is simpler, such as when there are participative and collaborative parents, a less-complicated diagnosis with less-interruptive behaviors in the classroom, or involved teachers and counselors who appreciate the client. The latter is important yet not always common. Teachers may struggle with collaboration when a student continually is causing concerns and related problems within the classroom. Most importantly, the students should have a significant voice when they have the capacity to make decisions related to their care (Dickey, Kiefner, & Beidler, 2002). Teaching students to self-advocate and assert their needs in their health care is ethically responsible. As counselors, we should educate students about advocacy while counseling them so they learn lifelong participation in their health care. As the mental health expert at the table, we should bring the necessary parties together and guide treatment.

Guided Practice Exercise 9.2

Interdisciplinary Teams at Work

Visit your local school district, and interview the school guidance counselor. Ask about how it is to work with an interdisciplinary team when developing the treatment plan for a minor client.

Guided Practice Exercise 9.3

Working With Minors and the State

Visit a counseling institution that houses and provides care for minors retained by the state. Ask about the special counseling needs of this group.

CASE STUDY 9.2

You are a professional counselor working at an at-risk youth camp for adolescent girls. Your client, Tameka, is African American, 15 years old, and the youngest of three children. In addition, Tameka has a 2-year-old daughter who lives at home with her mother, who has primary custody. Tameka has been estranged from her family and daughter for one and a half years. Tameka has been court ordered to the treatment camp by the judge for a minimum of six months due to her ongoing drug use, stealing, and truancy from school.

You have been working with Tameka for one month. Tameka shares with you during a counseling session that she has intense guilt related to behaviors she took part in while under the influence. Tameka discloses that while under the influence of marijuana and pain medicine, she hit a pedestrian who was crossing the street late at night. The image of the elderly lady flying over the car and hitting the pavement still haunts her. She states that she was with her friends, and after hitting the pedestrian, they went to a hotel room, continued to party, and never told anyone what happened that night. The next morning after it happened, she and her friends thought it was a dream, but then she saw it on the news and a reward for any information leading to the arrest of those responsible.

1. *How do you respond to Tameka after she shares this information? Do you have any questions for Tameka?*

2. *What are your ethical, legal, and moral concerns?*

3. *Who would you consult with following this counseling session?*

CULTURAL AND CONTEXTUAL COMPETENCE

Counselor competence when working with minor clients is similar to that of working with other populations. To practice ethically, we must have training to work with that particular population; if we begin working with a new population, we are required to have regular supervision. Hence, counselors working with minors should have spent considerable time training with adolescents because their mental health focus and needs are significantly different from adults even when diagnoses may be the same. Minor-focused laws, health care, and school regulations concern confidentiality and protection of the minor. Therefore, ethically based counseling must consider these related laws, regulations, and specific ethical codes when working with minor clients.

Adolescent clients have different cultural needs than those of adult clients. Often, culturally diverse minors deal with their own desires to assimilate to the dominant culture of their peers while also attempting to please parents who want acculturation only to the extent necessary. They often have to consider their parents' and grandparents' desires for their native cultural practices to remain intact while wanting to be more similar to their peers. Counselors working with this population may find they are working with two clients within one: the minor client and the family of the minor. The goals will evolve and transform as the minor develops. It may take time to build trust with the client and the family and to develop goals that will help to alleviate current discomfort.

Working with a minor and eventually the family requires sensitivity to the nuances of the minor's culture. We must be aware of the varying family roles in his or her particular culture. Is it a matriarchal culture in which the mother makes the health care decisions? Is it a culture in which outside mental health experts are regarded as having the answer to the client's problems without input from others? Or is it the opposite—a culture in which the family does not trust outside assistance for family mental health issues? Or is it a culture that does not even recognize mental health?

These questions have to be answered by the counselor and considered throughout treatment in addition to other considerations related to culture and ethical practice. Informed consent takes on added significance when we work with culturally different minors and their families. An explanation of confidentiality and the process and expectations of counseling are critical as most from non-Western countries are unfamiliar with the concept of counseling. As with minors of the dominant culture in America, we may want to share minimal information with the family while helping build the trust in the family and the client toward us in our role as counselor. We can explain to the family that we will share information with parents or guardians when it is necessary to retain trust and therefore provide the most proficient counseling of the minor client. This way the client may feel more comfortable opening up to us when he or she trusts that we will share only certain information with the family. When we are culturally aware and familiar with the client's cultural expectations, these conversations can be geared toward building that trust.

Ethical Code 9.9

B.5.b. Responsibility to Parents and Legal Guardians.

Counselors inform parents and legal guardians about the role of counselors and the confidential nature of the counseling relationship. Counselors are sensitive to the cultural diversity of families and respect the inherent rights and responsibilities of parents/

guardians over the welfare of their children/charges according to law. Counselors work to establish, as appropriate, collaborative relationships with parents/guardians to best serve clients.

Source: 2014 American Counseling Association Code of Ethics. Reprinted with permission from American Counseling Association.

At the same time, we have to ensure that we are not imposing our values or that of the dominant culture and assimilating a client around practices and behaviors that are typical for minors of the dominant culture but not that of the client's culture.

Ethical Code 9.10

A.4.b. Personal Values.

Counselors are aware of and avoid imposing their own values, attitudes, beliefs, and behaviors. Counselors respect the diversity of clients, trainees, and research participants, and seek training in areas in which they are at risk of imposing their values onto clients, especially when the counselor's values are inconsistent with the client's goals or are discriminatory in nature.

Source: 2014 American Counseling Association Code of Ethics. Reprinted with permission from American Counseling Association.

As with all counseling, staying focused on goals and regularly revisiting the client's needs in relation to those goals is critical for success with minors. Involving the family when the client wants them involved and in consideration of when the culture supports their involvement is important. Needs and goals will evolve, and the culturally competent counselor will continue to include the client's needs in relation to culture to those goals overall; working with minors of varying cultures will require a counselor with strong multicultural competence and an ability to build trust with potentially more than a few family members while also with the client.

Guided Practice Exercise 9.4

Minors in a Group Setting

Develop a counseling group for minors. Select a topic, develop the screening guidelines for selecting members, and write the rules for the group.

CASE STUDY 9.3

Jon is a new counselor at a local counseling agency that specializes in minors. Jon's new job requires him to provide intensive, outpatient counseling to children and adolescents, primarily in the client's home or school. Jon is nervous because this is his first real counseling job since he graduated with his master's degree last month. He wants to make sure that he does a good job and keeps this job. Not only does he need this job to support himself, but he also wants to get this post-master's experience toward independent licensure. In fact, he was just approved yesterday for his provisional license in his state. This is a big accomplishment for Jon, and he wants to make sure he does everything right. Jon's first couple weeks go well. He feels comfortable with observing other therapists with their clients and is now ready to handle his own caseload of clients.

The next week, Jon meets his four clients whom he will be seeing for intensive outpatient counseling several hours each week. All of his clients seem to react well to Jon and are open to counseling. However, one of his clients, Bobby, sticks out in Jon's mind. When Jon first met Bobby at his school, he seemed like a normal 10-year-old boy with some self-esteem and socialization issues. After speaking with Bobby, Jon began to become concerned about Bobby's home life. Bobby told Jon that he often has to take care of himself after school for several hours until his mother comes home from work. He not only takes care of himself, but also his younger brother, Jamal, who is 6 years old.

Jon is anxious to learn more about Bobby's home life, so he visits him at home the next day. When Jon arrives at Bobby's house, he sees many issues of concern. The lawn is overgrown, and there are pieces of rusted appliances and car parts scattered around the yard. The home's paint is peeling away and appears to be in disrepair. Upon entering the home, Jon notices that there are dog feces in several places and a strong smell. Bobby shares his bedroom with his younger brother, both of whom sleep in the same bed. Upon investigation of the kitchen, Jon notes that there is very little food in the home, and several of the appliances appear to be broken.

After visiting the home, Jon is very concerned. Children that young cannot be left at home alone per state law. Also, the home has several safety issues as well as being in poor condition. As a mandated reporter, it is Jon's duty to report any indication of child abuse or neglect.

1. *What are some of the issues in this case?*

2. *What impact would a report to Child Protective Services have on the new relationship with the client and family?*

3. *What impact does Jon's socioeconomic status have on his perspective on the state of his client's home?*

CONCLUSION

Working with children and adolescents, also known as minor clients, is a calling for many counselors. As you have learned in this chapter, there are some ethical challenges specific to this population. Understanding the concept of consent versus assent, the legalities of informed consent with minors, and involving family members are just some of the dilemmas counselors will encounter. Using this chapter as a foundation, you can begin to conceptualize how to approach the wonderful and challenging work of counseling children and adolescents in your practice.

KEYSTONES

- There are many laws that impact disclosure of information related to minors. Counselors must have a strong understanding of their state law and health care and local school system regulations.
- Minors are held to the legal construct that they cannot enter into contracts and thus have no right to privileged communication.
- Mandated reporting refers to those individuals and circumstances that require a breach of the minor's confidentiality regardless of whether the client or parents want the information disclosed.
- Informed consent is considered a legal agreement and must be documented according to state law in all 50 states.
- There are occasions in which a minor client may consent to his or her own treatment. For instance, children over the age of 16 who live independently and manage their own financial affairs can seek their own treatment. Federal law complements any state law that allows minors to seek treatment for drug or alcohol concerns without consent if the treatment provider receives federal funding.
- There are multiple parties who are involved and participate in the treatment of the student-client identified by a school system. When many individuals are involved in the treatment planning of one student-client, differing goals and needs can become intertwined, and the focus on the student-client can be lost.
- Minor clients have different cultural needs than adults. Culturally diverse minors wish to assimilate to the dominant culture while also trying to please their parents' and grandparents' desires for their native cultural practices to remain intact.
- It may take time to build trust in the client and the family and to develop goals that will help alleviate current discomfort. Informed consent takes on added significance when counselors work with culturally different minors and their families.

SUGGESTED BEST PRACTICES

- When working with minors, always consult state law and school regulations.
- Remember that the safety of the client should rule the decision to share information with parents and guardians.
- Following an EDM is the counselor's best strategy for making ethical decisions.
- When best applied, informed consent begins with the intake and continues as an ongoing part of the client–counselor relationship.
- When working with a school-based group, it is the counselor's responsibility to ensure that the client's needs are the focus of treatment planning and that treatment is appropriate.
- If you work in a school setting, you may have to help train school systems and personnel on the items of confidentiality and practices related to the mental health of students.
- As the school guidance counselor or clinical counselor, you help determine who should be involved in the treatment of the client.
- Teaching students to self-advocate and assert their health care needs is ethically responsible.
- Counselors working with minors should have spent adequate time training with minors because their mental health focus and needs are significantly different than adults even when diagnoses may be the same.
- An explanation of confidentiality and the process and expectations of counseling are critical when working with culturally diverse minor clients and their families.
- Counselors should educate students around advocacy while counseling them so they learn lifelong participation in their health care.
- Counselors working with school systems should ensure that the staff are educated regularly on the practice of sharing minimal information about a client and the practice of providing access to confidential information only to those who truly need it.
- As with minors of the dominant culture in America, you may want to share only minimal information with the family while helping build trust in the family and the client toward the counselor.
- Counselors must ensure that they are not imposing their values or that of the dominant culture onto their client or assimilating that client to practices and behaviors that are typical for minors of the dominant culture but not for the client's culture.
- Involving the family when the client wants them involved and in consideration of when the culture supports their involvement will be important.

ADDITIONAL RESOURCES

In Print

Henderson, K. L. (2013). Mandated reporting of child abuse: Considerations and guidelines for mental health counselors. *Journal of Mental Health Counseling, 35*(4), 296–309.

Hutchfield, J., & Coren, E. (2011). The child's voice in service evaluation: Ethical and methodological issues. *Child Abuse Review, 20*(3), 173–186. doi:10.1002/car.1142

Vernon, A., & Barry, K. L. (2013). *Counseling outside the lines: Creative arts intervention for children and adolescents, individual, small group, and classroom applications.* Champaign, IL: Research Press.

On the Web

Basics About Your Child's Rights. (n.d.). *Understood for Learning and Attention Issues.* http://www.ncld.org/parents-child-disabilities/ld-rights/advocating-for-your-school-aged-child

Child and Adolescent Issues. (n.d.). *GoodTherapy.* Retrieved from http://www.goodtherapy.org/therapy-children-teens.html

National Children's Advocacy Center. (n.d.). Retrieved from http://www.nationalcac.org/

REFERENCES

American Counseling Association (ACA). (2014). *ACA code of ethics.* Alexandria, VA: Author.

Baetens, I., Claes, L., Onghena, P., Grietens, H., Van Leeuwen, K., Pieters, C., Wiersema, J. R., & Griffith, J. W. (2014). Non-suicidal self-injury in adolescence: A longitudinal study of the relationship between NSSI, psychological distress and perceived parenting. *Journal of Adolescence, 37*(6), 817–826. doi:10.1016/j.adolescence.2014.05.010

Dickey, S. B., Kiefener, J., & Beidler, S. M. (2002). Consent and confidentiality issues among school-age children and adolescents. *The Journal of School Nursing, 18*(3), 179–186.

Gonzales, A. H., & Bergstrom, L. (2013). Adolescent non-suicidal self-injury (NSSI) Interventions. *Journal of Child & Adolescent Psychiatric Nursing, 26*(2), 124–130. doi:10.1111/jcap.12035

Gümüş, A., & Gümüş, M. (2009). Informed consent: Legal and ethical liabilities in counseling process. *Turkish Psychological Counseling & Guidance Journal, 4*(31), 1.

Krueger, M., & Labbe, D. (2012). Protecting a domestic abuse victim's priviledged counseling communications in family law cases. *New Hampshire Bar Journal, 53*(2), 38–43.

Mississippi State Code §73–30–17. (2013). Nondisclosure of information: Exceptions. Retrieved from http://law.justia.com/codes/mississippi/2013/title-73/chapter-30/section-73–30–17

Mississippi State Code § 97–5–51. (2013). Offenses effecting children. Retrieved from http://law.justia.com/codes/mississippi/2013/title-97/chapter-5/section-97–5–51

National Association of Counsel for Children. (2014). *Child maltreatment.* Retrieved from http://www.naccchildlaw.org/?page=childmaltreatment

Sherman, P., Moscou, S., & Dang-Vu, C. (2009). The primary care crisis and health care reform. *Journal of Health Care for the Poor and Underserved, 20,* 944–950.

Texas Family Code § 261.101. (2013). Investigation of report of child abuse or neglect. Retrieved from http://www.statutes.legis.state.tx.us/Docs/FA/htm/FA.261.htm

Texas Family Code. (2013). Chapter 32 consent to treatment of child by non-parent or child. Retrieved from http://www.statutes.legis.state.tx.us/Docs/FA/htm/FA.32.htm

Texas Office of the Attorney General. (2000). *Information held by governmental bodies deemed private or confidential by the Texas constitution and statutes.* Retrieved from https://www .texasattorneygeneral.gov/notice/privacy_statutes.htm

Title 42 C.F.R. (2014). *Electronic code of federal regulations; Title 42: Public health.* Retrieved from http://www.ecfr.gov/cgi-bin/text-idx?rgn=div5;node=42%3A1.0.1.1.2

U.S. Department of Health and Human Services. (2014). *Mandated reporters of child abuse and neglect.* Retrieved from https://www.childwelfare.gov/systemwide/laws_policies/statutes/ manda.pdf

Young, R., Sproeber, N., Groschwitz, R. C., Preiss, M., & Plener, P. L. (2014). Why alternative teenagers self-harm: Exploring the link between non-suicidal self-injury, attempted suicide and adolescent identity. *BMC Psychiatry, 14*(1), 1–25. doi:10.1186/1471–244X-14–137.

Zur, O. (2014). *Introduction to informed consent in psychotherapy, counseling, and assessment.* Retrieved from http://www.zurinstitute.com/informedconsent.html

Chapter 10

Ethics in Family and Group Counseling

Ray has been interning as a counselor in a mental health agency. He has become proficient at attending to verbal and nonverbal behaviors of his clients and managing the content his clients disclose. His supervisor tells him he is now ready to co-facilitate groups. Ray has to take that same level of focus he is used to providing a single client and apply it to a setting that requires a multilevel focus on an entire group, plus multiple dyads in the group, plus Ray's co-facilitator. . . . It can easily become overwhelming.

CHAPTER OVERVIEW

In this chapter the reader will consider group counseling and family counseling as separate but similar practices when learning about ethical practice. In both contexts the counselor works with more than one individual and must consciously identify the client. When working with families, the family unit typically is considered the client. When working with groups, each individual member typically is considered a client. There are different practices for counselors to utilize regarding the aspects of confidentiality, competency, and culture when working with clients who are comprised of more than one individual. While there are differences in counseling groups versus families, learning ethical practice when working with these two types of clients is easiest when the two are combined and compared. Hence, we do so in this chapter.

LEARNING OBJECTIVES

After reading this chapter you will be able to do the following:

1. Apply the specialized practices utilized when counseling a group or family in terms of the counseling relationship, role changes, protection of clients, screening, and termination.

2. Describe the competencies needed by group and family counselors and the consequences of leading a group without adequate training.

3. Explain the role of cultural competency in group and family counseling.

4. Employ ethical confidentiality practices in family and group work.

5. Examine how to advocate for clients and how to foster their skills to self-advocate.

CACREP STANDARDS

CACREP Core Standards

G.2.d. Individual, couple, family, group, and community strategies for working with and advocating for diverse populations, including multicultural competencies.

G.2.f. Counselors' roles in eliminating biases, prejudices, and processes of intentional and unintentional oppression and discrimination.

G.6.a. Principles of group dynamics, including group process components, developmental stage theories, group members' roles and behaviors, and therapeutic factors of group work.

G.6.b. Group leadership or facilitation styles and approaches, including characteristics of various types of group leaders and leadership styles.

G.6.c. Theories of group counseling, including commonalities, distinguishing characteristics, and pertinent research and literature.

G.6.d. Group counseling methods, including group counselor orientations and behaviors, appropriate selection criteria and methods, and methods of evaluation of effectiveness.

G.6.e. Direct experiences in which students participate as group members in a small-group activity, approved by the program, for a minimum of 10 clock hours over the course of one academic term.

CACREP Clinical Mental Health Standards

D.5. Demonstrates appropriate use of culturally responsive individual, couple, family, group, and systems modalities for initiating, maintaining, and terminating counseling.

E.2. Understands current literature that outlines theories, approaches, strategies, and techniques shown to be effective when working with specific populations of clients with mental and emotional disorders.

INTRODUCTION

There are multiple codes of ethics and practice guidelines for group facilitation and family counseling in the field of professional counseling. In addition to the ethical code of the American Counseling Association (ACA, 2014), which addresses group work, the Association for Specialists in Group Work, a division of ACA that supports and oversees group work in counseling, has its own set of practice guidelines. The American Association of Marriage and Family Therapy is the primary professional organization for the practice of marriage and family therapy and provides an ethical code for their members. Hence, counselors working primarily in group facilitation or family counseling have an ethical obligation to adhere to the ethical codes of all of the organizations that boundary their practice. These counselors also have an obligation to maintain best practices by keeping current with new literature and practices.

In group and family counseling, confidentiality becomes difficult if not impossible to guarantee because the counselor is not the only individual who has access to session information. Other members of a group or family may inappropriately disclose comments and issues raised in a confidential counseling session. This may harm other members of the group or family such as in family counseling when one partner uses the content of a counseling session to incriminate the other partner negatively. Maintaining the safety and therapeutic gain of the client may be more difficult when more than one person makes up the client. This is because the counselor must protect all members of the group or family while providing the most therapeutic effect for all involved. When working with a client who is comprised of more than one individual, identifying the client is critical. Terminating a member who is being disruptive to the group or blocking the group from therapeutic progress sometimes becomes a requirement for a good group counselor.

To help client members understand the boundaries and limits of group or family counseling sessions, counselors working with these populations do best when they establish rules for the counseling sessions on day one. This holds members accountable to behaviors that will result in the most therapeutic gain for all. Establishing group rules and reminding the family or group of those rules will keep everyone focused on their therapeutic goals versus getting caught up in individual issues. Let's take a look at how this works.

SPECIALIZED PRACTICES FOR GROUP AND FAMILY COUNSELING

As you can already see, there are many variances between individual and group or family counseling. Even the term *client* denotes something different in each type of counseling. In this section, we will discuss the various types of client–counselor relationships that exist, what happens when these roles change, how to protect clients from the group, the purpose of screening group members, and what to do in cases of terminating counseling with a group or individuals within a group.

The Counseling Relationship

When we work with more than one client, such as when working with families, couples, or groups, maintaining ethical practice can be multitiered and complex. We first must determine who the actual client is to make sound ethical decisions. When treating a couple, the couple is considered the client. However, if the couple separates or only one member of the couple continues to attend counseling, who is the client then? In a group setting, who is the client? And in a family?

In group counseling, the individual group members are considered individual clients. While notes are maintained on the group and the counselor facilitates the group members' interactions, for best therapeutic outcome, the counselor, or group leader, should attend to each individual member. When we lead a group, we must apply ethical practice to each individual member. We must protect each member of the group from other members who may become inappropriate in their responses.

The family or couple is considered the client when in counseling. If the couple should separate or one member stops attending sessions, the counselor is advised to begin a new file on the newly defined client. When working with a family, the family unit is considered the client, and a family systems perspective typically is followed. If one or more members of the family discontinue counseling, the remaining family members are the family client. However, if the family is reduced to one member, the counselor is advised to begin a new file and treat that family member as an individual. Maintaining focus on the client will guide the counselor with these populations and keep the sessions from getting off track with issues that involve only one member or one dyad within the family.

Role Changes

When a counselor has a change in roles—the counselor changes who the client is or they transition from counseling to a related practice such as mediation or evaluation—it is incumbent on the counselor to explain any related consequences of the role change to the client. These include but are not limited to consequences related to shifts in financial obligations or fees, legal impacts, therapeutic impacts, or related negatively concerns. Disclosures related to role changes are related directly to informed consent and checking in with the client for their understanding of the new roles and the change in approach. The counselor should cover role changes with a new written and verbal informed consent with the client. The new consent will clarify with the client the parameters of the new relationship. Its use provides an opportunity for the counselor and client to discuss the role changes and any potential resulting impacts on the client.

Ethical Code 10.1

A.6.d. Role Changes in the Professional Relationship.

When counselors change a role from the original or most recent contracted relationship, they obtain informed consent from the client and explain the client's right to refuse services related to the change. Examples of role changes include, but are not limited to

1. changing from individual to relationship or family counseling, or vice versa;

2. changing from an evaluative role to a therapeutic role, or vice versa; and

3. changing from a counselor to a mediator role, or vice versa.

Clients must be fully informed of any anticipated consequences (e.g., financial, legal, personal, therapeutic) of counselor role changes.

Source: 2014 American Counseling Association Code of Ethics. Reprinted with permission from American Counseling Association.

Protecting Clients

In a group setting, counselors must focus on individual members and the group as a whole. It is our responsibility to protect clients from physical, emotional, or psychological trauma that may be induced by the behavior of other members in the group.

Ethical Code 10.2

A.9.b. Protecting Clients.

In a group setting, counselors take reasonable precautions to protect clients from physical, emotional, or psychological trauma.

Source: 2014 American Counseling Association Code of Ethics. Reprinted with permission from American Counseling Association.

Additionally, we must be careful to avoid coercing members into participating in particular exercises when they are not comfortable with the exercise (Corey, Corey, & Corey, 2010; Jacobs, Masson, Harvill, & Schimmel, 2012). This is parallel to informed consent; clients must provide consent for activities and the therapeutic process. Activities meant for growth are not therapeutic when the client is not open to them. We should explain any upcoming activity and obtain informed consent from group members before moving forward. A key therapeutic piece to any activity is the time spent afterward processing the exercise. This helps members to reflect and conclude discussions that the activity may have facilitated, so members do not leave with open issues or triggers. Further, we must ensure that clients understand that they have the right to stop counseling when they choose.

Counselors working with families and couples have a similar responsibility to protect members of the family unit. We focus on the family unit or couple while not enabling or allowing other family members to harm one another in any way. We must be extra attentive to law and ethics when it comes to practice and note taking (Remley & Herlihy, 2014). Family law is not always parallel to laws pertaining to the individual. When stepparents or guardians are involved, confidentiality and related note taking can become complex. Perceived support of one family member over another can damage trust and counselor efforts with the client. We must check in frequently with the client (family unit or couple) in regard to their understanding of what is happening in the counseling session and their related perceptions. We must work with the client on multiple levels by listening to and treating them on all the different levels of interaction that occur.

CASE STUDY 10.1

Rick and Cindy have been attending couples counseling with Sam Gold, a marriage and family therapist for over 10 years. Cindy disclosed that Rick has been inattentive for the past seven years of their marriage, since Rick began studying to earn a graduate degree and their three adolescent children began to require much of their time at various sporting events. Cindy began to overspend to fulfill what felt like a "hole in her soul." She disclosed that she felt depressed, had difficulty sleeping, and was concerned about drinking too often and not eating enough. She admitted to having feelings of deep sadness and an inability to concentrate.

Cindy began an affair two years ago after speaking with Rick several times about his inattentiveness with no change on his part. Rick discovered the affair recently, became enraged, and stated that she must stop the affair, or he would file for divorce. She did not, so he angrily filed for divorce. The couple stopped attending appointments with Sam the week that Rick filed his paperwork. Two weeks later, Rick's attorney requested copies of all case notes taken during the couple's counseling sessions. Sam had maintained one set of notes for all sessions with the couple. He was detailed in his descriptions of what had been stated in the sessions. Rick has filed for custody of both of their children, claiming that Cindy is unfit as a mother and has poor decision-making skills.

1. What advice do you have for future couples counselors in regard to note taking?

2. What should Sam do with his notes at this time?

3. Should Sam respond immediately to the demand by the attorney for the notes?

Screening

One way to make group or family counseling more ethical and a smoother process is to screen potential members. This enables the counselor to screen out those clients who may be inappropriate for the group, such as members who have violent backgrounds or do not have the appropriate level of mental functioning. Interviewing members to ensure a better fit with the group can assist us in predetermining members who could become a problem, such as those who monopolize conversations, blame others, remain silent, are violent, are self-harming, or arc in severe crisis (Jacobs et al., 2012; Remley & Herlihy, 2014).

Inviting members with personality disorders into a group that is not focused on personality disorders could be detrimental to the group (Jacobs et al, 2012.). Groups that involve persons with personality or mood disorders and that have a focus that is not personality- or mood-based may be difficult to facilitate toward achievement of goals because of the nature of personality disorders. It is our responsibility to ensure the group process is therapeutically effective for all members and inviting members who will deter the group's progress toward goals could end in dissolution of the entire group.

Ethical Code 10.3

A.9.a. Screening.

Counselors screen prospective group counseling/therapy participants. To the extent possible, counselors select members whose needs and goals are compatible with the goals of the group, who will not impede the group process, and whose well-being will not be jeopardized by the group experience.

Source: 2014 American Counseling Association Code of Ethics. Reprinted with permission from American Counseling Association.

Counselors should screen for fit, which will produce a sense of cohesiveness among members. Norcross (2011) found that 80 percent of published studies supported that cohesion among group members led to the best client improvement. Screening for fit and cohesion is one of the best strategies a counselor group facilitator can implement for best outcome for the group members.

We also may screen families and couples prior to agreeing to meet. We should not work with populations with whom we have no expertise without adequate supervision. If a couple or family suffers from a particular issue of which we have no background, we should refer or seek supervision. Much like with group screening, we may choose to screen and refer family or couple inquiries when they are describing violent behavior or self-harm. The family counselor will want to confirm that these families or couples are stable before beginning therapeutic work on issues that could trigger a family or its members into negative behavior toward one another.

The screening process should include explaining the purpose of the group and the process. Not all prospective members are good candidates for some groups or group work in general. Discussing the goals of the group and the group's purpose will help some potential members to self-select out of the group or will assist the facilitator in assessing fit for the group.

As with individual clients, group members and family members also should be told that change can be stressful, and at times, undesirable consequences may occur, such as divorce (Jacobs et al., 2012). Jacobs and colleagues (2012) teach that screening is important because it often can uncover those members of the group or couple who are being coerced into attending counseling yet prefer not to. In these cases, the counselor may want to refer the couple or the involved individuals who want treatment to individual counseling.

Screening for groups also includes attending to final group size. Whether working with couples in a group or with a group of individuals, the number of members involved will affect the outcome and group interactions. Most experts in group counseling agree that a total of 8 to 12 members is adequate for group cohesion and therapeutic work to occur (Corey et al., 2010; Jacobs et al., 2012; Norcross, 2011). More than 12 or fewer than 8 can lead to members not having their needs met and difficulty in facilitation for the counselor.

Termination

As in individual counseling, ethical practice includes counselors terminating counseling groups (or families) when the client no longer benefits from counseling or if the counselor determines that the client is being harmed by the counseling process. We are also within our ethical rights to terminate counseling with clients who have not paid agreed-upon fees or if the client or a relation to the client threatens violence. We are not required to continue seeing persons who may do harm to us via lack of pay or personal injury. However, we should seek consultation and refer the client whenever possible so as not to face abandonment or neglect charges.

At times, members of counseling groups have to be terminated by the counselor prior to the group reaching its goals. When we must act to terminate a client who is not benefitting from the group and possibly disrupting the group and other members, we should work with the individual first and refer that individual to more appropriate counseling (Corey et al., 2010). We should then process with the remaining members the reasons for the individual leaving the group without disclosing anything that would be considered that member's right to confidentiality. The terminated member will have developed a place in the group, whether positive or not, and the absence should be processed.

Members also may choose to terminate counseling on their own. As part of the group rules, many groups will request that members desiring to leave prematurely tell the group first their reasons for leaving. When a member is leaving a group because he or she feels uncomfortable or not included, mentioning this to the rest of the group can encourage them to include that group member more openly (Remley & Herlihy, 2014). This can be therapeutic for the group members as well as the member who was thinking of terminating. All members of a group or family should be told in their informed consent and throughout the process that they are free to withdraw from the group at any time (Corey, Corey, & Callahan, 2011).

Clients should be referred in all possible situations when they are no longer benefitting from working with the counselor or are not pursuing agreed-upon behaviors. Whether a member chooses to terminate or the counselor chooses to terminate the member for the overall client's benefit, counselors should provide referral sources or treatment plan outlines or those behaviors the individual can pursue. Counselors treating groups or families ethically do not abandon members who are in need and work to assist them in obtaining the help they need after terminating with the counselor.

Ethical Code 10.4

A.11.c. Appropriate Termination.

Counselors terminate a counseling relationship when it becomes reasonably apparent that the client no longer needs assistance, is not likely to benefit, or is being harmed by continued counseling. Counselors may terminate counseling when in jeopardy of harm by the client or by another person with whom the client has a relationship, or when clients do not pay fees as agreed upon. Counselors provide pretermination counseling and recommend other service providers when necessary.

Source: 2014 American Counseling Association Code of Ethics. Reprinted with permission from American Counseling Association.

Guided Practice Exercise 10.1

Growing as a Group Counselor

Interview a group facilitator with more than 10 years' experience leading groups. Ask about his or her perceptions around the use of activities, group rules, and processes that lead to best outcomes for the members. Ask about how he or she terminates members who are disruptive.

COUNSELOR COMPETENCY

Counselors are required to receive appropriate supervision when working with a population or technique in which we have no special training.

Ethical Code 10.5

C.2.b. New Specialty Areas of Practice.

Counselors practice in specialty areas new to them only after appropriate education, training, and supervised experience. While developing skills in specialty areas, counselors take steps to ensure the competence of their work and protect others from possible harm.

Source: 2014 American Counseling Association Code of Ethics. Reprinted with permission from American Counseling Association.

This standard may seem obvious to you. However, consider a situation in which you accepted a new client, and in session three, the client mentions dealing with a severe trauma with which you have no specialized training; in fact, your education and training contained no work in trauma. The question becomes, then, do you refer the client after an alliance has been established, or do you continue to see the client and immediately seek (and receive) supervision in the specialized area of trauma? For each counselor, these questions surrounding specialty areas of practice will have to be answered and likely more than once.

Specialty Training

The subfield of group counseling and facilitation is framed more frequently by the professional counseling field as requiring specialty training in group counseling and facilitation (Association for Specialists in Group Work, 2012; Jacobs et al., 2012). Group facilitation is considered a highly specialized type of counseling, and those whose practices focus predominantly on group facilitation assert the need for specialty training in the topic. In fact, many postulate that it is unethical to lead a group without having specific training (beyond a master's level course) in leading groups (Corey et al., 2010; Jacobs et al., 2012). Corey and colleagues (2010) go a step further to state that group workers should receive supervision and group counseling in a group setting.

Jacobs and others (2012) assert that the most frequent unethical practice in group facilitation is when untrained leaders lead groups. Group counselors, like those working with individuals, have to be cautious regarding our own personal growth in a group and dual relationships that can occur. Inviting family or friends into counseling groups is not ethical practice for counselors. The ethical code (ACA, 2014) states that in cases where dual relationships may exist, we have the responsibility to "document boundary extensions." This includes informing the noncounselor party in the dual relationship of the boundaries or limits of the relationship, in other words, talking about the type of relationship that exists and where the boundaries will be drawn. Group counseling and facilitation takes a specialized approach.

Likewise, in family counseling, inadequate training can include questionable techniques such as paradoxical directives and inattention to gender bias (Corey et al., 2010). Counselors and counselors in training should be reminded regularly by supervisors and watched by supervisors to practice only within their level of competence. This may include but is not limited to not counseling families without educational course work and direct clinical internship hours in family counseling, that is, not conducting couples, family, group, or substance abuse counseling without course work and, hopefully, clinical training in such. We must be trained and competent to practice with new populations and approaches.

Ethical Code 10.6

C.2.a. Boundaries of Competence.

Counselors practice only within the boundaries of their competence, based on their education, training, supervised experience, state and national professional credentials, and appropriate professional experience. Whereas multicultural counseling competency is required across all counseling specialties, counselors gain knowledge, personal awareness, sensitivity, dispositions, and skills pertinent to being a culturally competent counselor in working with a diverse client population.

Source: 2014 American Counseling Association Code of Ethics. Reprinted with permission from American Counseling Association.

Another concern that may become an ethical issue for some includes competency in knowing when and how to stop working with clients. We must act ethically regarding issues that could be perceived as client abandonment or neglect. This can be especially complicated when working with group or family members who are disruptive to the group. It is important that we are detailed and clear in the informed consent and possibly repeat the group rules often regarding consequences for members who are disruptive to the therapeutic process. Regularly repeating or beginning each group or family session with a reminder of appropriate behavior can help to minimize members from leaving or being dismissed from the group. It also can serve to protect the counselor or other members from potential negative reactions from a member who is asked to leave but wasn't warned or reminded of the consequences. These clients can feel abandoned and may raise ethical complaints with licensure or professional boards or approach the counselor in other negative ways if they feel wrongly terminated. Repetition of terms for dismissal from the group or counseling sessions can help to thwart this possibility. We need to take precautions to avoid neglecting or abandoning clients.

Ethical Code 10.7

A.12. Abandonment and Client Neglect.

Counselors do not abandon or neglect clients in counseling. Counselors assist in making appropriate arrangements for the continuation of treatment, when necessary, during interruptions such as vacations, illness, and following termination.

Source: 2014 American Counseling Association Code of Ethics. Reprinted with permission from American Counseling Association.

CASE STUDY 10.2

Odette, licensed professional counselor (LPC), has been facilitating groups for four years in her local lesbian, gay, bisexual, transgender/transsexual, queer/questioning, intersex, asexual (LGBTQIA) community. She has been running a 10-week, closed group for gay men struggling with self-worth and the coming-out process. The group consists of six men between the ages of 18 and 26 of different ethnic and racial identities. During the seventh-week session, a group member, Mario, shares that "dealing with sexual confusion" has been hard on him and his family, especially his parents and siblings, and his family has asked for him to "try conversion therapy to work on his sexual issues." He asks the group to support his decision and starts to cite conversion theory information to promote his decision. Mario discloses that he has started conversion therapy and feels "nervous about the whole thing" and would like to continue with the group counseling. The other five group members become angry and saddened by Mario's decision and vocalize that they expect Odette to convince Mario of other alternatives. Odette can see that a few group members start to question the cohesion of the overall group and overall group goal of supporting group members through the coming-out process.

1. How should the group facilitator handle the situation with Mario promoting conversion therapy in a supportive gay counseling group?

2. What ethical implications can arise from a group member promoting a controversial treatment in a group counseling format?

3. What are the next steps Odette should take regarding the group's cohesion?

4. Should the group facilitator disclosure her own views on conversion therapy?

5. How do you think the Mario's presence would change the group dynamic if he continued group counseling or if he left the group?

Contributed by Mariaimee Gonzalez, PhD, visiting assistant professor, University of San Diego.

Cultural Competency

Facilitating groups and working with families from varying cultures or who are simply different from the counselor require special attention to client cultural context. We should be aware of our own biases and privileges to facilitate a therapeutic experience for a client. This is true when working with mixed groups as well as families or individuals. Family rules often are established within a cultural context. Whether or not a family will talk to a counselor or how comfortable they are with sharing family problems with an outside party is critical for a counselor to know prior to working with that family. From the opposite perspective, certain cultures will look to the counselor as the expert on a family issue and will expect the counselor to tell them what to do. We should be careful not to impose our own values in cases like this but to help the client determine the best next steps for the family.

When working with groups, counselor facilitators have to be aware of the varying cultures that may make up a group. One group may have members of varying races, religions, marital status, and socioeconomic status. All of these can impede the therapeutic process if not managed within the group. This is one way that screening can help us: screening prospective members for group fit and group goal attainment can help us to create a cohesive group. We must be aware of our own biases and of the various cultural contexts within a group to provide the best therapeutic outcome for the clients involved.

Guided Practice Exercise 10.2

Being a Group Member

What is the best way to learn about a group? Participate in one! Attend a counseling group as a member. Participate for a minimum of eight sessions, and then journal about your experience.

CONFIDENTIALITY AND PRIVACY

Confidentiality in group and family counseling can be complex. A family or group counselor never can guarantee the confidentiality of the other group or family members. While there are the obvious exceptions to confidentiality for the counselor, including harm of client self or harm by the client of another, even court-ordered breaking of confidentiality becomes sensitive to special circumstances and needs. For instance, family members in counseling have a right to the session notes. What if one spouse or partner wants to use the case notes to defame the other partner in a divorce case? What if a group member asks for notes from a session?

Guided Practice Exercise 10.3

Multiple Clients and the Law

Visit your state's licensure Web site. Review the laws and regulations that specifically pertain to group counseling. Compare those situations when the law is in favor of the group member versus the counseling group. Next, review the laws that specifically pertain to family counseling. Compare those situations when the law is in favor or the individual versus the family. Are their differences between group and family law in your state?

For these and other reasons, counselors working with groups are recommended to maintain minimal but effective notes; counselors working with families are advised to maintain separate notes on the various members of a family (Remley & Herlihy, 2014). An alternative is to use one set of notes on the family client and redact all information on the members who are not requesting the notes. For instance, if a couples counselor maintains one set of notes while counseling a couple and one partner requires copies of the notes after counseling has occurred, the counselor may redact all parts of the notes that have to do with the non-asking partner; that is, the counselor doesn't want to incriminate one partner to the other while providing confidential notes about both to one. Maintaining separate notes on the couple client will help to alleviate the work involved in redacting the correct information. Maintaining minimal group notes will help members from having access to the counselor's perceptions of other group members.

Ethical Code 10.8

B.4.b. Couples and Family.

In couples and family counseling, counselors clearly define who is considered "the client" and discuss expectations and limitations of confidentiality. Counselors seek agreement and document in writing such agreement among all involved parties regarding the confidentiality of information. In the absence of an agreement to the contrary, the couple or family is considered to be the client.

Source: 2014 American Counseling Association Code of Ethics. Reprinted with permission from American Counseling Association.

Many authors recommend the use of a confidentiality contract with client members (Bernstein & Harstell, 2004; Remley & Herlihy, 2014). A contract of this type is sometimes used as a deterrent to members breaking confidentiality. The contracts are in most cases not legally binding, but they can make members think first before acting in a harmful manner. This can help remind group clients of the importance of confidentiality. Bernstein and Hartsell (2004) suggest the use of a sign-in sheet when working with groups or families that reiterates the consequences of breaking confidentiality. A sign-in sheet can be a subtle but regular reminder of the rules of the group. We can also begin each session with a verbal reminder. This is similar to informed consent—reminding clients of what we are doing in session and checking for understanding. What will you do if a member breaks confidentiality?

Ethical Code 10.9

B.4.a. Group Work.

In group work, counselors clearly explain the importance and parameters of confidentiality for the specific group.

Source: 2014 American Counseling Association Code of Ethics. Reprinted with permission from American Counseling Association.

When confidentiality must be broken, such as in cases of court-ordered situations or harm of self or another, we are required by ethical code to disclose only that information that is necessary. This harkens back to the previous paragraph in which we discussed the process of redacting or cutting back notes to include only information that is necessary and that has content that only the individual requesting the notes has stated. In other words, the counselor is not providing notes that include things the other partner has stated, which can lead to harm of the other partner.

Ethical Code 10.10

B.2.e. Minimal Disclosure.

To the extent possible, clients are informed before confidential information is disclosed and are involved in the disclosure decision-making process. When circumstances require the disclosure of confidential information, only essential information is revealed.

Source: 2014 American Counseling Association Code of Ethics. Reprinted with permission from American Counseling Association.

This leads to another issue related to confidentiality—naming the client. Defining who the client is can help to guide the goals of counseling. For instance, when working with families, the family typically is considered the client—not one of the family members or the individual family members. This is to help the counselor retain clarity regarding who is being helped and to whom the therapeutic goals pertain. In the process of defining the client, we have to be careful not to make things better for one member of the group or family while simultaneously making things worse for another (Corey et al., 2010). This can be more difficult than it sounds. We should remind the family that their goals are the focus and not individual needs. This communication helps to maintain informed consent while keeping the client focused on the family as a whole. Hence, we must always be thinking of who the client is and maintaining the balance of therapeutic change around the goals of the client versus one individual.

Contradictorily, while the counselor may view the family as the client, the law typically sees the individuals of a family as the client or at least having rights (Remley & Herlihy, 2014). Because of this, we must stay abreast of family law in our state. Family laws can differ from state to state and are often revised. We have to not only know our own craft when practicing with the public; we have to be very aware of current and trending laws and regulations that impact the populations with which we work.

Ethical Code 10.11

B.4.b. Couples and Family.

In couples and family counseling, counselors clearly define who is considered "the client" and discuss expectations and limitations of confidentiality. Counselors seek agreement and document in writing such agreement among all involved parties regarding the confidentiality of information. In the absence of an agreement to the contrary, the couple or family is considered to be the client.

Source: 2014 American Counseling Association Code of Ethics. Reprinted with permission from American Counseling Association.

ADVOCACY

Counselors and counselors in training have an ethical obligation to advocate for clients who need assistance and to teach clients to self-advocate. Advocacy can be with members of counseling groups as well as families. When our society or parts thereof, interfere or keep our clients from attaining counseling goals or steps toward health and wellness, it is our responsibility to advocate for the client in the face of society. This often involves working with schools that client family members may attend; social workers, psychiatrists, and other mental health workers who our clients may see; and local agencies that may be able to provide more services to a client with particular needs (e.g., a client for whom travel to your office has become a hindrance, yet there is a mental health agency one block from his or her home). We are mental health experts and can work with all of these people in ways that will make things better for the client. We work with these parties to help clients gain services and hopefully to overcome barriers in society that may work against their achievement of mental health and wellness.

Ethical Code 10.12

A.7.a. Advocacy.

When appropriate, counselors advocate at individual, group, institutional, and societal levels to address potential barriers and obstacles to inhibit access and/or the growth and development of clients.

Source: 2014 American Counseling Association Code of Ethics. Reprinted with permission from American Counseling Association.

While advocacy is something that counselors are bound to implement, prior to doing so, we have to inform the client of advocacy options and obtain their consent to be advocated for. So while it may seem obvious to us that we help the client through advocacy efforts (attending individualized education program [IEP] meetings with a family at their child's school or calling a local agency for a group member), it is still an ethical requirement that we obtain the client's permission to begin advocacy efforts. This should occur in an informed consent type of discussion. We must inform the client of the advocacy options and help them select the options that make the most sense for them.

Advocacy always should include client education and participation in the advocacy efforts. Clients should be made aware of what we are doing and engage in the efforts. When they participate, they learn how to advocate for themselves. Teaching clients how to advocate for themselves is at the heart and foundation of counselor advocacy efforts. When clients learn how to advocate for themselves, dependency on the counselor is minimized, and client efficacy is enhanced.

Ethical Code 10.13

A.7.b. Confidentiality and Advocacy.

Counselors obtain client consent prior to engaging in advocacy efforts on behalf of an identifiable client to improve the provision of services and to work toward removal of systemic barriers or obstacles that inhibit client access, growth, and development.

Source: 2014 American Counseling Association Code of Ethics. Reprinted with permission from American Counseling Association.

CONCLUSION

We started this chapter with a scenario imagining what it might be like to feel reasonably confident and secure in your individual work, only to be thrown into a group dynamic. As you have learned, group facilitation and family counseling are complex processes requiring separate guidelines and, in most cases, ethics and practices that are distinct from individual counseling. Understanding the challenges to confidentiality, as well as the inherent power dynamics at play in groups and families, help beginning counselors conceptualize how their skills as individual counselors might transfer to working with families and groups. To wrap up this discussion of one of the more complicated aspects of counseling, we offer you some suggestions and best practices.

KEYSTONES

- A family or group counselor can never guarantee the confidentiality of the other group or family members because other members of the group may disclose comments and issues raised in the counseling sessions.
- When counselors work with more than one client, such as when working with families, couples, or groups, maintaining ethical practice can be multitiered and complex.
- The family or couple is considered the client when in counseling.
- In group counseling, the individual group members are considered individual clients. In a group setting, counselors must pay attention to individual members and the group as a whole. It is our responsibility to protect all clients from any trauma that could be provoked by other members in the group.
- The counselor has to be extra attentive to law and ethics when it comes to practice and note taking.
- Counselors may terminate counseling groups or families when the client no longer benefits from counseling or if the client is being harmed by the counseling process. We are also within our ethical rights to terminate counseling with clients who have not paid agreed-upon fees or if the client threatens violence.
- Counselors working with groups are recommended to maintain minimal but effective notes, and those working with families are recommended to maintain separate notes on the various members of the family.
- Counselors and counselors in training have an ethical obligation to advocate for clients and to teach clients to self-advocate.

SUGGESTED BEST PRACTICES

- You must first determine who the actual client is to make sound ethical decisions.
- A role of the group counselor is to protect clients from physical, emotional, or psychological trauma that may be induced by the behavior of other members in the group.

- As a group facilitator, it is your responsibility to protect all members from other members and not to coerce members into participating in particular exercises.
- With families and couples, maintain focus on the family unit or couple while not enabling or allowing other family members to harm one another in any way.
- When setting up a counseling or therapeutic group, you will need to screen prospective members. The screening process should include explaining the purpose of the group and the process.
- Ethical practice includes counselors terminating counseling groups (or families) when the client no longer benefits from counseling or actually is being harmed by the counseling process.
- Terminating a group member from a group is hard. You will work with the individual first and refer that individual to more appropriate counseling. You will then then process with the remaining members what happened with the particular member.
- If you treat groups or families, you cannot abandon a member who is in need. Instead, you will have to work to assist them in getting the help they need from another source.
- The subfield of group counseling and facilitation is framed by the professional counseling field as requiring specialty training in group counseling and facilitation.
- When you have to change roles as a counselor—going from family to individual or making a transition from counseling to a related practice such as mediation or evaluation—it is incumbent on you to explain any related consequences of the role change to the client.
- When confidentiality has to be broken, such as in cases of court-ordered situations or self-harm or harm of another, disclose only the information that is necessary.
- Be aware of your own biases and of the various cultural contexts within a group to provide the best therapeutic outcome for the clients involved.

ADDITIONAL RESOURCES

In Print

Belmont, J. (2008). *The therapeutic toolbox: 103 group activities and TIPs.* Eau Claire, WI: PESI.

Hartshorne, T. S., Sperry, L., & Watts, R. E. (2010). Ethical issues in open-forum family counseling or education: Johnny still wets his pants. *Journal of Individual Psychology, 66*(2), 144–151.

Shaw, E. (2014). Relational ethics and moral blindness: Startling incongruities in couple and family life. *Australian & New Zealand Journal of Family Therapy, 35*(4), 493–509. doi:10.1002/anzf.108

On the Web

Group Work for School Counselors: http://www.schoolcounselor.org/asca/media/asca/Position Statements/PS_Group-Counseling.pdf

The Professional School Counselor and Group Counseling. (n.d.). *The Association for Specialists in Group Work.* Retrieved from http://www.asgw.org/

REFERENCES

American Counseling Association (ACA). (2014). *ACA code of ethics.* Alexandria, VA: Author.

Association for Specialists in Group Work (ASGW). (2012). *Multicultural and social justice competence principles for group workers.* Retrieved from http://www.asgw.org/pdf/ASGW_MC_SJ_Priniciples_Final_ASGW.pdf

Bernstein, B. E., & Hartsell, T. L., Jr. (2004). *The portable lawyer for mental health professionals: An A-Z guide to protecting your clients, your practice and yourself* (2nd ed.). Hoboken, NJ: John Wiley & Sons.

Corey, G., Corey, M. S., & Callahan, P. (2011). *Issues and ethics in the helping professions* (8th ed.). Belmont, CA: Brooks/Cole.

Corey, M. S., Corey, G., & Corey, C. (2010). *Groups: Process and practice* (8th ed.). Belmont, CA: Brooks/Cole.

Jacobs, E. E., Masson, R. L., Harvill, R. L., & Schimmel, C. J. (2012). *Group counseling: Strategies and skills* (7th ed.). Belmont, CA: Brooks/Cole.

Norcross, J. C. (2011). *Psychotherapy relationships that work: Evidence-based responsiveness* (2nd ed.). New York: Oxford University Press.

Remley, T. P., & Herlihy, B. (2014). *Ethical, legal, and professional issues in counseling* (4th ed.). Upper Saddle River, NJ: Pearson/Merrill Prentice Hall.

Chapter 11

COUNSELOR EDUCATION AND SUPERVISION

In the second year of her counseling program, Marnie is assigned to Dr. Whitaker for supervision. During the supervisory process, Marnie becomes aware of some personal issues that are blocking her from being successful in her internship. Dr. Whitaker helps her define these areas and suggests ways Marnie can work on them. One suggestion is for Marnie to seek personal counseling. Marnie would like to, but her time is limited being a full-time graduate student and working her internship full-time. She has a great relationship with Dr. Whitaker and knows that she could work through these concerns in supervision. She asks Dr. Whitaker to work with her on these issues and is surprised when Dr. Whitaker refuses while reiterating her suggestion that Marnie seek counseling. What should Marnie do? How should Dr. Whitaker proceed with Marnie's supervision?

CHAPTER OVERVIEW

This chapter introduces the reader to the many and varied ethical responsibilities of the individuals accountable for the education and training of counselors in training (CITs). In doing so, it details various types of relationships inherent in the education and training process and the associated ethical codes and curriculum requirements. Readers will learn about the dual relationships characteristic of supervision and education and what to expect from them. American Counseling Association (ACA) ethical codes and related Council for Accreditation of Counseling & Related Educational Programs (CACREP) standards are presented.

LEARNING OBJECTIVES

After reading this chapter you will be able to do the following:

1. Analyze the ethical responsibilities of counselor educators related to curriculum, field experience, career development, and their relationships with students.

2. Analyze the ethical gatekeeping responsibilities of counselor educators related to orientation, evaluation, and remediation of students.

3. Examine the responsibilities of clinical supervisors and relationships between supervisors and supervisees.

4. Evaluate the ethical responsibilities of counseling students.

5. Apply concepts of culture and context to provide effective counseling to individuals with diverse backgrounds.

CACREP STANDARDS

CACREP Core Standards

G.1.b. Professional roles, functions, and relationships with other human service providers, including strategies for interagency or interorganization collaboration and communications.

G.1.d. Self-care strategies appropriate to the counselor role.

G.1.e. Counseling supervision models, practices, and processes.

G.1.f. Professional organizations, including membership benefits, activities, services to members, and current issues.

G.1.g. Professional credentialing, including certification, licensure, and accreditation practices and standards, and the effects of public policy on these issues.

G.1.h. The role and process of the professional counselor advocating on behalf of the profession.

G.1.j. Ethical standards of professional organizations and credentialing bodies, and applications of ethical and legal considerations in professional counseling.

CACREP Clinical Mental Health Standards

A.5. Understands a variety of models and theories related to clinical mental health counseling, including the methods, models, and principles of clinical supervision.

INTRODUCTION

Counselors in training are required to adhere to the ACA (2014) Code of Ethics and their state laws when counseling clients even while in training. They are as liable to client suit as are their supervisors; hence, ethical practice is critical.

Ethical Code 11.1

Section F. Introduction.

Counselor supervisors, trainers, and educators aspire to foster meaningful and respectful professional relationships and to maintain appropriate boundaries with supervisees and students in both face-to-face and electronic formats. They have theoretical and pedagogical foundations for their work; have knowledge of supervision models; and aim to be fair, accurate, and honest in their assessments of counselors, students, and supervisees.

Source: 2014 American Counseling Association Code of Ethics. Reprinted with permission from American Counseling Association.

Students should study the ACA code and their practice diligently and must speak openly to their supervisors—both faculty and site—about their experiences with clients so that everyone involved can keep a close watch on the developing CIT as well as the client.

The manner in which CITs are evaluated and then remediated and either dismissed or endorsed to the profession are described in this chapter. Counselor educators and supervisors are responsible for providing regular feedback to students through evaluation. When a student experiences difficulties in training or encounters a challenging area, it is important that the educators and supervisors provide feedback and remediation, with detailed guidelines to assist the student's improvement in this area. Likewise, if a student does not improve, the ACA Code of Ethics requires that educators and supervisors dismiss the CIT from the field or program. It can be difficult for students to understand that their faculty and licensed supervisors have the ethical mandate to refuse to graduate any student who is not a fit for the profession. This allows for subjective assessment on the part of the supervisor or educator in regard to the student's skills and development. Hence, an open relationship, with appropriate boundaries, is critical for the developing CIT.

This chapter is organized by ACA ethical codes that relate to counselor educators, those related to students, and those related to clinical supervisors. The terms *student* and *CIT* are used interchangeably throughout the chapter.

COUNSELOR EDUCATORS

Counselor educators play a crucial role in the development of CITs. They create, implement, and supervise educational programs and provide students with the most current knowledge and research in the profession. We will explore their roles, responsibilities, and relationships with students in this section.

Responsibilities

Counselor educators have many varied responsibilities to provide an educational program that meets ethical and professional counseling standards while also attending to the professional and sometimes personal development of students and the program (Corey, Corey, & Callahan, 2011).

Curriculum

In addition to educating and supervising students and serving as role models within the profession, counselor educators are responsible for regularly revising their counseling curriculum to keep up with the literature base as well as their own areas of expertise (Morrissette & Gadbois, 2006). Curriculum continually must reflect the most recent findings in the field and be immersed with ethics and the multicultural aspects of the core courses (Pack-Brown, Thomas, & Seymour, 2008). If little empirical evidence exists on a course topic or content, the educator has the responsibility to ensure that students understand that the information is not fully developed. This means that there could be risks associated with such information and that the information may change over time (Hartsell & Bernstein, 2008). Counseling curriculum should be based empirically and infused with ethics and multiculturalism throughout.

Ethical Code 11.2

F.7.a. Counselor Educators.

Counselor educators who are responsible for developing, implementing, and supervising educational programs are skilled as teachers and practitioners. They are knowledgeable regarding the ethical, legal, and regulatory aspects of the profession; are skilled in applying that knowledge; and make students and supervisees aware of their responsibilities. Whether in traditional, hybrid, and/or online formats, counselor educators conduct counselor education and training programs in an ethical manner and serve as role models for professional behavior.

F.7.b. Counselor Educator Competence.

Counselors who function as counselor educators or supervisors provide instruction within their areas of knowledge and competence and provide instruction based on current information and knowledge available in the profession. When using technology to deliver instruction, counselor educators develop competence in the use of the technology.

F.7.c. Infusing Multicultural Issues/Diversity.

Counselor educators infuse material related to multiculturalism/diversity into all courses and workshops for the development of professional counselors.

F.7.d. Integration of Study and Practice.

In traditional, hybrid, and/or online formats, counselor educators establish education and training programs that integrate academic study and supervised practice.

F.7.e. Teaching Ethics.

Throughout the program, counselor educators ensure that students are aware of the ethical responsibilities and standards of the profession and the ethical responsibilities of students to the profession. Counselor educators infuse ethical considerations throughout the curriculum.

F.7.g. Student-to-Student Supervision and Instruction.

When students function in the role of counselor educators or supervisors, they understand that they have the same ethical obligations as counselor educators, trainers, and supervisors. Counselor educators make every effort to ensure that the rights of students are not compromised when their peers lead experiential counseling activities in traditional, hybrid, and/or online formats (e.g., counseling groups, skills classes, clinical supervision).

F.7.h. Innovative Theories and Techniques.

Counselor educators promote the use of techniques/procedures/modalities that are grounded in theory and/or have an empirical or scientific foundation. When counselor educators discuss developing or innovative techniques/procedures/modalities, they explain the potential risks, benefits, and ethical considerations of using such techniques/procedures/modalities.

Source: 2014 American Counseling Association Code of Ethics. Reprinted with permission from American Counseling Association.

When teaching from actual client cases or from student experiences, educators must receive permission first from the client or student, or they must change the details enough to protect the identity of the persons involved. Students and clients have a right to know if their stories will become teaching tools, otherwise the educator risks breach of confidentiality and trust and accusations of unethical practice. Within this realm, educators continually model effective counseling techniques and demeanors in their interactions with students. This can be difficult with challenging students. Yet, the opportunity for students to experience effective counseling and interpersonal skills firsthand can be quite impactful. Counselor educators have the added responsibility of safeguarding the rights of those involved in any teaching demonstration.

Ethical Code 11.3

F.7.f. Use of Case Examples.

The use of client, student, or supervisee information for the purposes of case examples in a lecture or classroom setting is permissible only when (a) the client, student, or supervisee has reviewed the material and agreed to its presentation, or (b) the information has been sufficiently modified to obscure identity.

Source: 2014 American Counseling Association Code of Ethics. Reprinted with permission from American Counseling Association.

Field Experience Supervision

A significant aspect of counseling curriculum involves field experience. Counseling program faculty develop relationships with community agencies that provide a comprehensive counseling experience for students. This experience requires clinical supervision by a trained and experienced supervisor who teaches the student skills through application. The learning curve in this type of environment can be steep for a student and risky to say the least. Appropriate supervision comprises weekly time with the supervisor in which a minimum of an hour (or consecutive 50 minutes) is spent directly attending to client issues that have arisen for the student. Supervision should be proactive and train students on how to manage crisis situations and the general operations of the agency before a crisis occurs. Students must learn to advocate for themselves on their site and also to report issues and concerns about their site to their faculty supervisors in group supervision. This will ensure the best care for the clients and the most appropriate training for the student.

Faculty supervisors are responsible for monitoring their students' learning onsite (for their field experience). They should remain in regular contact with site supervisors about students' development and areas needing more focus. Council for Accreditation of Counseling & Related Educational Programs (CACREP, 2009) requires that educators have biweekly interaction with site supervisors during practicum and regular contact during internship. This ensures that the faculty and site supervisors are in agreement when training the student, thereby minimizing student confusion regarding client treatment.

There are many roles and responsibilities of the student, supervisor, and counselor educators involved in a field experience. Counselor educators are responsible for documenting that students, supervisors, and other faculty are aware of the responsibilities that each member has in the field experience. Further, faculty supervisors (educators) are required to help students understand the significance of communicating their training status (student or CIT) to clients. Faculty also need to ensure that students communicate to clients that information discussed in session likely will be disclosed to supervisors. Clients seen by a student must be aware that their discussions will be shared and that the student is just that—a student. This helps to minimize client confusion and may lower the client's expectations of the student, which can be beneficial. Some clients can be more open and cooperative because they are working with a student. Students have many responsibilities in field experience, but faculty members have the ethical responsibility to organize educational experiences that define and clarify these responsibilities, so students have support during the learning process.

Ethical Code 11.4

F.7.i. Field Placements.

Counselor educators develop clear policies and provide direct assistance within their training programs regarding appropriate field placement and other clinical experiences. Counselor educators provide clearly stated roles and responsibilities for the student or supervisee, the site supervisor, and the program supervisor. They confirm that site supervisors are qualified to provide supervision and inform site supervisors of their professional and ethical responsibilities in this role.

Source: 2014 American Counseling Association Code of Ethics. Reprinted with permission from American Counseling Association.

Career Development

Another important component to counselor education that takes place during the final terms of a student's program involves career development. New to the 2014 ACA Code of Ethics is the call for counselor educators to teach their students about the lifelong and important concept of professional development and to create awareness of local employment opportunities. Ongoing professional development throughout a counselor's career should be stressed from the beginning of a program and should be infused throughout the curriculum. Students should understand the importance of keeping up with recent empirical findings in the field and also the field's requirement to do so. Most state licensure boards call for continuing education for sustained licensure; some states require that a portion of that education regards ethics.

Graduate job placement typically occurs in conjunction with discussions of continued professional development. This can happen more frequently in rural areas and communities with few counseling and social work degree programs. Yet, it is also seen in larger and even saturated communities where the counselor education programs have a strong track record of developing skilled counselors for their communities. Program faculty must make the time to develop relationships and maintain regular communications with local agencies regarding job placement and provide that information to students. Faculty are responsible ethically to help their students find job opportunities; effective faculty also will teach their students how to prepare for the national exams and pursue licensure and specialty certification.

Ethical Code 11.5

F.8.b. Student Career Advising.

Counselor educators provide career advisement for their students and make them aware of opportunities in the field.

Source: 2014 American Counseling Association Code of Ethics. Reprinted with permission from American Counseling Association.

Guided Practice Exercise 11.1

Comparing and Contrasting Ethical Codes

Review the ethical codes of ACA and the Association for Counseling and Supervision and pick out those codes that are not repeated or are different between the two.

Relationships Between Counselor Educators and Students

Relationships between supervisors and educators with current and former students or supervisees are best when kept on a professional level. While this may seem obvious, counseling can be an intimate experience, and education, training, and supervision also can be intimate experiences. In this context, intimate is defined as deep and personal experiences in a caring setting (not sexual experiences). When educators, supervisors, students, and supervisees are continually in confidential settings discussing the care and development of others, caring feelings naturally can evolve. This occurs between clients and their counselors for the same reasons. For some students, experiencing supervision in a counseling training program may be one of the few times they have experienced another individual caring for them and showing empathy. The natural response is to care back. However, counselor educators and supervisors are in positions of power over students and have multiple, overlapping roles with students.

Kolberg, Morgan, and Brendel (2002) emphasize that while counselor educators may see a dual relationship with a student as harmless—because they know what they are thinking—the student doesn't know what the faculty member is thinking and may have a different perception of the relationship. Therefore, it is necessary for educators to monitor the actual experience of the student–faculty relationship so as to maintain clear and accurate perceptions of the definition of that relationship and defined boundaries around behavior. For this reason, the ACA (2014) Code of Ethics no longer supports counseling of students by faculty. Confusion between responsibilities and acceptable behavior can be high when these roles are intermingled. Counselor educators must be mindful of boundaries and the potential for student misperception about the relationship in counselor education and supervision.

Ethical Code 11.6

F.10.a. Sexual or Romantic Relationships.

Counselor educators are prohibited from sexual or romantic interactions or relationships with students currently enrolled in a counseling or related program and over whom they have power and authority. This prohibition applies to both in-person and electronic interactions or relationships.

F.10.e. Counseling Services.

Counselor educators do not serve as counselors to students currently enrolled in a counseling or related program and over whom they have power and authority.

Source: 2014 American Counseling Association Code of Ethics. Reprinted with permission from American Counseling Association.

Educators and supervisors are responsible for maintaining professional boundaries and to model and explain the reasons they exist. Modeling these boundaries can help students learn how to do the same with their clients—not doing so may lead to students having weak boundaries with their own clients (Downs, 2003). Downs found that students who had romantic relationships with faculty were more likely to have romantic relationships with clients. Hence, an inappropriate relationship between educator and student can lead to an inappropriate relationship between counselor (or CIT) and client. Educators and supervisors need to clarify their roles when working with students, and if boundaries are crossed, it is ethical practice to help the student understand why the boundaries are in place and how they translate to the learning experience and the clinical experience.

Protection from harassment is also the educator's responsibility. Students are required to participate in self-growth activities by ethical code, and exposing personal stories during self-growth experiences can leave them open to harassment. Counselor educators must manage these experiences in ways that protect students from unknown harm. For instance, faculty should provide informed consent regarding self-growth in their syllabus as well as before and after any experiential activity. The faculty should caution students to think through the content that they want to share and should step in and provide further warning if a student seems to be disclosing something exceptionally deep and personal that may not relate directly to the classroom experience.

Faculty also should remind students regularly of confidentiality regarding other students' disclosures during self-growth experiences. Students may be tempted to discuss others' experiences in the hallway or during a break. Repeating private information that another student disclosed becomes the easy target of program gossip. Yet, this practice breaks confidentiality and, therefore, is unethical, and students are warned by faculty not to engage in it. Many programs have policies around breaking confidentiality of self-disclosures that result in dismissal from or remediation in the program. Additionally, protection from sexual harassment during self-growth as well as at any other time in the program is a responsibility of all in the program.

Ethical Code 11.7

F.10.b. Sexual Harassment.

Counselor educators do not condone or subject students to sexual harassment.

Source: 2014 American Counseling Association Code of Ethics. Reprinted with permission from American Counseling Association.

It is a small world when dealing with relationships and smaller yet when dealing with dual relationships. On occasion, and especially in smaller communities, relationships between educators or supervisors and students, clients, and even relatives of students and clients seem imminent. Yet, educators and supervisors are cautioned against having nonacademic relationships with students, former students, supervisees, clients, or relatives of clients. In rare instances, these relationships may be considered helpful by both parties and fall within the bounds of an acceptable relationship; however, ethical code mandates open discussions between both parties regarding the definition of the relationship and potential effects of the relationship on both parties. Those involved should be clear about the roles of the relationship and how the relationship is serving a beneficial purpose. The faculty member or supervisor has the responsibility of ensuring that the party with less power (student or relative) understands the relationship and that there are no misperceptions.

Ethical Code 11.8

F.10.c. Relationships With Former Students.

Counselor educators are aware of the power differential in the relationship between faculty and students. Faculty members discuss with former students potential risks when they consider engaging in social, sexual, or other intimate relationships.

F.10.d. Nonacademic Relationships.

Counselor educators avoid nonacademic relationships with students in which there is a risk of potential harm to the student or which may compromise the training experience or grades assigned. In addition, counselor educators do not accept any form of professional services, fees, commissions, reimbursement, or remuneration from a site for student or supervisor placement.

F.10.f. Extending Educator–Student Boundaries.

Counselor educators are aware of the power differential in the relationship between faculty and students. If they believe that a nonprofessional relationship with a student may be potentially beneficial to the student, they take precautions similar to those taken by counselors when working with clients. Examples of potentially beneficial interactions or relationships include, but are not limited to, attending a formal ceremony; conducting hospital visits; providing support during a stressful event; or maintaining mutual membership in a professional association, organization, or community. Counselor educators discuss with students the rationale for such interactions, the potential benefits and drawbacks, and the anticipated consequences for the student. Educators clarify the specific nature and limitations of the additional role(s) they will have with the student prior to engaging in a nonprofessional relationship. Nonprofessional relationships with students should be time limited and/or context specific and initiated with student consent.

Source: 2014 American Counseling Association Code of Ethics. Reprinted with permission from American Counseling Association.

CASE STUDY 11.1

Professor Jackie Garrett was a counselor educator working with master and doctoral students. Professor Garrett admired the work ethic and insight of a particular student, a second-year master's student named Jose Gonzalez. Professor Garrett collaborated with Jose on research projects and community volunteer opportunities throughout his second

(Continued)

(Continued)

year. In Jose's third year, Professor Garrett found herself spending more time with Jose and felt they had a special connection. One evening while working closely, Jose leaned in to kiss Professor Garrett, and she kissed him back. The evening ended with no discussion regarding what had happened. In the ensuing days, Professor Garrett and Jose found themselves texting romantic messages on a daily basis, along with hour-long phone calls. Eventually Professor Garrett and Jose's relationship elevated to a sexual relationship that both were happy about. No discussion had occurred about the relationship, including no talk of the power differential and related ethical choices and codes.

Other students in Jose's cohort began to hear about their relationship, creating tension between Jose and his classmates. Professor Garrett was worried that she would lose her position and respect from her colleagues, but as there was no official university policy prohibiting consensual sexual relationships between professors and students, she continued with the relationship. During an advising appointment with a student in Jose's cohort, the advisee told Professor Garrett, "Many students are talking about you and Jose. We are all concerned that we cannot truly trust you with our concerns and personal problems because we feel that you will tell Jose." Following the meeting, Professor Garrett reflected on how her relationship with a student might have wounded her relationships with other students and her colleagues.

1. *Although the university allows for professor and student consensual romantic relationships, what does the ACA (2014) Code of Ethics state about faculty and CIT romantic relationships?*

2. *What consequences do you think can arise from consensual faculty–student romantic relationships?*

3. *What are the appropriate steps Professor Garrett should take in regard to her relationship with Jose?*

4. *How do you think a consensual romantic relationship can affect a CIT? Include your thoughts related to personal growth, boundary formation, professional development, relationships with peers and faculty, objectivity, self-awareness, and impact on others.*

5. *How do you think the intersection of gender and hierarchy play a part in the formation of consensual romantic relationships between faculty and CITs? What are other demographic variables that could be intersected when power imbalances are formulated?*

Contributed by Mariaimee Gonzalez, PhD, visiting assistant professor, University of San Diego.

Guided Practice Exercise 11.2

Romantic Relationships at the University Level

Visit your university Web site, and search for university policy regarding romantic relationships among faculty and students. If there are none, consider writing a letter to your university administration requesting policies be drafted according to ethical practice.

GATEKEEPING: ORIENTATION, EVALUATION, AND REMEDIATION

In addition to creating and maintaining curriculum, supervising field experience, assisting with career development, and establishing and growing relationships with students, counselor educators must participate in gatekeeping activities, which include the orientation, evaluation, and remediation of students within the counseling program.

Orientation

When beginning any new job or profession, orientation is critical to an individual's success. The same holds true when beginning a clinical professional educational program that leads to entering a profession (as determined by affiliated licenses, certifications, and usually, ethical codes). Professional educational programs that are clinical and professional in nature require attention to the varied details associated with the educational content, program experiences, and the associated profession. Learning all the requirements of being a licensed professional counselor (LPC) can confuse even an experienced CIT. Understanding all of the details that must be attended to while in the program, while training in an internship, applying for supervision of clinical hours, and preparing for professional licensure can be equated to learning a foreign language. Orientation to the program and profession will help students to organize their learning.

Often, students and CITs benefit from hearing details many times to fully understand their responsibilities in getting and remaining licensed as a professional counselor. Students must learn the details of field experience, including counseling and interpersonal skills work, management of crises and essential topics in treatment, diagnoses and pathology, theory and application, note taking, self-care, treatment team planning and case conceptualizations, and of course, ethical codes and state law. They must learn the details of practice and getting licensed, including taking national and state exams, supplying supervisor credentials for supervision approval, providing education information for licensure, and learning how to read the various state board requirements. Pacing the orientations and reiterating the information at key times during the program may assist students to develop a working knowledge of the program and profession. Hence, an orientation to the program curriculum and the counseling profession at the beginning of a student's program is supported by the ACA code of ethics and will help the student to determine that he or she is in the appropriate program and profession.

Orientation should be ongoing and should not end with an introduction to the program curriculum and field. Providing orientations to the program, field experience, and postgraduation responsibilities and next steps helps students prepare for the interviewing process and understand what to look for in a prospective job.

Orientation also helps determine student fit with a particular program—that is, is this the right program for a particular student—and to determine student fit with the profession—that is, is this student fit to enter the profession? The ACA Code of Ethics requires counselor educators and supervisors to graduate only students who are a fit with the profession. It is the responsibility of counselor educators and supervisors not to graduate those students who lack interpersonal or clinical counseling skills, openness to supervision, and understanding of ethical practice. This responsibility is one that prospective and active students should keep in mind: counselor educators and supervisors are the gatekeepers to the profession. This is a subjective perspective on the part of the counselor educator but is supported by the profession because of the counselor educator's education, clinical experience, and mostly, adherence to ethical practice in which the counselor educator will not discriminate against a student and will impose only restrictions that protect the general public where the student is concerned. Close attention to specific information regarding postgraduation is helpful to students in the later stages of their degree programs.

The ACA (2014) Code of Ethics outlines several components that a counselor education program should cover in the orientation of new students. Those components include informing prospective students of the principles of the profession, the level of skill and knowledge required to complete the degree, program curriculum, evaluation and dismissal procedures, the inclusion of self-growth as part of the curriculum, and field experience.

Ethical Code 11.9

F.8.a. Program Information and Orientation.

Counselor educators recognize that program orientation is a developmental process that begins upon students' initial contact with the counselor education program and continues throughout the educational and clinical training of students. Counselor education faculty provide prospective and current students with information about the counselor education program's expectations, including

1. the values and ethical principles of the profession;

2. the type and level of skill and knowledge acquisition required for successful completion of the training;

3. technology requirements;

4. program training goals, objectives, and mission, and subject matter to be covered;

5. bases for evaluation;

6. training components that encourage self-growth or self-disclosure as part of the training process;

7. the type of supervision settings and requirements of the sites for required clinical experiences;

8. student and supervisor evaluation and dismissal policies and procedures; and

9. up-to-date employment prospects for graduates.

Source: 2014 American Counseling Association Code of Ethics. Reprinted with permission from American Counseling Association.

Evaluation and Remediation

As mentioned, counselor education programs have the responsibility of informing students of the evaluation process during the initial orientation and throughout the program. The evaluation process of a counseling program has the unique components of measuring the self-growth and related self-awareness of a developing student in addition to assessing the student's academic development and skills acquisition; this measurement is ongoing, and feedback to the student is important. Hence, the evaluation process in a counselor education program will include measurement of the student's development in knowledge, skills, self-awareness, and personal growth, and the evaluation process and related feedback is continual throughout the program.

Students have the right to know which of their self-growth experiences will be shared with others—including in class—and must agree to such. To develop as counselors, students need ongoing feedback that describes the skills and awareness issues in which they are succeeding and those which need improvement, but they also have the right to agree to the sharing of these skills with others. Ethical code requires that educators and supervisors who use a student's exercise experience as a teaching tool obtain the student's consent for doing so. The instructor usually accomplishes this by providing an informed consent to students when they begin a self-growth activity.

Ethical Code 11.10

F.9.a. Evaluation of students.

Counselors clearly state to students, prior to and throughout the training program, the levels of competency expected, appraisal methods, and timing of evaluations for both didactic and clinical competencies. Counselor educators provide students with ongoing feedback regarding their performance throughout the training program.

F.8.c. Self-Growth Experiences.

Self-growth is an expected component of counselor education. Counselor educators are mindful of ethical principles when they require students to engage in self-growth experiences. Counselor educators and supervisors inform students that they have a right to decide what information will be shared or withheld in class.

Source: 2014 American Counseling Association Code of Ethics. Reprinted with permission from American Counseling Association.

When students are having difficulties developing appropriately, counselor educators must provide an evaluation process that includes due process and an opportunity to improve. It is important that students know the program's expectations in regard to developing skills and that the faculty are clear regarding the items (self-growth, skills, or knowledge) that need improvement. An ethical program will provide students with options for assistance when they are struggling with developmental components. This may include referrals to counseling services or the completion of academic projects to support their continued development. Documentation of these options is inherent in the process, and students should be provided copies of the documentation of their remediation or referral process. The evaluation process (and remediation process) of a program should be clearly defined and discussed with prospective and active students. Programs are required to provide informed consent regarding evaluation and remediation to their students.

Ethical Code 11.11

F.9.b. Limitations.

Counselor educators, throughout ongoing evaluation, are aware of and address the inability of some students to achieve counseling competencies. Counselor educators do the following:

1. assist students in securing remedial assistance when needed,

2. seek professional consultation and document their decision to dismiss or refer students for assistance, and

3. ensure that students have recourse in a timely manner to address decisions requiring them to seek assistance or to dismiss them and provide students with due process according to institutional policies and procedures.

F.9.c. Counseling for Students.

If students request counseling, or if counseling services are suggested as part of a remediation process, counselor educators assist students in identifying appropriate services.

Source: 2014 American Counseling Association Code of Ethics. Reprinted with permission from American Counseling Association.

CLINICAL SUPERVISORS

While counselor educators teach students in the classroom, clinical supervisors assist students in the field. Their primary role is to observe and monitor the counseling skills of counselors and CITs. This allows supervisors to help them improve their clinical performance and professional development. We will examine their responsibilities and relationships with supervisees in this section.

Responsibilities

Supervision is the oversight of training of a developing counselor. It takes place during the counseling program curriculum in clinical courses, including field experience as well as postgraduation (but prior to licensure). In the best counselors, it continues post licensure and is a lifelong pursuit. Primarily, supervision is the training of a counselor through oversight of the counseling in which the CIT is engaged; that is, it is the direct oversight of the client. The oversight occurs through review of the CIT's case notes and other written assessments; observation of the CIT's actual counseling, either through video or audio taping or directly observing counseling; and self-reporting from the CIT. The supervisor is responsible for reviewing the CIT at work, providing feedback regarding areas that need growth, and also to provide learning experiences for the CIT.

CITs must explain clearly their level of training and student status to clients. Supervisors ensure that their CITs communicate the limits of their competence, their level of training, and confidentiality—particularly the fact that the supervisor will have access to the contents of counseling sessions between the CIT and the client. This information typically is covered in the informed consent process provided by the CIT to the client. It is the supervisor's responsibility to ensure that the CIT specifies the aspects of the counseling process that may be unique for the client because he or she is being seen by a CIT. Supervisors also must adhere to the ethical code provided by the Association for Counselor Education and Supervision (ACES, 1995).

Ethical Code 11.12

F.1.a. Client Welfare.

A primary obligation of counseling supervisors is to monitor the services provided by supervisees. Counseling supervisors monitor client welfare and supervisee performance and professional development. To fulfill these obligations, supervisors meet regularly with supervisees to review the supervisees' work and help them become prepared to serve a range of diverse clients. Supervisees have a responsibility to understand and follow the ACA Code of Ethics.

F.1.b. Counselor Credentials.

Counseling supervisors work to ensure that supervisees communicate their qualifications to render services to their clients.

F.1.c. Informed Consent and Client Rights.

Supervisors make supervisees aware of client rights, including the protection of client privacy and confidentiality in the counseling relationship. Supervisees provide clients with professional disclosure information and inform them of how the supervision process influences the limits of confidentiality. Supervisees make clients aware of who will have access to records of the counseling relationship and how these records will be stored, transmitted, or otherwise reviewed.

Source: 2014 American Counseling Association Code of Ethics. Reprinted with permission from American Counseling Association.

The supervisor must have protocol for emergency contact in place. Just as a counselor is required to have information and protocol in place for clients when a mental health crisis occurs, the supervisor must have contact information and protocol in place for those times when the CIT is in a crisis situation with a client. Because the supervisor is responsible for the client, it is important that he or she establishs procedures for the CIT to follow when a crisis occurs, so the CIT can receive supervision (help) on how to handle the crisis. Supervisors always should be within contact of a CIT when the CIT is counseling clients.

Ethical Code 11.13

F.4.a. Informed Consent for Supervision.

Supervisors are responsible for incorporating into their supervision the principles of informed consent and participation. Supervisors inform supervisees of the policies and procedures to which supervisors are to adhere and the mechanisms for due process appeal of individual supervisory actions. The issues unique to the use of distance supervision are to be included in the documentation as necessary.

F.4.b. Emergencies and Absences.

Supervisors establish and communicate to supervisees procedures for contacting supervisors or, in their absence, alternative on-call supervisors to assist in handling crises.

F.4.c. Standards for Supervisees.

Supervisors make their supervisees aware of professional and ethical standards and legal responsibilities.

Source: 2014 American Counseling Association Code of Ethics. Reprinted with permission from American Counseling Association.

It may seem like common sense that counseling supervisors have appropriate training in clinical supervision of CITs. However, the similar professions of social work and counseling psychology share the training and education of counseling students in many parts of the country (though in other parts this sharing is not permitted). Community agencies are managed by licensed counselors, social workers, or psychologists. This places these professionals in the role of supervising counseling interns (or supervising supervisors of counseling interns). Supervision is one of the primary ways new counselors and interns develop their professional identities (Bernard & Goodyear, 2009). Therefore, it is necessary that supervisors not only have experience supervising but have experience and training in the clinical supervision of counselors. For CITs to develop professional identity as a counselor and to learn comprehensive counseling (rather than social work or another treatment approach to mental illness), they must be trained by individuals who were trained in the clinical supervision of counselors. When these supervisors also are licensed counselors, the assurance of a strong counselor identity is even greater.

Ethical Code 11.14

F.2.a. Supervisor Preparation.

Prior to offering supervision services, counselors are trained in supervision methods and techniques. Counselors who offer supervision services regularly pursue continuing education activities, including both counseling and supervision topics and skills.

F.2.b. Multicultural Issues/Diversity in Supervision.

Counseling supervisors are aware of and address the role of multiculturalism/diversity in the supervisory relationship.

Source: 2014 American Counseling Association Code of Ethics. Reprinted with permission from American Counseling Association.

Relationships Between Clinical Supervisors and Supervisees

The supervisor–supervisee relationship has similar components to the client and counselor relationship. Informed consent, the quality of the relationship, and performance evaluation are significant components to supervision. Supervisors have the duty to provide informed consent that delineates the roles and responsibilities of the parties, various protocols that will be followed throughout the relationship, and the manner in which termination can occur. The supervisor must remain in the position of supervisor and not blur boundaries with the CIT so that the CIT may experience an accepting and professional place for growth.

Supervisors are discouraged from sharing other supervisory roles with the CIT, such as administrative supervisor. This type of dual relationship may lead to role confusion for the developing CIT, which can impair growth and indirectly may harm client welfare. The supervisory relationship should be defined clearly and adhered to by both parties. It is critical that CITs understand their responsibilities to provide the best counseling services to clients. Components of effective counseling can be neglected when the CIT is unaware of responsibilities that they have in the counselor–client relationship. This is covered in their informed consent to clients and also in the informed consent between the supervisor and supervisee.

Ethical Code 11.15

F.3.a. Extending Conventional Supervisory Relationships Counseling.

Supervisors clearly define and maintain ethical professional, personal, and social relationships with their supervisees. Supervisors consider the risks and benefits of extending current supervisory relationships in any form beyond conventional parameters. In extending these boundaries, supervisors take appropriate professional precautions to ensure that judgment is not impaired and that no harm occurs.

Source: 2014 American Counseling Association Code of Ethics. Reprinted with permission from American Counseling Association.

Supervisors also are discouraged from engaging in nonprofessional relationships with supervisees. Sexual contact and romantic relationships between supervisors and supervisees are prohibited, primarily because of the power differential that exists in the relationship. A romantic relationship often will distort the objectivity of the supervisor (Barnett & Johnson, 2010). Supervisees may develop feelings for a caring supervisor, believe that they have a special relationship, and then may act on that belief. The opposite also can occur, and supervisors can take advantage of their power (and influence grades and endorsement to the profession) over the supervisee by proposing a romantic relationship. Either way, a romantic relationship between the supervisor and supervisee is prohibited by ethical code due to its negative impact on the CIT's development and its potential indirect influence on the client–counselor relationship and the welfare of clients of the involved counselors.

Ethical Code 11.16

F.3.b. Sexual Relationships.

Sexual or romantic interactions or relationships with current supervisees are prohibited. This prohibition applies to both in-person and electronic interactions or relationships.

Source: 2014 American Counseling Association Code of Ethics. Reprinted with permission from American Counseling Association.

Counseling supervisors also are discouraged from supervising friends, romantic partners, or relatives in a clinical relationship. Like the client–counselor relationship, power differentials and associated displacement of judgment may result.

Ethical Code 11.17

F.3.d. Friends or Family Members.

Supervisors are prohibited from engaging in supervisory relationships with individuals with whom they have an inability to remain objective.

Source: 2014 American Counseling Association Code of Ethics. Reprinted with permission from American Counseling Association.

Relationships that can be defined as therapeutically beneficial for the CIT, such as attending ceremonies, visiting the supervisee in the hospital and providing support, or collaborating at professional conferences and organizations, are permissible. However, the supervisor must have open discussions with the CIT regarding inherent risks involved in the relationship and how introductions and potential outcomes of the relationship will be managed. Supervisors have the duty to carry out these discussions and then document the reasons for the nonprofessional relationship and how it is beneficial.

Ethical Code 11.18

F.10.f. Extending Educator–Student Boundaries.

Counselor educators are aware of the power differential in the relationship between faculty and students. If they believe that a nonprofessional relationship with a student may be potentially beneficial to the student, they take precautions similar to those taken by counselors when working with clients. Examples of potentially beneficial interactions or relationships include, but are not limited to, attending a formal ceremony; conducting hospital visits; providing support during a stressful event; or maintaining mutual membership in a professional association, organization, or community. Counselor educators discuss with students the rationale for such interactions, the potential benefits and drawbacks, and the anticipated consequences for the student. Educators clarify the specific nature and limitations of the additional role(s) they will have with the student prior to engaging in a nonprofessional relationship. Nonprofessional relationships with students should be time limited and/or context specific and initiated with student consent.

Source: 2014 American Counseling Association Code of Ethics. Reprinted with permission from American Counseling Association.

The quality of the supervisor–supervisee relationship has been found to be as important as that of the client and counselor (Barnett, Cornish, Goodyear, & Lichtenberg, 2007). Supervisors must nurture the relationship to create an environment wherein the CIT can experience clinical and personal growth. CITs should feel accepted and comfortable enough to grow and also to feel unencumbered when self-reporting on counseling with clients. Supervisees inadvertently may omit important information in supervision if they are concerned with being unfairly judged or assessed in the process. Countertransference and transference likely will occur in the supervisory relationship as it does in a professional counseling relationship. Hence, supervisors must juggle the roles of teacher, consultant, and counselor while supervising (Bernard & Goodyear, 2009). Transition among these roles, as well as knowing when to work from which role, creates an effective and strong supervisory relationship (Bernard & Goodyear, 2009). The supervisor must be aware of his or her role in the supervisory relationship while also closely observing the CIT and client relationship.

Termination of the relationship is as much a possibility in the supervisory relationship as it is in a client–counselor relationship. Because of that, termination protocol should be delineated at the outset of the supervisory experience. Reasons for termination as well as referral processes or where to receive additional supervision and provision of notice are important for both parties to consider. When termination occurs due to a conflict in the supervisory relationship, the supervisor and CIT have a professional responsibility to work through their difficulties. If the issues cannot be resolved, the supervisor is required to work with the CIT until the CIT is referred to another qualified supervisor in the area or the CIT leaves the relationship on his or her own decision. Termination of the relationship is a significant event, and reasons for and action steps should be documented for both parties.

Ethical Code 11.19

F.4.d. Termination of the Supervisory Relationship.

Supervisors or supervisees have the right to terminate the supervisory relationship with adequate notice. Reasons for considering termination are discussed, and both parties work to resolve differences. When termination is warranted, supervisors make appropriate referrals to possible alternative supervisors.

Source: 2014 American Counseling Association Code of Ethics. Reprinted with permission from American Counseling Association.

Evaluation, Remediation, and Endorsement

Parallel to counselor education and the educational process, the supervisory process also includes evaluation, remediation, and endorsement of the CIT. Counselor education programs and supervisors of clinical sites are responsible for assessing the readiness of a CIT and providing a recommendation of the CIT to the profession. The evaluation process occurs weekly during the counselor's training. It includes informal and formal feedback in written and verbal evaluations discussing the CIT's skills and provides the CIT with defined areas of growth.

Supervisors indicate areas of challenge for the supervisee and work with the supervisee to develop skills in all areas; they also provide appropriate referrals for counseling when necessary. When CITs do not improve and are not a fit with the profession despite repeated documented attempts at development by the supervisor, it is the ethical responsibility of the supervisor not to endorse or recommend the CIT for graduation or licensure. As long as the CIT has been provided the opportunity to develop and these opportunities were documented, the CIT has been provided due process, and therefore the supervisor does not support graduation and endorsement to the field.

Ethical Code 11.20

F.6.a. Evaluation.

Supervisors document and provide supervisees with ongoing feedback regarding their performance and schedule periodic formal evaluative sessions throughout the supervisory relationship.

F.6.b. Gatekeeping and Remediation.

Through initial and ongoing evaluation, supervisors are aware of supervisee limitations that might impede performance. Supervisors assist supervisees in securing remedial assistance when needed. They recommend dismissal from training programs, applied counseling settings, and state or voluntary professional credentialing processes when those supervisees are unable to demonstrate that they can provide competent professional services to a range of diverse clients. Supervisors seek consultation and document their decisions to dismiss or refer supervisees for assistance. They ensure that supervisees are aware of options available to them to address such decisions.

F.6.c. Counseling for Supervisees.

If supervisees request counseling, the supervisor assists the supervisee in identifying appropriate services. Supervisors do not provide counseling services to supervisees.

Supervisors address interpersonal competencies in terms of the impact of these issues on clients, the supervisory relationship, and professional functioning.

F.5.d. Endorsement.

Supervisors endorse supervisees for certification, licensure, employment, or completion of an academic or training program only when they believe supervisees are qualified for the endorsement. Regardless of qualifications, supervisors do not endorse supervisees whom they believe to be impaired in any way that would interfere with the performance of the duties associated with the endorsement.

Source: 2014 American Counseling Association Code of Ethics. Reprinted with permission from American Counseling Association.

STUDENTS AND COUNSELORS IN TRAINING

Students also have responsibilities in the supervisory relationship. First and foremost, they are responsible for appropriate and adequate counseling to the client. They must provide informed consent, including disclosing their training status to clients, and know and adhere to ethical codes and their state laws—just as licensed counselors do. This is a lot of responsibility for the developing CIT—to know codes and laws in addition to theory and technique takes much effort and attention. Too often students may not comprehend fully that they are responsible for these items and that they too can be sued by a client. They may become caught up in all of their responsibilities and not realize that they and the supervisor are accountable to the client.

Ethical Code 11.21

F.5.c. Professional Disclosure.

Before providing counseling services, students and supervisees disclose their status as supervisees and explain how this status affects the limits of confidentiality. Supervisors ensure that clients are aware of the services rendered and the qualifications of the students and supervisees rendering those services. Students and supervisees obtain client permission before they use any information concerning the counseling relationship in the training process.

Source: 2014 American Counseling Association Code of Ethics. Reprinted with permission from American Counseling Association.

CASE STUDY 11.2

Shawnda is a third-year master's student nearing the end of her internship experience. With two months to the completion of her internship, Shawnda is given a new client by the site agency. She provides a strong informed consent, informing the client about her student status, the process of counseling, anticipated risks and rewards, timeliness, and so on. In her second session with this particular client, Shawnda requests to audio tape their next session. She is distracted by noises outside of their session and thinking about if the tape machine is working. Because of these distractions, she only verbalizes to the client that the tape is a requirement of the course; she forgets to mention that others will view the tape, including her site and faculty supervisors and the class of students when she presents the tape as a case conceptualization project. The client agrees and signs the consent without review. The written consent describes in full who will view the tape, how the tape will be used, and when the tape will be destroyed. The session occurs and is taped. Shawnda thanks the client for permission to tape and proceeds on her class project. She tells the faculty supervisor that she received permission to tape and that the client received informed consent regarding the taped session.

1. *Is the last sentence of the illustration accurate? Did Shawnda receive permission to tape, and was the client adequately informed?*

2. *What codes of ethics apply to this illustration? Which laws would be broken in your state by a student intern who did not inform the client that the class and instructor would view the tape but told the instructor that she had?*

3. *What charges or consequences would occur in your state if this situation occurred?*

4. *What can you recommend to your peers, and keep in mind yourself, to help you remember critical pieces in counseling practice when there is often the potential to become distracted and forget?*

It is essential that students and CITs maintain personal and professional mental health and that they not counsel when they are impaired. The latter often occurs when CITs experience difficult times such as losing a close relative, attending to substance abuse issues, going through a divorce, or other personal concerns. When counselors and CITs experience personal difficulty, it may interfere with their judgment and objectivity with clients. They may be at higher risk for a greater amount of countertransference and an inability to see such. CITs have the responsibility to seek professional counseling when they experience difficult times and their skills are compromised and not to return to counseling others until they are healthy.

Ethical Code 11.22

F.5.b. Impairment.

Students and supervisees monitor themselves for signs of impairment from their own physical, mental, or emotional problems and refrain from offering or providing professional services when such impairment is likely to harm a client or others. They notify their faculty and/or supervisors and seek assistance for problems that reach the level of professional impairment, and if necessary, they limit, suspend, or terminate their professional responsibilities until it is determined that they may safely resume their work.

Source: 2014 American Counseling Association Code of Ethics. Reprinted with permission from American Counseling Association.

Guided Practice Exercise 11.3

What Does Your State Say?

Visit the Web site for your state's regulations related to counseling, and select those that relate to counselor education and supervision. Develop questions for those areas that are unclear, and discuss as a group.

CULTURE AND CONTEXT

Counselor education programs and related supervisors have the professional duty to adhere to and attend to issues related to multiculturalism. Ethical code and professional standards require that multiculturalism be present not just in one course or one section of the curriculum but infused throughout the counseling program. Multiculturalism is inherent in any counseling relationship and the counselor's understanding of the client. Students and CITs must learn to identify personal constructs of a client—those things by which an individual identifies —to provide effective counseling. These constructs—age, ableism, race, ethnicity, religious orientation, sexual orientation, profession, marital status, parental status, and so on—are all parts of our identity. Counseling curriculum must not only teach the knowledge behind the differences inherent in all of us but must help students develop the skills to apply this knowledge.

Ethical Code 11.23

F.11.c. Infusing Multicultural Issues/Diversity.

Counselor educators actively infuse multicultural/diversity competency in their training and supervision practices. They actively train students to gain awareness, knowledge, and skills in the competencies of multicultural practice.

Source: 2014 American Counseling Association Code of Ethics. Reprinted with permission from American Counseling Association.

To fully encompass the multicultural aspect, counselor education programs work to recruit faculty and students from diverse backgrounds. Diversity in the faculty ranks better helps faculty and students to embrace and understand cultural aspects. Diversity in student ranks provides a similar experience; students feel part of a diverse society and learn from others with different backgrounds when they are in shared experiences.

Ethical Code 11.24

F.11.a. Faculty Diversity.

Counselor educators are committed to recruiting and retaining a diverse faculty.

F.11.b. Student Diversity.

Counselor educators actively attempt to recruit and retain a diverse student body. Counselor educators demonstrate commitment to multicultural/diversity competence by recognizing and valuing the diverse cultures and types of abilities students bring to the training experience. Counselor educators provide appropriate accommodations that enhance and support diverse student well-being and academic performance.

F.11.c. Infusing Multicultural Issues/ Diversity.

Counselor educators actively infuse multicultural/diversity competency in their training and supervision practices. They actively train students to gain awareness, knowledge, and skills in the competencies of multicultural practice.

Source: 2014 American Counseling Association Code of Ethics. Reprinted with permission from American Counseling Association.

Multiculturalism also must be included and attended to in supervisory experiences. Clinical experiences provide opportunities for the knowledge surrounding diversity and multiculturalism to be applied through skills. Effective supervisors present opportunities to help students infuse attention to multiculturalism throughout a client relationship and not just in the intake session. They can help students attend to multiculturalism by writing specifically of the diversity-related issues that may occur for a client in their case notes (Henning & Pangelinan, 2007). When students are asked to search for and pay special attention to the diversity of a client and how that diversity affects the issues they discuss in counseling, students can learn to make multiculturalism second nature in their counseling.

Ethical Code 11.25

F.2.b. Multicultural Issues/Diversity in Supervision.

Counseling supervisors are aware of and address the role of multiculturalism/diversity in the supervisory relationship.

Source: 2014 American Counseling Association Code of Ethics. Reprinted with permission from American Counseling Association.

Guided Practice Exercise 11.4

Heard in the Hallway?

What would you do if you heard classmates discussing a personal disclosure related to sexual orientation by a classmate in the hallways? Discuss in small groups the ethical codes that relate to this concern, and present your thoughts to the class.

CONCLUSION

Relationships are the focus and key aspect of the counseling relationship between the client and the counselor; they are also the focus and key aspect of the relationship between the supervisor and supervisee as well as the counselor educator and CIT. This chapter highlighted some of the ethical responsibilities of these relationships and how counselors, supervisors, and CITs can navigate these difficult waters. In addition, attention to context and culture was emphasized.

KEYSTONES

- Counselor educators have many varied responsibilities to provide an educational program that meets ethical and professional counseling standards while also attending to the professional and personal development of students and the program. Counseling curriculum should be based empirically and infused with ethics and multiculturalism throughout.
- Faculty and site supervisors frequently interact to maintain agreement when training the student and to minimize student confusion regarding client treatment.
- Relationships between supervisors and educators with current and former students or supervisees are best when left on a professional level.
- Supervision is the oversight of training of a developing counselor. It occurs during clinical courses, field experience, and postgraduation. It involves the review of the CIT's written assessments, observation of counseling sessions, and self-reporting from the CIT.
- The supervisor–supervisee relationship has similar components to the client and counselor relationship. Informed consent, the quality of the relationship, and performance evaluation are significant components to supervision. The quality of the supervisor–supervisee relationship has been found to be as important as that of the client and counselor.
- Termination of the supervisor–supervisee relationship is a significant event, and reasons for the termination and action steps should be documented for both parties.
- Relationships that can be defined as therapeutically beneficial for the CIT, such as attending ceremonies, visiting the supervisee in the hospital and providing support, or collaborating at professional conferences and organizations, are permissible. However, it is incumbent on the supervisor to have open discussions with the CIT regarding the inherent risks involved.
- CITs have the responsibility to seek professional counseling when they experience difficult personal times and their skills are compromised and not to return to counseling others until they are healthy.
- Ethical code and professional standards require that multiculturalism be infused throughout the counseling program. Multiculturalism is inherent in any counseling relationship and the counselor's understanding of the client, so it must be included in counseling curriculum and supervisory experiences.

SUGGESTED BEST PRACTICES

- Not all counselors become counselor educators or supervisors, but most of us will engage in some of these roles at some point in our careers.
- Counselors who teach ethics should also practice ethics.

- As counselor educators, look to infuse ethics throughout the curriculum rather than just treating it as a stand-alone course.
- Counselor educators should teach courses in which they are subject matter experts.
- If you bring client stories into the classroom or a training event, the client data must be presented in such a way to protect the identity of the client.
- Most of us will serve as a supervisor at some point. Remember what you liked and disliked about supervision and let that help drive your approach.
- Step up to the role of gatekeeper. You don't want to be responsible for an incompetent or dangerous CIT to graduate or get licensed.
- Be a lifelong learner, and teach others around you to be lifelong learners as well.
- Be professional in your interactions with faculty, students, supervisors, and supervisees, no matter your role.
- Just say no to romantic relationships with faculty, students, supervisors, supervisees, and clients.
- Keep student and supervisee development confidential to the extent possible given your role. Do not gossip about shortcomings.
- If you practice supervision, have a documented plan for assessing and remediating perceived deficits.
- Supervisors also should have a plan in place to protect the clients under your care.

ADDITIONAL RESOURCES

In Print

Borders, L. D., Bernard, J. M., Dye, H. A., Fong, M. L., Henderson, P., & Nance, D. W. (1991). Curriculum guide for training counseling supervisors: Rationale, development, and implementation. *Counselor Education & Supervision, 31*(1), 58–81.

Crocket, K., & Kotze, E. (2012). Counsellors becoming counsellor educators: A New Zealand example. *British Journal of Guidance and Counselling, 40*(3), 247–260. doi:10.1080/030698 85.2012.678288

Pack-Brown, S. P., Thomas, T. L., & Seymour, J. M. (2008). Infusing professional ethics into counselor education programs: A multicultural/social justice perspective. *Journal of Counseling & Development, 86*(3), 296–302. doi:10.1002/j.1556–6678.2008.tb00512.x

Smith, R. D., Riva, M. T., & Erickson-Cornish, J. A. (2012). The ethical practice of group supervision: A national survey. *Training and Education in Professional Psychology, 6*(4), 238–248. doi:10.1037/a0030806

On the Web

Association for Counselor Education and Supervision (ACES). (2011). *Best practices in clinical supervision: ACES task force report.* Retrieved from www.saces.org/Resources/Documents/aces_best_practices.doc

Curriculum Development for Counselor Education Programs. (n.d.). Retrieved from http://www
.counseling.org/knowledge-center/clearinghouses/syllabus-clearinghouse
Graduate Student Committee With the Association for Counseling and Supervision. (n.d.).
Retrieved from http://www.acesonline.net/about-aces/students/

REFERENCES

American Counseling Association (ACA). (2014). *ACA code of ethics.* Alexandria, VA: Author.

Association for Counselor Education and Supervision (ACES). (1995). Ethical guidelines for counseling supervisors. *Counselor Education and Supervision, 34*(3), 270–276. doi:10.1002/j.1556–6978.1995.tb00248.x

Barnett, J. E., Cornish, J. A. E., Goodyear, R. K., & Lichtenberg, J. W. (2007). Commentaries on the ethical and effective practice of clinical supervision. *Professional Psychology: Research and Practice, 38*(3), 268–275.

Barnett, J. E., & Johnson, W. B. (2010). *Ethics desk reference for counselors.* Washington, DC: American Counseling Association.

Bernard, J. M., & Goodyear, R. K. (2009). *Fundamentals of clinical supervision* (4th ed.). Upper Saddle River, NJ: Merrill.

Corey, G., Corey, M. S., & Callahan, P. (2011). *Issues and ethics in the helping professions* (8th ed.). Belmont, CA: Brooks/Cole.

Council for Accreditation of Counseling & Related Educational Programs (CACREP). (2009). *CACREP 2009 standards.* Retrieved from http://www.cacrep.org/doc/2009%20Standards%20with%20cover.pdf

Downs, L. (2003). A preliminary survey of relationships between counselor educators' ethics education and ensuing pedagogy and responses to attractions with counseling students. *Counseling and Values, 48*(1), 2–13. doi:10.1002/j.2161–007X.2003.tb00270.x

Hartsell, T. L., Jr., & Bernstein, B. E. (2008). *The portable ethicist for mental health professionals: A complete guide to responsible practice* (2nd ed.). Hoboken, NJ: John Wiley & Sons.

Henning, S. L., & Pangelinan, J. (March, 2007). *Developmental supervision model for advanced skill integration and multicultural competence.* Poster presented at the American Counseling Association Convention, Detroit, MI.

Kolberg, J. B., Morgan, B., & Brendel, J. M. (2002). Faculty and student perceptions of dual relationships within counselor education: A qualitative analysis. *Counselor Education and Supervision, 41,* 193–206.

Morrissette, P. T., & Gadbois, S. (2006). Ethical consideration of counselor education teaching strategies. *Counseling and Values, 50*(2), 131–141. doi:10.1002/j.2161–007X.2006.tb00049.x

Pack-Brown, S. P., Thomas, T. L., & Seymour, J. M. (2008). Infusing professional ethics into counselor education programs: A multicultural/social justice perspective. *Journal of Counseling & Development, 86*(3), 296–302. doi:10.1002/j.1556–6678.2008tb00512.x

Chapter 12

CHALLENGES TO ETHICAL PRACTICE IN THE 21ST CENTURY

Zoe is a recent graduate of an accredited master's program in clinical mental health counseling. She is working as an adult outpatient counselor with the local mental health center. Over the next two years, she will accrue supervised clinical hours toward licensure in her state. Many of Zoe's clients are young and technology savvy, just like Zoe. She often receives Facebook friend requests and texts from her clients and recently had a client ask if he could see her via Skype to avoid the lengthy commute into town for services. Although Zoe is excited to offer cutting-edge services to her clients, she is unsure what her limits are in these cases. Many of her colleagues have been employed at the agency for more than 20 years and do not have the same interest in technology as Zoe. What should she do?

CHAPTER OVERVIEW

This chapter introduces the reader to many of the primary ethical challenges facing the 21st-century counselor. Many of these challenges have to do with scope of practice, such as the role of the counselor in medication management. In addition, counselors are faced with policy and procedure challenges in work environments, interdisciplinary challenges in collaboration and consultation, and training and employment standards. Of primary importance in the revised American Counseling Association (ACA, 2014) Code of Ethics is the use of technology and social media. In this chapter, we will review ethical codes and choices that impact your role as a professional counselor. Key ACA ethical codes and the related Council for Accreditation of Counseling & Related Educational Programs (CACREP, 2009) standards are also denoted for your use.

LEARNING OBJECTIVES

After reading this chapter you will be able to do the following:

1. Identify personal challenges to wellness and self-care.

2. Apply research-based strategies to promote self-care.

3. Describe employer and ethical issues that may arise with outside employment.

4. Examine policy challenges experienced by practicing counselors including prescription privileges, testing privileges, and licensure reciprocity.

5. Analyze ethical dilemmas in distance counseling and technology use.

CACREP STANDARDS

CACREP Core Standards

G.1.g. Professional credentialing, including certification, licensure, and accreditation practices and standards, and the effects of public policy on these issues.

G.1.j. Ethical standards of professional organizations and credentialing bodies, and applications of ethical and legal considerations in professional counseling.

CACREP Clinical Mental Health Standards

A.1. Understands the history, philosophy, and trends in clinical mental health counseling.

A.2. Understands ethical and legal considerations specifically related to the practice of clinical mental health counseling.

INTRODUCTION

Counselors take on many roles in the course of our work. We serve as a listener, confidant, and mentor and advocate among others. Working in such diverse roles, it is not surprising that the challenges we encounter are diverse as well. While much of this text is dedicated to addressing those diverse challenges, this chapter will highlight challenges that are related to living and working in the 21st century.

PERSONAL CHALLENGES

We live in a high-paced, high-stress society. As counselors, we are expected to be of good mental health, self-aware, culturally sensitive, open-minded, ethical, competent, trustworthy, objective, and inviting to clients (Hackney & Cormier, 2013). That's a tall order! Consider yourself at this point in your training. Are there lessons in your courses that teach you things about yourself that you never knew? Are there times when you need a mental health day? Perhaps there are times when you feel less competent or are not interested in being around others. Does this make you an unethical counselor? Of course not. These experiences make you human. And being a counselor does not supersede your right to be human.

We have already discussed impairment in Chapter 5, but what we haven't discussed as much is how we as counselors can take care of ourselves. Counselor self-care is one of the primary challenges of our profession. The introduction to Section C of the ACA (2014) code states "counselors engage in self-care activities to maintain and promote their own emotional, physical, mental, and spiritual well-being to best meet their professional responsibilities" (p. 6). Activities such as exercise, yoga, relaxation, and meditation previously may have been considered self-indulgent but now are regarded as an ethical necessity (Williams, Richardson, Moore, Gambrel, & Keeling, 2010).

Researchers support a number of elements that may contribute to counselor self-care. Some are work related, such as maintaining a reasonable client load, participating in supervision, and having a supportive work environment (Killian, 2008). Others occur outside of the work site, such as exercise, spirituality, and family connections (Killian, 2008). Self-awareness and mindfulness also rise to the top of well-researched approaches to self-care (Richards, Campenni, & Muse-Burke, 2010). Self-care requires us to focus inward because of all the time we spend focusing outward with clients (Shallcross, 2013). While this chapter cannot explore all of the ways that self-care can benefit counselors and our clients ethically, it is the hope of your text authors that you will look for self-care activities that work for you and continue them throughout your career.

EMPLOYMENT CHALLENGES

As professional counselors, we dedicate our time to helping others. Many of us work in agencies, schools, or private practice. In fact, we may work in several settings. School counselors who are licensed professional counselors or licensed clinical mental health counselors may see private clients at the end of the school day, on weekends, or during the summer. Agency counselors may serve as consultants in other institutions. Private practice counselors may see individual clients in their offices as well as perform hospital consults. Unless their work contract prohibits outside employment, we generally view these occupational opportunities as being allowed at the discretion of the counselors looking to expand their practices.

Let's take a look at a case study.

CASE STUDY 12.1

Darlene is a licensed professional counselor (LPC) working for a state-funded agency in her hometown. She serves as a child and adolescent counselor and has been employed with her agency for five years. Darlene has always liked working with adult clients as well. Because she sees only children and adolescents at her agency, she opens a small private practice in an independent office space seeing adults two or three evenings per week after work. She does not solicit clients from work and advertises online and through word of mouth. In addition to the professional satisfaction of seeing adults, Darlene has many student loans from her graduate program, and the extra money is helpful in paying off this debt. Is this ethical?

1. *What are your initial thoughts about this case? About Darlene?*

2. *How do you relate to Darlene's dilemma?*

3. *If she were your friend from graduate school, how would you advise Darlene?*

Many of us sympathize with Darlene. She enjoys working with a population that she is unable to work with at her primary job. In addition, the extra money is helpful. She is not stealing clients from her agency, and there may not be a specific ethical code that opposes her outside employment. But what if her agency contract contains a moonlighting clause? A moonlighting clause is a term used in contracts to ensure that employees do not engage in outside employment (Robinson, 2009). Employers of counselors often include such clauses to ensure that clients are not stolen from their agencies. While Darlene's behavior may be ethical, it may be illegal under contract law.

What if Darlene found another way to make money? For example, what if she decided to take a few shifts waitressing to help pay off her loans? It may be that such employment would not violate an agency contract. However, if these shifts went late into the night, Darlene would have to assess her ability to function well at her primary job. Perhaps she would elect to sell kitchen products on the side instead. As long as these work opportunities did not interfere with her primary job, and her agency allowed outside employment, most of us would not have an ethical problem with Darlene finding ways to supplement her income. Let's take it a step further.

What if Darlene went to work as a dancer in a gentlemen's club? Again, we will assume that there is no outside employment clause in her contract. It is likely that some of you reading this had an immediate opinion about this line of work that was different from your opinion about waitressing or selling kitchen products. The challenge of practicing in the 21st century is deciding how far individuals can go personally without impacting themselves professionally. The code of ethics is largely silent on these matters. What would you do?

One element to consider is moral turpitude. Moral turpitude is a legal concept that refers to conduct that violates or is contrary to generally acceptable standards of morality or justice (Moore, 2008). Most licensure boards include crimes involving moral turpitude as a rationale for denying, suspending, or revoking a license. Would Darlene's choice of outside employment fall under the realm of moral turpitude? That would be up to the individual licensure board to decide as there is no direct ethical code that addresses her choice.

POLICY CHALLENGES

As professional counselors, we are subject to ethical codes as well as federal laws. In addition, we are impacted by various policies that also may be evidenced in state law. In this section, we will address concerns that vary state by state and impact counselors as a result. Specifically, we will look at prescription privileges, testing privileges, and licensure reciprocity.

Prescription Privileges

As master's level counselors, we do not receive prescription privileges in any of the 50 U.S. states. However, this often is confusing to clients. Think about the course you took as an introduction to the counseling profession. It is likely that you lacked some clarity about the differences among counselors, social workers, psychologists, and psychiatrists. Let's briefly review for our own purposes in this text.

Social workers are licensed at the bachelor's degree level. Certainly, social workers can receive master's and doctorate degrees, which may change the level of licensure they are eligible for, but a basic social work degree needed to work in most agencies is a bachelor's degree. Conversely, counselors are licensed at the master's degree level. Again, counselors can receive doctorates, but it is not necessary for practice. Psychologists are licensed at the doctoral level. The education level of social workers, counselors, and psychologists is only one of many variables that distinguish these helping professions from one another. Finally, psychiatrists have a medical doctorate (MD) with a specialty in psychiatry. Of these professions, MDs are afforded prescription privileges across all 50 states.

Psychologists have pushed for the right to prescribe in recent years, but currently only two states, New Mexico and Louisiana, allow this practice (American Psychological Association, 2014). In these two states, licensed psychologists who meet certain criteria are allowed to prescribe specified medications for the psychiatric disorders of their clients. Professional counselors, who are often in a position to explain both the necessity of medication in treatment and maintain ongoing evaluation of compliance and side effects, do not have such privileges.

In an age of integrated behavioral health care models, professional counselors often work hand in hand with medical practitioners who prescribe. In 2002, researchers surveyed members of the American Mental Health Counselors Association (AMHCA) to determine their perceptions of mental health counselors being allowed similar rights (Scovel, Christensen, & England, 2002). While 41 percent of respondents thought mental health counselors should have independent prescribing privileges, 64 percent were of the opinion that dependent prescribing privileges would be helpful. Dependent prescribing privileges mean that the professional counselor could prescribe certain psychotropic medications when under the oversight of a physician.

Researchers have found that wait times and cost of screening by psychiatrists can be prohibitive to clients seeking psychotropic medication (Caccavale, Reeves, & Wiggins, 2012). As such, counselors need to have some understanding of how to help clients who may need psychotropic medications. The following case study highlights a common challenge to practicing counselors.

CASE STUDY 12.2

Dakota has been working in her small town as an LPC for many years. Over the years, she has developed good working relationships with local medical providers. One day, her client Sami is in her office displaying signs of psychosis. Dakota is concerned that Sami needs a psychiatric evaluation, but the soonest available appointment is three months away. Dakota calls Sami's primary care physician, who agrees to provide interim assistance. He asks Dakota what she thinks the best medication option should be as he is not a psychiatrist. Dakota has a lot of work experience with antipsychotic medication but no real training.

1. *What is Dakota's competence in this area?*

2. *Is providing a suggestion unethical?*

3. *What could Dakota do to become more competent in psychopharmacology?*

Testing Privileges

Formal assessments are within the scope of practice of professional counselors. Counselors often use test instruments to develop treatment plans, provide appropriate referrals, and assess treatment progress. Test publishers establish the guidelines for education, training, and experience needed to purchase and use each assessment instrument. If, for example, you wanted to use a symptom screener to assess clients at intake, you would simply locate the instrument you wanted to use and determine if you meet the criteria for using the instrument.

What does it take to meet criteria? Each publishing house sets the minimum educational and training level required to purchase and use the assessment. The publisher then sets forth criteria for A-, B-, and C-level assessments (PAR, 2012). Typically, A-level assessments require no special qualifications. Anyone can purchase and use these assessments. B-level assessments require a degree in counseling, psychology, or a related field plus completion of course work in test use and interpretation, instrument development, and statistics. A license in the field also typically meets these criteria. Finally, C-level assessments may be purchased and used by those with a higher level of training, such as a doctoral degree in the field.

As you likely can discern, master's level counselors have the requisite training to purchase and use A- and B-level assessments, which matches the mandate in our code of ethics.

Ethical Code 12.1

E.2.a. Limits of Competence.

Counselors use only those testing and assessment services for which they have been trained and are competent. Counselors using technology-assisted test interpretations are trained in the construct being measured and the specific instrument being used prior to using its technology-based application. Counselors take reasonable measures to ensure the proper use of assessment techniques by persons under their supervision.

Source: 2014 American Counseling Association Code of Ethics. Reprinted with permission from American Counseling Association.

Some counselors have additional training, making them eligible to purchase and use C-level assessments. However, state laws often say otherwise. In many states, licensed counselors who are ethically eligible and competent to use certain assessments are prohibited from using those assessments because a restricted testing law has been passed.

A restricted test law allows a state psychology board the right to establish a restricted test list. This list, once entered into state law, prohibits qualified counselors from using tests that the test publisher finds them to be eligible and qualified to use. It is a way for psychology boards to control the provision of services in the state and maintain control over testing. As counselors, we do not see restricted test laws as being fair. Assuming we meet the standards deemed necessary to administer and interpret the instrument, we believe we should be able to do so across states.

Another entity believes this as well and works on behalf of counselors and others. That entity is called the Fair Access Coalition on Testing (FACT). FACT is a nonprofit formed in 1996 to educate professionals not credentialed as psychologists who have been affected adversely by restrictions on assessment practices imposed by state psychology licensure boards. Such restrictions are the object of concern for diverse professional groups whose members utilize and have an interest in protecting the right to use psychological, educational, vocational, industrial, or other assessment instruments. The FACT board is comprised of representatives from test publishers, school psychologists, speech and language therapists, the National Board for Certified Counselors (NBCC), ACA, the Association for Assessment in Counseling (AACE), and others (Watson & Sheperis, 2010).

Because counselors use assessments to aid in treatment provision and evaluation of clients, paying careful attention to this ongoing contemporary concern is essential. It is not enough simply to know what tests are restricted in your state and follow along. Professional counselors must serve as advocates for the profession and the clients we serve. By prohibiting the ethical use of certain assessments, professional counselors are unable to provide the best possible services for their clients. In essence, counselors who are subject to test restrictions may be forced to provide lesser quality, and thus less ethical, services to clients.

CASE STUDY 12.3

Belinda is an LPC working in a multidisciplinary mental health clinic. She decides to administer the 16 Personality Factor Questionnaire (16PF) to a client to aid in diagnosis and treatment. While staffing the case with her clinical director, who is a psychologist, she is told that she is not allowed to give the 16PF as an LPC. When Belinda was in graduate school, she was trained on the instrument and learned that LPCs in her state were able to use this assessment.

1. *What should Belinda do to confirm her understanding of state law?*

2. *How should she approach her supervisor about this seemingly contradictory information?*

Licensure Reciprocity

Another critical area of concern for ethical counselors practicing in the 21st century is licensure. Licensure laws are developed, passed, and regulated by each state. Counselors are unique in the helping professions in that licensure standards vary greatly from state to state. Social work, psychology, and other professions have what is known as licensure reciprocity. Licensure reciprocity means that if a practitioner is licensed in one state and has no complaints or other infractions, then the license can be transferred to another state. Because individual state licensure laws differ, this is not the case for counselors.

Recently, ACA reported on a licensed counselor who had been practicing in her home state for more than 20 years. She had a perfect licensure record, kept up her continuing education units (CEUs), and renewed faithfully. This particular counselor had the good fortune to fall in love. The challenge was that her fiancée lived in another state, and based on that state's licensure laws, she was not eligible to be licensed there (Kaplan, 2012). Imagine your own development as a professional counselor. You may have a clear idea of where you plan to live and work, but as you know, plans can change. Is it ethical to keep a licensed counselor from practicing when he or she moves?

One group that is working to take on this issue is the American Association for State Counseling Boards (AASCB). AASCB is an organization of all state licensure boards designed to improve communication among boards and develop a cohesive identity for licensed counselors across all 50 states (AASCB, 2014). In addition to states having differing regulations for education and supervised hours, states adopt codes of ethics for their licensees to follow. Many states use the ACA Code of Ethics, while others use the AMHCA code. Still other states, like Texas, have developed their own codes. This is confusing to clients, counselors, insurance panels, and the general public. As such, a unified licensure plan with reciprocity would make the professional identity of counselors clearer for all stakeholders.

Guided Practice Exercise 12.1

A Path to Licensure

Although you may be early in your journey to become a professional counselor, you probably already have thought about licensure. Because licensure varies widely from state to state, it is important to begin considering your potential licensure needs. For this activity, research state laws for the licensing of professional counselors in your state and another state of your choice. Specifically, consider the following:

(Continued)

(Continued)

1. What is the name of the license in the state you researched?

2. What types of degrees qualify one for licensing in this state?

3. How many semester hours of graduate course work are required to become license eligible?

4. In what areas is course work required? Does your degree from your university meet these requirements? If not, what additional course work would you need?

5. How many total clock hours of supervised clinical practice are required for licensure? How many of these hours can come from pre-degree supervised practicums and internships?

6. How many hours of post-degree supervision are required? Who can provide supervision to pre-licensed counselors?

7. Are candidates required to pass any examinations to be licensed? If so, what examinations?

8. How do the two states compare? What would it take to be licensed in both places? With this information, how will you proceed in your training?

TECHNOLOGICAL CHALLENGES

As you would likely expect, many of the challenges associated with 21st-century counseling have to do with technology. Prior to the digital age, these technological challenges primarily had to do with the use of telephones and answering machines. For those of you too young to remember, cell phones have not always existed. For years, the only way for counselors to contact clients was using landline home phones. These home phones also may have had answering machines that could be listened to by the whole family. As a result, counselors were cautioned against calling clients or leaving voice messages.

Nowadays, counselors face more and more technological challenges. Most people have private cell phones even if they also have a home phone, reducing the risk of a voice-mail message being heard by another person. But does that make it OK to leave a voice-mail on a cell phone? Like many other ethical dilemmas, the answer is, "It depends." What are some other ethical concerns with technology for 21st-century counselors?

While the ACA Code of Ethics always has addressed technology at some level, the 2014 code contains an entire section expressly devoted to technological challenges for counselors. Today's counselors must understand the ethics behind the use of e-mail, texting, social media, chat, video calls, and distance counseling. That is a lot of new technology—much of which appeared within the last 10 to 15 years! Not surprisingly, the ethics around these technological advances are not formed fully. Let's take a look at some of the primary considerations.

Distance Counseling

As of 2009 there were more than 4 million online Web sites dedicated to counseling (Haberstroh, 2009). While not all of these sites are related to distance counseling, many link clients to such options. You already may have formed an opinion about distance counseling, but we would ask you to consider this: distance counseling has been found to be as effective as face-to-face counseling (Barak, Hen, Boniel-Nissim, & Shapira, 2008). Surprised? We thought you might be.

When students are asked about distance counseling, they typically indicate a negative impression, citing the need for verbal and nonverbal cues to develop the therapeutic relationship. However there are some client populations for whom distance counseling is preferable. Take, for example, the rural client who lacks transportation to a counselor many hours away. Rather than have no access to services, distance video counseling offers the client an option. In addition, some clients are not verbal due to expressive language disorders or other conditions that impede speech. For this client, encrypted chat counseling may be more efficient. Finally, some clients travel or are overseas and wish to continue services. For them, distance counseling may be an option.

Because distance counseling is relatively new and evolving, we reached out to a private practitioner who utilizes distance counseling in her practice. A brief interview with Katarzyna Peoples, PhD, LMHC, LPC, follows:

What drew you to distance counseling?

Dr. Peoples: *The biggest reason I chose to do distance counseling was convenience. I travel a lot, and staying in one consistent area over a period of years is not likely for me. I didn't want to keep starting over. I wanted to build a distance counseling practice so that I could take it with me throughout any move I might make.*

What types of clients do you serve?

Dr. Peoples: *I typically work with clients who are struggling in their marriages and romantic partnerships. I also work with people who have anxiety and depression issues due to all kinds of reasons—health issues, work issues, general anxiety, and so on.*

I work with couples a lot, and because I offer distance counseling, it is a real benefit for couples who live in separate areas of the country (or world). They have an opportunity to work on relationship issues prior to committing to a move.

What is your process for starting with and seeing a new client?

Dr. Peoples: *I always set up a telephone call that is free of charge. I assess the client at that time for appropriateness. This also allows the client to ask any questions he or she might have and to assess if this is a good fit for him or her. If both of us feel it is a good fit, I discuss the process of online therapy and how sessions work, billing works, and technical issues are dealt with.*

What are the advantages of distance counseling? Disadvantages?

Dr. Peoples: *The biggest advantage of distance counseling is convenience. People can log on from their computers at home at almost any time and spend an hour with a therapist. I provide therapy via video conferencing, so it's a real personal experience. Also, if someone needs to reschedule, it is a bit easier to do that with short notice. I find that most people are still very respectful of my time, but emergencies and unexpected events do happen. If someone needs to cancel an hour before the session, it is usually fine because I have not driven to the office to meet them.*

Disadvantages of distance counseling are the severity of issues one can work with. If someone is actively suicidal or living in a high-crisis situation, online counseling is typically not the best avenue for him or her. That person may need to work with someone local who has access to crisis intervention facilities. However, sometimes an unanticipated crisis situation does come up with a client. In those instances, I make sure that I work with his or her network of medical professionals (psychiatrist, medical doctor, etc.) and family members to establish a crisis intervention plan. I continue to see that person as long as it's appropriate. This varies depending on each situation.

Another disadvantage is technical difficulties. There will always be a glitch once in a while with the Internet, but I have a process for that, and clients usually know that is a common challenge in online counseling.

What ethical challenges have you encountered, and how have you dealt with them?

Dr. Peoples: *I had one client who started out stable and appropriate for online therapy who later ended up having some destructive behaviors around suicidal patterns. Ethically, it was difficult because I had developed a relationship with her that was productive, and she struggled with abandonment issues. Referring her out would have made things worse. In this instance, we continued to work together, and I had her sign consents for her psychiatrist and her family members. I kept in close contact with everyone, so we could have a supportive network for her and could address any crises immediately. For example, if the client called me about wanting to harm herself, I could immediately call her mom, psychiatrist, and so on, and they could work with her locally on crisis intervention issues. With this arrangement, the client felt supported rather than abandoned, and our therapeutic relationship was much stronger. She progressed really well.*

I also had some other issues that a local therapist might not ever encounter. These issues are truly online therapy specific and will need to be addressed further in online counseling ethics as the profession evolves.

For example, a client decided he was going to bring a glass of wine into the session. He was in China, and I was in the United States, so the time zones were significantly different. Naturally, he had a glass of wine at night and thought it was appropriate for the online session. As the session proceeded, his buzz got a little more pronounced. He wasn't drunk by any means, but how appropriate is a glass of wine in a therapy session? What are the cultural implications of that scenario?

Another client lived in a very strict part of the world where video conferencing was not allowed by law. She chose to do therapy via Skype and rerouted her address to be a U.S. address, so she would not get into any legal troubles. I was torn ethically in this situation because it would seem that I was putting her at legal risk each time we met online. I wasn't aware of this issue until we were well along in our therapy. Should I end the therapy sessions? What would be the consequences of that? Who would I even refer her to if I chose to end the sessions?

Last, I had another client who wore his bathrobe to therapy (again, we were across the world from one another, and the time zone was a factor). No indecent exposure happened, but the potential of that was a bit too close of a call than I would be comfortable with. This is a boundary issue and a delicate issue to address. Would I offend the client in asking him to put on more clothes? Was this a cultural issue? How appropriate or inappropriate was this for him?

Source: Personal communication, K. Peoples, March 24, 2015.

As the authors of your text, we want to state clearly that developing a distance counseling practice is not for new graduates in the profession. Independent licensure at the state level, national credentialing, and a rich clinical background are essential to embarking on such an endeavor. As always, consultation and supervision are keys to best practice.

Guided Practice Exercise 12.2

Marketing Distance Counseling

Conduct a Web search for online counseling providers. Find three to compare. As you review the Web sites, consider the following:

1. Is the Web site inviting and engaging?
2. Are the counselor's credentials and qualifications readily apparent?
3. How does the counselor provide services? Is it through video consult, encrypted chat, or some other means?
4. What privacy measures are in place for online work with this counselor?
5. Does the counselor provide a distance counseling informed consent that covers emergency procedures?

Social Media

It is likely that you have a social media account. Perhaps you use Facebook, Twitter, Vine, or some other mass communication site to connect with friends and family. Not unexpectedly, the desire to connect professionally has followed a similar trend. Applications such as LinkedIn allow for professional contacts and networking. In addition, you probably have noticed that your grocery store, dry cleaner, hair salon, and favorite restaurants all invite you to connect with them via social media. But what about the use of social media to market a practice and connect with counseling clientele?

Kaplan, Wade, Conteh, and Martz (2011) described a counselor who was using Twitter ethically as a way to connect with adolescents in a group setting. In essence, the counselor found that the clients were not always forthcoming during the actual group meeting but would participate in check-ins between group sessions. These check-ins were contained to a closed Twitter loop that allowed the members to respond to each other and maintained the confidentiality of the group and its members. The counselor was pleased with the results, and the use of this social media outlet became a viable way to work productively with her group members.

Unfortunately, not all efforts to use social media have such positive—or ethical—results. When a counselor decides to friend a client on Facebook, for example, the counselor opens the door to breaching client confidentiality simply by being in an open relationship with the client. Even if the client initiates the request, this still is not considered ethical. The code of ethics requires counselors to establish boundaries related to social media in their informed consent.

Ethical Code 12.2

H.6.b. Social Media as Part of Informed Consent.

Counselors clearly explain to their clients, as part of the informed consent procedure, the benefits, limitations, and boundaries of the use of social media.

Source: 2014 American Counseling Association Code of Ethics. Reprinted with permission from American Counseling Association.

Kaplan and colleagues (2011) provide a number of cautions for counselors wishing to use social media. They suggest that counselors start the process of protecting clients' privacy by not searching out clients on these sites. It seems logical, but if we don't want our clients finding our personal pages, it is probably a good idea not to look for theirs! The ACA Code of Ethics mentions this specifically in Standard H.6.c.

Ethical Code 12.3

H.6.c. Client Virtual Presence.

Counselors respect the privacy of their clients' presence on social media unless given consent to view such information.

Source: 2014 American Counseling Association Code of Ethics. Reprinted with permission from American Counseling Association.

Second, Kaplan and colleagues (2011) suggest creating a set of professional social media accounts that are separate from your personal accounts. They should carry your professional name (e.g., Dr. Donna Sheperis) and not be linked to any personal pages. Further, any personal pages should be somewhat professional. If your current Twitter handle is FluffyBunny1983, you might want to consider a change! Finally, Kaplan and others (2011) also remind us to double-check all agency, school, or institutional policies around the use of social media so that we are not in violation of employment or other contracts.

Cell Phones and Texting

In a modern clinical setting, you likely will use cell phone contact with clients. However, this contact must be addressed explicitly at the onset of services. In your informed consent, you will want to inform the client if you intend to try to sched-ule them via phone, ensure that such messages can be left on voice mail, and determine if there are other ways to reach the client. If you have a professional cell phone, let the client know if your voice mail is confidential and who, if anyone, can access your phone. If you choose to engage clients via text, be sure to include your response expectations in your informed consent. As Kaplan and colleagues (2011) point out, you don't want a client who is considering suicide to reach out to you via text if you don't routinely check your text messages.

Fax and E-Mail

The use of fax and e-mail communication, while convenient, also can be chal-lenging. For example, how do you determine that the person you intend to read the message is actually the person who receives it? Oftentimes, fax machines are placed in the center of an office for all to access. There is no guarantee of privacy. As a result, faxing confidential information becomes difficult when the sender cannot guarantee who will see the sheets of paper shooting out of the machine. The code of ethics does not address fax machines specifically but does ask that counselors take reasonable precautions to protect client confidentiality when transmitting records electronically.

Ethical Code 12.4

H.2.d. Security.

Counselors use current encryption standards within their Web sites and/or technology-based communications that meet applicable legal requirements. Counselors take reasonable precautions to ensure the confidentiality of information transmitted through any electronic means.

Source: 2014 American Counseling Association Code of Ethics. Reprinted with permission from American Counseling Association.

E-mail may be considered the dinosaur of electronic communication to younger counselors and clients. However, it is still the most traditional method for client–counselor communication (Kaplan et al., 2011). If you use e-mail in your practice, how can you ensure that the correspondence reaches the intended party? Some professionals use encrypted e-mail but many simply restrict the use of e-mail to scheduling issues only and include this use in their informed consent.

CASE STUDY 12.4

Nora has been practicing as a professional counselor for more than 10 years. She routinely uses e-mail to schedule and confirm appointments. Her informed consent includes the statement that e-mail is used for administrative purposes only and will not contain any personal information or information about session content. Nora has been working with Clarissa, a woman about her age who has been showing tremendous progress in individual sessions. Because of the scheduling reminders, Clarissa has Nora's work e-mail address and often responds to the scheduling reminder with a brief update on how her week has been and progress toward goals. Although such updates are not expected, Nora finds these e-mails helpful and believes they expedite the work she and Clarissa do in counseling.

1. *Is this ethical?*

2. *In what ways might this practice compromise confidentiality?*

3. *What steps could Nora take to protect Clarissa?*

Electronic Storage and Transmission

Counselors are responsible for keeping records of the services they provide to clients. These records include case notes, assessment data, billing, insurance claims, and administrative ledgers. While some records are kept on paper and under lock and key, the modern counseling office often utilizes electronic storage of records. Systems may be as simple as using a therapy note-taking app on a tablet or iPad or as involved as complete electronic health record (EHR) and practice management (PM) software. According to the ACA Code of Ethics, counselors are expected to follow all laws when using technology in record keeping and to inform clients of the process.

Ethical Code 12.5

H.5.a. Records.

Counselors maintain electronic records in accordance with relevant laws and statutes. Counselors inform clients on how records are maintained electronically. This includes, but is not limited to, the type of encryption and security assigned to the records, and if/for how long archival storage of transaction records is maintained.

Source: 2014 American Counseling Association Code of Ethics. Reprinted with permission from American Counseling Association.

HIPAA

If you have visited any form of medical office since 2003, you are probably familiar with the Health Insurance Portability and Accountability Act (HIPAA) of 2007. This act was passed by Congress to protect clients and their health information from fraud and unauthorized access. As counselors, we generally legally are required to follow HIPAA mandates, although if our practice does somehow fall into a loophole, we are encouraged to follow HIPAA as a matter of aspirational ethics and best practices (Freeburg & McCaughan, 2008). What does this mean for you? Although a full discussion of HIPAA mandates is outside of the scope of this text, there are some simple precautions all counselors should take.

Counselors should ensure that all physical records are locked and protected from unauthorized access. Likewise, electronic records must be secured using passwords or safe software. Make sure that computers and other work spaces are out of public view. We are responsible for all employees, even contract employees who come into the office, and we must protect client information from technical support help, maintenance workers, and others. Finally, when transmitting data electronically, we must take every precaution to determine that the person who is intended to receive the data actually receives it (Freeburg & McCaughan, 2008). What is heartening for counselors to know is that the ACA Code of Ethics and HIPAA are in harmony with one another, and we generally can be assured that if we follow HIPAA, we are practicing ethically (Lawley, 2012).

CONCLUSION

This chapter has addressed some of the common challenges that counselors may face when practicing in the 21st century. Counselors must understand the role of licensure in practice and the presence or absence of portability between states. Wellness and self-care are areas of focus for ethical counselors in modern practice. In addition, outside employment conflicts and potential for prescription privileges must be visible on the radar of professional counselors.

Finally, we addressed technology in modern counseling. In our personal lives, we are probably quite adept at using our laptops, cell phones, tablets, and other electronic devices to communicate. Many of us have social media accounts such as Facebook and Twitter. However competent we are at using this technology in the digital age, it is not likely that we fully understand how to integrate that knowledge into ethical clinical practice. Ongoing review of the ACA Code of Ethics, consultation, and supervision will allow counselors to develop best practices in these emerging areas for ethical dilemmas in our profession.

KEYSTONES

- Counselor self-care is one of the primary challenges of our profession. Researchers support a number of elements that may contribute to counselor self-care, including maintaining a reasonable client load, having a supportive work environment, exercising, and having self-awareness.
- Unless a work contract prohibits outside employment, we generally view these occupational opportunities as being allowed at the discretion of the counselors looking to expand their practices. However, employers of counselors often include moonlighting clauses to ensure that clients are not stolen from their agencies.
- The education level of social workers, counselors, and psychologists is one of many variables that distinguish these helping professions from one another.
- Master's level counselors do not receive prescription privileges in any of the 50 U.S. states. In New Mexico and Louisiana, licensed psychologists who meet certain criteria are allowed to prescribe specified medications for the psychiatric disorders of their clients. Dependent prescribing privileges mean that the professional counselor could prescribe certain psychotropic medications when under the oversight of a physician.
- Formal assessments are within the scope of practice of professional counselors. Master's level counselors have the requisite training to purchase and use A- and B-level assessments. However, counselors may be prohibited from using certain assessments if a restricted testing law has been passed. A restricted test law is one that allows a state psychology board the right to establish a restricted test list. FACT is a

nonprofit formed in 1996 to educate professionals not credentialed as psychologists who have been adversely affected by restrictions on assessment practices imposed by state psychology licensure boards.

- Licensure laws are developed, passed, and regulated by each state. Counselors are unique in the helping professions in that licensure standards vary greatly from state to state. The AASCB is an organization of all state licensure boards designed to improve communication among boards and develop a cohesive identity for licensed counselors across all 50 states.

- Distance counseling has been found to be as effective as face-to-face counseling. Client populations for which distance counseling is preferable include rural clients, clients who are not verbal, or those who travel or are overseas.

- Social media, e-mail, cell phones, and texting can be positive means of keeping in contact with clients. However, confidentiality and counselor–client boundaries always must be considered.

- The modern counseling office often utilizes electronic storage of records. Counselors should ensure that all physical records are locked and protected from unauthorized access and electronic records are secured using passwords or safe software. HIPAA protects clients and their health information from fraud and unauthorized access. The ACA Code of Ethics and HIPAA are in harmony with one another.

SUGGESTED BEST PRACTICES

- Yes, you are a counselor, but don't forget you are human. We all have limits.
- Wellness and self-care are not just about avoiding impairment; they also are intended to help us get even healthier. Practice them.
- Check your workload for unnecessary stressors.
- Maintain close family and friend relationships as emotional support.
- It has been said before, but we will say it again: seek your own counseling. We think it is unwise to sit in the counselor's chair if you have never sat in the client's chair.
- Engage in continuing education related to psychopharmacology—not so that you could prescribe medications but so that you can understand the medications that may best benefit your clients.
- Engage in integrated behavioral health care models when possible. Including mental health care in physical care offers clients the best wraparound service possible.
- Know your testing limits in terms of education and competency as well as in terms of state law and scope of practice.
- Advocate for testing privileges for counselors.
- Stay abreast of licensure laws in your state and others.
- If you choose to engage in distance counseling, consider becoming a distance credentialed counselor through the Center for Credentialing & Education.

- Be aware of your presence on social media. If your neighbors can see your posts on social media, so can your clients.
- Consider creating separate social media accounts for your professional and private purposes.
- Have clear limits to cell phone, texting, and e-mail use with clients.

ADDITIONAL RESOURCES

In Print

Centore, A. J., & Milacci, F. (2008). A study of mental health counselors' use of and perspectives on distance counseling. *Journal of Mental Health Counseling, 30*(3), 267–282.

Kaplan, D., & Martz, E. (2014). New concepts in the ACA code of ethics: Distance counseling, technology, and social media. *Counseling Today, 57,* 22–24.

McAdams, C. R., III, & Wyatt, K. L. (2010). The regulation of technology-assisted distance counseling and supervision in the United States: An analysis of current extent, trends, and implications. *Counselor Education & Supervision, 49*(3), 179–192.

On the Web

American Association of State Counseling Boards (AASCB). (n.d.). Retrieved from http://www .aascb.org/aws/AASCB/pt/sp/home_page

Bray, B. (2014). *Facebook: Don't let friends' cries for help go unanswered.* Retrieved from http:// ct.counseling.org/tag/social-media/

Fair Access Coalition on Testing (FACT). (n.d.). Retrieved from http://www.fairaccess.org/

Ostrowski, J. (2014). *HIPAA compliance: What you need to know about the new HIPAA-HITECH rules.* Retrieved from http://www.nbcc.org/assets/HIPAA_Compliance.pdf

REFERENCES

American Association for State Counseling Boards (AASCB). (2014). *Mission of AASCB.* Retrieved from http://www.aascb.org/aws/AASCB/pt/sp/about

American Counseling Association (ACA). (2014). *ACA code of ethics.* Alexandria, VA: Author.

American Psychological Association (APA). (2014). *Can psychologists prescribe medications for their patients?* Retrieved from https://www.apa.org/support/about/psych/prescribe .aspx#answer

Barak, A., Hen, L., Boniel-Nissim, M., & Shapira, N. (2008). A comprehensive review and a meta-analysis of the effectiveness of internet-based psychotherapeutic interventions. *Journal of Technology in Human Services, 26*(2–4), 109–160.

Caccavale J., Reeves J. L., & Wiggins, J. (2012). *The impact of psychiatric shortage on patient care and mental health policy: The silent shortage that can no longer be ignored.* Retrieved from http://abbhp.org/survey.pdf

Council for Accreditation of Counseling & Related Educational Programs (CACREP). (2009). *CACREP 2009 standards.* Retrieved from http://www.cacrep.org/doc/2009%20Standards%20 with%20cover.pdf

Freeburg, M., & McCaughan, A. (2008). HIPAA for dummies: A practitioner's guide. In G. R. Walz, J. C. Bleuer, & R. K. Yep (Eds.), *Compelling counseling interventions: Celebrating VISTAS' fifth anniversary* (pp. 305–312). Alexandria, VA: American Counseling Association.

Haberstroh, S. (2009). Strategies and resources for conducting online counseling. *Journal of Professional Counseling: Practice, Theory, and Research, 37*(2), 1–20.

Hackney, H. L., & Cormier, S. (2013). *The professional counselor: A process guide to helping* (7th ed.). Upper Saddle River, NJ: Pearson.

Kaplan, D. (2012). Licensure reciprocity: A critical public protection issue that needs action. *Counseling Today: Online Features.* Retrieved from http://ct.counseling.org/2012/01/licensure-reciprocity-a-critical-public-protection-issue-that-needs-action/

Kaplan, D. M., Wade, M. E., Conteh, J. A., & Martz, E. T. (2011). Legal and ethical issues surrounding the use of social media in counseling. *Counseling and Human Development, 43*(8), 1–12.

Killian, K. D. (2008). Helping till it hurts? A multimethod study of compassion fatigue, burnout, and self-care in clinicians working with trauma survivors. *Traumatology, 14*(2), 32–44. doi:10.1177/1534765608319083

Lawley, J. S. (2012). HIPAA, HITECH and the practicing counselor: Electronic records and practice guidelines. *The Professional Counselor, 2*(3), 192–200.

Moore, D. (2008). "Crimes involving moral turpitude": Why the void-for-vagueness argument is still available and meritorious. *Cornell International Law Journal, 41*(3), 813–843.

PAR. (2012). *Qualification levels.* Retrieved from http://www4.parinc.com/Supp/Qualifications.aspx

Richards, K. C., Campenni, C. E., & Muse-Burke, J. L. (2010). Self-care and well-being in mental health professionals: The mediating effects of self-awareness and mindfulness. *Journal of Mental Health Counseling, 32*(3), 247–264.

Robinson, J. (2009). *Do employees have a right to moonlight?* Retrieved from http://www.workforce.com/articles/do-employees-have-the-right-to-moonlight

Scovel, K. A., Christensen, O. J., & England, J. T. (2002). Mental health counselors' perceptions regarding psychopharmacological prescriptive privileges. *Journal of Mental Health Counseling, 24*(1), 36–50.

Shallcross, L. (2013). Who's taking care of Superman? *Counseling Today, 55*(7), 42–46.

Watson, J. C., & Sheperis, C. J. (2010). *Counselors and the right to test: Working toward professional parity (ACAPCD-31).* Alexandria, VA: American Counseling Association.

Williams, I. D., Richardson, T. A., Moore, D. D., Gambrel, L., & Keeling, M. L. (2010). Perspectives on self-care. *Journal of Creativity in Mental Health, 5*(3), 320–338. doi:10.1080/15401383.2010.507700

Chapter 13

RESOLVING ETHICAL ISSUES

Shawn is a licensed professional counselor (LPC) with a thriving private practice. To supplement his client work, Shawn provides continuing education hours around the state for fellow LPCs. As a National Board of Certified Counselors (NBCC) approved provider, he conducts seminars and offers hours that are accepted by the state licensure board. Shawn shares an office space with Nelah, a fellow LPC whom he has known for years. This year, Nelah was not able to get all of her contact hours in time for her renewal. She asks Shawn for a certificate from one if his supervision workshops, saying they have talked about supervision so much that she has earned the contact hours. Plus, she says, she is willing to pay for the cost of a seminar.

CHAPTER OVERVIEW

This chapter introduces the reader to an overview of how ethical complaints are heard and adjudicated. Because individual counselors are licensed and credentialed differently, knowing who can hear and adjudicate cases is essential. Professional memberships, organizations, and licensure boards serve as entry points for making an initial complaint. This chapter walks through the typical process of filing a complaint and the sanctions that may occur. Within this chapter you also will find ways to prevent ethical misconduct through risk management and aspirational practice. Finally, tips for approaching a colleague you suspect of unethical behavior along with steps to take if you are the one who is accused are presented. Key American Counseling Association (ACA) ethical codes and the related Council for Accreditation of Counseling & Related Educational Programs (CACREP, 2009) standards also are denoted for your use.

LEARNING OBJECTIVES

After reading this chapter you will be able to do the following:

1. Distinguish between ethics and the law.

2. Examine the ways in which counselors are held to the ethical codes of licensure boards, professional members, and credentialing.

3. Analyze steps in the adjudication processes in professional organizations and licensure boards.

4. Describe what to do when counselors are accused of ethical misconduct and explain risk management strategies to avoid.

5. Summarize steps to take if you suspect someone of an ethical transgression.

CACREP STANDARDS

CACREP Core Standards

G.1.j. Ethical standards of professional organizations and credentialing bodies, and applications of ethical and legal considerations in professional counseling.

CACREP Clinical Mental Health Standards

A.2. Understands ethical and legal considerations specifically related to the practice of clinical mental health counseling.

INTRODUCTION

The majority of this text has been devoted to helping counselors and counselors in training (CITs) develop a discerning eye regarding ethical dilemmas. As many of the ethical decision-making models (EDMs) we studied in Chapters 2 through 4 attest, determining that an ethical dilemma exists is a starting point for resolving it. Until this point, we primarily have discussed how to follow an EDM and involve our clients in the process. However, some decisions require that we go beyond the client–counselor relationship and involve professional organizations and licensure boards. This chapter will address the resolution of ethical issues, including the involvement of licensure boards and professional organizations.

In addition, this chapter will address what to do when you are accused and what to do when you suspect another professional of an ethical transgression.

ETHICS VERSUS THE LAW

Many of the issues we have discussed throughout this text have related to ethical and legal issues. However, there are clear distinctions between ethics and law. Ethics arise out of values and morals and comprise a code adopted by individuals in their personal ethics and organizations. Laws are standards that we, as a society, have agreed to uphold. Laws come with inherent punishments. If someone breaks a law and is caught, that person is punished. Ethics are slightly different.

Codes of ethics adopted by organizations, such as ACA, can result in consequences if the organizations deem them to be needed. However, those consequences apply only to members of the organization. The process of adjudication of cases is outlined clearly by each organization and varies from organization to organization. However, many state boards and ACA have specific adjudication policies that we will discuss later in this chapter.

Do ethics and law always align? Not necessarily. A perfect example is part of the discussion in Chapter 9 on working with minor clients. As you know, our ethical codes ask us always to put client welfare first. Most of us who work with children and adolescents view that individual as our client. Because children have no legal right to enter into contracts, the law does not view a minor as the client. Instead, the adult parent or guardian is the legal client. This can create complications for the counselor trying to balance ethics and the law.

ETHICS IN CREDENTIALING BODIES

The licenses, credentials, and professional memberships held by the counselor can play a role in addressing ethical dilemmas. Each of these entities may hold a code of ethics to which we are responsible. We are required to understand the codes under which we fall, but individuals pursuing ethical complaints against us must understand them as well. This section addresses the various ways that counselors may be held to the ethical codes of licensure boards, professional memberships, and credentialing.

Licensure Boards

State licensure boards have the authority and responsibility to confer licenses to counselors who meet their minimum requirements. There are three general components of licensure for professional counselors: educational requirements, competency exam, and supervised clinical experience (Buckley & Henning, 2015). The specifics of these components vary from state to state but have the three fundamental concepts in common. Every counselor licensed by a state board agrees to uphold the code of ethics set forth by the state licensure board. There are 52 ACA jurisdictions: the 50 states, Puerto Rico, and the District of Columbia. Of these 52 jurisdictions, 19 of them have adopted ACA Code of Ethics for their state licensure boards (ACA, 2014c).

Other states elect to adopt a version of ACA code or another code. However, the code they use is outlined clearly in state LPC law and available to practitioners and consumers in the state. Regardless of the origination of the code of ethics, when a counselor is licensed in a state, that counselor agrees to uphold the ethics for that state.

Professional Membership and Credentialing

As we discussed, licensure often is required for counselors to practice in their state. However, counselors also voluntarily seek out national credentials and membership in professional organizations in addition to licensure status. Understanding these voluntary activities in addition to state licensure sets the stage for understanding how to approach ethical issue resolution.

Ideally, counselors are introduced to professional membership in our graduate degree programs. A professional organization "is a group of people in a learned occupation who are entrusted with maintaining control or oversight of the legitimate practice of the occupation" (Harvey, 2014, para. 6). The counseling profession is full of such organizations, and many of them have their own codes of ethics.

American Counseling Association. We have spent a great deal of time discussing ACA and its ethical code. ACA is the flagship professional membership for counselors. With membership, counselors join an organization of more than 53,000 peers who participate in ongoing professional development, stay abreast of current trends, lobby for legislative advances, and network with peers (ACA, 2014b). Members also receive discounts on liability and other insurances, continuing education opportunities, and professional directory or advertising services.

ACA is the umbrella organization under which many other divisions in counseling fall. To date, there are 20 divisions of ACA tailored to specific areas of interest and practice. Professional divisions include organizations such as the Association for Assessment and Research in Counseling, Association for Counselor Education and Supervision, and the American School Counselor Association. Some of these divisions contain their own codes of ethics in addition to ACA code.

ACA (2014a) Code of Ethics serves as the gold standard of ethics for our profession. Members of ACA and its divisions are held to ACA code as well as their related division codes. As a result, members may be held to many ethical standards. ACA has an ethics committee that is charged with adjudicating ethical cases. This will be discussed in greater detail in the section titled "Adjudication Processes." At this point, it is important to recognize that ACA members must be mindful of their division ethical codes along with ACA Code of Ethics.

American School Counselors Association. ASCA is both a division of ACA and an independent professional organization for school counselors. What this means is that members of ASCA do not necessarily have to be members of ACA. There are approximately 30,000 members of ASCA, making this one of the larger professional organizations for counselors of any type. ASCA is a powerful resource of school counselors providing continuing education, legislative activities, and support for members. In addition, ASCA has its own code of ethics that specifically governs the role of the school counselor and protects stakeholders (ASCA, 2014a).

American Mental Health Counselors Association. AMHCA is a voluntary professional membership for clinical mental health counselors. AMHCA has about 7,000 members who join to work with other clinical mental health counselors on public policy legislation, networking, and clinical practice issues (AMHCA, 2013). AMHCA has its own code of ethics, and counselors who belong to AMHCA agree to adhere to its standards.

Just as joining a professional organization is a voluntary process, so is credentialing. While licensure is legislated, defined, and monitored at the state level, various credentialing bodies may offer their own certifications to counselors. These credentialing bodies often have their own ethical codes to which counselors must be responsive. Let's begin with one of the most common credentialing bodies, NBCC.

The National Board of Certified Counselors. NBCC is an independent nonprofit credentialing body offering voluntary national certification to counselors (NBCC, 2014). It was founded by ACA as a way of bringing national credentialing to the profession while states were determining state licensure laws. The primary credential offered by NBCC is the National Certified Counselor (NCC), which is held by more than 55,000 counselors. These counselors voluntarily take the National Counseling Exam and apply for credentialing through NBCC. Other credentials offered by NBCC include the Master Addictions Counselor (MAC), Certified Clinical Mental Health Counselor (CCMHC), and National Certified School Counselor (NCSC). Separate from licensure, these certifications show the public that the counselor has met a high level of national standards through training, examination, and clinical practice.

NBCC has its own code of ethics that governs all who are credentialed as an NCC, MAC, CCMHC, or NCSC. This code was updated in 2012 and is available on the NBCC Web site: http://www.nbcc.org/InteractiveCodeOfEthics/. Similar to ACA code, the NBCC code is more concise and governs the work of all credentialed under its banner. In addition, NBCC has an adjudication process that manages ethical complaints against those holding NCC, MAC, CCMHC, or NCSC credential. This process will be explored further in the adjudication section of this chapter.

→ *Association for Play Therapy.* A specialty organization that credentials counselors is the Association for Play Therapy (APT). APT is an organization of mental health professionals promoting the use of play therapy with a variety of populations (APT, n.d.). In addition to advancing the use of play therapy, APT offers two credentials: the Registered Play Therapist (RPT) and the Registered Play Therapist-Supervisor (APT-S). To become an RPT, counselors already must hold a state license as a professional counselor. In addition, RPT candidates must have specific course work and clinical experience in play therapy (APT, 2014). Rather than a formal code of ethics, RPTs are asked to follow play therapy best practices, which closely parallel the codes of ethics we have studied thus far and provide the basis for ethical decision making as a play therapist (APT, 2012).

National Association of Forensic Counselors. Another credentialing body is the National Association for Forensic Counselors (NAFC). NAFC offers a number of credentials for counselors including the Forensic Counselor, Criminal Justice Specialist, and Sex Offender Treatment Specialist. NAFC was the first to credential forensic counselors and criminal justice specialists (NAFC, 2009). NAFC has a code of ethics that governs those it credentials. However, there does not seem to be an adjudication process for NAFC, which will become relevant as we discuss handling ethical complaints. Not all credentialing bodies have a code of ethics or adjudication process. As a result, adjudicating ethical complaints can become complicated both for the practicing counselor and the general public for whom these codes are developed to protect.

ADJUDICATION PROCESSES

Because ethics are not laws, they are not heard in courts. Rather, they are adjudicated by the boards or organizations that govern the person accused. To adjudicate means to make a formal judgment or decision about a dispute or dilemma (Adjudicate, 2014). Licensure boards, professional organizations, and credentialing bodies have the option to develop adjudication processes for members. All state licensure boards have an adjudication process. However, not all professional organizations and certification bodies have a means of handling ethical complaints, even when they have an identified code of ethics.

For example, AMHCA has its own code of ethics that can be easily located on the www.amhca.org Web site. This code addresses many elements of clinical mental health practice and provides more guidance to those clinicians in its code of ethics than ACA code. However, AMHCA clearly states in Section IV of its code that the organization does not hear or rule on ethical matters (AMHCA, 2010). Members are encouraged to follow ethical decision-making practices to address ethical dilemmas, but no recourse is available via the organization.

What, then, is the proper way to have an ethical case heard? Section I of ACA (2014a) Code of Ethics covers aspects of resolving ethical issues. At their core, codes of ethics are written to guide our behavior as counselors and to protect the public. In addition, ACA code asks that counselors "hold other counselors to the same standards and are willing to take appropriate action to ensure that standards are upheld" (ACA, 2014a, p. 19). To do so, we are encouraged to communicate directly with other counselors about potential transgressions.

Ethical Code13.1

I.2.a. Informal Resolution.

When counselors have reason to believe that another counselor is violating or has violated an ethical standard and substantial harm has not occurred, they attempt to first resolve the issue informally with the other counselor if feasible, provided such action does not violate confidentiality rights that may be involved.

Source: 2014 American Counseling Association Code of Ethics. Reprinted with permission from American Counseling Association.

Informal Resolution

Virtually all codes of ethics consider an informal resolution between counselors to be the first action step in resolving ethical dilemmas. Remember the case presented at the beginning of the chapter? Shawn was asked by Nelah to fake her attendance at a workshop, so she could have the appropriate number of continuing education units for her license. It is likely that after thoughtful consideration and consultation, Shawn would be able to speak candidly with Nelah about why her request would violate his professional ethics. To maintain harmonious relations, he also may suggest some online opportunities for her to access continuing education with her schedule. While it may be an inconvenience for Nelah, Shawn will have responded ethically via informal resolution.

Formal Adjudication

If informal resolution is unsuccessful or not possible, formal adjudication may be necessary. ACA (2014a) Code of Ethics outlines how to handle formal resolution for all types of counselors. It provides guidance for the next steps by asking counselors and others to consider the various licensure boards, professional organizations, and memberships through its discussion of the concept of jurisdiction.

Ethical Code 13.2

I.2.b. Reporting Ethical Violations.

If an apparent violation has substantially harmed or is likely to substantially harm a person or organization and is not appropriate for informal resolution or is not resolved properly, counselors take further action depending on the situation. Such action may include referral to state or national committees on professional ethics, voluntary national certification bodies, state licensing boards, or appropriate institutional authorities. The confidentiality rights of clients should be considered in all actions. This standard does not apply when counselors have been retained to review the work of another counselor whose professional conduct is in question (e.g., consultation, expert testimony).

Source: 2014 American Counseling Association Code of Ethics. Reprinted with permission from American Counseling Association.

Jurisdiction as it relates to ethical adjudication simply means that the board in question has the authority to interpret the codes and determine recourse. For example, ACA has jurisdiction only over ACA members. That jurisdiction is enacted through ACA Ethics Committee.

ACA Ethics Committee

ACA Ethics Committee is a board of nine ACA members appointedby ACA president-elect for three-year terms (ACA, 2005). The committee has a number of duties, including educating the membership and public at large about ethical considerations in counseling. The committee meets, at minimum, three times per year explicitly to process ethical complaints. It follows a clear process to ensure the rights of both the client and the accused counselor are protected.

First, the counselor must be a member of ACA. If the counselor is not a member, then the committee has no jurisdiction. Many clinicians elect not to join a professional organization, leaving the committee no ability to help the complainant. If the counselor is an ACA member, a complainant can file the alleged violation with ACA. Because the complainant is typically a client, that person is given a number of protections and assistance by ACA. The complainant can work directly with ACA ethics manager to complete the necessary paperwork to file a complaint. The ethics manager will assist the complainant in connecting the narrative of his or her complaint to existing ACA ethical codes. The complaint is then passed to the cochair of the ethics committee. That person is responsible for determining what codes are in question and if the points in the complainant's narrative are true. This step is not a determination of fact; rather, it is a way of connecting the narrative to the codes. If the narrative cannot be matched to a code, then the issue is not an ethical one (ACA, 2005).

The complainant is informed that the committee will share the documentation of the complaint with the accused. In other words, there are no anonymous complaints heard by ACA. The accused ACA member has every right to the documentation submitted and to develop an appropriate defense. Most liability and malpractice insurance policies cover attorney consultation and representation for the practicing counselor. At the hearing, held in person or via conference call, both the complainant and the accused may present their sides. As in court cases, each side has the right to legal counsel and to call witnesses. However, because this is not a court of law, judicial rules of evidence do not apply. What this means is that documents and witnesses that may not be admissible in court are admissible in ACA ethics hearings. Like a court of law, the ethics committee must meet minimum criteria for the burden of proof to rule against the accused. It is not the responsibility of the accused to prove him or herself right; rather, it is the complainant's responsibility to prove that the accused was in the wrong. After the evidence is heard, the ethics committee meets to discuss, deliberate, and determine judgment.

Guided Practice Exercise 13.1

Ethical Adjudication in Your State

Visit your state licensure board Web site, and learn how ethical cases are adjudicated. Are the hearings open or public? Are the cases and outcomes made available on the Web site? If so, look through the case summaries and types of sanctions offered to get a sense of the ethical transgressions that occur or have occurred in your state.

When a complaint is found to have merit, ACA Ethics Committee has several responses at its discretion. Sanctions within the committee's purview include remediation, probation, suspension, and expulsion (ACA, 2005). Remediation includes activities to increase the accused's awareness of ethical transgressions and ethical decision making, such as attendance at mandatory ethics workshops. Probation may occur along with remediation in that the counselor is on probation until he or she complies with the remediation activities. Suspension may be imposed while awaiting compliance, and in this case, ACA membership is not active during the time of remediation. Finally, the accused, if found to be at fault, may be expelled from ACA permanently with no opportunity for return. Expulsion occurs when more atrocious ethical transgressions have transpired for which remediation is not deemed possible and is rarely used, according to ACA Chief Professional Officer David Kaplan (as cited in Boodman, 2005).

Guided Practice Exercise 13.2

When a Colleague Is Accused

A new client tells you that she recently discontinued working with Sal, a counselor in your local area. She further discloses that she became uncomfortable when Sal asked her to go for coffee after a session to "get to know her better." What are your next steps?

Another question to consider is why is expulsion so uncommon? If an organization, such as ACA, permanently expels a member, it has no ability to govern or sanction the ex-member's work as a counselor in the future. It is only in these most extreme cases that counselors are expelled from membership. While expulsion creates a challenge for professionals and is a blemish on their professional record, the real consequences of ethical case adjudication come via the state licensure boards.

State Licensure Boards

As has been discussed, the state licensure board governs the practice of professional counseling. Counselors can belong to professional organizations without being licensed. They can hold certifications from national credentialing bodies such as NBCC. But professional counselors cannot practice independently without a state license.

Because the state license is the ticket to independent practice, it is a desirable part of professional counselor functioning. Without it, a counselor may work in some select agency settings or in another field, but he or she may not see clients and bill them for services independently. As such, maintaining the standards of the state board is essential to the licensed counselor.

Although state licensure laws differ, there are similarities when it comes to adjudicating ethical complaints. These complaints typically are handled via a process that is very similar to ACA process previously described. Complainants must first determine if the counselor is licensed in the state. Then a complaint may be filed with the state board. State boards meet monthly or several times per year and hear cases that are found to have merit.

CASE STUDY 13.1

A complaint is made against a counselor indicating that he conducted an assessment unethically with Sharla, the client making the accusation. In her complaint, Sharla states that the counselor evaluated her for work with the local police academy then reported those results to the police academy before sharing them with her. She felt this was a breach of her personal confidentiality and filed a complaint. When contacted by the board, the counselor in question produces a contract indicating that the work was commissioned by the police academy, and the terms of the agreement were that the results would be communicated to the police academy directly, before they were shared with the client. The complaint is dismissed as lacking in merit.

1. *Was the board correct in dismissing the case?*

2. *If you were the counselor charged, how might this case impact how you practice with clients?*

As an example, let's take a look at how the state of Oregon handled ethical complaints. The state of Oregon Board of Licensed Professional Counselors and Therapists' Web site, http://www.oregon.gov/oblpct, contains both a practitioner section and a consumer section. The consumer section includes a copy of the code of ethics, expectations of counselors, information about filing an ethical complaint, and the confidential complaint form. After a complaint is received and jurisdiction is established, the board acknowledges the complaint and solicits additional information as needed. The board then contacts the licensee and requests a response in 21 days. Upon receipt of the response, the board interviews the parties involved and gathers any needed information to make a determination. Within 120 days, the board takes action on the complaint (Oregon.gov, n.d.b.).

In Oregon, this case has several possible outcomes. First, if no merit is found to the complaint, the complaint can be dismissed. If the board has concerns about the allegations, but does not find that there is sufficient evidence to rule against the licensee, it can dismiss the complaint but issue a letter of concern. Another option is to propose disciplinary action similar to ACA remediation. In Oregon, any discipline imposed by the board is provided to the counselor and posted on the board's Web site. The outcome also is reported to a national data bank of disciplinary actions against health care and mental health providers known as the Healthcare Integrity & Protection Data Bank (Oregon.gov, n.d.a.). Examples of disciplines offered by the Oregon board range from monthly mandatory supervision, a child abuse reporting course, and license revocation in the case of counselors who were involved sexually with their clients (Oregon.gov, 2014).

While this chapter has illustrated Oregon, most states follow a similar pattern. As we saw in the case of professional organizations, revocation of license is a rare outcome with disciplinary actions. This is because when the board removes licensure from the counselor, that person can no longer be governed by the board. Having a counselor maintain licensure status with conditions allows the board to monitor the counselor's activities, require regular reporting, and keep the professional accountable to the licensure board.

You may recall that unlicensed counselors can work in a variety of settings but cannot operate independently. Consider the following case example:

Case Example

Peter is a master's level LPC in private practice conducting child custody evaluations in an urban area. He has a thriving practice alongside a clinical psychologist. Many of his clients and their families call him "doctor," and he does not discourage this. The nature of his work requires that Peter conduct a variety of assessments for the court system. He finds that employing counseling interns and clerical staff is a great way to complete these assessments. He then signs these reports as if he had done the assessment and goes to court to provide the results. Peter views this as the best use of his time as administering most of the assessments is pretty much clerical anyway.

A complaint is made against Peter with his state LPC board indicating that he encourages his clients to call him "doctor." The state LPC board issues a cease and desist letter to Peter asking him to fully inform his clients of his credentials.

Over the years, Peter built a larger and larger business with the court system. He came to the decision that mothers are better able to parent children after divorce than fathers. As a result, his assessments tend to skew in favor of mothers. At times, he even submits reports as if he had conducted a home visit with both parents when he did not. A complaint eventually is filed with the LPC board about Peter's practices.

> *The complainant lost his children due to Peter's erroneous assessment and created a Web site to gather other fathers to join him in challenging Peter's competency. The board suspends Peter's license and requires a remediation plan. Several additional complaints and lawsuits follow. Eventually, the board is forced to revoke Peter's license due to his ongoing ethical transgressions.*
>
> *When he can no longer practice independently, Peter moves to another state. He does not secure licensure there because states require copies of previous licenses as well as verification from that state that the license is in good standing or was not renewed voluntarily. He works for some time in that state but later returns to his home state. He now works for the state department of mental health managing their group home systems. In other words, the very state that revoked his license now employs him in a counseling role.*

The case example is rooted in a series of similar cases familiar to your text authors. What are your emotional reactions to this case? We find that many students and counselors initially are appalled. Many focus on the fact that he can continue to work with vulnerable populations without a license. Remember that these emotions, the gut check, if you will, are elements of many EDMs. Let's consider some of the challenges inherent in this case. For example, is it illegal or unethical to call yourself *doctor?* Take a moment to look at your ACA Code of Ethics, and determine your response. It would seem reasonable that C.3. would apply, but that is only about advertising. What about accurately representing yourself with your existing clients? Many ethical boards would see this as a violation.

Now return to Chapter 1, and visit the ethical decision-making traps discussed. Recall that these traps are simply ways that we take a first step on the slippery slope to poor ethical choices. We may start with good intentions but let the behavior slide, if you will, into unethical territory. The first time a client calls you "doctor," would you redirect? When you consider allowing an administrative assistant to conduct the assessment, you have begun the journey down that slippery slope. It is only when you allow it to occur, and even more so when you sign your name to it, that you have crossed the line.

- What ACA ethical codes did Peter violate? Is it illegal to call yourself *doctor?*
- What ethical decision-making traps from Chapter 1 may have contributed to Peter's poor choices?
- What remediation plans would you want to see Peter engage in early on to avoid losing his license?
- What are your thoughts on unlicensed counselors working in state systems?

CASE STUDY 13.2

Richard A. Cohen holds a master's degree in counseling psychology and is a former ACA member. His primary area of practice was conversion therapy. As someone who states that he used to be gay but is now heterosexual, he works with others who want to convert from being gay. Mr. Cohen authored a book titled Coming Out Straight, *which describes his experiences in his own sexual identity development. His practice is exclusively with gay men who wish to become heterosexual.*

Mr. Cohen is not licensed in any state and operates as a coach rather than a counselor. He has a charitable organization that helps fund his endeavors. Mr. Cohen shared with a Washington Post *reporter that touch is a central component of his therapy practice. He believes that close, intimate mentorship with a heterosexual male is conducive to change.*

Mr. Cohen was brought up on numerous ethical charges in an ACA complaint brought forward by a former client. The complaint contained concerns about Mr. Cohen's approach to therapy, and the former client felt forced to be a part of workshops and lectures for Mr. Cohen. According to the adjudicated complaint, Cohen was found in violation of multiple codes of ethics including those related to imposing values, fostering autonomy, and exploiting client trust (Boodman, 2005).

1. *What are your initial reactions as you read this case?*

2. *Do you agree with Mr. Cohen's approach to counseling? Why or why not?*

3. *Would you refer a client to Mr. Cohen? Why or why not?*

Adjudication by the Numbers

As you read through the steps to adjudication and the various outcomes, the process should seem relatively straightforward. While it is straightforward, it is important to know that a full case adjudication is less common than you may think. One of the best ways to illustrate this is with the annual report data provided by the ACA Ethics Committee.

Each year, ACA receives a number of ethical inquiries. Those numbers have increased dramatically in recent years. Inquiries include calls, e-mails, letters, and faxes to ACA office to ask questions about ethics. In 2004, there were 758 such inquiries (Anderson & Freeman, 2006). By 2012 and 2013 there were more than 6,000 inquires (ACA, 2012; ACA, 2013). This is an almost 700 percent increase in less than 10 years! Imagine if all of these inquiries turned into actual cases to be adjudicated. It would take a lot more than the current ethics committee infrastructure to manage such a deluge of cases.

Why such an increase? It is likely that ACA Ethics Committee has done a good job of educating practitioners and the public as to its role. In addition, counseling students have become more aware, and many of the questions are coming from that population of beginning professionals (personal communication, E. Martz, 2011). Finally, the culture of our country is increasingly litigious, and the practice of protecting oneself is more common than in the past. Now let's take a look at what happens to all these cases.

In fiscal year 2011 to 2012, there were 6,231 inquiries and only four formal complaints (ACA, 2013). Of those four complaints, only two were accepted for adjudication as the others were filed against nonmembers, or the complaint could not be matched with relevant ethical codes required to meet the standard for hearing the case. This extremely small percentage of cases moving from inquiry to adjudication is due to a number of factors. Many of the inquiries may be found not to be ethical dilemmas at all. Additionally, the queries may have to do with non-ACA members. Finally, the complainant may decide the process of filing the complaint is not worthwhile or that the idea of the complaint being made public is personally difficult. As you can see, the numbers that reach adjudication are very manageable at the national level and are likely mirrored at the state licensure board level.

WHAT COUNSELORS SHOULD DO WHEN THEY ARE ACCUSED OF ETHICAL MISCONDUCT

Perhaps the biggest fear that counselors carry is the fear that a client will accuse them of ethical misconduct via an ethics complaint or lawsuit. As a result, counselors are advised to carry independent malpractice policies even if working for an agency or practice that carries a group policy. Large professional organizations, such as ACA and AMHCA, offer malpractice insurance to students as part of their membership to cover the work they do as interns. Once graduated, beginning counselors must shop for and purchase their own coverage to meet their personal needs.

Having such a policy is a benefit in the event that a counselor is accused of ethical misconduct. As you have seen from the statistics, formal complaints against counselors are rare, but they do occur. Being the target of such a complaint can be an overwhelming professional experience. Because ethical cases that go to the state board or are heard in a court of law are made public, these events can also be career shattering. Having an understanding of ethics, the use of an EDM, and a good malpractice insurance policy are preventative actions all counselors should take.

According to Walk-In Counseling Center, a nonprofit mental health consultation organization providing resources for counseling professionals, a counselor may hear that there is an ethical concern in a number of ways (Walk-In Counseling

Center, n.d.). The counselor may receive a grievance directly from the client in the form of a conversation, letter, or other means. This informal complaint may be handled quickly and directly, especially if the client is asking for session fees to be returned. The counselor should consult, of course, but may want to refund the money to avoid costly litigation of a formal complaint.

The counselor may receive first notification that there is a problem when a formal complaint is filed with an agency, institution, or school where the counselor is employed. Or, a counselor may receive a call from the state licensure board or attorney general's office if the complaint is filed at the state level. Finally, the counselor may receive a subpoena or subpoena *duces tecum*. A subpoena is a court order requiring that the counselor appear before the court in a case while a subpoena *duces tecum* is an order filed through the court by an attorney requesting the production of records or evidence, such as case files (Subpoena, 2013).

Many counselors likely handle informal complaints made directly to them by clients on a regular basis, but what happens after a formal case is filed? The first step a counselor should take is to cease and desist all communication with the client. When the client opens the complaint, he or she loses all right to confidentiality as the counselor is free to develop a defense. Contacting the insurance company and beginning to go over the case with the provided attorney are the next steps.

When You Are Contacted

In general, there are some rules of thumb to follow when you are contacted by a professional board regarding a potential ethical transgression (Zur, 2014). First, treat all contacts seriously. These are not matters to be trivialized or ignored. As tempting as it may be to decide that the claim lacks any validity, it still must be addressed professionally and quickly—but not too quickly. Always consult legal counsel before replying, even to your own state licensure board. It is important to maintain control of all client files and contacts until you are authorized to release them by your attorney. Perhaps most important is that those careful files you kept must not be altered in any way after contact about the issue.

All communication, written or in person, should occur with your attorney's involvement. Even if the client, client's attorney, or a board representative appears on your doorstep, do not engage without your own counsel present. We discussed informal resolution with the client earlier in this section, but once a formal complaint has been filed, there should be no further discussion with the client. In fact, your discussions should be kept to a minimum and include only your attorney, supervisor, and partner. It will be tempting to talk openly about the case, but this is ill advised in case it works against you in court or in a hearing. Finally, it is recommended widely that filing a countersuit is not in your best interests.

Remember that the client is still the vulnerable party in the eyes of the law and in codes of ethics, and you want to avoid the appearance of a power play (Zur, 2014).

Above all, we want to impress upon you as practicing counselors that lawsuits and ethical charges are relatively rare. When they do occur, they can be life altering. It is imperative to practice self-care along the way to ensure that you are still functioning well for existing clients and that you are able to live a reasonably content life in spite of this challenge. As you know, the codes of ethics exist to help you govern your own behavior.

Risk Management

A counselor is five times more likely to have a state board charge filed against him or her than to be a party in a lawsuit; however, being prepared is critical (Zur, 2014). An essential component of risk management is to have adequate liability insurance coverage. As previously mentioned, students may acquire such insurance as a function of several professional memberships, such as ACA, AMHCA, and ASCA. ASCA even offers some insurance coverage to U.S.-based school counselor professional members (ASCA, 2014b). ACA has a partnership with Healthcare Providers Service Organization (HPSO) to provide liability insurance to members at a reduced rate (ACA, 2014b). Other private malpractice providers exist to serve counselors as well. Counselors need to consider how much coverage to purchase annually. Some providers suggest that counselors have a policy that offers them $1 million for each claim and up to $5 million maximum coverage (HPSO, 2014). These types of policies are intended to supplement employer policies and protect the individual rather than the agency.

Hopefully, this is a policy you will never use! In the event that you do have a concern, the policy typically will offer disciplinary defense coverage. In other words, your insurance policy will assist you with legal counsel in the event of a lawsuit or board hearing. In addition, these policies often include personal injury protection. This is not to cover you for physical assaults, necessarily; rather, personal injury protection covers claims related to slander, libel, and privacy violations. Given that so many ethical challenges are related to privacy considerations and HIPAA, having coverage for these pitfalls is helpful for risk management purposes (HPSO, 2014).

Having insurance is one component of risk management. Using the various EDMs discussed throughout the text is another. In addition, counselors must stay informed regarding changes to ethical codes and current trends in ethics cases. This is best accomplished through continuing education opportunities, belonging to professional organizations, and networking with others in the field. Finally, one of the most important components of preemptive risk management is good documentation and record-keeping practices (Zur, 2014).

Record keeping and documentation are elements of professional practice that counselors may complain about the most. Who loves paperwork? Not counselors, by and large. We are people oriented, not paper oriented, and prefer to spend our time in the active service of others. However, it is essential to keep accurate and timely case notes. As mentioned earlier in the text, part of a good ethical decision-making process is to document consultation and decision-making practices as well. We should follow the motto, "If it isn't written, it didn't happen," and be diligent in recording our work with clients and any potential pitfalls (and resolutions) that occur along the way.

Practice Aspirationally and Relationally

Recall from our discussion in Chapter 1 that aspirational ethics mean that counselors serve the client beyond the letter of the law. Practicing aspirationally means keeping our client's welfare in the forefront at all times. It is an elevated level of practice that protects the client, follows relevant codes and laws, and as such, serves to protect us as well. This text has made a point of focusing on the relation aspect as well. Whenever possible, involve your client and relevant stakeholders in ethical decisions. When you do so and the client has buy-in to the decision, there is less risk of a lawsuit or case being brought before a board.

Next we will examine your role when someone else's behavior is in question.

WHAT TO DO WHEN YOU SUSPECT SOMEONE ELSE OF AN ETHICAL TRANSGRESSION

Throughout this text you have applied the codes of ethics to case studies of fictional counselors. We hope that we have made it clear that codes of ethics exist to allow us to monitor our own behavior. However, there may be times that you are faced with knowledge of an ethical transgression that requires your attention and, perhaps, intervention. Let's take a closer look at what to do when someone else may be crossing ethical lines.

Your own ethics training and EDM should alert you to signs of an ethical dilemma. During conversations with colleagues, these dilemmas will become apparent. Remember that you have an ethical decision-making process to follow, and while it may be tempting to point an accusatory finger, your EDM requires you to take a step-by-step approach. First, make sure the dilemma you have identified truly is an ethical dilemma and violates a distinct ethical principle or law. If you cannot connect the perceived transgression to a particular ethical code, then no ethical dilemma exists.

Guided Practice Exercise 13.3

When You Are Accused

You are having a wonderful day at the office when a process server arrives. It seems that a former client, who has a history of litigation against service providers of all types, is suing you for malpractice. Her suit alleges that you promised her that she would be relieved of her depression after six sessions, but she is still depressed. You know that you did not make that promise and have a clause in your informed consent indicating all possible outcomes of counseling. What steps should you take next?

Assuming there is an ethical transgression occurring, however, how should you handle it? You initially will want to consider the evidence, or lack thereof. Very few ethical transgressions happen in public with witnesses and corroborating evidence (Koocher & Keith-Spiegel, 2012). One exception is when you learn of a non-licensed counselor advertising as though he or she is a licensed counselor. In these cases, state boards will issue a cease and desist letter based on the public advertising.

Ethical transgressions are more likely to occur in private between the client and counselor and be reported after the fact. You may learn about it via conversation with the counselor, or perhaps you begin to see a new client who tells you about a former counselor. In these instances, you should consider the information provided and check your own motives for taking on this dilemma. Are you acting as an advocate for your profession? Have you always been suspicious of that counselor and now have a way to get him or her? Do you enjoy the conflict that comes with being the righter of wrongs? It is likely that you have time to consult before acting on the matter, and these motives should be discussed in your consultation. Remember the importance of consultation in all ethical decisions—consulting about confronting a colleague's ethical transgression is no different.

Koocher and Keith-Spiegel (2012) warn counselors against taking covert action to address the behavior in a less direct and professional way. They state that counselors can be tempted to avoid the confrontation by simply sharing their knowledge with others in the field to prevent further harm to clients. If other counselors know of the problem, perhaps they will not refer clients to the practitioner. You can see how this may diminish the frequency of future cases but not address the real problem. A second covert action these authors describe is the counselor who sends an anonymous note to the suspected offender letting him or her know that you are on to them. The counselor attempting to right the wrong may even go so far as to send a copy of the relevant ethical code to send the message that the accused must stop. As you can see, both of these options lack the transparency that our profession expects in collegial interactions and do not take into account that the presumed offender may have been incorrectly judged. To address the ethical concern in such a manner violates the spirit of aspirational ethics and is simply not professional.

When a true dilemma seems to be at hand, and you determine that an informal resolution is the best option, make an appointment rather than engaging in an ambush. It may be tempting to catch them in the hallway or to pull them aside at a staff luncheon, but a professional dilemma requires professional behavior on your part. Ask for some time with the colleague without being threatening or menacing. Set a tone for the meeting that is not critical but open to your having misunderstood the information. For example, you may wish to start with simple facts that contain no judgment so that your peer can agree or disagree with your understanding of events. If there is still an ethical dilemma present, outline your concerns allowing your colleague to offer any explanations along the way. Be sure to let the counselor in question know your role: Are you acting on behalf of a client or as a fellow counselor? Do you have personal knowledge of the behavior (as in the case between Shawn and Nelah at the start of the chapter), or are you acting on hearsay? Be clear, nonjudgmental, nonthreatening, and nondefensive. Remember that this is your colleague in the profession. If you are unable to come to a resolution, you may need to take this further. However, in the moment, you are there to share your concern and listen to your colleague (Koocher & Keith-Spiegel, 2012). If an informal intervention is unsuccessful, you may need to move forward with the steps to address the transgression with the ACA or your state licensure board.

CASE STUDY 13.3

Juli is a counselor working in a private practice with Laura, a fellow counselor. Both Juli and Laura see clients of all ages, but Laura specializes in child and adolescent care. When Juli sees a client under the age of 18 who reveals the use of alcohol or drugs, she reports that use to the parent or guardian. She informs both parent and child of this policy in her informed consent. This reporting is legal and occurs when the parent meets with Juli about the child's progress. Laura does not agree with this policy and has told Juli how she handles these disclosures. Laura wonders if she should report Juli to the state ethics board or the ACA. When she calls the ACA ethics manager, she learns that Juli's behavior is legal and does not explicitly violate a code of ethics that could be pursued. While Juli may lose the trust and therapeutic relationship with the child as a result of the report to the guardian, she is up front about how she views this illegal behavior and follows the policy consistently with her clients.

1. *What are your personal reactions to Juli's process?*

2. *Do you identify more with Juli or Laura in how they handle these disclosures?*

3. *If Laura came to you for advice, what would you tell her?*

CONCLUSION

Learning the ins and outs of ethical codes is essential to becoming a professional counselor. As we have seen in this chapter, understanding how those codes are used to adjudicate cases in professional organizations and legal cases is also a critical component of professional practice. When a colleague is suspected of unethical behavior, an informal resolution is the preferred approach. However, there are times when a formal action must occur. Knowing the professional memberships and licenses of the accused counselor will direct the process as those are the only organizations that can hear or adjudicate a complaint. When counselors are accused, there are a number of steps they must follow under the guidance of legal counsel. Although lawsuits and ethical adjudications are relatively rare, it is important to protect your practice using risk management and aspirational approaches.

KEYSTONES

- Ethics arise out of values and morals and comprise a code adopted by individuals in their personal ethics and organizations, while laws are standards that we as a society have agreed to uphold.
- State licensure boards have the authority and responsibility to confer licenses on those counselors who meet their minimum requirements. Every counselor licensed by a state board must uphold the code of ethics provided by that board.
- A professional organization "is a group of people in a learned occupation who are entrusted with maintaining control or oversight of the legitimate practice of the occupation" (Harvey, 2014, para. 6). The counseling profession has many professional organizations, each with its own code of ethics.
- Virtually all codes of ethics consider an informal resolution between counselors to be the first action step in resolving ethical dilemmas. If informal resolution is unsuccessful or not possible, formal adjudication may be necessary.
- Jurisdiction as it relates to ethical adjudication simply means that the board in question has the authority to interpret the codes and determine recourse.
- Sanctions within ACA Ethics Committee's purview include remediation, probation, suspension, and expulsion. Remediation includes activities to increase the accused's awareness of ethical transgressions and ethical decision making, such as attendance at mandatory ethics workshops. Probation may occur along with remediation in that the counselor is on probation until there is compliance with the remediation activities. Suspension may be imposed while waiting compliance, and in this case, the membership is not active during the time of remediation.
- Adjudication of ethical complaints by the state board is similar to the process used by ACA. Complainants must determine if the counselor is licensed in the state, then they can file with the state board. State boards meet monthly or several times per year and hear cases that have merit.

- Counselors should practice risk management. One way of doing so is to purchase liability insurance. Large professional organizations, such as ACA and AMHCA, offer malpractice insurance to students as part of their membership to cover the work they do as interns. We also should practice aspirationally and relationally and, whenever possible, involve the client and relevant stakeholders in ethical decisions.
- When suspecting someone else of an ethical transgression, remember that you have an ethical decision-making process to follow, and while it may be tempting to point an accusatory finger, your EDM requires you to take a step-by-step approach.

SUGGESTED BEST PRACTICES

- Remember that ethical codes are written to guide your behavior, not to police the behavior of your peers.
- Consider what codes you would be willing to break and why. Consider what laws you would be willing to break and why. If the answer is none, what will you do when ethics and law collide?
- Know all of the ethical codes under which you fall.
- Know the educational requirements, competency exam, and supervised clinical hours requirements for your state.
- Join professional organizations, and participate in their activities, such as conferences and interest groups.
- Select voluntary credentials that help showcase your expertise to clients and the public.
- Understand the basics of the adjudication process so that you can better understand how to approach ethical decisions.
- Pay close attention to the steps to informal resolution. You may be called upon to talk with a colleague about unethical behavior.
- Have a liability policy, and know how to use it.
- Have an attorney with whom you can consult in the event of an ethical dilemma.
- Get involved with your state licensure board if possible.
- Visit your state licensure board Web site, and read cases that have been adjudicated to remain apprised of the trends in your state.

ADDITIONAL RESOURCES

In Print

Bolin, J. N., Mechler, K., Holcomb, J., & Williams, J. (2008). An alternative strategy for resolving ethical dilemmas in rural healthcare. *American Journal of Bioethics, 8*(4), 63–65. doi:10.1080/15265160802147231

Sheperis, D. S., & Goodnough, G. (2010). ACA ethics committee overview. *Counseling Today, 52*(11), 78.

Thomas, J. T. (2014). Disciplinary supervision following ethics complaints: Goals, tasks, and ethical dimensions. *Journal of Clinical Psychology, 70*(11), 1104–1114. doi:10.1002/jclp.22131

Woody, R. H. (2008). Obtaining legal counsel for child and family mental health practice. *American Journal of Family Therapy, 36*(4), 323–331. doi:10.1080/01926180701686171

On the Web

O'Neal, A. J. (2014). *Legal issues and the mental health counseling profession.* Retrieved from http://www.newsrecord.co/legal-issues-and-the-mental-health-counseling-profession/

Risk management. (n.d.). ACA. Retrieved from http://www.counseling.org/knowledge-center/ethics/risk-management

REFERENCES

Adjudicate. (2014). In *Merriam-Webster's dictionary.* Retrieved from http://www.merriam-webster.com/dictionary/adjudicate

American Counseling Association (ACA). (2005). *ACA policies and procedures for processing complaints of ethical violations.* Retrieved from http://www.counseling.org/docs/ethics/policies_procedures.pdf?sfvrsn=2

ACA. (2012). *Ethics committee summary–FY 2012.* Retrieved from http://www.counseling.org/knowledge-center/ethics

ACA. (2013). *Ethics committee summary–FY 2013.* Retrieved from http://www.counseling.org/knowledge-center/ethics

ACA. (2014a) *ACA code of ethics.* Alexandria, VA: Author.

ACA. (2014b). *Member exclusive benefits.* Retrieved from http://www.counseling.org/membership/membership-benefits

ACA. (2014c). *States that have adopted the ACA code of ethics.* Retrieved from http://www.counseling.org/docs/default-source/licensure/state-licensure-boards-that-have-adopted-the-aca-code-of-ethics-%28pdf%29.pdf?sfvrsn=2

American Mental Health Counselors Association (AMHCA). (2010). *AMHCA Code of Ethics.* Retrieved from https://www.amhca.org/assets/news/AMHCA_Code_of_Ethics_2010_w_pagination_cxd_51110.pdf

AMHCA. (2013). *About AMHCA.* Retrieved from http://www.amhca.org/about/default.aspx

American School Counselors Association (ASCA). (2014a). *About ASCA.* Retrieved from https://www.schoolcounselor.org/school-counselors-members/about-asca-%281%29

ASCA. (2014b). *Liability insurance.* Retrieved from https://www.schoolcounselor.org/school-counselors-members/member-benefits-info/liability-insurance

Anderson, D., & Freeman, L. T. (2006). Report of the ACA ethics committee: 2004–2005. *Journal of Counseling & Development, 84*(2), 225–227.

Association for Play Therapy (APT). (n.d.). *About APT.* Retrieved from http://www.a4pt.org/?page=AboutAPT

APT. (2012). *Play therapy best practices.* Retrieved from http://c.ymcdn.com/sites/www.a4pt.org/resource/resmgr/Publications/Play_Therapy_Best_Practices.pdf

APT. (2014). *Credentialing guide.* Retrieved from http://c.ymcdn.com/sites/www.a4pt.org/resource/resmgr/RPT_and_RPT-S_Credentials/RPTS_Guide.pdf

Boodman, S. G. (2005). A conversion therapist's unusual odyssey. *The Washington Post.* Retrieved from http://www.washingtonpost.com/wp-dyn/content/article/2005/08/15/AR2005081501063.html

Buckley, M. R., & Henning, S. (2015). Education, credentialing, and professional development. In D. S. Sheperis & C. J. Sheperis (Eds.), *Clinical mental health counseling: Fundamentals of applied practice.* Upper Saddle River, NJ: Pearson.

Council for Accreditation of Counseling & Related Educational Programs (CACREP). (2009). *CACREP 2009 standards.* Retrieved from http://www.cacrep.org/doc/2009%20Standards%20with%20cover.pdf

Harvey, L. (2014). Analytic quality glossary. *Quality Research International.* Retrieved from http://www.qualityresearchinternational.com/glossary/

Healthcare Providers Service Organization (HPSO). (2014). *Individual professional liability insurance for counselors.* Retrieved from http://www.hpso.com/profession/counselor.jsp

Koocher, G. P., & Keith-Spiegel, P. (2012). *"What should I do?"—Ethical risks, making decisions, and taking action.* Retrieved from http://www.continuingedcourses.net/active/courses/course050.php

National Association for Forensic Counselors (NAFC). (2009). *About the NAFC and certification.* Retrieved from http://www.nationalafc.com/?Home:About_NAFC

National Board of Certified Counselors (NBCC). (2014). *About NBCC.* Retrieved from http://www.nbcc.org/Footer/AboutNBCC

Oregon.gov. (2014). *Oregon board of licensed professional counselors and therapists disciplinary report.* Retrieved from http://www.oregon.gov/oblpct/ActionDocs/discipline_list_web_7_23_2014.pdf

Oregon.gov. (n.d.a.). *Board of licensed professional counselors and therapists.* Retrieved from http://www.oregon.gov/oblpct/Pages/index.aspx

Oregon.gov. (n.d.b.). *Oregon board of licensed professional counselors and therapists complaint process.* Retrieved from http://www.oregon.gov/oblpct/Pages/index.aspx

Subpoena. (2013). *Columbia Electronic Encyclopedia* (6th ed.). Retrieved from http://www.infoplease.com/encyclopedia/society/subpoena.html

Walk-In Counseling Center. (n.d.). *Resources for professionals.* Retrieved from http://www.walkin.org/resources-for-professionals

Zur, O. (2014). *When the board comes knocking: How to respond to a licensing board investigation and protect your license, professional career, and livelihood.* Retrieved from http://www.zurinstitute.com/board_investigation.html

Chapter 14

SOCIAL JUSTICE AND ADVOCACY

Deidre is a licensed counselor in a state where counselors cannot be Medicaid providers. In her rural area, Medicaid recipients may seek services at the local mental health center but may not secure their own providers without paying out of pocket. Deidre begins to worry that clients in her community lack the choices that more affluent clients with private insurance are afforded. Because of this injustice, she works with her state licensed professional counselor (LPC) organization and begins to advocate at the state level for counselors to be Medicaid providers.

CHAPTER OVERVIEW

This chapter introduces the reader to an overview of professional counselors' ethical imperative to operate from a social justice perspective and engage in advocacy. Beginning with the foundation of social justice as an ethical imperative, counselors learn to focus on the empowerment needs of the clients and communities they serve. In addition, counselors engage in advocacy activities to promote the well-being of clients and promote the aims of the counseling profession. This chapter will help you frame your understanding of social justice concerns and develop advocacy efforts that target these concerns. In addition, resources such as advocacy models, tips, and strategies are offered. The ethical mandate to serve as an advocate is emphasized.

LEARNING OBJECTIVES

After reading this chapter you will be able to do the following:

1. Define the concept of social justice.

2. Identify professional organizations related to social justice issues in counseling.

(Continued)

311

(Continued)

3. Examine client populations where social justice concerns exist.

4. Analyze the concept of advocacy, its competencies, and various models.

5. Describe how to advocate for the counseling profession.

6. Evaluate personal advocacy practices.

CACREP STANDARDS

CACREP Core Standards

G.1.g. Professional credentialing, including certification, licensure, and accreditation practices and standards, and the effects of public policy on these issues.

G.1.h. The role and process of the professional counselor advocating on behalf of the profession.

G.1.i. Advocacy processes needed to address institutional and social barriers that impede access, equity, and success for clients.

CACREP Clinical Mental Health Standards

E.2. Understands the effects of racism, discrimination, sexism, power, privilege, and oppression on one's own life and career and those of the client.

E.4. Understands effective strategies to support client advocacy and influence public policy and government relations on local, state, and national levels to enhance equity, increase funding, and promote programs that affect the practice of clinical mental health counseling.

E.5. Understands the implications of concepts such as internalized oppression and institutional racism as well as the historical and current political climate regarding immigration, poverty, and welfare.

E.6. Knows public policies on the local, state, and national levels that affect the quality and accessibility of mental health services.

INTRODUCTION

Throughout this text, we have provided you with the building blocks of ethics, ethical decision making, and ethical dilemmas. As we wrap up our study of ethics, we believe it critical to return to the first code listed in the ACA (2014) Code of

Ethics: "A.1.a. The primary responsibility of counselors is to respect the dignity and promote the welfare of clients" (p. 4). It is the belief of the authors that we best serve our clients through a lifelong commitment to social justice and advocacy. This ethical imperative is the focus of the final chapter. In this chapter, we provide an overview of social justice and advocacy as well as specific models, tips, and strategies for executing advocacy efforts to promote the welfare of clients and ethically serve our profession.

SOCIAL JUSTICE

Counselors are called to participate in social justice. However, many of us are unclear as to what that really means. Social justice often is rooted in an internal sense of fairness that may manifest as our conscience or even a spiritual obligation (Ellis & Carlson, 2009). While an empowering statement, that fulfilling a counseling role comes from within, it does not provide us with much practical guidance. Social justice is further defined by Nilsson, Schale, and Khamphakdy-Brown (2011) as our foundational value of fairness and equality for all regardless of societal standing. This definition most closely mirrors the ethical principle of justice as originally discussed in Chapter 1. In essence, social justice stands for a society that is fair, equitable, and safe (Center for Nonviolence and Social Justice, 2014).

Social justice further means treating all with fairness and integrity (Chang & Gnilka, 2010). Counselors recognize that the goal of social justice is to ensure that every individual has an opportunity to the basic resources of employment, health, and mental health (Chang, Crethar, & Ratts, 2010). The ideals of social justice sound almost utopian, don't they? Everyone deserves fair and equitable treatment, but we know that does not happen in reality. Translating social justice ideals into practical action is more challenging.

Lewis (2011) stated that social justice counseling is, in fact, "eminently practical" (p. 184). She further outlined some of the reservations that counselors bring into the social justice arena. Counselors may find the work of advocacy somewhat daunting. We see the big picture problems but are unsure where to begin. One way to start the process is to ask ourselves: rather than focusing on deficits, how can I frame this client's challenges from a position of empowerment? What assets and strengths does the client possess? How has this client's progress been hindered by oppression, discrimination, or persecution? What counseling approaches are tailored best to address barriers that create marginalization? Finally, what environmental assets may exist already to benefit this client, and what assets are lacking and need to be developed (Lewis, 2011)? Asking these types of questions allows us to keep an empowerment focus and begin to address client concerns from individual, institutional, and societal levels.

As you are probably aware, social justice is not new to counseling. In fact, social justice was identified in the early stages of our profession by some of the founders, Clifford Beers, Frank Parsons, and Carl Rogers, who advocated for client care and the profession of counseling in their writings (Chung & Bemak, 2012). Beers was a patient in a mental hospital who wrote about the inhumane conditions he experienced. By these writings, he advocated for change in the way we treated persons with mental illness in the early 1900s. Frank Parsons, considered the father of the vocational guidance movement, highlighted the disparity of treatment for youth, women, and the poor in his writings. Finally, Carl Rogers, the founder of person-centered therapy, saw the need to empower the client personally and politically to combat existing oppression (Kiselica & Robinson, 2001). These forefathers provided us with some essential elements of social justice counseling.

Counselors for Social Justice

Counselors are not isolated in our social justice efforts. We are organized under Counselors for Social Justice (CSJ), a division of the ACA. CSJ works to promote social justice counseling among practitioners and to combat oppressive systems that marginalize our clients (CSJ, 2013). CSJ works tirelessly with legislative, advocacy, and public policy initiatives to promote its goals. A primary initiative of CSJ is the publication of position statements. Position statements articulate the organization's view on topics of interest to members and are considered the official stance of the organization. They are vetted by the executive board and membership before approval. CSJ has published a number of position statements that are worthy of the attention of counselors who wish to practice ethically in a changing world. Specifically, CSJ has position statements on the infusion of advocacy competencies in counselor education, sexism and heterosexism, racism, equity in education, and rights of indigenous persons worldwide (CSJ, 2013).

In addition to position statements vetted and approved by the membership and executive board, CSJ also has developed and had ratified two resolutions by ACA. These resolutions are put through a rigorous evaluation process by the ACA Governing Council and stand as the position of ACA. The two resolutions put forward by CSJ are related to protecting intersex children and socially responsible counseling.

What makes these resolutions powerful is that they stand as the position of the ACA and must be followed by ethical counselors. The first of these was approved in 2004 and addresses the medical reality of intersex children. In the resolution, ACA supports the stance that as many as 1 in 2,000 children are born with nonconforming sexual anatomy and that these children may be subjected to medical intervention without their knowledge or consent. While children may not have legal rights to consent to medical treatment, we have discussed their ethical right to assent. The intersex resolution urges medical personnel to employ ethical best practices when communicating about such decisions with children and their care-givers (CSJ, 2004). The entire resolution is available via the CSJ Web site (http://www.counselorsforsocialjustice.net/PDF/IntersexResolution.pdf).

Second, a series of resolutions was passed by the ACA Governing Council in 2005 that support social justice counseling. These eight resolutions are contained in one document titled "Resolutions Promoting a Socially Responsible Approach to Counseling" and address an approach to counseling based on the teaching of Dr. Martin Luther King (CSJ, 2005). Within this master resolution, ACA addresses the negative impact of racism, sexism, ableism, ageism, and other beliefs or actions of privilege. While the resolution does not prescribe specific ethical actions on the part of professional counselors, it serves as a cornerstone for best practices within the profession from a social justice perspective. The series of resolutions is avail-able via the CSJ Web site at http://www.counselorsforsocialjustice.net/PDF/ResponsibleApproachCounseling.pdf.

Social Justice Concerns in Counseling

Now that we have covered social justice and social justice counseling as a global initiative, what are some areas in which counselors may see social justice concerns in their communities or with their clients?

Ethnic and Cultural Minorities

Ethnic and cultural minority clients suffer more injustices than members of the majority culture (Chang & Walsh, 2015). Ethnic and minority clients do not expe-rience privilege. Privilege occurs when one group has attitudes and behaviors that perpetuate the belief that its members are superior to other groups. Consequently, members of the privileged group consciously or unconsciously exercise control and power over the other groups (Ancis & Chang, 2008). This control results in oppression.

Oppression exists and impacts our clients. Ethnic and cultural minorities have been subjugated to a history of social and legal oppression in the United States. In an oppressive system, access to services, rewards, benefits, and privileges are based on or influenced by membership in a particular majority group (Chang & Walsh, 2015). As such, ethnic minority clients often have a more difficult time and may need the assistance and advocacy of others.

Counselors committed to serving ethnic and cultural minority clients often join the Association for Multicultural Counseling and Development (AMCD), a division of ACA. "AMCD is charged with the responsibility of defending human and civil rights as prescribed by law" (AMCD, n.d., para. 2). Within the AMCD, counselors have the opportunity to participate in public policy initiatives specific to ethnic and cultural minority concerns. Networking with other like-minded practitioners and mentorships are also benefits of joining this organization. For counselors working with ethnic and cultural minority clients, AMCD provides a strong voice for advocacy efforts.

Sexual Minorities

Sexual minority clients are often referred to as lesbian, gay, bisexual, transgender, and questioning or queer (LGBTQ) clients. Like ethnic and cultural minority clients, sexual minority clients do not experience privilege. Heterosexism is defined as negative attitudes and beliefs held by sexual majority individuals (e.g., heterosexuals) toward sexual minorities (Perrin, Bhattacharyya, Snipes, Calton, & Heesacker, 2014). Heterosexism must be addressed to develop LGBTQ allies. Counselors can work to address their own heterosexism through self-awareness activities that illuminate personal values that may contrast with ethical practice.

In addition, counselors committed to serving sexual minority clients may join the Association for Lesbian, Gay, Bisexual, and Transgender Issues in Counseling (ALGBTIC), a division of ACA. ALGBTIC recognizes the issues inherent at the individual and societal level when viewing the conflux or intersection of "race, ethnicity, class, gender, sexual orientation, ability, age, spiritual or religious belief system, [and] indigenous heritage" (ALGBTIC, 2014, para. 1). ALGBTIC works to promote best practices with sexual minority clients and publishes empirical research related to such efforts. In addition, ALGBTIC contains language in its mission statement that directly addresses social justice counseling by striving to identify client barriers to the development of LGBTQ clients and secure access when these barriers are identified.

CASE STUDY 14.1

Geneva has been seeing her counselor, Justin, since her sophomore year in high school. Over the course of her junior year, he was really helpful in her coming-out process with her family and friends. Now that Geneva is comfortable being herself at home and at school, she is excited that she can bring her new girlfriend, Lyda, to the senior prom. They have been shopping for prom outfits already, have rented a limo, and can't wait to join their friends in this wonderful time. A member of the school's parent–teacher organization has learned that Geneva and Lyda will be attending as a couple and wants the school to ban their admission, saying that only male–female couples are allowed at the prom. Deep in the prom guidebook, there is a line that reads: "At the beginning of prom, each female senior will be presented by her male escort and date to the audience." The parent is using this as proof that Geneva and Lyda are not allowed to attend.

1. *What is Justin's responsibility to his client?*

2. *What is Justin's responsibility to this situation?*

3. *If you were Justin, what would your next step be?*

4. *How might Justin's advocacy choices impact his relationship with Geneva?*

ADVOCACY IN COUNSELING

Advocacy involves the influence of public policy or the allocation of resources to benefit an individual, institution, or society. Advocacy is a fundamental activity of counselors.

Ethical Code 14.1

A.7.a. Advocacy.

When appropriate, counselors advocate at individual, group, institutional, and societal levels to address potential barriers and obstacles that inhibit access and/or the growth and development of clients.

Source: 2014 American Counseling Association Code of Ethics. Reprinted with permission from American Counseling Association.

Let's begin with a consensus definition of our role as counselors to serve as a foundation for this endeavor. In 2005, the ACA began a process known as the 20/20 Vision, which brought together stakeholders in the profession to brainstorm about the future of counseling. As part of this initiative, a comprehensive definition of counseling emerged: "Counseling is a professional relationship that empowers diverse individuals, families, and groups to accomplish mental health, wellness, education, and career goals" (Kaplan, Tarvydas, & Gladding, 2014, p. 368). With a clear emphasis on empowerment, the role of advocacy is highlighted.

Advocacy also is highlighted in accreditation standards. The Council for Accreditation of Counseling & Related Educational Programs (CACREP) defines advocacy as any "action taken on behalf of clients or the counseling profession to support appropriate policies and standards for the profession; promote individual human worth, dignity, and potential; and oppose or work to change policies and procedures, systemic barriers, long-standing traditions, and preconceived notions that stifle human development" (2009, p. 59). Finally, advocacy is mentioned directly in the ACA (2014) Code of Ethics, which states "(w)hen appropriate, counselors advocate at individual, group, institutional, and societal levels to address potential barriers and obstacles that inhibit access and/or the growth and development of clients" (p. 5). In other words, advocacy is not only ethical; it is a mandate from our profession.

ACA Advocacy Competencies

In 2003, the ACA Governing Council endorsed a series of advocacy competencies first written by Lewis, Arnold, House, and Toporek (2003). These competencies address the role of counselor advocacy from six specific perspectives:

1. Client/Student Empowerment: Ethical counselors approach work with clients and students from an empowerment perspective. We appreciate the impact of social, cultural, and political factors on the development of our clients and students.

2. Client/Student Advocacy: Ethical counselors who become aware of barriers hindering the growth of clients or students may respond via advocacy efforts.

3. Community Collaboration: Ethical counselors are in unique positions to note recurring barriers at the individual, system, and societal levels. When noted, we may choose to approach these barriers by joining with existing organizations effecting change. We would then become an ally to be helpful to the organization.

4. Community Collaboration Counselor Competencies: Ethical counselors are also in unique positions to note recurring environmental factors that impede the growth of clients and students. When such impediments are noted, we identify and offer our skills to collaborate with organizations impacting these factors.

5. Systems Advocacy: Ethical counselors identify barriers within existing systems that impact clients and students. When those barriers are identified, we understand that creating change takes leadership and that leadership may be fulfilled best by counselors as change agents.

6. Social/Political Advocacy: Ethical counselors understand the impact of public policy on client and student development and engage in such efforts as needed. We seek out allies and support them as change agents.

This list is merely a summary of the advocacies as they were approved. You can review the full set of competencies endorsed by ACA at http://www.counseling .org/docs/competencies/advocacy_competencies.pdf?sfvrsn=3. As counselors, we clearly serve as advocates to our clients and the profession of counseling. As a profession rooted in the belief that clients are empowered with the concept of autonomy, we are almost hardwired as a profession to champion the rights of our clients. However passionate we may be about this concept and its social justice implications, we may not have the knowledge of advocacy models necessary to bring our thoughts to fruition.

Advocacy Models

While advocacy efforts have existed since the conception of the profession, formal advocacy models began to emerge in the later part of the 20th century (Chi Sigma Iota, 1999; Eriksen, 1997). Not unlike the ethical decision-making models (EDMs) discussed in Chapters 2 through 4 of this text, advocacy models have evolved from basic guidelines to those specific to counseling theories or populations. Foundationally, let's begin with the reality that just as we have confidentiality in the work we do with clients, we also adhere to confidentiality in advocacy models.

Ethical Code 14.2

A.7.b. Confidentiality and Advocacy.

Counselors obtain client consent prior to engaging in advocacy efforts on behalf of an identifiable client to improve the provision of services and to work toward removal of systemic barriers or obstacles that inhibit client access, growth, and development.

Source: 2014 American Counseling Association Code of Ethics. Reprinted with permission from American Counseling Association.

While keeping this fundamental awareness on protecting the confidentiality of the client, we will now explore a few relevant models to help you develop your own style and sense of client and professional advocacy.

TRAINER Model

The TRAINER model is a seven-step advocacy process that is collaborative in nature (Hof, Dinsmore, Barber, Suhr, & Scofield, 2009). It is best utilized in situations where additional information is needed for the audience to understand the advocacy concern. The developers of the TRAINER model believe this form of instruction or explanation is necessary in virtually all advocacy efforts and suggest that it is appropriate as a foundation to most advocacy situations. The acronym TRAINER represents the following concepts:

1. *Target* the group in need of advocacy efforts and the specific needs of the identified group.

2. *Respond* to this need by determining the specific advocacy competencies to use.

3. *Articulate* a plan of action.

4. *Implement* the plan.

5. *Network* during the training to build upon advocacy efforts.

6. *Evaluate* the training.

7. *Retarget* any unmet advocacy needs.

Figure 14.1 TRAINER Model

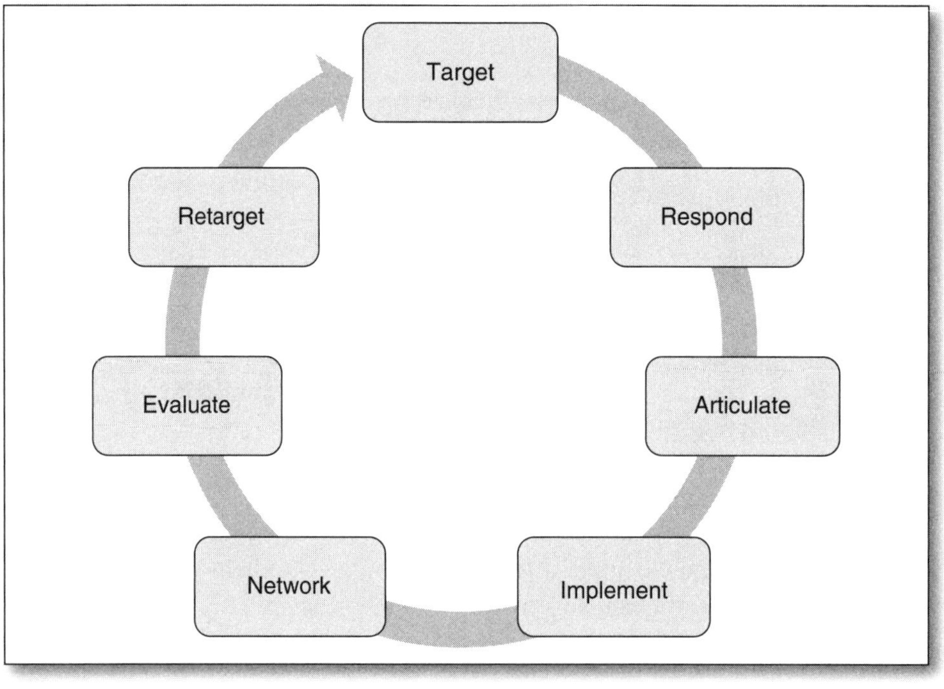

The advantage of the TRAINER model is twofold. First, it focuses on the power of information. By educating stakeholders regarding barriers they face or barriers they may contribute to, counselors can serve as change agents. Second, this model follows assessment best practices and allows for a continuous feedback loop to inform subsequent efforts at advocacy. As such, the TRAINER model is a good starting point for counselors interested in advocacy efforts.

CASE STUDY 14.2

Samantha, an elementary school counselor, has been providing services to Kendrick, a third grader in her school. Kendrick has an Individual Educational Plan (IEP) that designates he should receive pull-out services such as speech therapy, occupational and physical therapy, as well as accommodations for standardized testing. At the beginning of the year, Samantha noticed that these were all occurring regularly. However, the speech therapist has been out sick a lot, and when she has been at the school, she has not seen Kendrick. Samantha is concerned that there seem to be no accommodations in place for the upcoming state exams. Her administrator has said "not to worry" and "he will be just fine." Kendrick's mother is unaware that her son is not receiving all of his services.

1. *What can Samantha do within her school structure to benefit Kendrick?*

2. *How should Samantha involve Kendrick's mother?*

3. *What is Samantha's responsibility for representing Kendrick at the next IEP meeting?*

Three-Tiered Model of Advocacy

The Three-Tiered Model of Advocacy proposed by Chang, Hays, and Milliken (2009) suggests that counselors need to approach advocacy from the two perspectives of client advocacy and professional advocacy. These efforts often are intertwined, though there are some differences between them. Within each paradigm (client and professional), counselors must advocate in light of three elements: self-awareness, individual practice, and community collaboration.

The element of self-awareness is key because advocacy in this model is considered to be constructivist in nature. A constructivist approach says that we learn best when we learn through ourselves (Quale, 2014). In other words, we do not learn just by being told but by experiencing. Self-awareness is the key to unlocking those experiences that will allow us to see the need for advocacy. When we are aware of marginalization, barriers, and oppression in our own lives, it makes us better able to see these challenges in the lives of our clients and others.

Our individual practice is integral to this three-tiered model as it informs our understanding of how social, political, environmental, and other systems impact the clients with whom we work (Chang et al., 2009). Appreciating the client's worldview allows us to move away from stereotypes and generalizations and advocate at an individualized level.

The third tier of this model is community collaboration. By reaching beyond our own awareness and the needs of our clients, we can begin to impact society at a larger level. Examples of community collaboration include advocating for inclusion in a particular managed care company. Doing so creates change at the institutional level and offers the benefits of this change to others who have this same insurance. Legislative lobbying efforts also are considered community collaboration in the Three-Tiered Model of Advocacy (Chang et al., 2009).

Feminist Relational Model

While the previous advocacy models were appropriate for a variety of settings, some models address advocacy from a feminist or multicultural perspective. The model proposed by Hoffman and colleagues (2006) was developed in response to the belief that the elements of culture, such as race, ethnicity, and gender, impact the way advocacy efforts are framed and executed. A feminist or multicultural approach takes the clients' worldview as the expert perspective on their goals and needs for advocacy. Similarly, the Feminist Relational Model (Goodman, Glenn, Bohlig, Banyard, & Borges, 2009) builds further on the work of Hoffman and others (2006) to include the need for the counselor as advocate to partner with the client. Much like the Relational Ethical Decision-Making Model presented in Chapter 4, the Feminist Relational Model views the dynamic of the client and counselor in the change process as empowering to the client.

Specifically, the Feminist Relational Model suggests that considering cultural factors such as race, gender, and ethnicity is the most ethical approach to advocating for client concerns. It includes the following principles in the advocacy process:

- Valuing the Feminist Narrative: Ethical efforts at advocacy place the women's, that is client's, needs first.
- Honoring Mutuality and the Relationship: The counselor as advocate and the client must have an authentic and genuine relationship.
- Emotional and Instrumental Support: These support systems must be intertwined to provide the most beneficial social justice outcomes.
- Attention to External Forms of Oppression: The advocate recognizes that race, gender, and class oppression contribute to the experience of the client, and these realities must be factored into the advocacy plan.

Effective and ethical advocates must understand both foundational models of advocacy as well as specialty models for addressing the needs of the broadest base of their clientele and the profession. However, these efforts come with a price. One final model addresses this reality in advocacy.

Guided Practice Exercise 14.1

An Opportunity to Advocate

Nikki is a new counseling student in your program. As a second-year student, you were involved in the orientation held in the department and now share a graduate assistant office with her. When talking with Nikki, she shared with you that she suffers from cerebral palsy and uses a walker or cane when traveling long distances. She can ambulate around the classroom without assistance but uses a device to walk into the building and down the hallway.

One of the things you most admire about Nikki is her fierce independence and commitment to social justice. You notice that although your building meets minimum code standards per the Americans With Disabilities Act (ADA), it lacks single-push entry automatic door buttons that would allow her to enter the building doors or the women's restrooms with ease. She is forced to set her walker to the side and manually open these doors.

Following the Three-Tiered Model of Advocacy, you recognize this as an opportunity for professional advocacy that would serve not just your new colleague but the department and university membership as a whole. From a self-awareness perspective, you consider what these barriers might mean for you. From an individual perspective, appreciating Nikki's worldview informs your efforts as she may not want you to advocate for her without her approval. Finally, community collaboration looks to all stakeholders involved, including the department, other departments in the building, the office of disability services, the physical plant of the university, and disability groups in the area.

Now you can apply the directives of the Feminist Narrative Model to inform your next steps. You value Nikki's personal narrative and avoid making overtures without understanding her perspective. Second, you wish to honor your relationship and ensure that your desire to help is in line with her needs by involving her in the process. Third, you determine if her needs are best met by your emotional support or a more active, instrumental approach. Finally, you consider what other systems of oppression (race, ethnicity, disability status, etc.) may impact this effort. With a collaborative, relational approach built on the three legs of self-awareness, individual requirements, and community involvement, you and Nikki may reach a consensus on an advocacy plan that best suits her needs. Compose a letter to your university detailing your concerns and suggested outcomes. Be clear, informative, and persuasive in your argument.

Advocacy Serving Model

In addition to foundational advocacy models and relational-cultural advocacy models, researchers developed an advocacy model that perhaps best embodies the spirit of the profession. The Advocacy Serving Model is rooted in the belief that to serve as ethical advocates, counselors must attend to their own health and wellness in the process (Warren, Klepper, Lambert, Nunez, & Williams, 2011). Similar to the idea that counselors can suffer from vicarious trauma or compassion fatigue when they serve as receptacles for their client's trauma, the Advocacy Serving Model stresses the importance of advocate care throughout the process.

The Advocacy Serving Model suggests that the implementation of Buddhist principles can help advocates focus their advocacy efforts and allow for protection of the heart, mind, and spirit of the counselor as advocate. Specifically, this model views serving through advocacy as made up of five interconnected parts:

1. The Serving Being: The counselor as advocate has a servant approach to life. We view oppression and barriers as obstacles to challenge and are able to face them with a desire to create change.

2. The Serving Heart: Counselor advocates care about the work they do. While we do not use this word enough in our profession, counselors truly have compassion for those they serve, and this compassion transcends the more-often discussed element of empathy.

3. The Serving Mind: The counselor as advocate avoids rigid expectations and practices acceptance. In doing so, the advocacy process is more fluid and open to change, allowing for multiple outcomes to emerge that may be in line with initial expectations.

4. The Serving Practice: A counselor advocate's world is full of distractions and complications, but practicing mindfulness can serve as a buffer to these intrusions. Not only does mindfulness enhance the health and wellness of the advocate, but it also serves to focus the advocacy efforts more clearly.

5. The Serving Community: Healthy counselors as advocates do not operate in a vacuum. They appreciate the power of a professional and personal community. These advocates engage with peers and stakeholders to support their work but also maintain a connection to the larger world outside of counseling, including family, friendships, art, nature, and spirituality.

If this all sounds a little too New-Agey for some of you, bear with us. We assert and the research supports that a healthier counselor makes for a healthier servant and advocate (Cashwell, Bentley, & Bigbee, 2007; Myers & Sweeney, 2008; Roysircar, 2009).

PROFESSIONAL ADVOCACY

We would be remiss if we did not discuss explicitly how advocating for the profession of counseling is a unique form of advocacy. While we have mentioned the idea that advocacy encompasses those efforts aimed at benefiting the client's well-being as well as those directed at change in the larger social or political landscape, we have not discussed how to go about professional advocacy.

Let's start by revisiting licensure. As discussed in previous chapters (see Chapter 12), licensure varies from state to state. What it takes to be qualified as a licensed counselor in one state may not meet the requirements for another state. Similarly, testing privileges and scope of practice vary greatly across state lines. As you can imagine, these realities create complications for counselors who live near state lines and may have practices in multiple states or for those of us who move during our careers. The American Association of State Counseling Boards (AASCB) is an organization that works to advocate for the profession of counseling in its efforts toward unified licensure laws. The Fair Access Coalition of Testing (FACT) champions the fight against restricted test laws in many states. While these organizations devote their purpose to professional advocacy, how can you be involved?

As you may be aware from your counselor education program, Chi Sigma Iota (CSI) is the international counseling honor society. One of the aims of CSI is to promote professional excellence in counseling. The CSI Advocacy Committee develops policy position statements to encourage students and professional counselors to be involved in the advocacy process. Following the passage of the Mental Health Parity and Addiction Equity Act of 2008 (see http://www.dol.gov/ebsa/mentalhealthparity/), the CSI Advocacy Committee challenged members to get involved (Chi Sigma Iota, 2009). The Mental Health Parity and Addiction Equity Act legislated that insurance plans treat mental health and substance treatment the same as other health concerns in terms of coverage and deductibles (U.S. Department of Labor, 2008). However, CSI recognized that not all coverage is the same for all clients. Medicare recipients can utilize only licensed psychologists and licensed clinical social workers for such services. As such, the CSI Advocacy Committee suggested that students and counselors could engage in legislative lobbying efforts to address this Medicare disparity at the congressional level by writing and phoning senators and representatives, joining with organizations who were lobbying already for change, such as the ACA and the American Mental Health Counselors Association (AMHCA), and educating the public on this disparity and inequity.

How do you go about finding your state or U.S. representative? There are several Web sites to assist those of us who may not be particularly politically savvy.

Table 14.1

Finding Your U.S. or State Legislator	
U.S. House of Representatives	http://www.house.gov/representatives/find/
U.S. Senate	http://www.senate.gov/
State Legislators	http://www.votesmart.org

Guided Practice Exercise 14.2

Legislative Advocacy

Using the links in your text, determine who your senators and representatives are at the state and national level. You are aware that LPCs are not eligible to bill Medicare for services. From an advocacy perspective, compose a letter to your representatives detailing your concerns related to this issue. How does it affect clients? How would allowing LPCs to bill Medicare benefit clients and your state? Focus on the barriers to client care, lack of parity in services available to Medicare recipients, restrictions on choice, and so on. In addition to a focus on discriminatory practices, be sure to include the benefits of increased mental health care options. Be clear, concise, and persuasive.

It is our hope that you see advocacy not just as a requirement for ethical practice but a right and a responsibility for counselors. We all choose this profession because of a desire to serve others. Advocacy is one of the many ways in which we serve our clients and our profession.

SOCIAL JUSTICE AND ADVOCACY: FOUNDATIONS OF ETHICAL PRACTICE

It is no coincidence that we elected to end our text on the themes of social justice and advocacy. As practicing counselors holding multiple state licenses and national certifications, as well as counselor educators across three institutions, we strongly believe a commitment to social justice and advocacy will help inform ethical decision making in a host of contexts. Our experiences have shown that a desire to practice from a relational perspective, to involve the client in the ethical decision-making process, and to strive to empower the marginalized and disenfranchised client make us more aware of inequities that demand to be righted. To embark on your own journey of advocacy, it is suggested that you consider the following:

1. What are your own experiences with advocacy? Consider large and small efforts to effect change in your own life and the lives of others.

2. What hinders your success in advocacy? What holds you back? Is it fear, lack of knowledge, or something else?

3. Who do you rely on when you need someone to advocate for you? What qualities do you look for in an advocate, and which of these qualities do you share?

4. What additional social justice and advocacy qualities do you need to develop to be an effective change agent? How can you develop these?

5. Identify professional counselors whom you see doing social justice and advocacy work. How can you network with these people to inform your own efforts?

Social justice and advocacy is as much a philosophy as it is an action (Cruikshanks & Burns, n.d.). We anticipate that you have part of the philosophy already as you have elected to become a professional counselor. It is our hope that this chapter further inspires the action component of social justice and advocacy.

CONCLUSION

This chapter has addressed critical foci for counselors practicing in the 21st century: social justice and advocacy. The counseling profession is built on a philosophy of empowering the individual, which is directly in line with the theme of social justice. It is vital for counselors to understand systems of marginalization and oppression that have impacted us personally and impact our clients. Developing a sense of self and other awareness allows us to contextualize social justice concerns and see the inherent challenges for clients.

When counselors take social justice concerns and translate them into action, they are engaging in advocacy. Advocacy efforts occur at the individual, institutional, and societal levels and incorporate concerns for clients and the profession of counseling. This chapter explored how advocacy is an ethical mandate. In addition, we reviewed models and methods for engaging in advocacy activities to practice social change.

KEYSTONES

- Counselors are called to participate in social justice, which is a foundational value of fairness and equality for all regardless of standing in society. Its goal is to ensure that every individual has an opportunity to basic resources. Social justice was identified in the early stages of our profession by some of the founders: Clifford Beers, Frank Parsons, and Carl Rogers.

- CSJ works to promote social justice counseling among practitioners and to combat oppressive systems that marginalize our clients. This division passed two resolutions through ACA promoting social justice initiatives.
- Ethnic and cultural minority clients suffer more injustices than members of the majority culture. Like ethnic and cultural minority clients, sexual minority clients do not experience privilege. Heterosexism is defined as negative attitudes and beliefs held by sexual majority individuals (e.g., heterosexuals) toward sexual minorities.
- Advocacy involves the influence of public policy or the allocation of resources to benefit an individual, institution, or society.
- In 2005, the ACA began a process known as 20/20 Vision, which brought together stakeholders in the profession to brainstorm about the future of counseling. Counseling is defined by the ACA as a professional relationship that empowers diverse individuals, families, and groups to accomplish mental health, wellness, education, and career goals. Advocacy also is highlighted in accreditation standards.
- The ACA advocacy competencies address the role of counselor advocacy from six specific perspectives: client and student empowerment, client and student advocacy, community collaboration, community collaboration counselor competencies, systems advocacy, and social and political advocacy.
- Formal advocacy models have evolved from very basic guidelines to those specific to counseling theories or populations. These models include the TRAINER model, Three-Tiered Model of Advocacy, Feminist Relational Model, and Advocacy Serving Model.
- CSI is the international counseling honor society, which promotes professional excellence in counseling. The CSI Advocacy Committee develops policy position statements to encourage students and professional counselors to be involved in the advocacy process.

SUGGESTED BEST PRACTICES

- Take some time to reflect on your own definition of social justice. When have you been part of a marginalized population? How did social justice initiatives benefit you?
- Consider the following: How do you practice social justice today? How will you take those practices into your work with clients?
- Use social justice initiatives to build on the ethical principle of autonomy. Our goal is to empower the client.
- Educate yourself on the history of mental health care. Understanding the lengths that treatment has come can help you better explain current practices to your clients.
- Get involved in CSJ at the national (ACA) and at your state level
- Make it your mission to identify and serve ethnic and cultural minorities as part of your practice.

- Contact your state organizations to gain an understanding of advocacy efforts in your area. Then participate in them!
- Read the advocacy bulletins put forward by the ACA, particularly as they relate to legislative issues.
- Review the advocacy competencies, and identify how you meet those competencies in each of the identified areas.
- When you engage in advocacy activities, use a model.
- Educate yourself on licensure reciprocity and the efforts toward that end. Know your state standards for licensure as well as surrounding states or states where you may move.
- Serve as a professional advocate by promoting excellence in counseling.
- Know your state and area representatives in Congress and your state legislature. Know how to contact them and make sure that you do!

ADDITIONAL RESOURCES

In Print

The Counselors for Social Justice (CSJ). (2011). Code of ethics. *Journal for Social Action in Counseling & Psychology, 3*(2), 1–21.

Murray, C. E., Pope, A. L., & Rowell, P.C. (2010). Promoting counseling students' advocacy competencies through service learning. *Journal for Social Action in Counseling and Psychology, 2*(2), 29–47.

Rees-Turyn, A. (2007). Coming out and being out as activism: Challenges and opportunities for mental health professionals in red & blue states. *Journal of Gay & Lesbian Psychotherapy, 11*(3/4), 155–172. doi:10.1300/J236v11n03.09

On the Web

American Counseling Association (ACA). (2003). Advocacy competencies. Retrieved from http://www.counseling.org/resources/competencies/advocacy_competencies.pdf

Chi Sigma Iota (CSI). (2015). *Professional advocacy.* Retrieved from http://www.csi-net.org/?page=Advocacy

Counselors for Social Justice (CSJ). (n.d.). Retrieved from http://www.counselorsforsocialjustice.net/advocacy.html

Mental Health America. (n.d.). Retrieved from http://www.mentalhealthamerica.net/policy-advocacy

REFERENCES

American Counseling Association (ACA). (2014). *ACA code of ethics.* Alexandria, VA: Author.

Ancis, J., & Chang, C. (2008). Oppression. In F. Leong (Ed.), *Encyclopedia of counseling* (Vol. 3, pp. 1246–1248). Thousand Oaks, CA: Sage. doi:http://dx.doi.org/10.4135/9781412963978.n419

Association for Lesbian, Gay, Bisexual, and Transgender Issues in Counseling (ALGBTIC). (2014). *Mission statement.* Retrieved from http://www.algbtic.org/mission.html

Association for Multicultural Counseling and Development (AMCD). (n.d.). *About AMCD.* Retrieved from http://www.multiculturalcounseling.org/index.php?option=com_content&view=article&id=62&Itemid=82

Cashwell, C. C., Bentley, D. P., & Bigbee, A. (2007). Spirituality and counselor wellness. *Journal of Humanistic Counseling, Education, and Development, 46*(1), 66–81.

Center for Nonviolence and Social Justice. (2014). *What is social justice?* http://www.nonviolenceandsocialjustice.org/FAQs/What-is-Social-Justice/43/

Chang, C. Y., Crethar, H. C., & Ratts, M. J. (2010). Social justice: A national imperative for counselor education and supervision. *Counselor Education and Supervision, 50*(2), 82–87.

Chang, C. Y., & Gnilka, P. (2010). Social advocacy: The fifth force in counseling. In D. G. Hays & B. T. Erford (Eds.), *Developing multicultural counseling competency: A systems approach* (pp. 53–71). Columbus, OH: Pearson Merrill/Prentice Hall.

Chang, C. Y., Hays, D. G., & Milliken, T. F. (2009). Addressing social justice issues in supervision: A call for client and professional advocacy. *The Clinical Supervisor, 28*(1), 20–35.

Chang, C. Y., & Walsh, M. E. (2015). Professional and social advocacy in clinical mental health. In D. S. Sheperis & C. J. Sheperis (Eds.), *Clinical mental health counseling: Fundamentals of applied practice* (pp. 83–106). Upper Saddle River, NJ: Pearson.

Chi Sigma Iota. (1999). *Counselor advocacy leadership conference reports.* Greensboro, NC: Author.

Chi Sigma Iota. (2009). Counselor advocacy tips: Advocating for counselors of tomorrow. *Exemplar, 24*(2), 13.

Chung, R., & Bemak, F. (2012). *Social justice in counseling: The next step beyond multiculturalism.* Thousand Oaks, CA: Sage.

Council for Accreditation of Counseling & Related Educational Programs (CACREP). (2009). *The 2009 standards.* Retrieved from http://www.cacrep.org/doc/2009%20Standards%20with%20cover.pdf

Counselors for Social Justice (CSJ). (2004). *Intersex resolution.* Retrieved from http://www.counselorsforsocialjustice.net/PDF/IntersexResolution.pdf

CSJ. (2005*). Resolutions promoting a socially-responsible approach to counseling.* Retrieved from http://www.counselorsforsocialjustice.net/PDF/ResponsibleApproachCounseling.pdf

CSJ. (2013). *What is Counselors for Social Justice?* Retrieved from http://www.counselorsforsocialjustice.net/

Cruikshanks, D. R., & Burns, S. T. (n.d.) *Why worry about professional advocacy?* Retrieved from http://www.statelicensedcounseloradvocate.org/why-worry-about-professional-advocacy.html

Ellis, C. M., & Carlson, J. (Eds.). (2009). *Cross-cultural awareness and social justice in counseling.* New York: Routledge.

Erikscn, K. (1997). *Making an impact: A handbook on counseling advocacy.* Washington, DC: Accelerated Development.

Goodman, L. A., Glenn, C., Bohlig, A., Banyard, V., & Borges, A. (2009). Feminist relational advocacy processes and outcomes from the perspective of low-income women with depression. *The Counseling Psychologist, 37*(6), 848–876.

Hof, D. D., Dinsmore, J. A., Barber, S., Suhr, R., & Scofield, T. R. (2009). Advocacy: The TRAINER model. *Journal for Social Action in Counseling and Psychology, 2*(1), 15–28.

Hoffman, M. A., Phillips, E. L., Noumair, D. A., Shullman, S., Geisler, C., Gray, J., . . . Ziegler, D. (2006). Toward a feminist and multicultural model of consultation and advocacy. *Journal of Multicultural Counseling and Development, 34*(2), 116–128.

Kaplan, D. M., Tarvydas, V. M., & Gladding, S. T. (2014). 20/20: A vision for the future of counseling: The new consensus definition of counseling. *Journal of Counseling & Development, 92*(3), 366–372.

Kiselica, M. S., & Robinson, M. (2011). Bringing advocacy counseling to life: The history, issues, and human dramas of social justice work in counseling. *Journal of Counseling & Development, 79*(4), 387–397.

Lewis, J. A. (2001). Operationalizing social justice counseling: Paradigm to practice. *Journal of Humanistic Counseling, 50*(2), 183–191.

Lewis, J. A., Arnold, M. S., House, R., & Toporek, R. (2003). *Advocacy competencies.* Retrieved from http://www.counseling.org/Resources/Competencies/Advocacy_Competencies.pdf

Myers, J. E., & Sweeney, T. J. (2008). Wellness counseling: The evidence base for practice. *Journal of Counseling & Development, 86*(4), 482–493.

Nilsson, J. E., Schale, C. L., & Khamphakdy-Brown, S. (2011). Facilitating trainees' multicultural development and social justice advocacy through a refugee/immigrant mental health program. *Journal of Counseling & Development, 89*(4), 413–422.

Perrin, P. B., Bhattacharyya, S., Snipes, D. J., Calton, J. M., & Heesacker, M. (2014). Creating lesbian, gay, bisexual, and transgender allies: Testing a model of privilege investment. *Journal of Counseling & Development, 92*(2), 241–251. doi:10.1002/j.1556–6676.2014 .00153.x

Quale, A. (2014). Ethics: A radical-constructivist approach. *Constructivist Foundations, 9*(2), 256–261.

Roysircar, G. (2009). The big picture of advocacy: Counselor, heal society and thyself. *Journal of Counseling & Development, 87*(3), 288–294.

U.S. Department of Labor. (2008). *Mental Health Parity Act.* Retrieved from http://www.dol.gov/ ebsa/mentalhealthparity/

Warren, J., Klepper, K. K., Lambert, S., Nunez, J., & Williams, S. (2011). Applying Buddhist practices to advocacy: The advocacy-serving model. *Journal of Creativity in Mental Health, 6*(2), 132–148.

EPILOGUE

From the Authors' Chair

Writing a text book is part research—part experience—but mostly the articulation of the author's unique perspective on practice and profession. Each author has made personal decisions on how to organize the book and what, from the mass of information available, should be included. These decisions reflect the author's bias—personal interest—values and professional identity. We, as editors of the series, have invited each author to respond to the following questions as a way of providing the reader a glimpse into the 'person' and not just the product of the author.

It is our hope that these brief reflections will provide a little more insight into our view of our profession—and our selves as professionals.

Richard Parsons and Naijian Zhang

Question: There is certainly an abundance of insightful points found within this text. But if you were asked to identify a single point or theme from all that is presented that you would hope would stand out and stick with the reader, what would that point or theme be?

Donna Sheperis: *What I would hope the reader would find to be a primary takeaway is that ethical decision making is a process. Over time in our profession, the content of dilemmas has changed but the need to incorporate a process into our decision making has been a constant. Secondly, I would hope that the reader would see the value in consultation. By consultation I mean not just talking through a dilemma with a trusted colleague but involving the client in the process as well. So many obstacles could be sidestepped in ethical decision making if we would simply involve our clients in the process!*

Stacy Henning: *For me, one of the keys to learning ethics is understanding the significance of ethical decision making. Too many of us bypass important steps in decision making and devolve to where we "go with our gut" when presented with an ethical dilemma. While gut reactions are useful, for ethical as well as legal purposes, it is more useful to think through and document a thorough decision making process in regard to the concern. Making an on the spot decision also tends to be "encouraged" by the fact that most ethical decisions occur with the client in session—so many counselors may not feel they have the ability to process the issue and related decision—they feel on the spot with the client and that they have to have the exact solution or next step at that immediate moment. Learning to implement an evidence based decision making model and then documenting such will increase the opportunity for the decision to be strong and ethical and will support best practice for the counselor.*

Michael M. Kocet: *The main "take-away" that I hope readers get from this book is that the study, reflection, and application of ethics into one's professional practice can be exciting and energizing. Oftentimes, counselors perceive ethics as dry, boring, and a requirement to attend for continuing education. However, ethics is so much more than that. It is rich with new discoveries and ways of practicing the art and science of counseling.*

Question: In the text there is a great deal of research cited—theories presented. Could you share from your own experience how the information presented within the text may actually look—or—take form in practice?

Donna Sheperis: In this text, the relevant research is presented to show best practice in addressing common ethical dilemmas. Many of the examples are provided in the form of case studies. From working in the field, however, we know that people are not case studies. We are complex creatures who often have a convergence of ethical challenges that need to be addressed. Because of this, research can only be used to inform our decisions. The decision itself must be made in the context in which the dilemma arises.

Stacy Henning: There are actually many real case scenarios and application exercises throughout the text. These exercises include thought provoking questions for the reader and provide a firsthand account of instances where the particular ethical code was called into question.

Michael M. Kocet: When writing a book on ethical decision-making it is critical that students and professionals engage in the research and theories about ethics in practical ways that can be used in day-to-day practice—what is sometimes referred to as applied ethics. Having served on professional ethics boards for professional associations, I have seen how ethical violations have severed professional relationships and torn apart long lasting friendships. Ethical behavior doesn't just affect one's professional practice, but one's personal life as well.

Question: As author(s) of this text—what might this book reveal about your own professional identity?

Donna Sheperis: I hope that this text shows how passionate I am about the profession of counseling. As a professional counselor, I am ethically responsible for promoting the autonomy of clients and working with their welfare first and foremost in mind. I value the role of the counselor but, as importantly, I value and honor the client in the relationship.

Stacy Henning:	*I have a strong identity as a counselor educator and one who is interested in the use of ethical decision making models becoming the norm. Using a model will help the counselor to protect the client and further advance their treatment to be the best and most proficient.*
Michael M. Kocet:	*Being a self-proclaimed "ethics geek" I am passionate about engaging students and counseling professionals in the importance of ethical reflection. There is no such thing as a "perfect ethical counselor." We all make mistakes, but it is essential that we reflect on our actions, our ethical intentions, and identify ways to become more effective, more competent, more ethical counselors through our missteps and through challenging ethical conundrums. Serving on ethics boards of professional associations, as well as getting to lead the revision of our professional code of ethics has been the highlight of my professional career thus far. It has been a true privilege working with some of our ethics experts in the field.*

Question: What final prescription—direction—might you offer your readers as they continue in their journey toward becoming Professional Counselors?

Donna Sheperis:	*My hope would be that readers will find their passion in the larger profession of counseling. To do so, it is my belief that beginning counselors need to open themselves to a variety of experiences in order to find their best fit for future practice. Some of us come into this profession with a clear sense of the work we want to do as counselors but, for others, our true talents emerge within our work experiences. In addition, I have found that a work experience sometimes teaches you as much about what you don't want to do as what you do want to do! In either case, being open to the process and learning from each experience is key.*
Stacy Henning:	*Consult, consult, consult; document, document, document. Counseling is a career that involves life-long learning and supervision, hence, regular consultation with peers can only make you stronger.*

Michael M. Kocet: *Always ask questions- never be satisfied with taking the quickest or easiest way out of an ethical dilemma. Consult supervisors, the literature, reflect on your own personal and professional judgment, and most importantly, to engage the client and other stakeholders in the ethical decision-making process whenever possible.*

INDEX